INUBAKA

CRAZY FOR DOGS

7

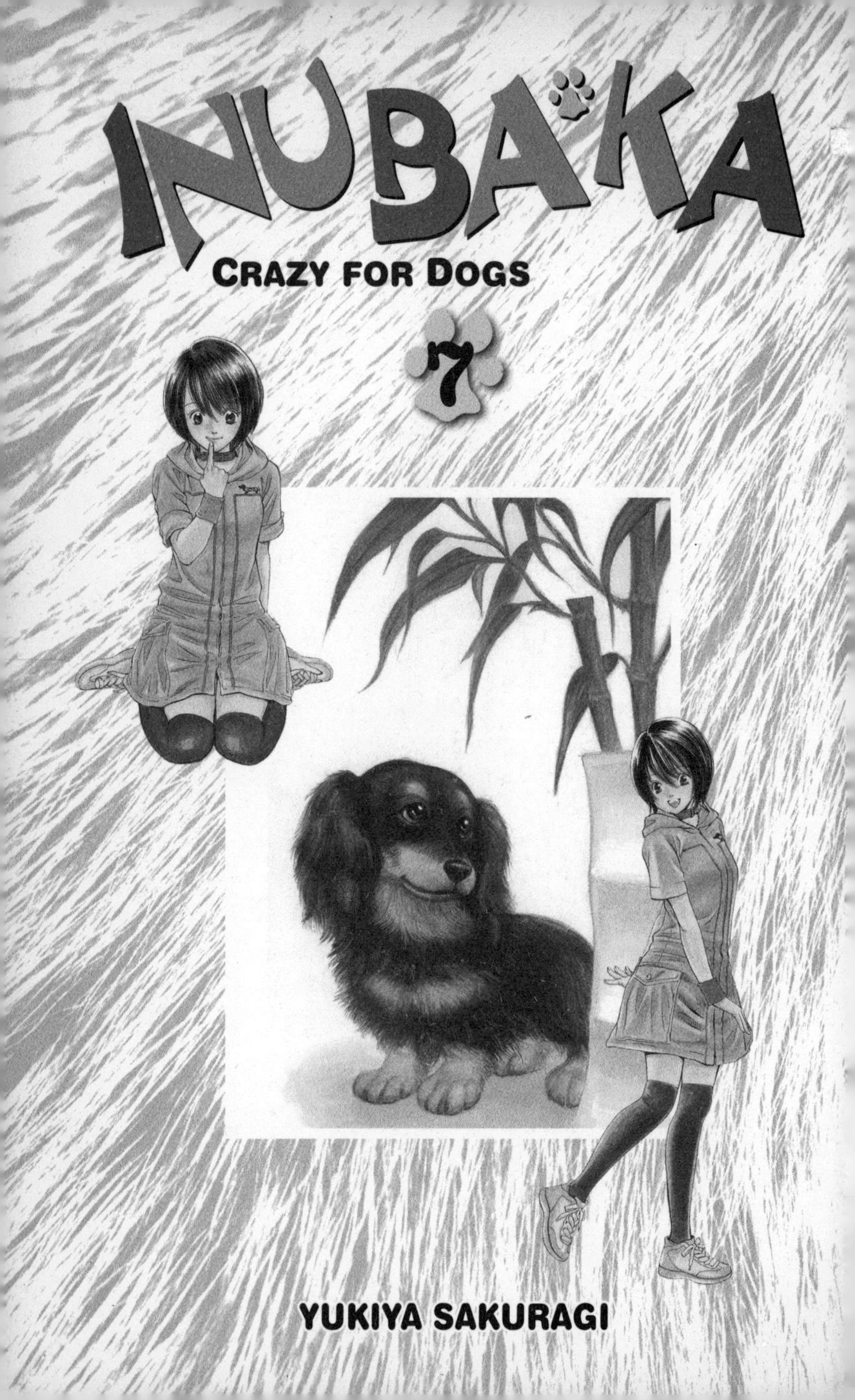

YUKIYA SAKURAGI

Contents

Story thus far

Teppei is the manager of the recently opened pet shop Woofles. He intended to breed his black Labrador Noa with a champion dog, but instead Noa was "taken advantage of" by an unknown and unfixed male dog!

The unknown dog's owner was Suguri Miyauchi and her dog was a mutt named Lupin. Suguri is now working at Woofles to make up for her dog's actions.

Suguri's enthusiasm is more than a little unique. She has eaten dog food (and said it was tasty), caught dog poop with her bare hands, and caused dogs to have "happy pee" in her presence. Teppei is starting to realize that Suguri is indeed a very special girl.

Hidden treats seem to be at every turn when Noa, the dog belonging to Suguri's boss, stumbles across an abandoned kitten! Amazing cuteness follows when Noa nurtures the kitten as if it were her very own.

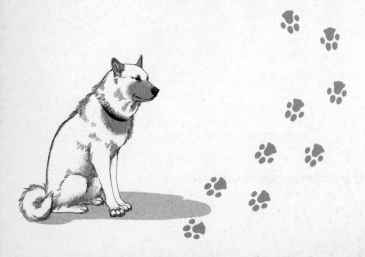

CHARACTERS

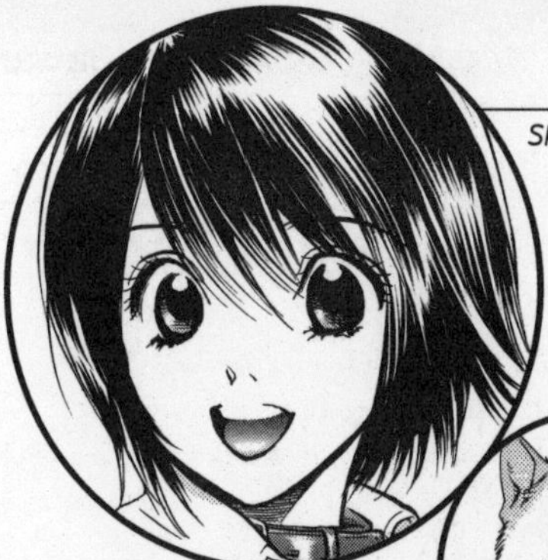

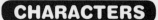

Suguri Miyauchi

She seems to possess an almost supernatural connection with dogs. When she approaches them they often urinate with great excitement! She is crazy for dogs and can catch their droppings with her bare hands. She is currently a trainee at the Woofles Pet Shop.

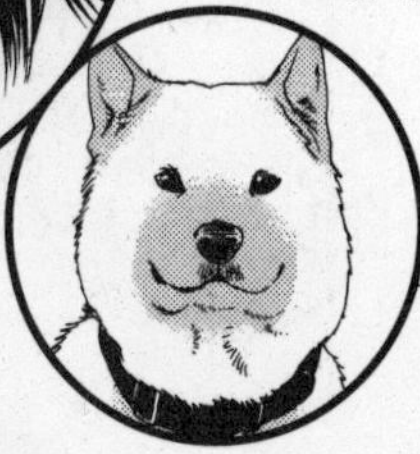

Lupin

♂ *Mutt (mongrel)*

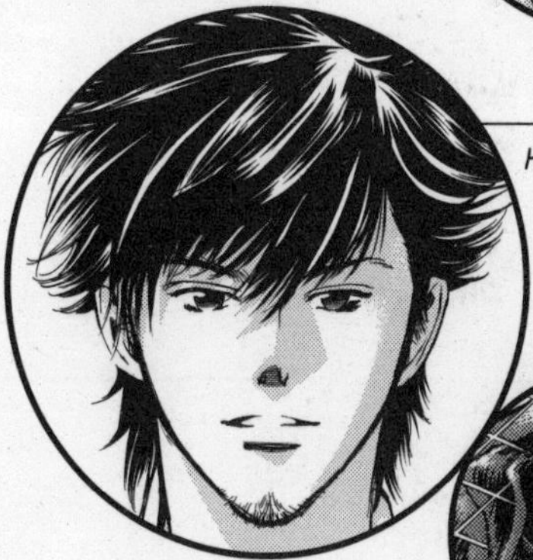

Teppei Iida

He is the manager of the recently opened pet shop Woofles. He is aware of Suguri's special ability and has hired her to work in his shop. He also lets Suguri and Kentaro crash with him.

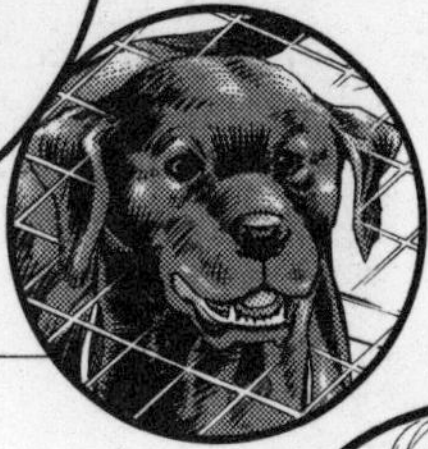

Noa

♀ *Labrador retriever*

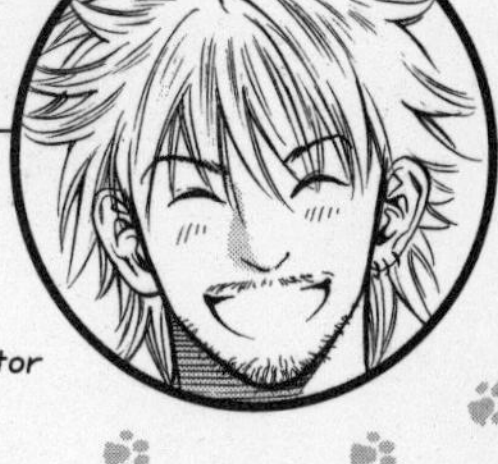

Kentaro Osada

A wanna-be musician and buddy of Teppei's from high school. Teppei saved Kentaro when he was a down-and-out beggar. He has a crush on the piano instructor Kanako, but not her dog...

Melon

♂ *Chihuahua*

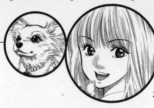

Chizuru Sawamura

She adopted a Chihuahua, Melon, after her long-time pet Golden Retriever Ricky alerted her that he was ill. She works at a hostess bar to repay Melon's medical fees.

Kanako Mori

She teaches piano on the second floor of the same building as Woofles. Her love for her dog, Czerny, is so great that it surprises even Suguri!

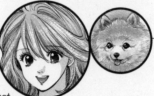

Czerny

♀ *Pomeranian*

Zidane

♂ *French bulldog*

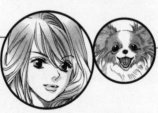

Hiroshi Akiba

Pop-idol otaku turned dog otaku. His dream is to publish a photo collection of his dog, Zidane. He is a government employee.

Mari Yamashita

She is a model whose nickname is Yamarin. She decided to keep an unsold Papillon, Lucky, who was her co-star in a bread commercial.

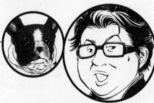

Lucky

♂ *Papillon*

Chanta

♀ *Shiba*

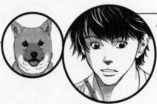

Kim

A Korean friend of Kentaro. He had a phobia of dogs, but he has been working hard to get over it in order to get close to Suguri, whom he has a crush on. He bought a Shiba dog!

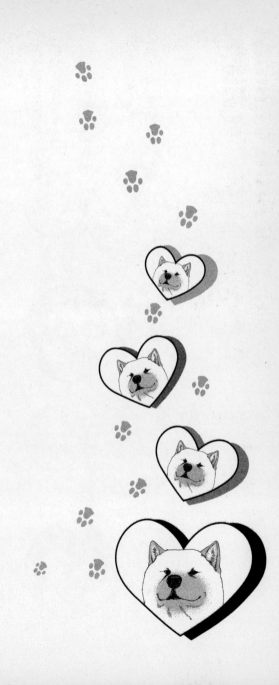

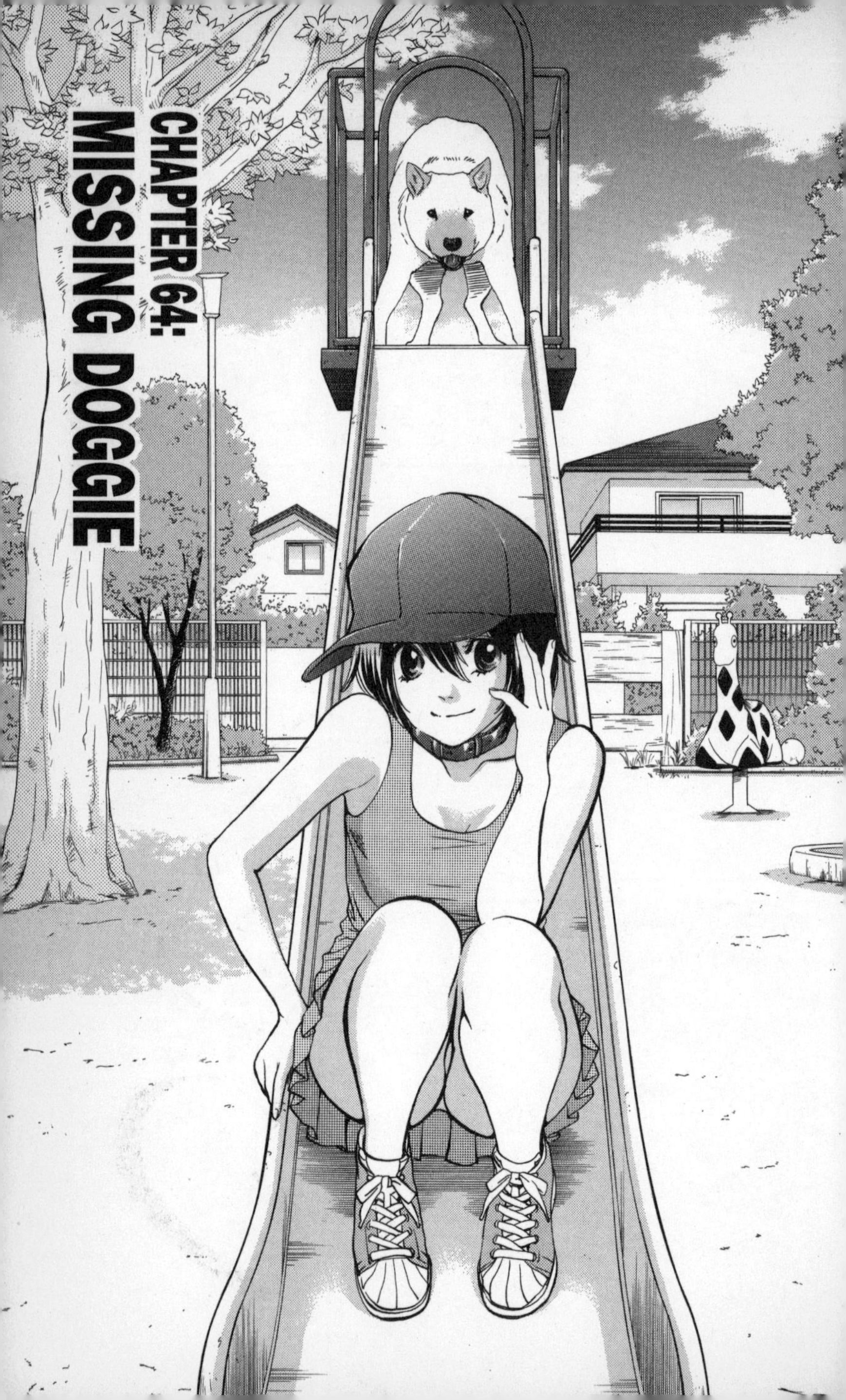
CHAPTER 64:
MISSING DOGGIE

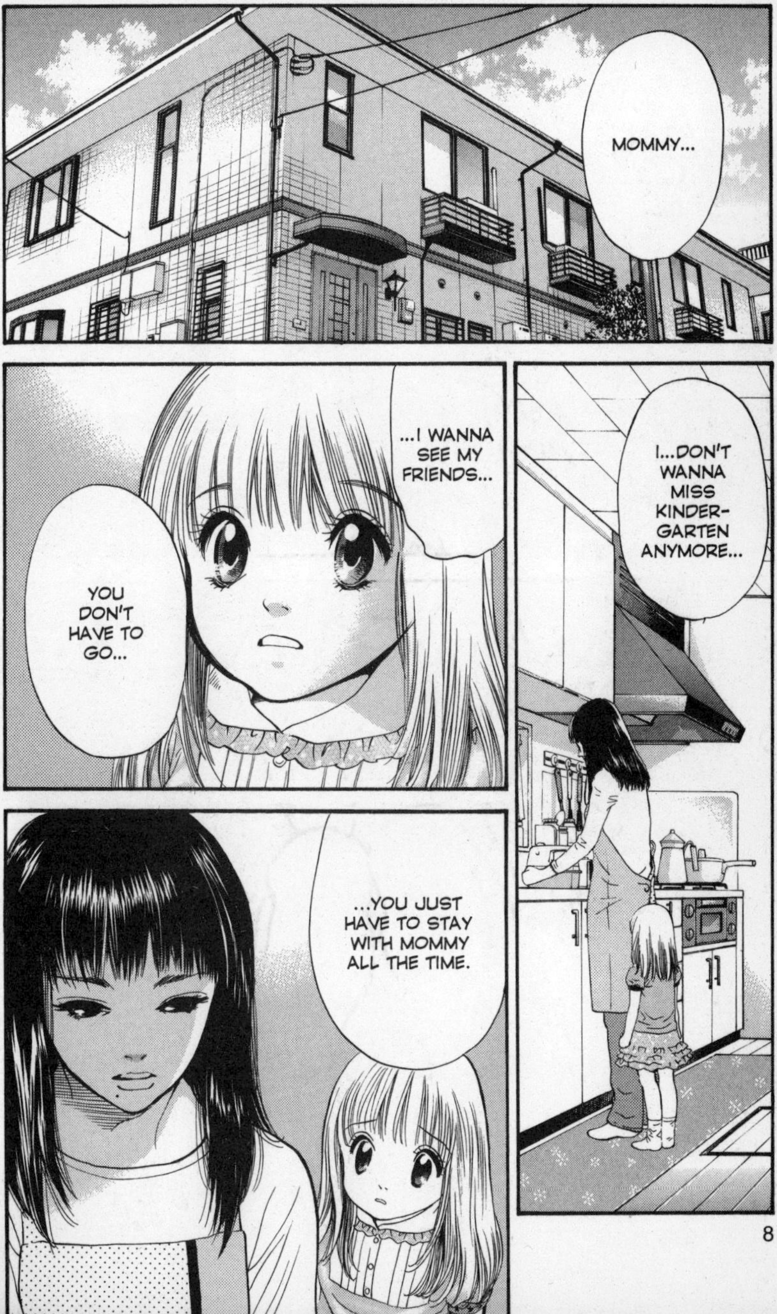
MOMMY...
I...DON'T WANNA MISS KINDER-GARTEN ANYMORE...
...I WANNA SEE MY FRIENDS...
YOU DON'T HAVE TO GO...
...YOU JUST HAVE TO STAY WITH MOMMY ALL THE TIME.

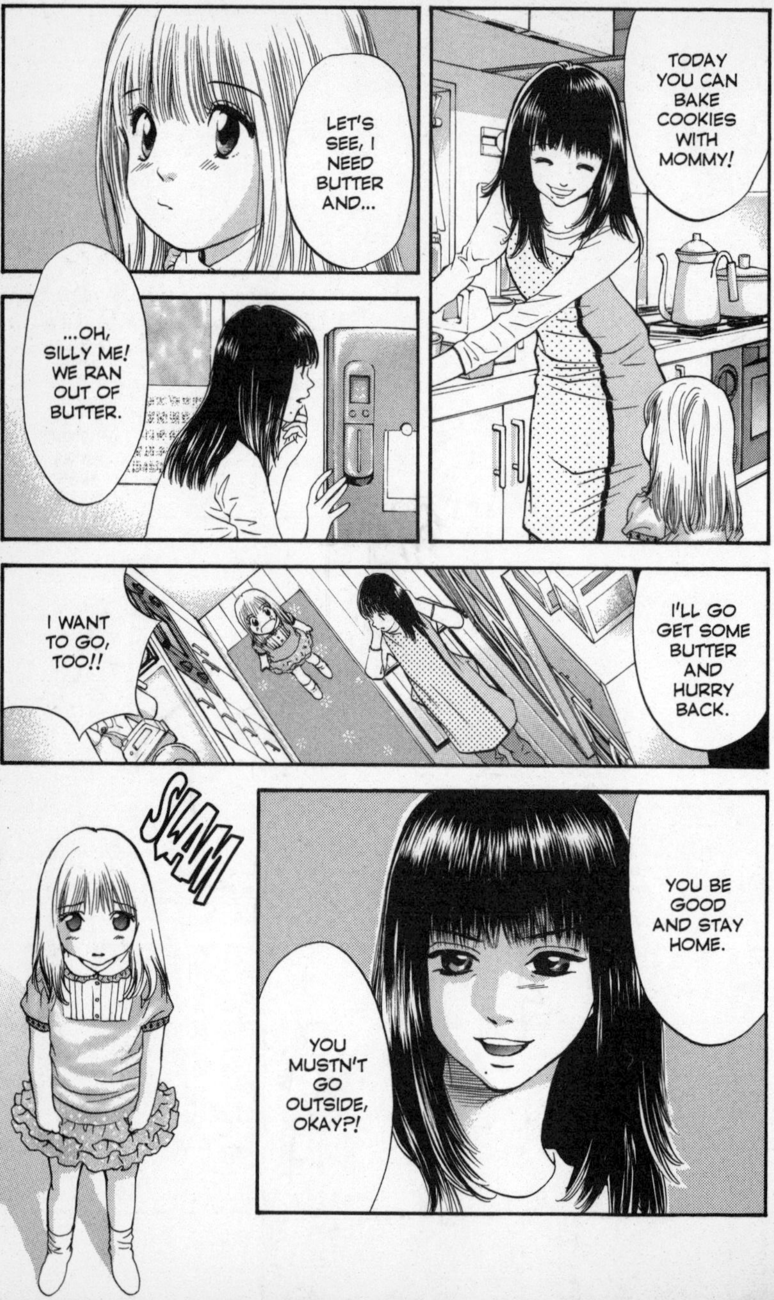
TODAY YOU CAN BAKE COOKIES WITH MOMMY!
LET'S SEE, I NEED BUTTER AND...
...OH, SILLY ME! WE RAN OUT OF BUTTER.
I'LL GO GET SOME BUTTER AND HURRY BACK.
I WANT TO GO, TOO!!
YOU BE GOOD AND STAY HOME.
YOU MUSTN'T GO OUTSIDE, OKAY?!
SLAM

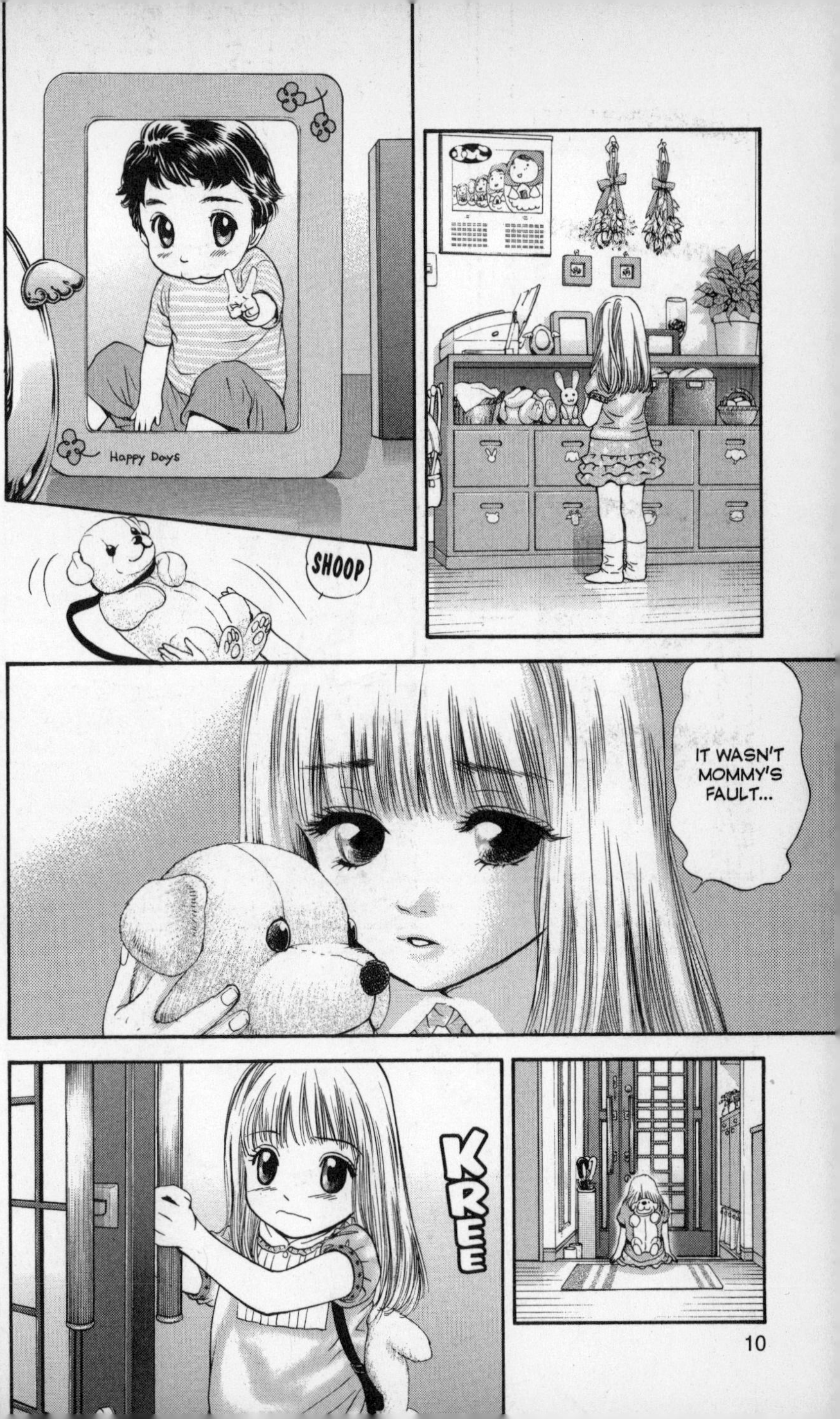
Happy Days
SHOOP
IT WASN'T MOMMY'S FAULT...
KREE

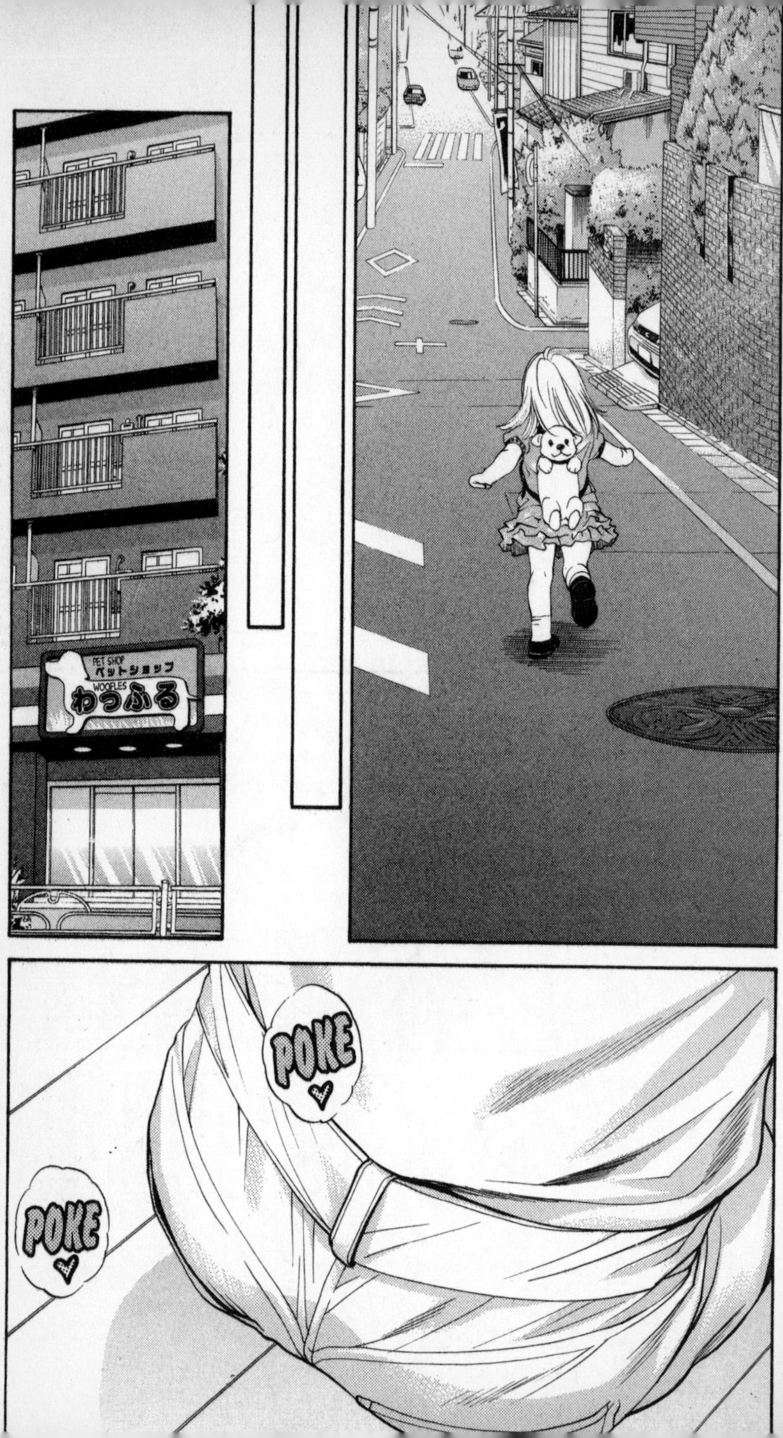
PET SHOP
ペットショップ
WOOFLES
わっふる
POKE ♥
POKE ♥

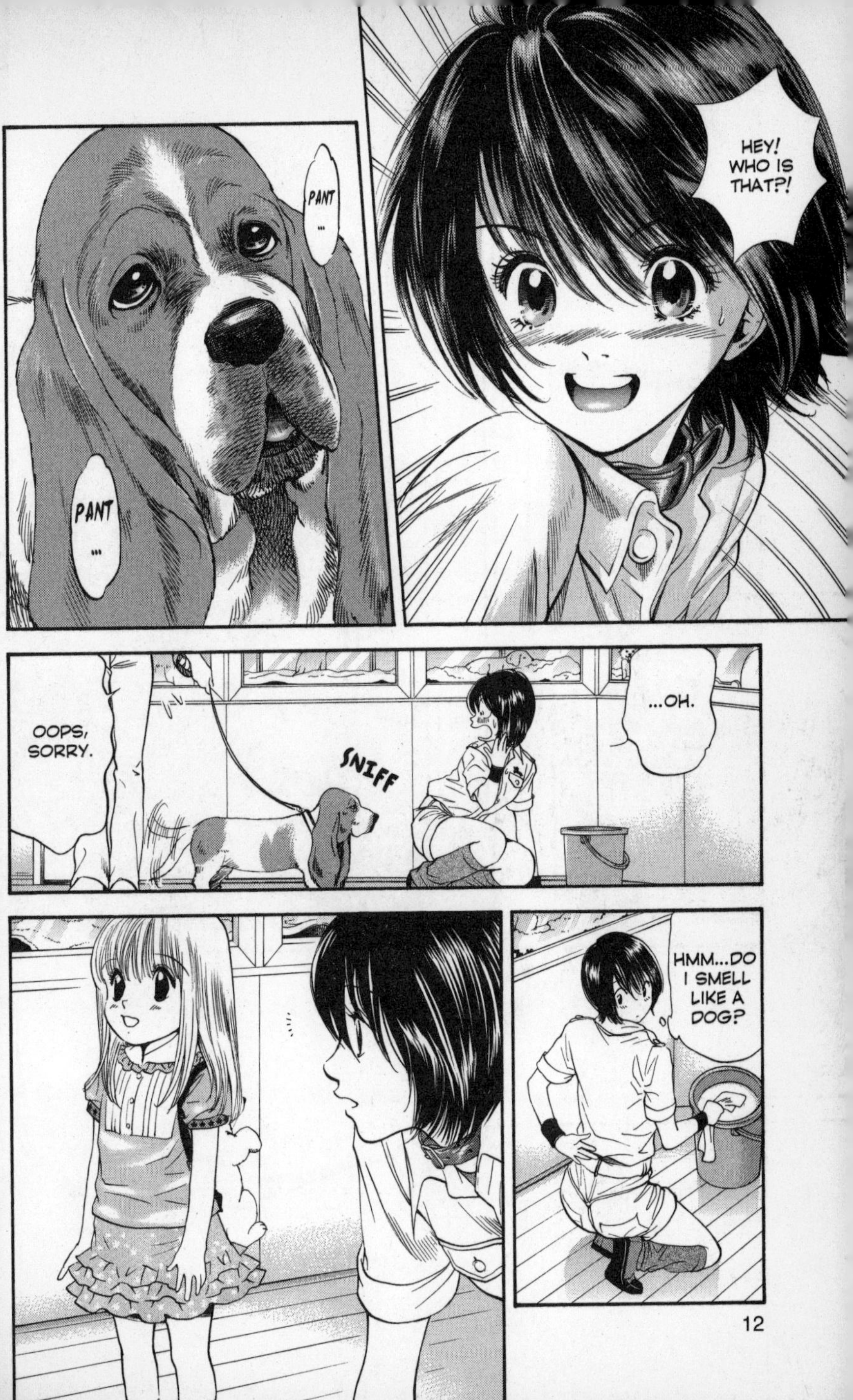
HEY! WHO IS THAT?!
PANT ...
PANT ...
...OH.
SNIFF
OOPS, SORRY.
HMM...DO I SMELL LIKE A DOG?

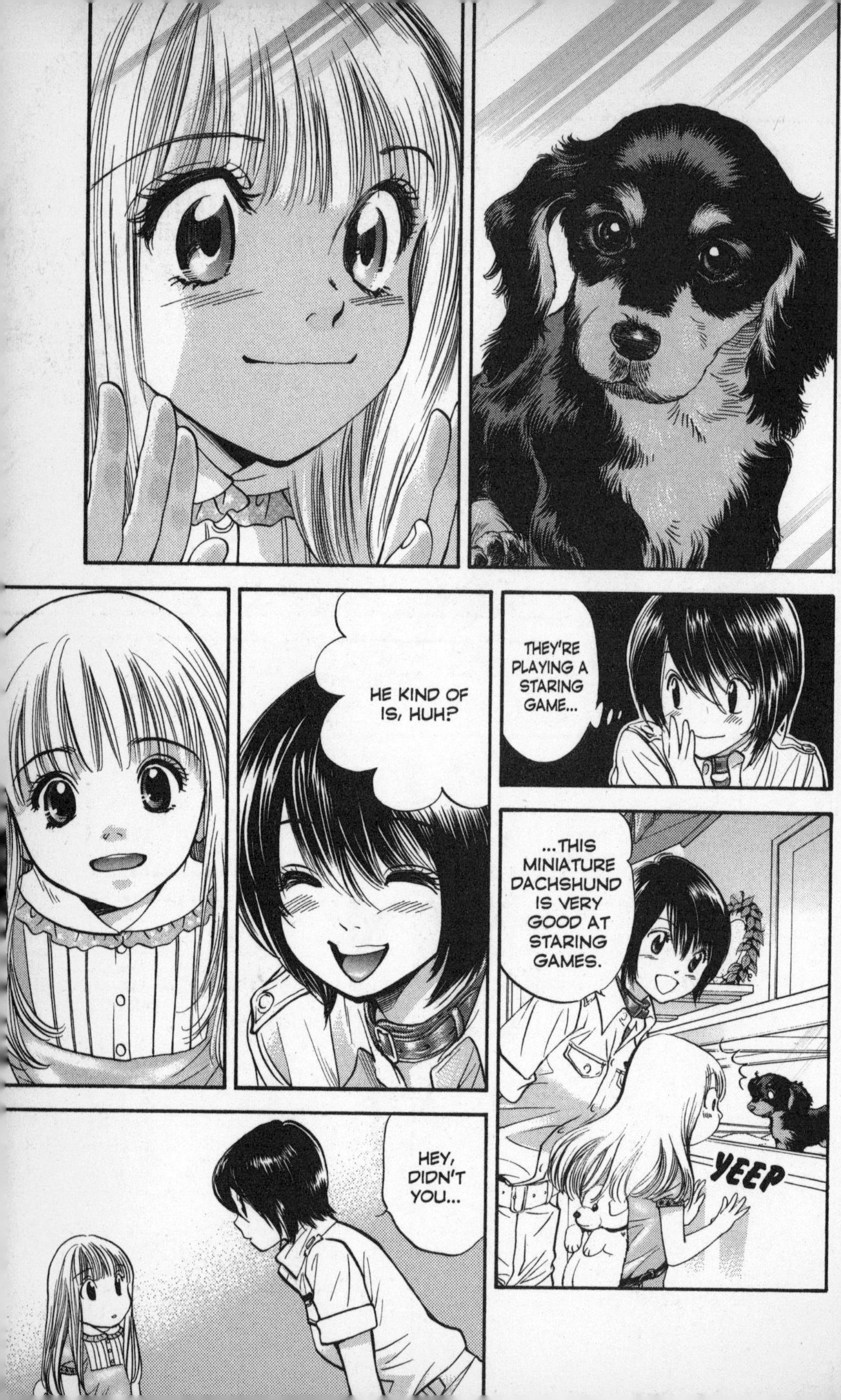
THEY'RE PLAYING A STARING GAME...
...THIS MINIATURE DACHSHUND IS VERY GOOD AT STARING GAMES.
YEEP
HE KIND OF IS, HUH?
HEY, DIDN'T YOU...

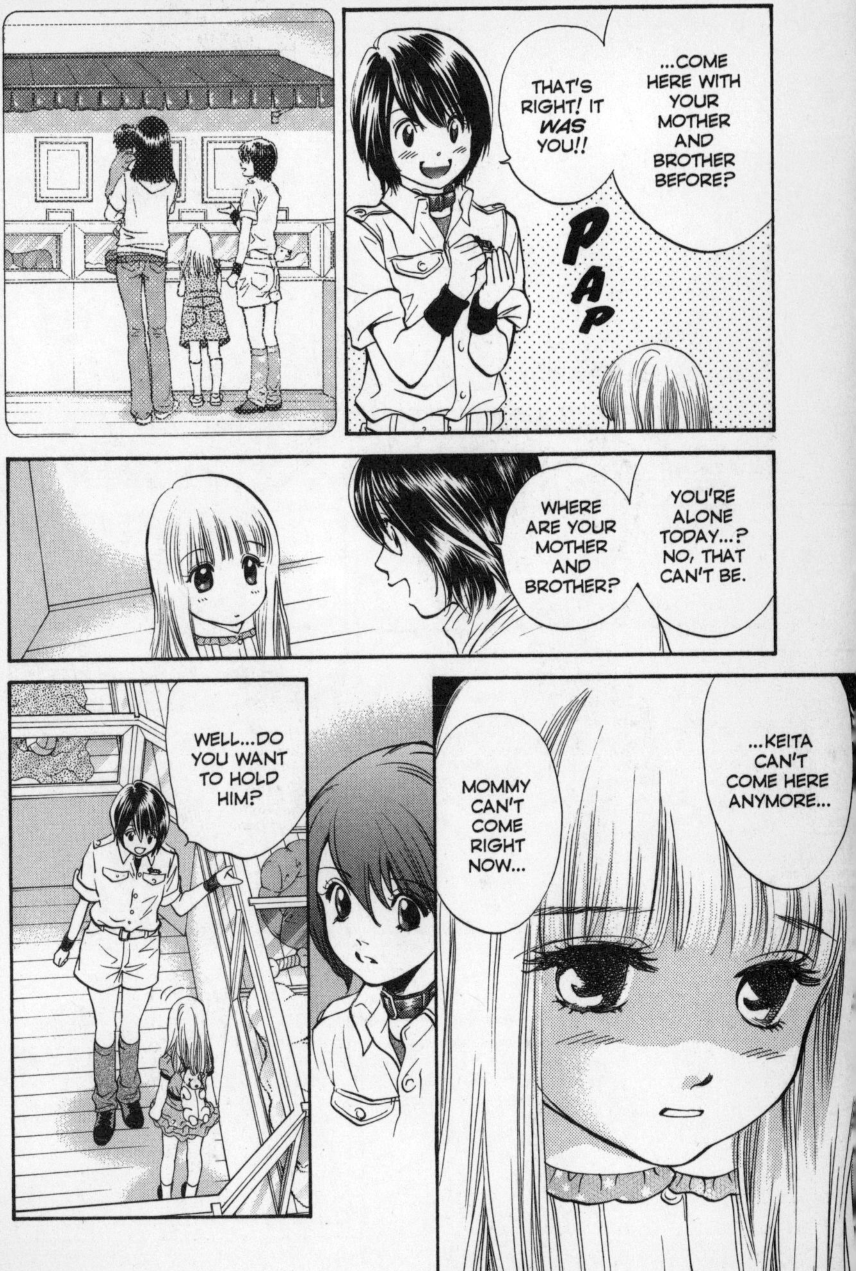
...COME HERE WITH YOUR MOTHER AND BROTHER BEFORE?
THAT'S RIGHT! IT *WAS* YOU!!
PAP
YOU'RE ALONE TODAY...? NO, THAT CAN'T BE.
WHERE ARE YOUR MOTHER AND BROTHER?
...KEITA CAN'T COME HERE ANYMORE...
MOMMY CAN'T COME RIGHT NOW...
WELL...DO YOU WANT TO HOLD HIM?

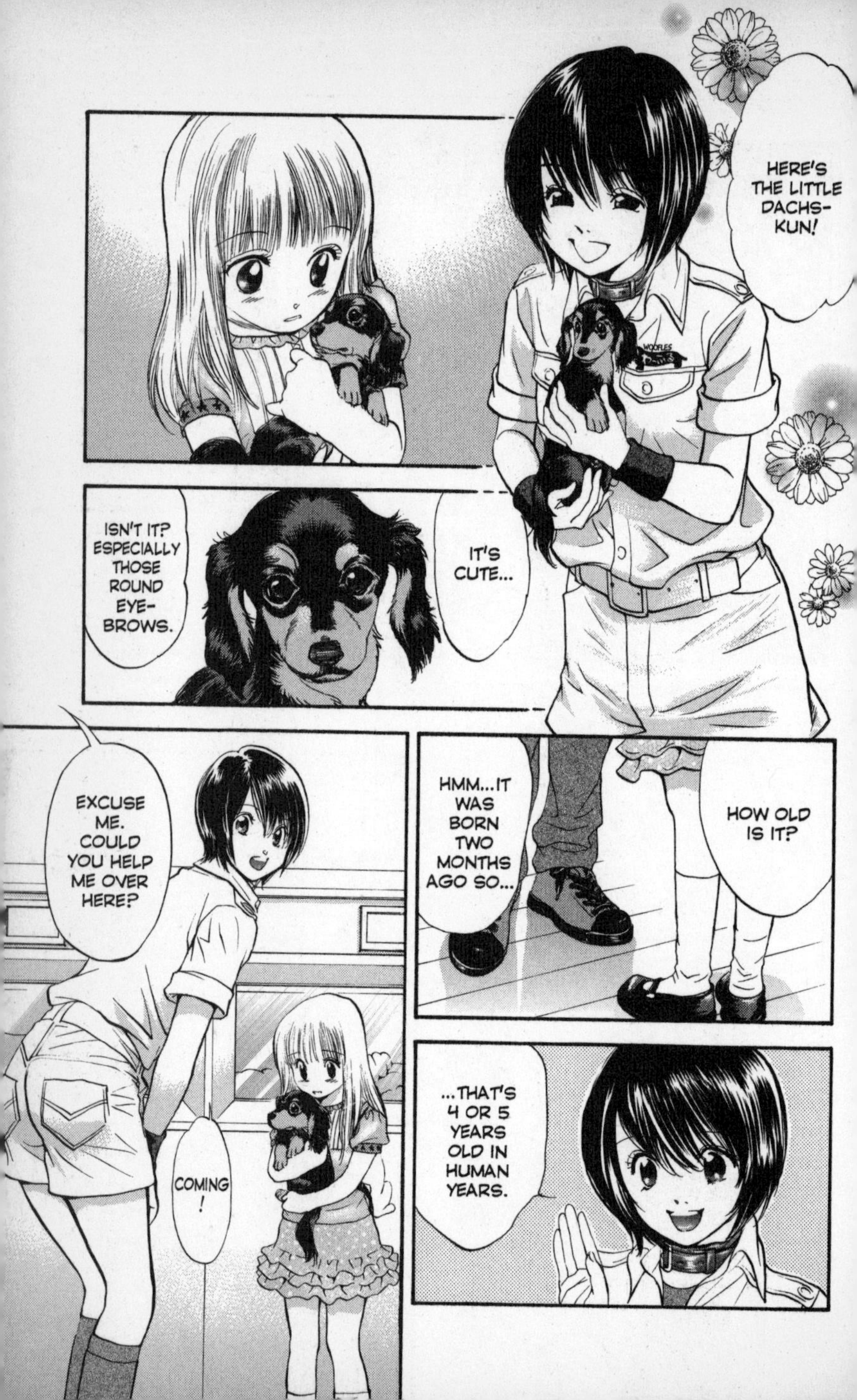
HERE'S THE LITTLE DACHS-KUN!
IT'S CUTE...
ISN'T IT? ESPECIALLY THOSE ROUND EYE-BROWS.
HOW OLD IS IT?
HMM...IT WAS BORN TWO MONTHS AGO SO...
...THAT'S 4 OR 5 YEARS OLD IN HUMAN YEARS.
EXCUSE ME. COULD YOU HELP ME OVER HERE?
COMING!

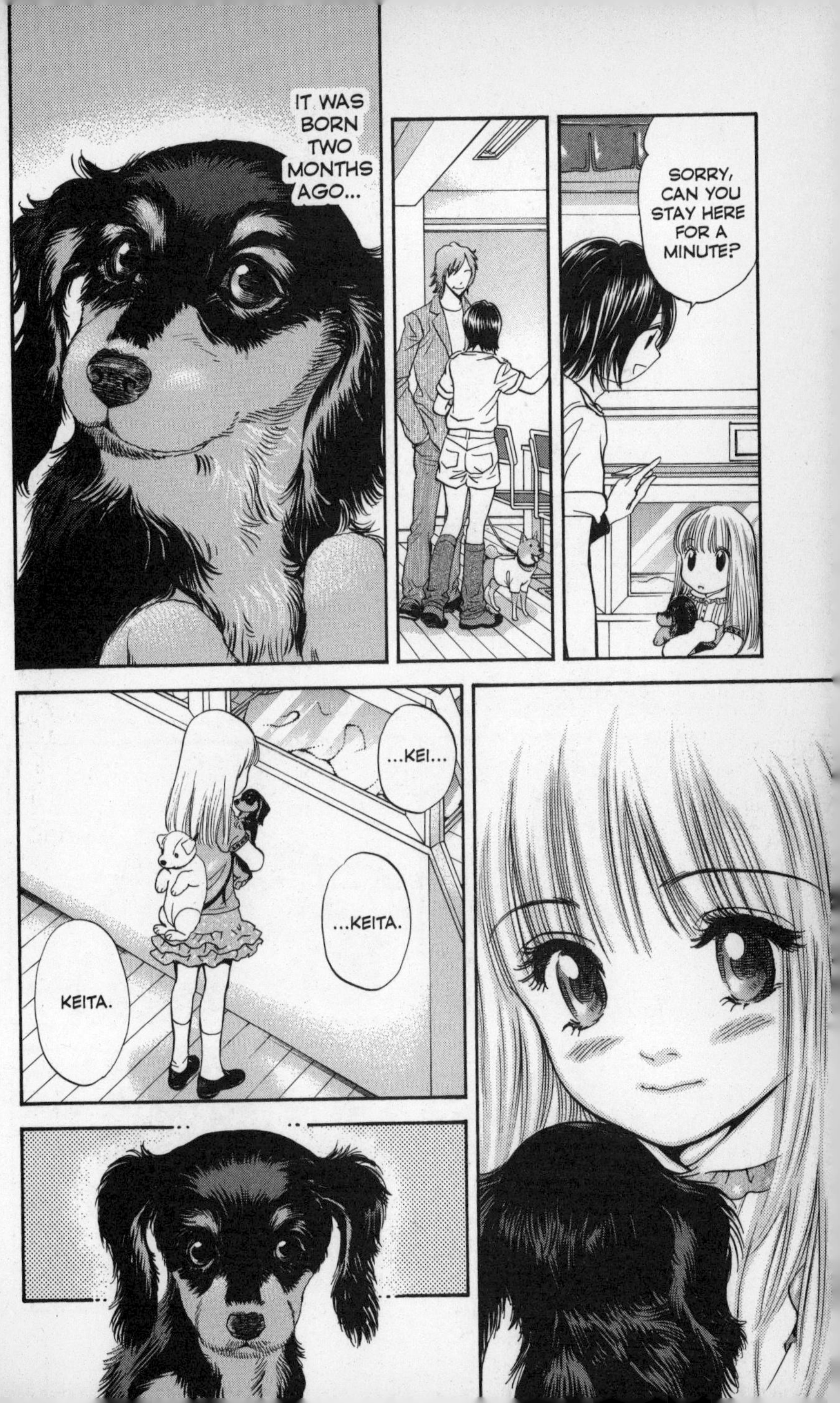
SORRY, CAN YOU STAY HERE FOR A MINUTE?
IT WAS BORN TWO MONTHS AGO...
...KEI...
...KEITA.
KEITA.

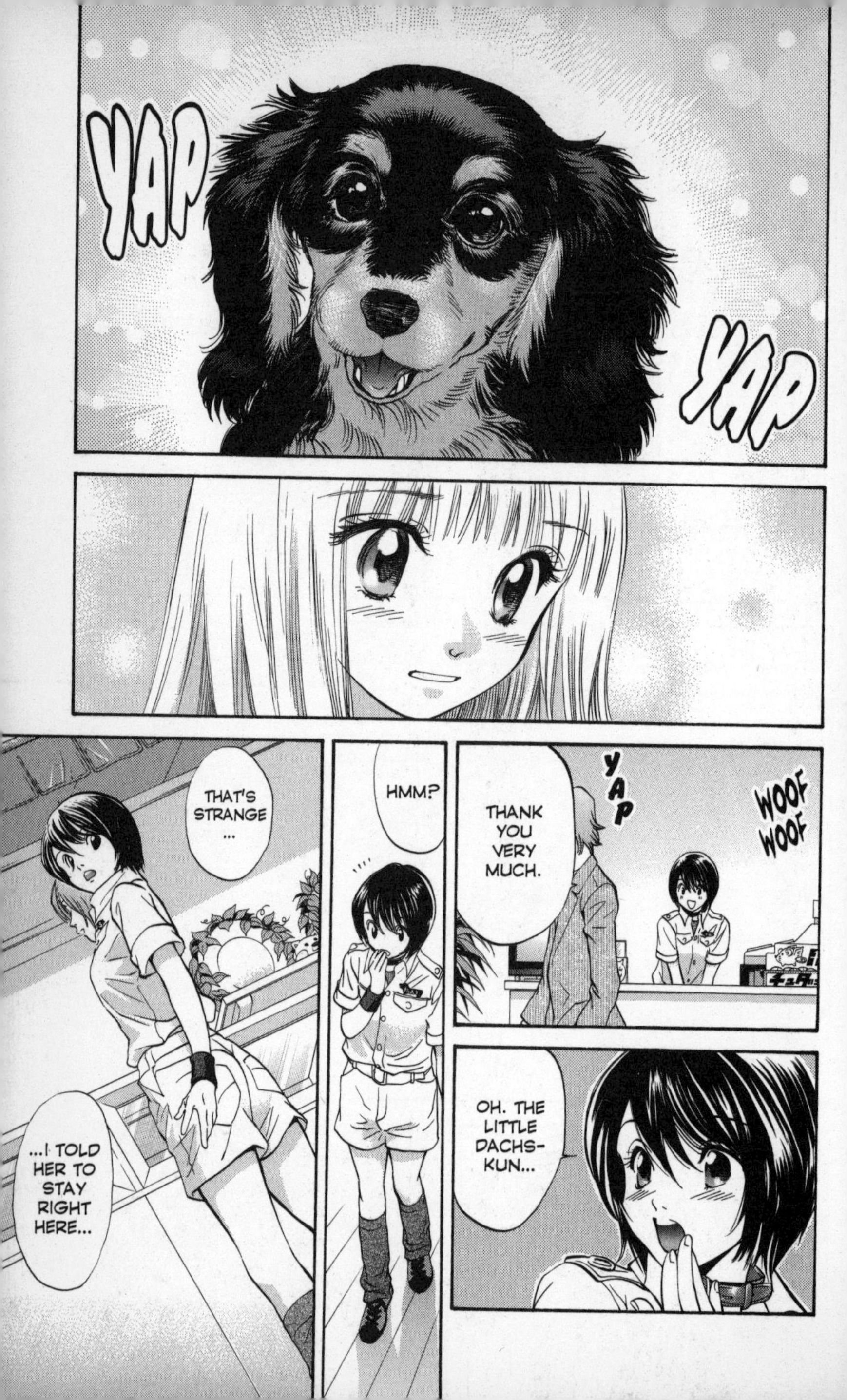
YAP
YAP
WOOF WOOF
YAP YAP
THANK YOU VERY MUCH.
OH. THE LITTLE DACHS-KUN...
HMM?
THAT'S STRANGE ...
...I TOLD HER TO STAY RIGHT HERE...

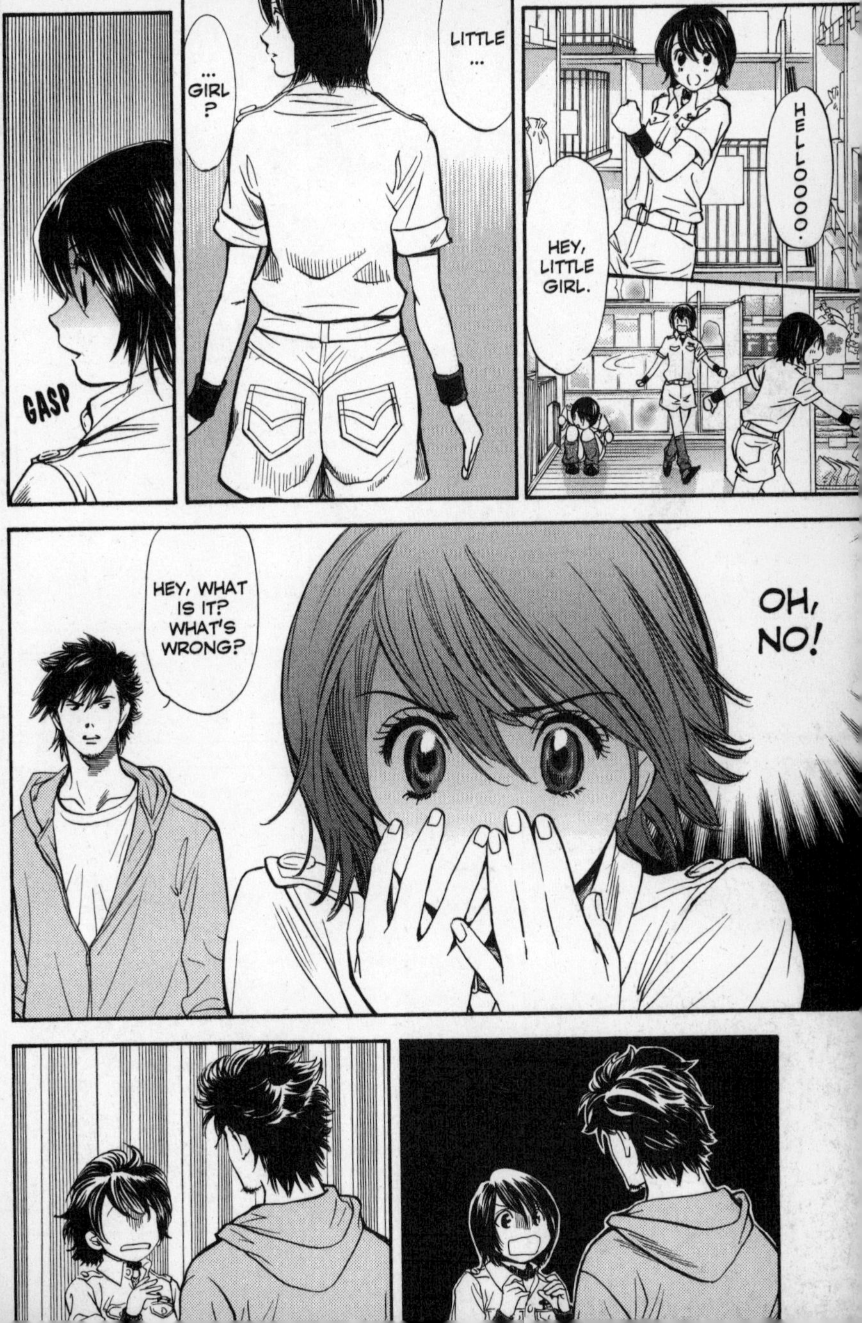
HELLOOOO.
HEY, LITTLE GIRL.
LITTLE ...
... GIRL ?
GASP
OH, NO!
HEY, WHAT IS IT? WHAT'S WRONG?

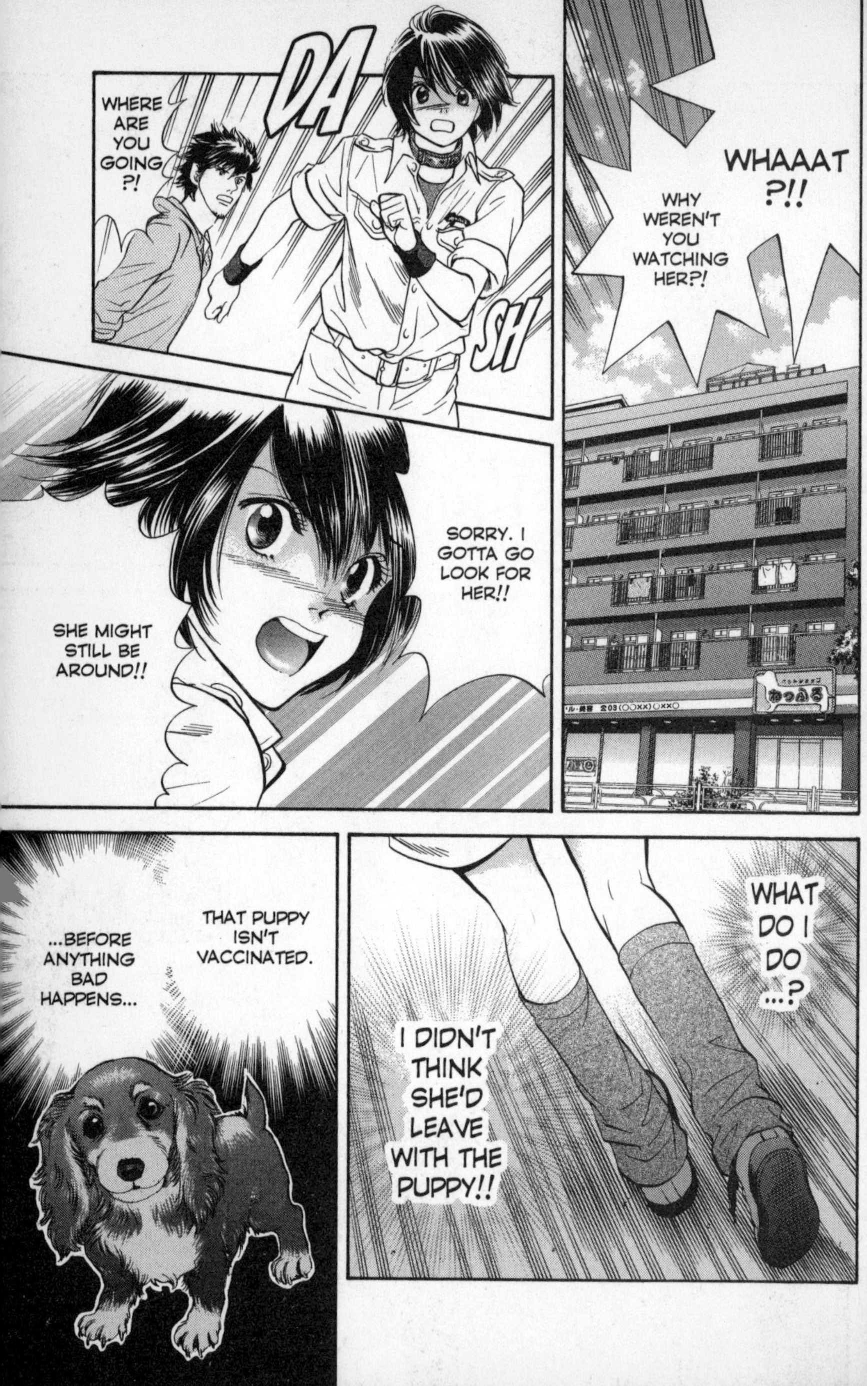
WHAAAT ?!!
WHY WEREN'T YOU WATCHING HER?!
DASH
WHERE ARE YOU GOING ?!
SORRY. I GOTTA GO LOOK FOR HER!!
SHE MIGHT STILL BE AROUND!!
WHAT DO I DO ...?
I DIDN'T THINK SHE'D LEAVE WITH THE PUPPY!!
THAT PUPPY ISN'T VACCINATED.
...BEFORE ANYTHING BAD HAPPENS...

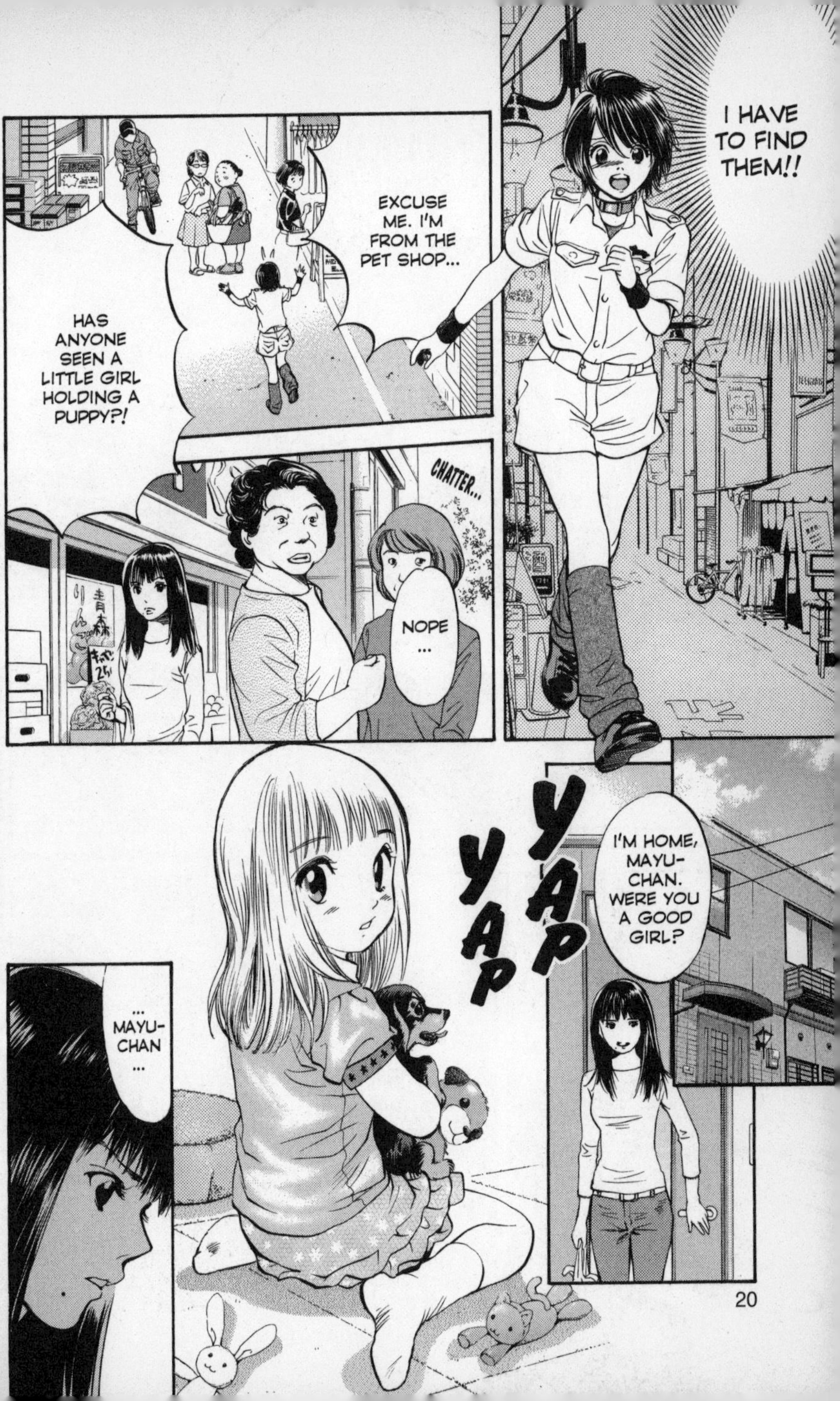
I HAVE TO FIND THEM!!
EXCUSE ME. I'M FROM THE PET SHOP...
HAS ANYONE SEEN A LITTLE GIRL HOLDING A PUPPY?!
CHATTER...
NOPE ...
I'M HOME, MAYU-CHAN. WERE YOU A GOOD GIRL?
YAP YAP
YAP YAP
... MAYU-CHAN ...

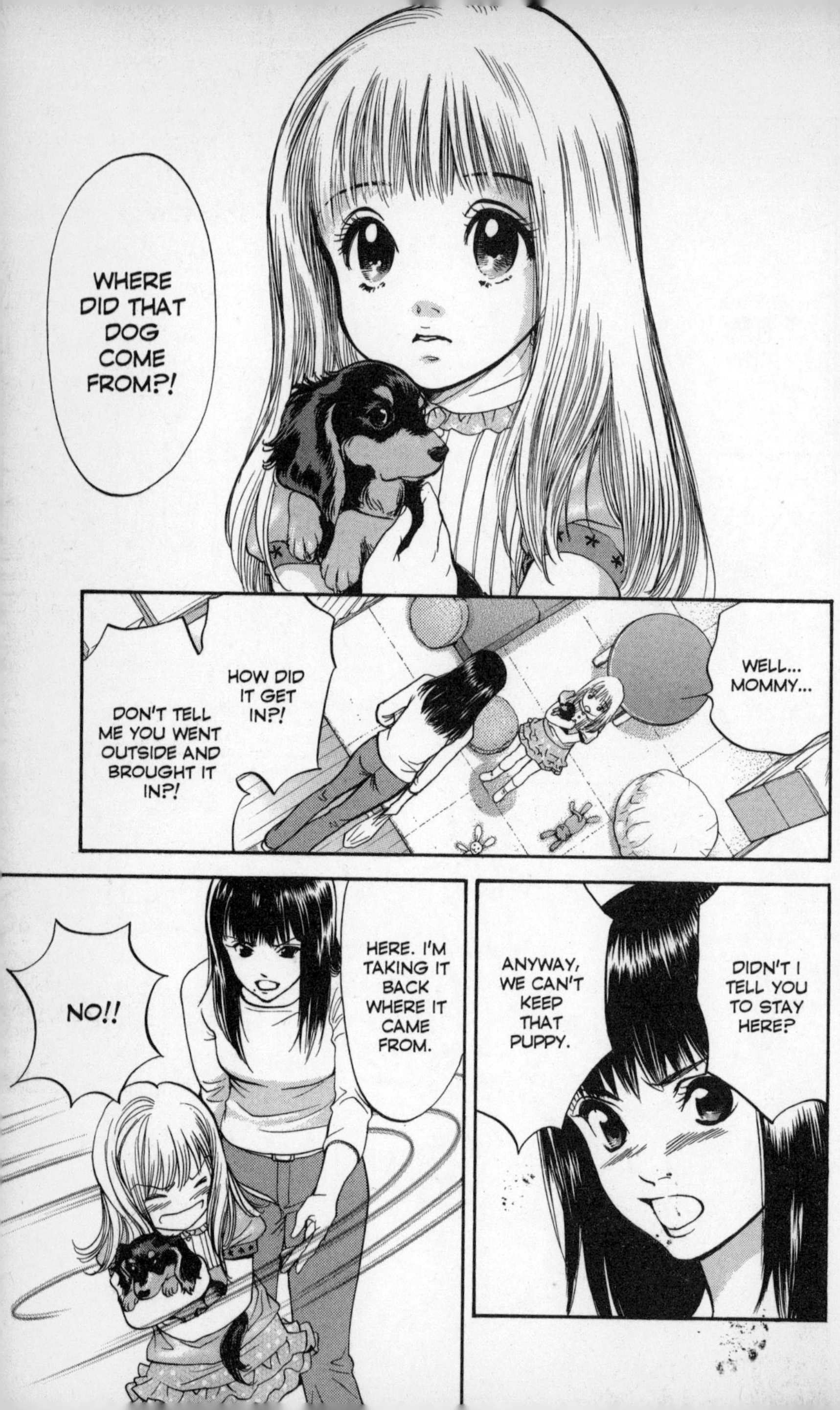
WHERE DID THAT DOG COME FROM?!
WELL... MOMMY...
HOW DID IT GET IN?!
DON'T TELL ME YOU WENT OUTSIDE AND BROUGHT IT IN?!
DIDN'T I TELL YOU TO STAY HERE?
ANYWAY, WE CAN'T KEEP THAT PUPPY.
HERE. I'M TAKING IT BACK WHERE IT CAME FROM.
NO!!

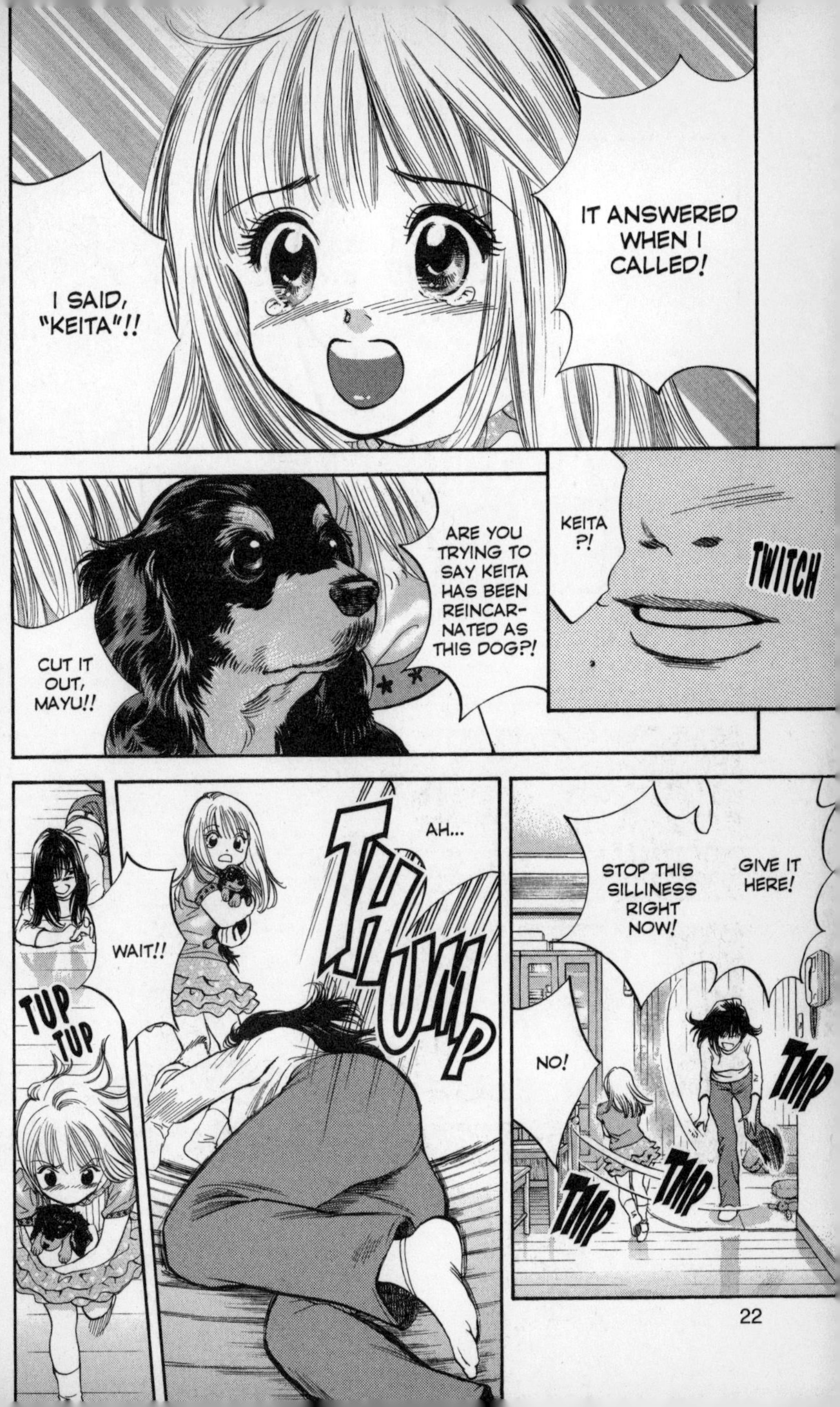
IT ANSWERED WHEN I CALLED!
I SAID, "KEITA"!!
KEITA?!
TWITCH
ARE YOU TRYING TO SAY KEITA HAS BEEN REINCARNATED AS THIS DOG?!
CUT IT OUT, MAYU!!
GIVE IT HERE!
STOP THIS SILLINESS RIGHT NOW!
NO!
TMP
TMP
TMP
AH...
THUMP
WAIT!!
TUP TUP

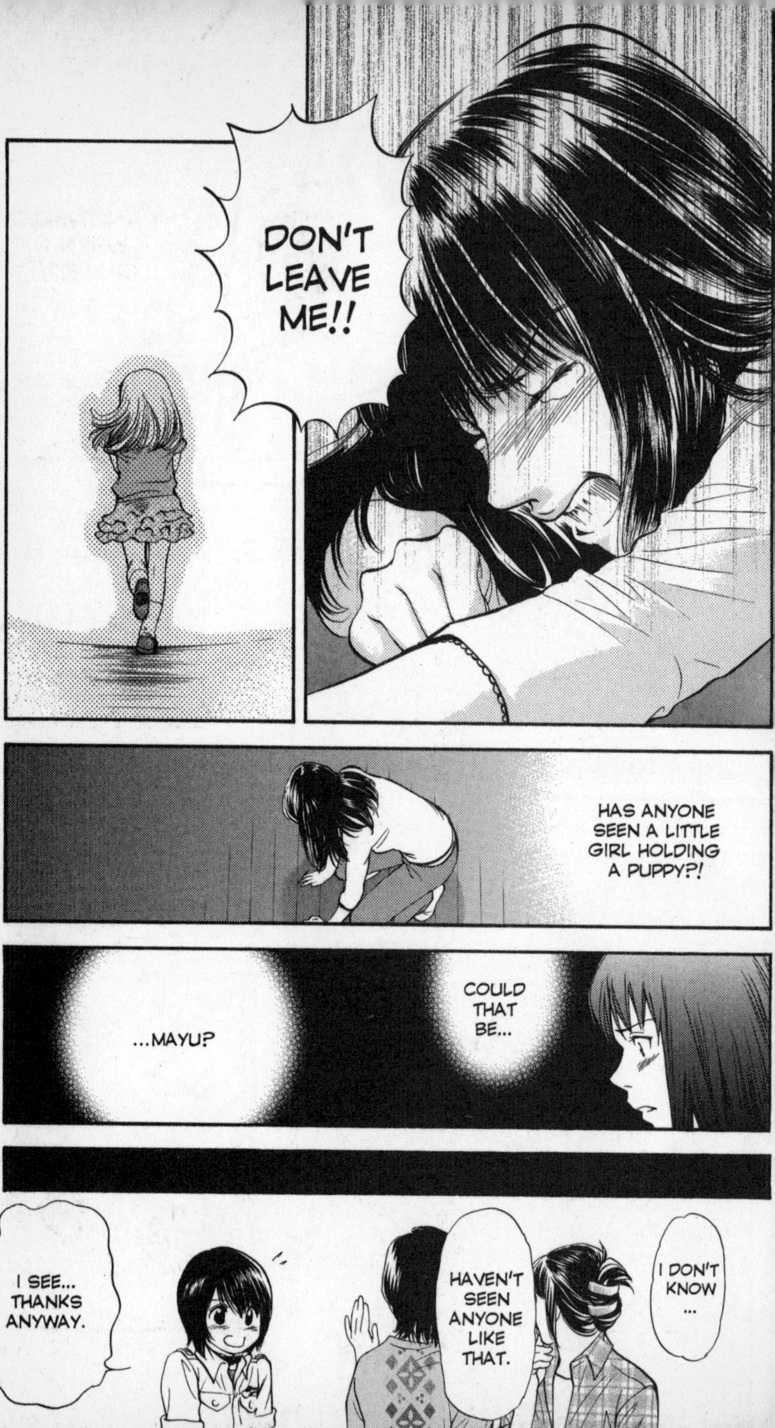
DON'T LEAVE ME!!
HAS ANYONE SEEN A LITTLE GIRL HOLDING A PUPPY?!
COULD THAT BE...
...MAYU?
I DON'T KNOW ...
HAVEN'T SEEN ANYONE LIKE THAT.
I SEE... THANKS ANYWAY.

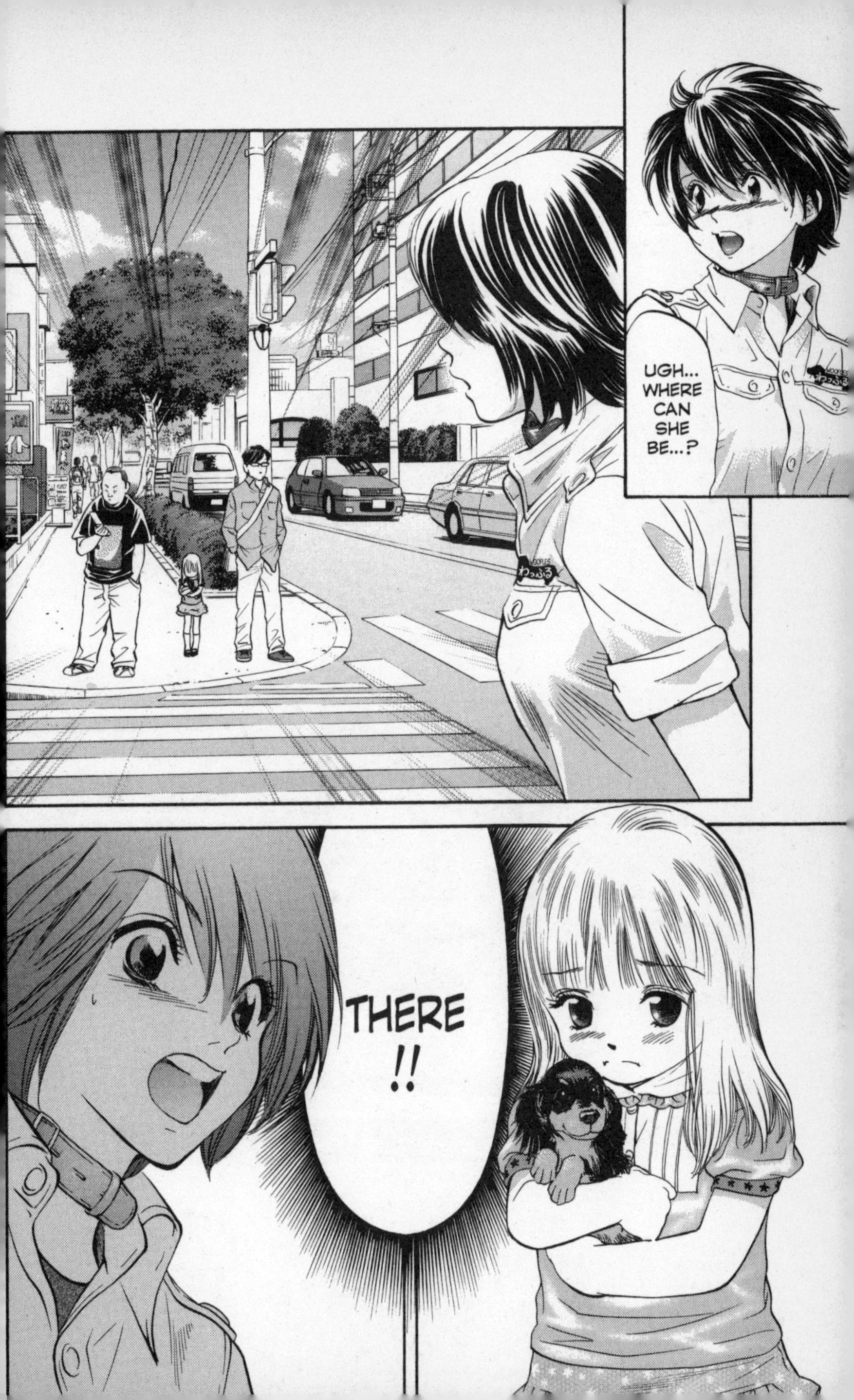
UGH... WHERE CAN SHE BE...?
THERE !!

CHAPTER 65:
GOING AFTER THE DOGGIE!!

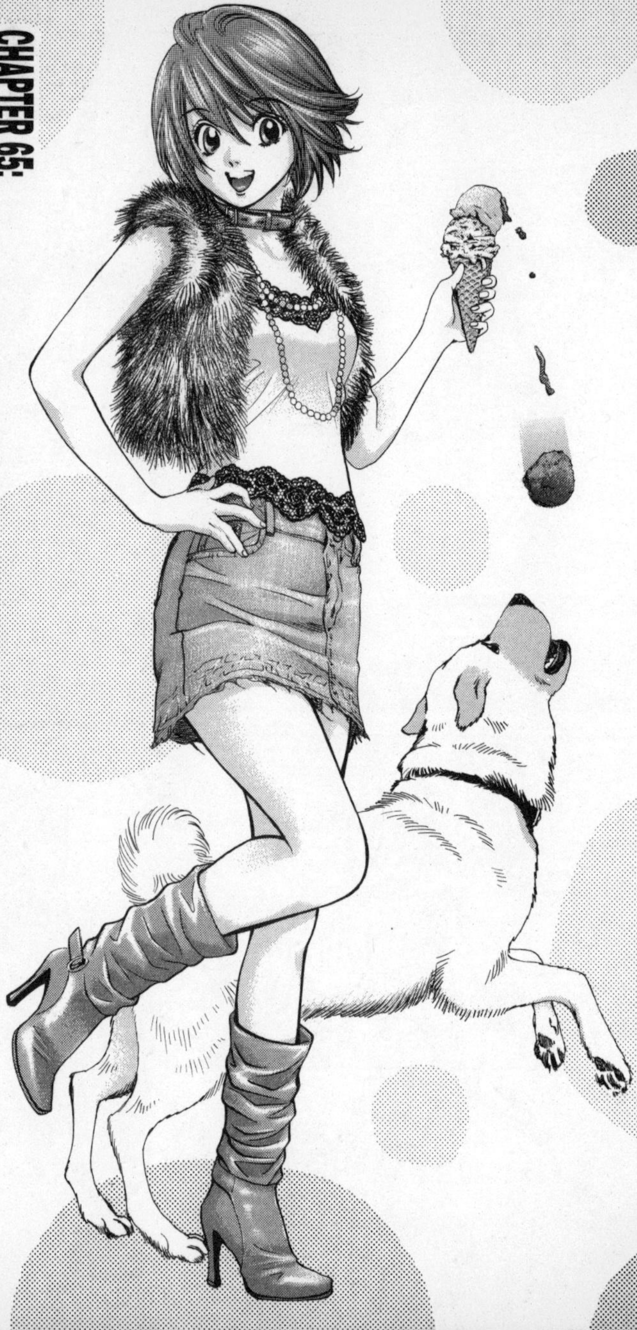

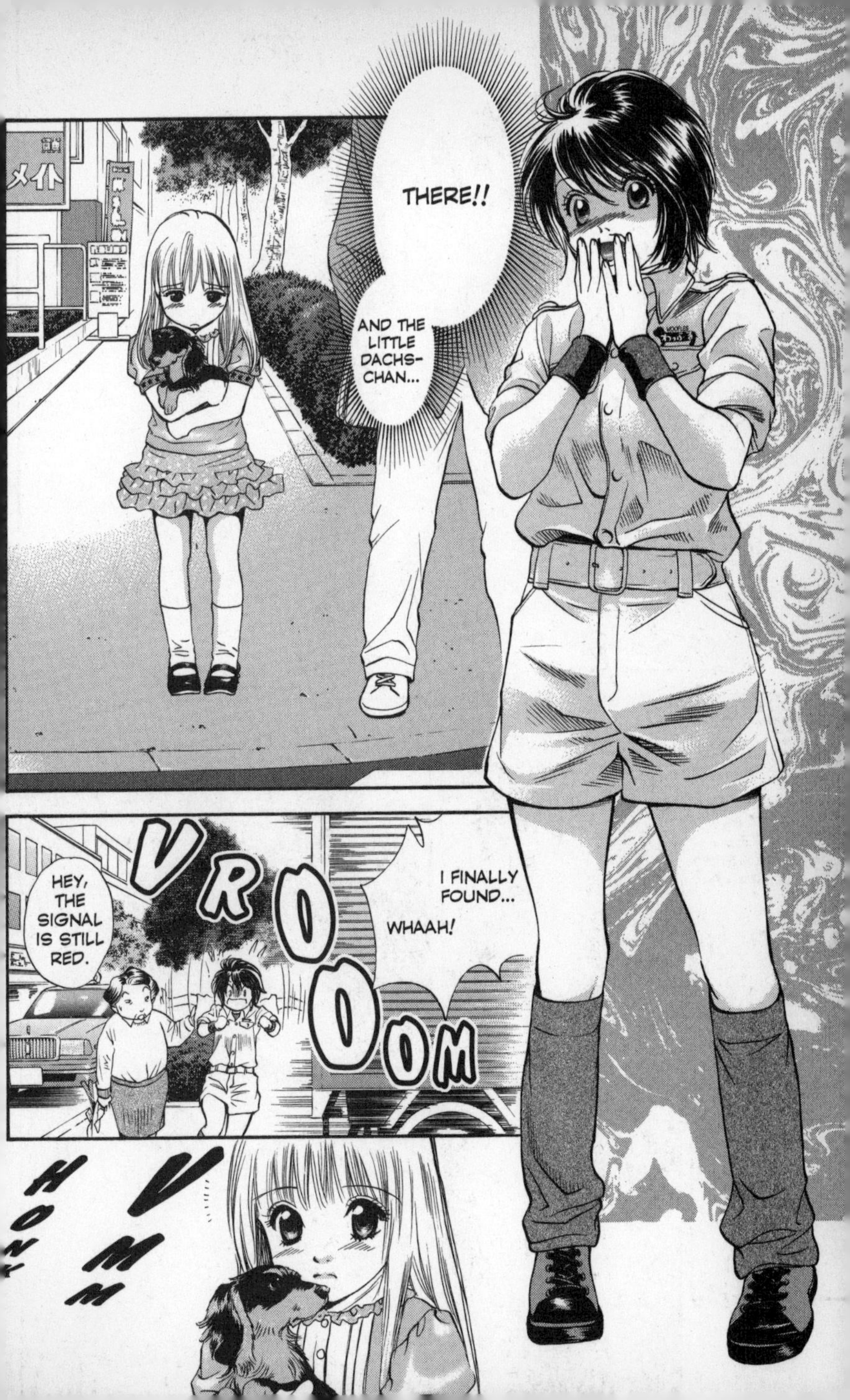
THERE!!
AND THE LITTLE DACHS-CHAN...
I FINALLY FOUND...
WHAAH!
VROOOOM
HEY, THE SIGNAL IS STILL RED.
VMMM
HONK

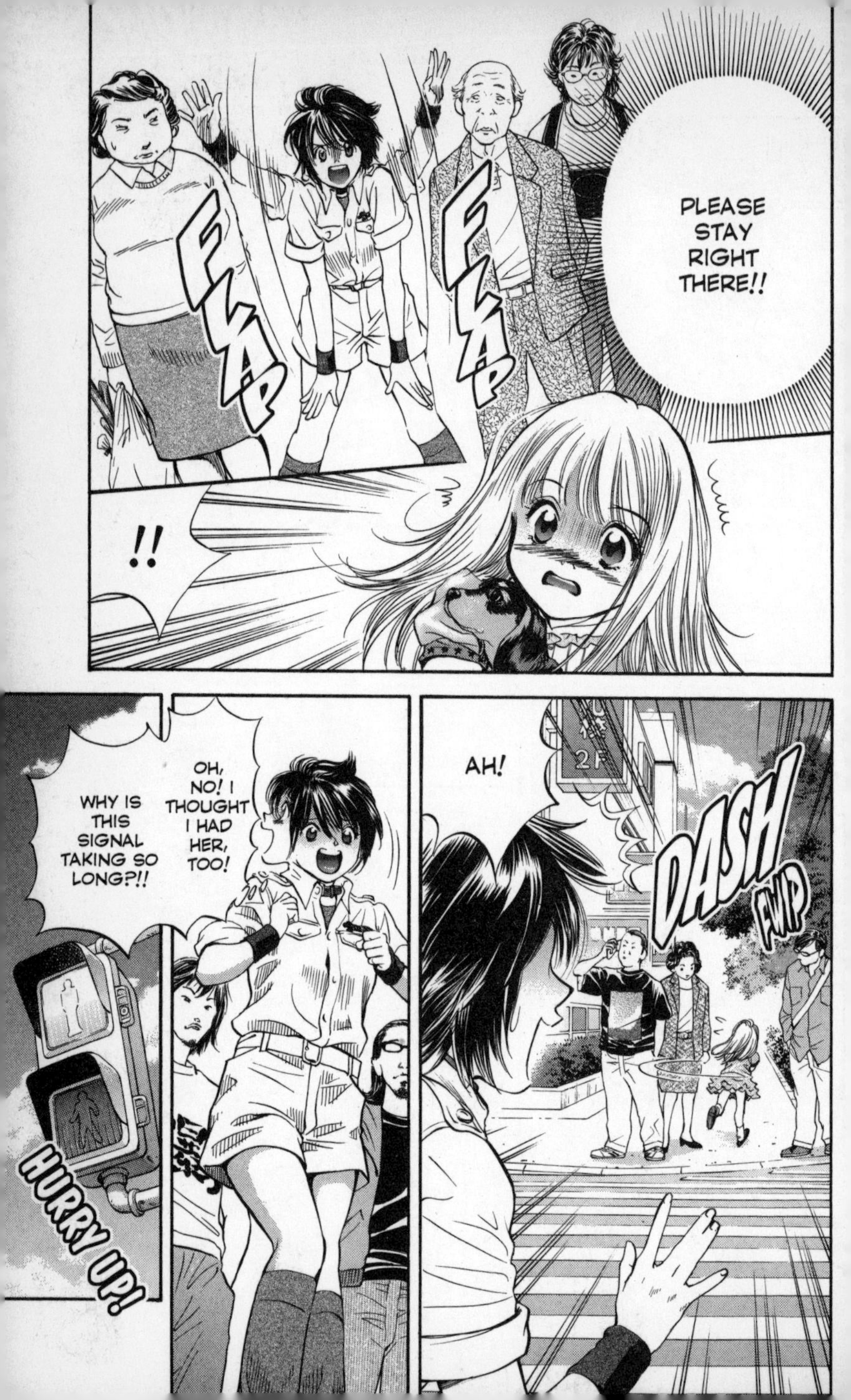
PLEASE STAY RIGHT THERE!!
FLAP
FLAP
!!
AH!
DASH
FWIP
OH, NO! I THOUGHT I HAD HER, TOO!
WHY IS THIS SIGNAL TAKING SO LONG?!!
HURRY UP!

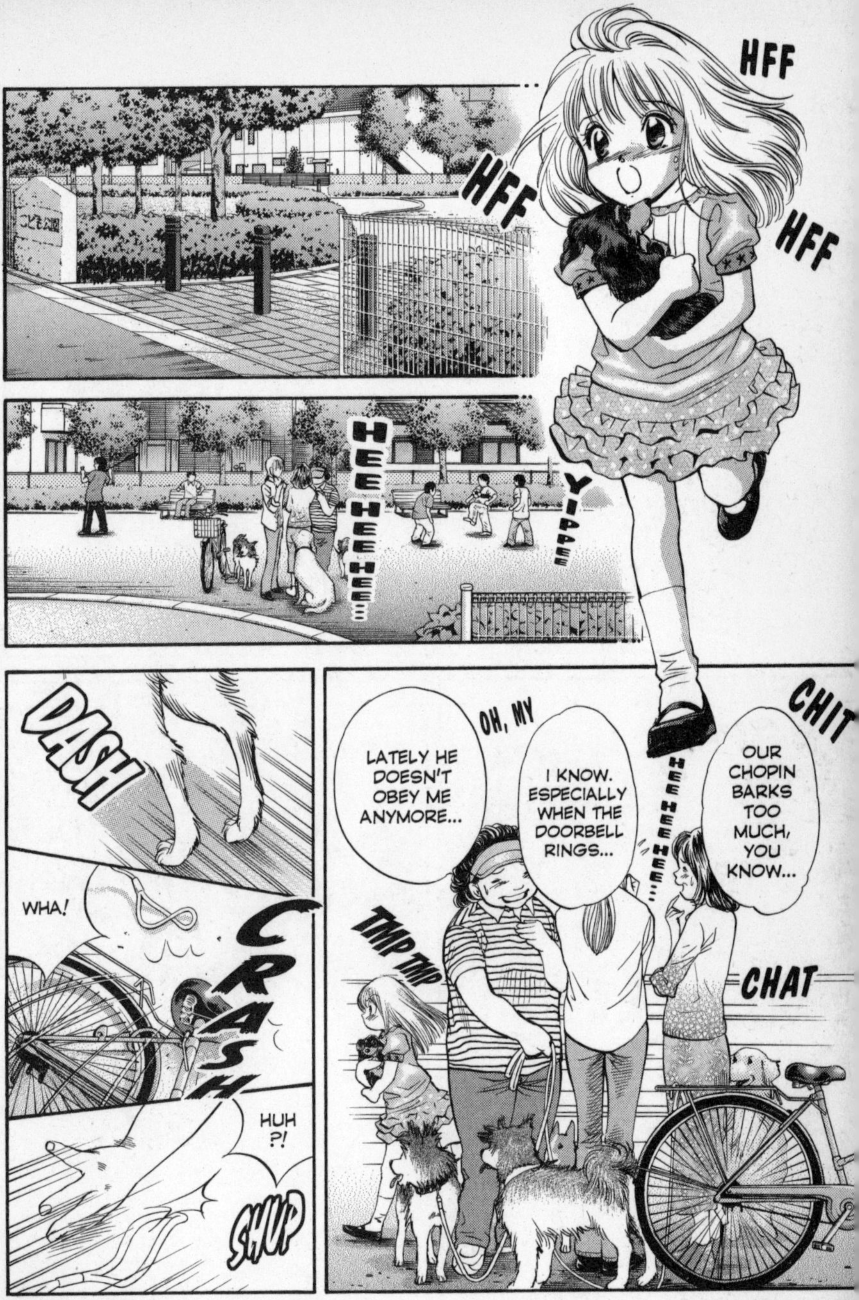

HFF
HFF
HFF
HEE HEE HEE...
YIPPEE
CHIT
OUR CHOPIN BARKS TOO MUCH, YOU KNOW...
I KNOW. ESPECIALLY WHEN THE DOORBELL RINGS...
OH, MY
LATELY HE DOESN'T OBEY ME ANYMORE...
HEE HEE HEE...
CHAT
TMP TMP
DASH
WHA!
CRASH
HUH ?!
SHUP

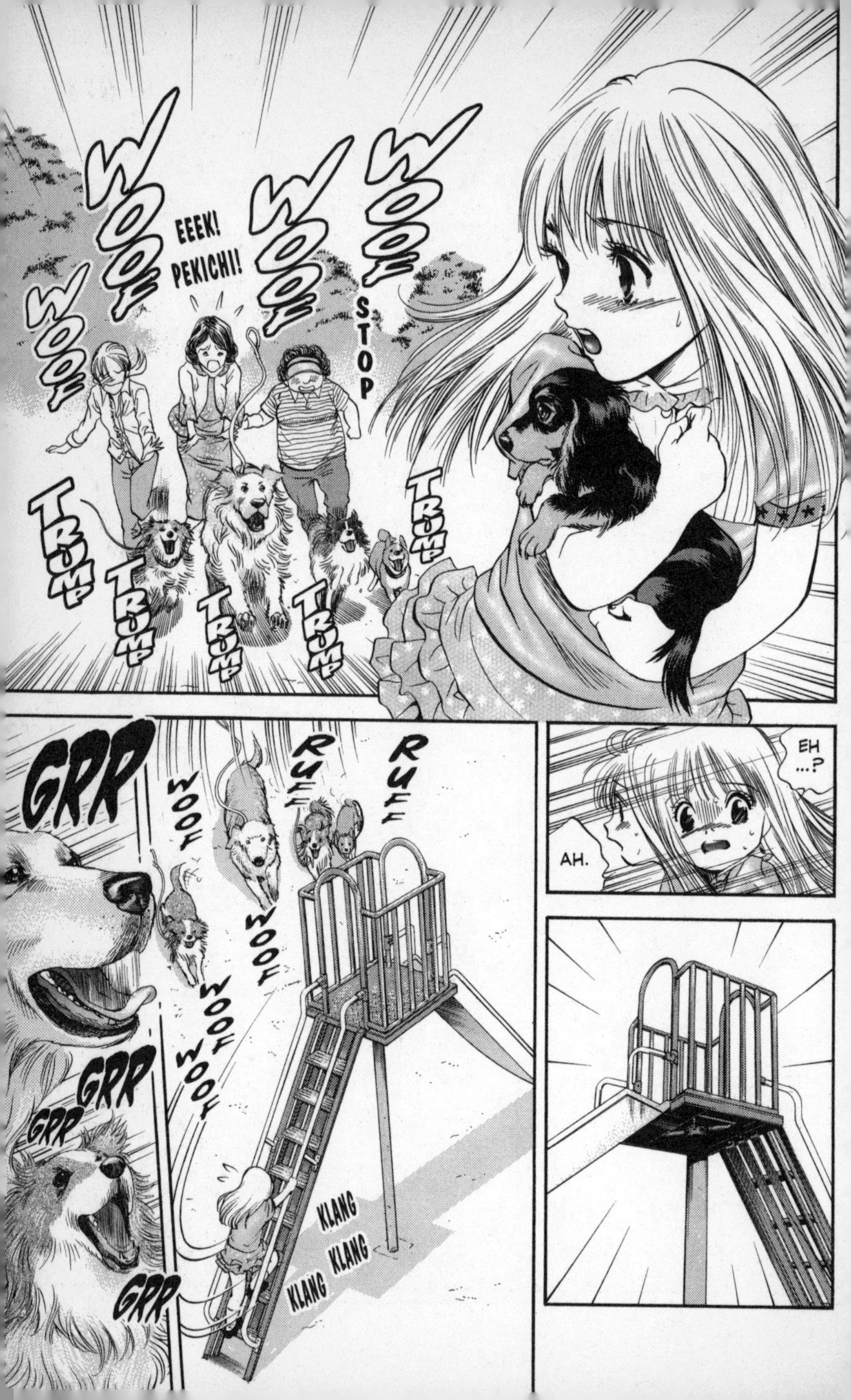
WOOOF!
STOP
WOOOF!
EEEK! PEKICHI!
WOOOF!
WOOF!
TRUMP
TRUMP
TRUMP
TRUMP
TRUMP
EH ...?
AH.
RUFF
RUFF
WOOF
WOOF
WOOF
WOOF WOOF
GRR
GRR
GRR
GRR
KLANG
KLANG
KLANG

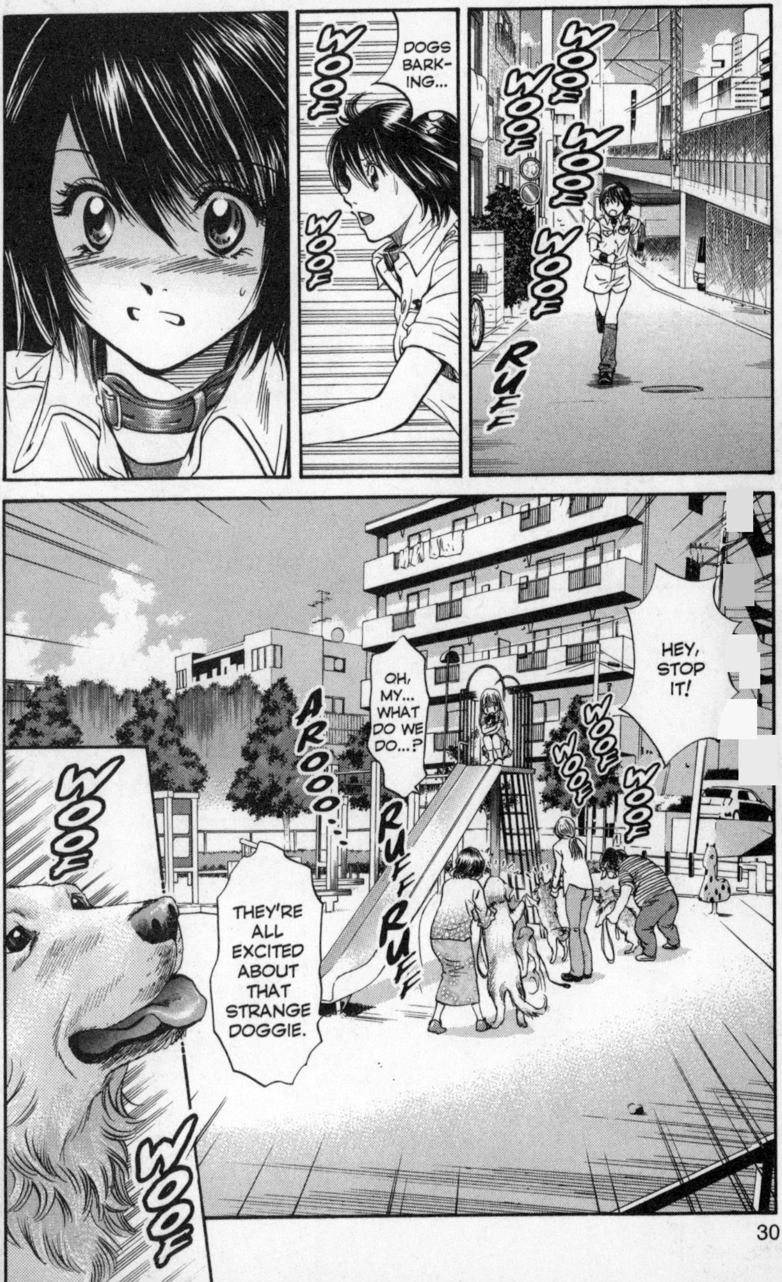

WOOF
WOOF
WOOF
WOOF
WOOF
RUFF
DOGS BARKING...
WOOF
WOOF
HEY, STOP IT!
WOOF
WOOF
WOOF
OH, MY... WHAT DO WE DO...?
AROOO...
RUFF RUFF
WOOF
THEY'RE ALL EXCITED ABOUT THAT STRANGE DOGGIE.
WOOF

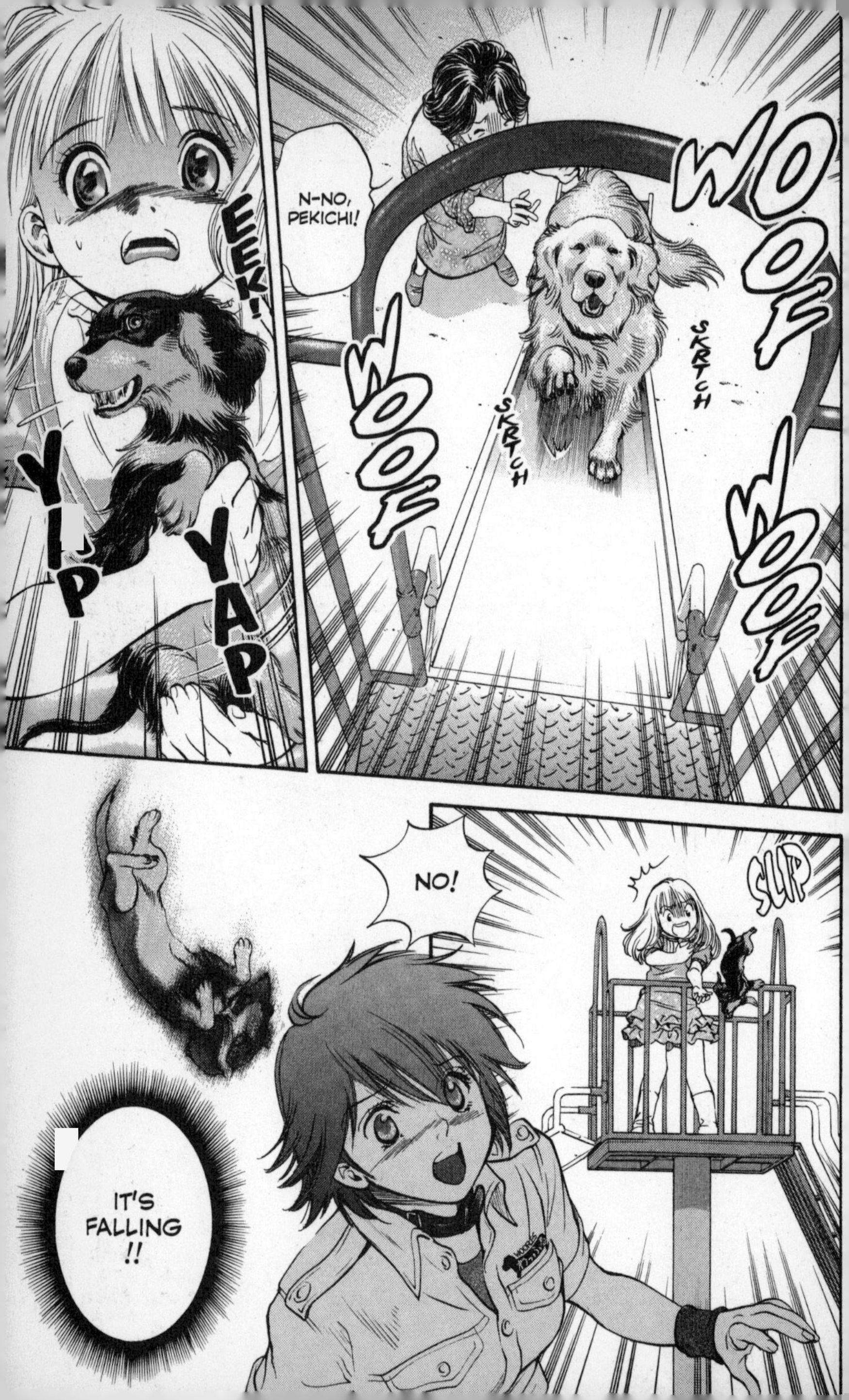
WOOF
N-NO, PEKICHI!
SKRTCH
WOOF
SKRTCH
WOOF
EEK!
YAP
YIP
SLIP
NO!
IT'S FALLING!!

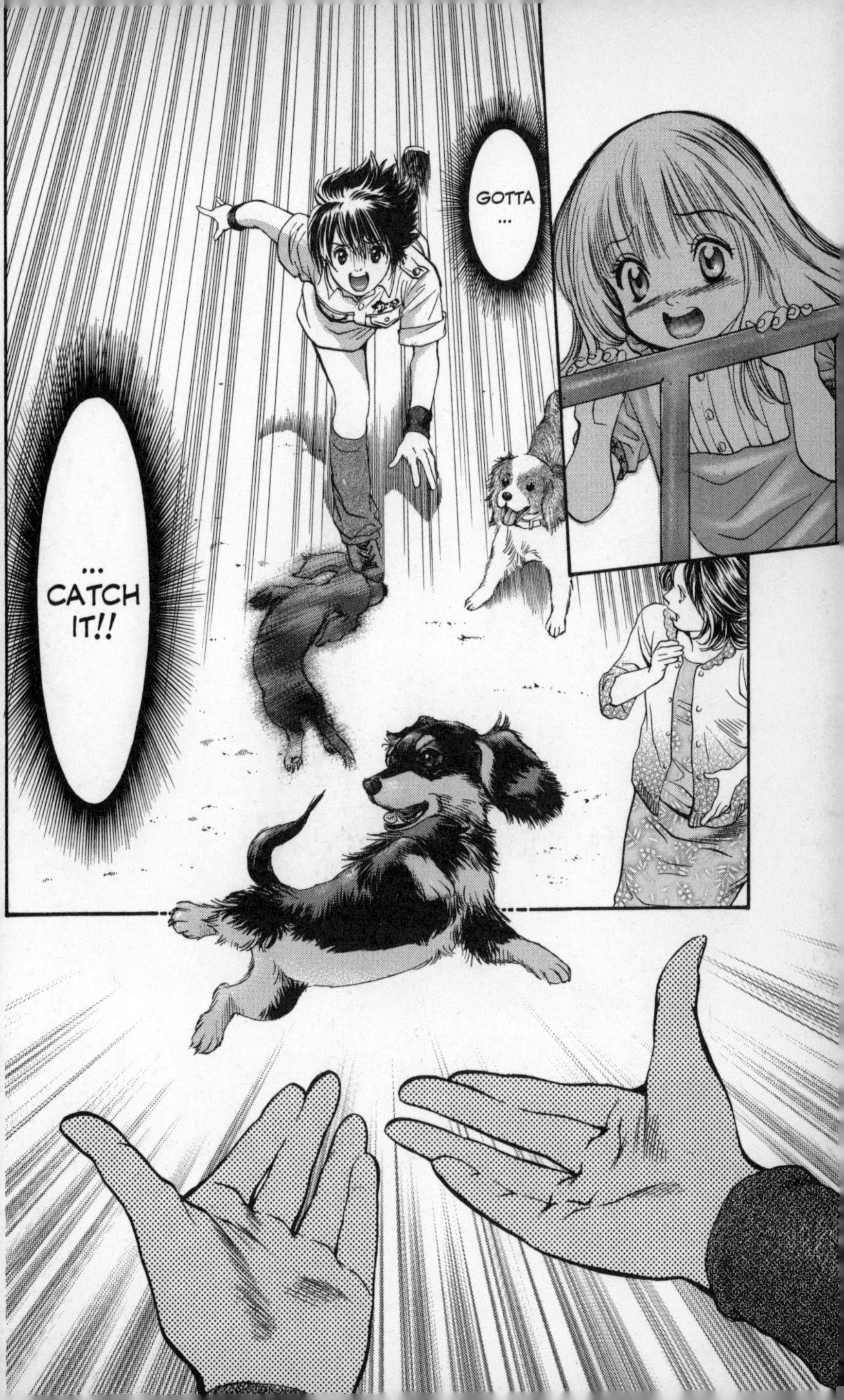
GOTTA ...
... CATCH IT!!

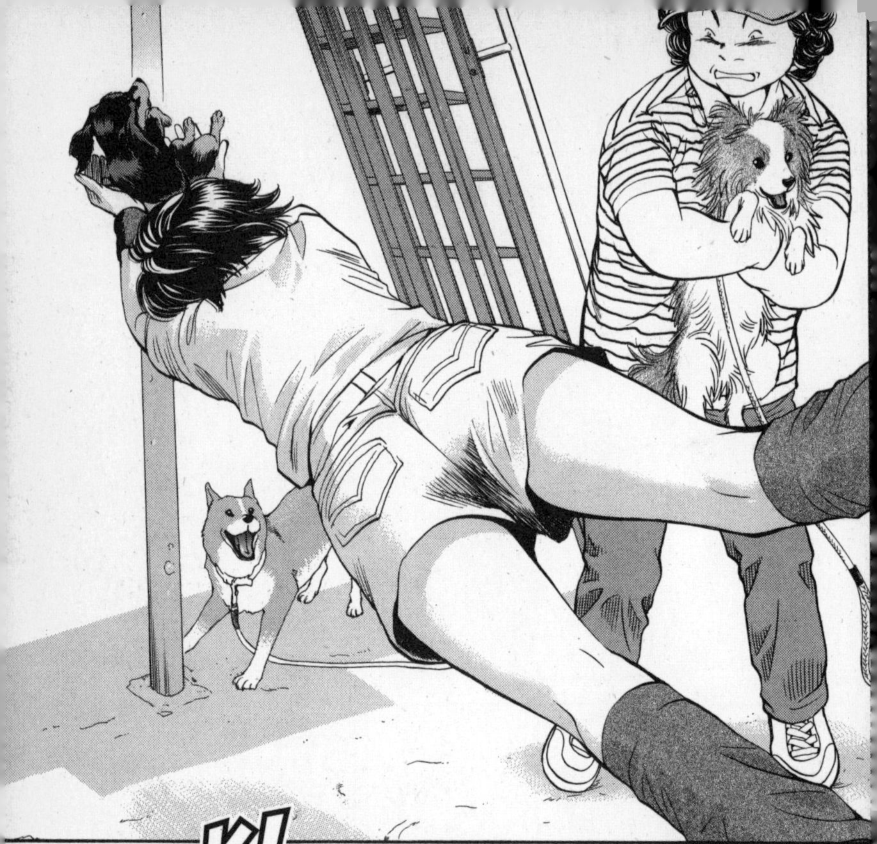
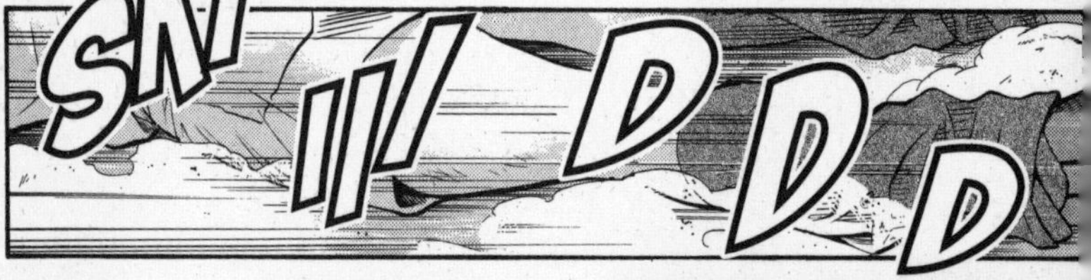
SKIIIDDD
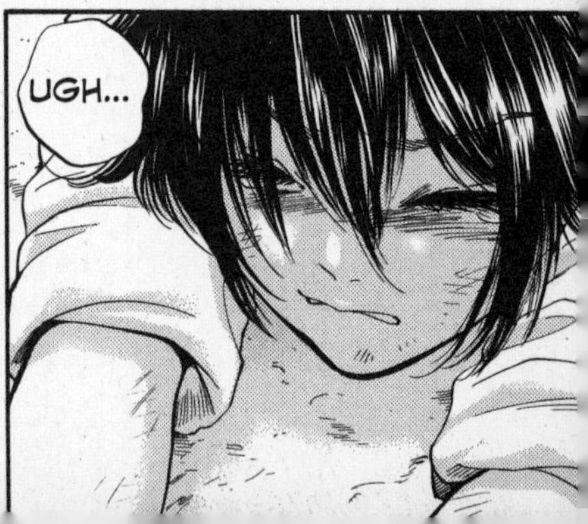
UGH...
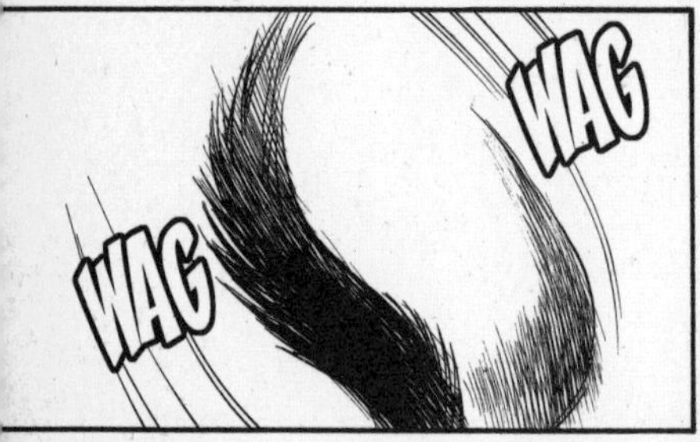
WAG
WAG

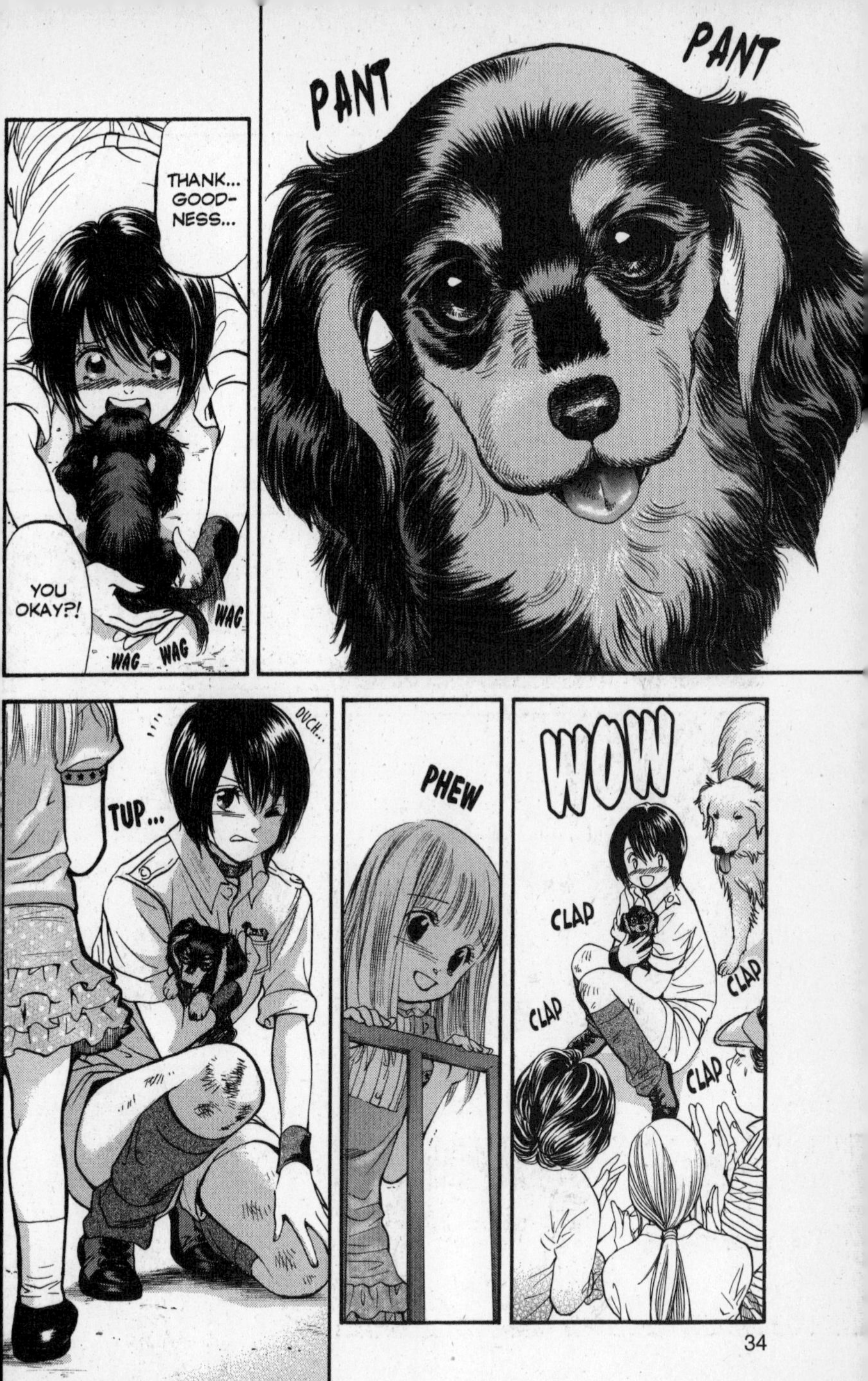
PANT
PANT
THANK... GOODNESS...
YOU OKAY?!
WAG
WAG
WAG
WOW
CLAP
CLAP
CLAP
CLAP
PHEW
OUCH...
TUP...

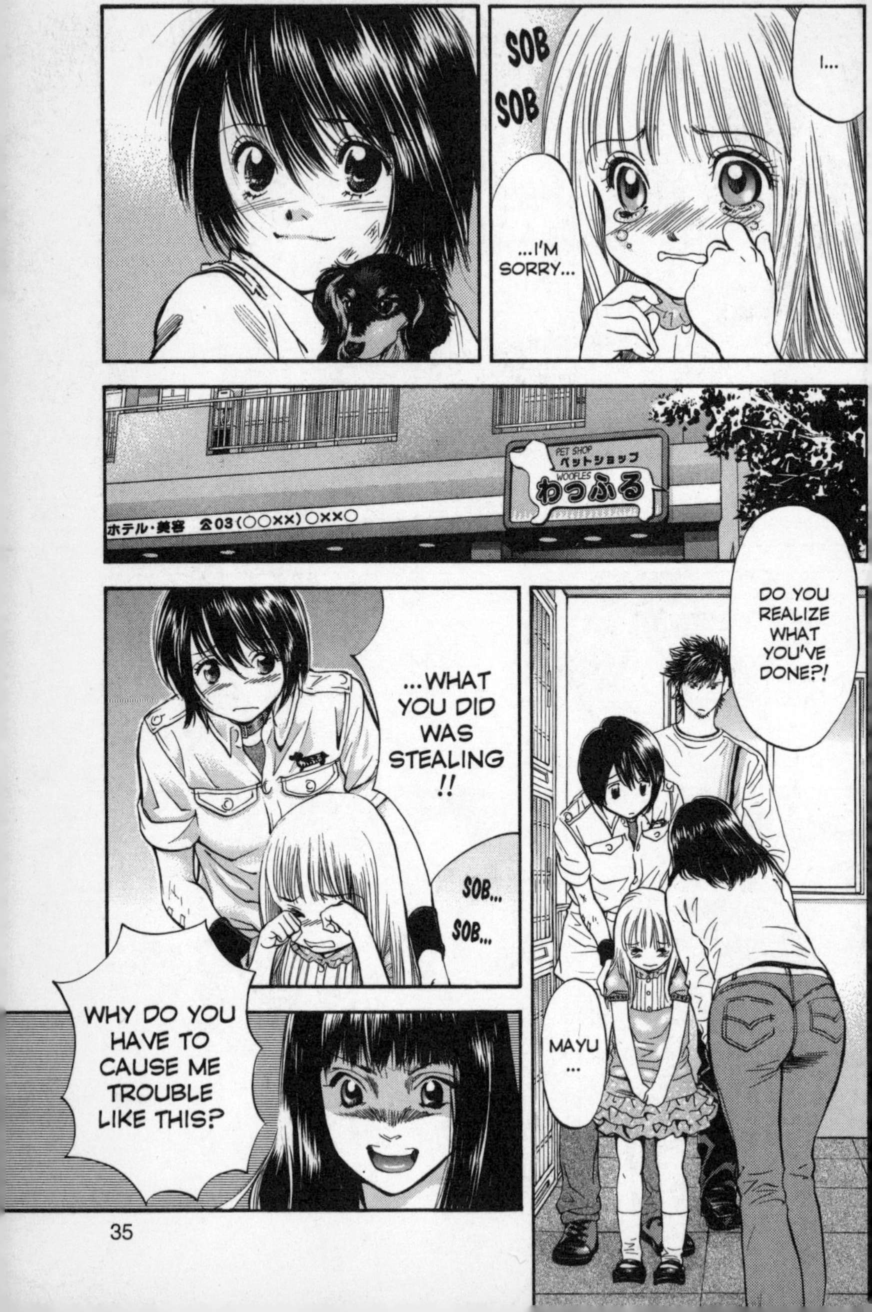
I...
SOB
SOB
...I'M SORRY...
PET SHOP
ペットショップ
WOOFLES
わっふる
ホテル・美容 ☎03(○○××)○××○
DO YOU REALIZE WHAT YOU'VE DONE?!
MAYU...
...WHAT YOU DID WAS STEALING!!
SOB... SOB...
WHY DO YOU HAVE TO CAUSE ME TROUBLE LIKE THIS?

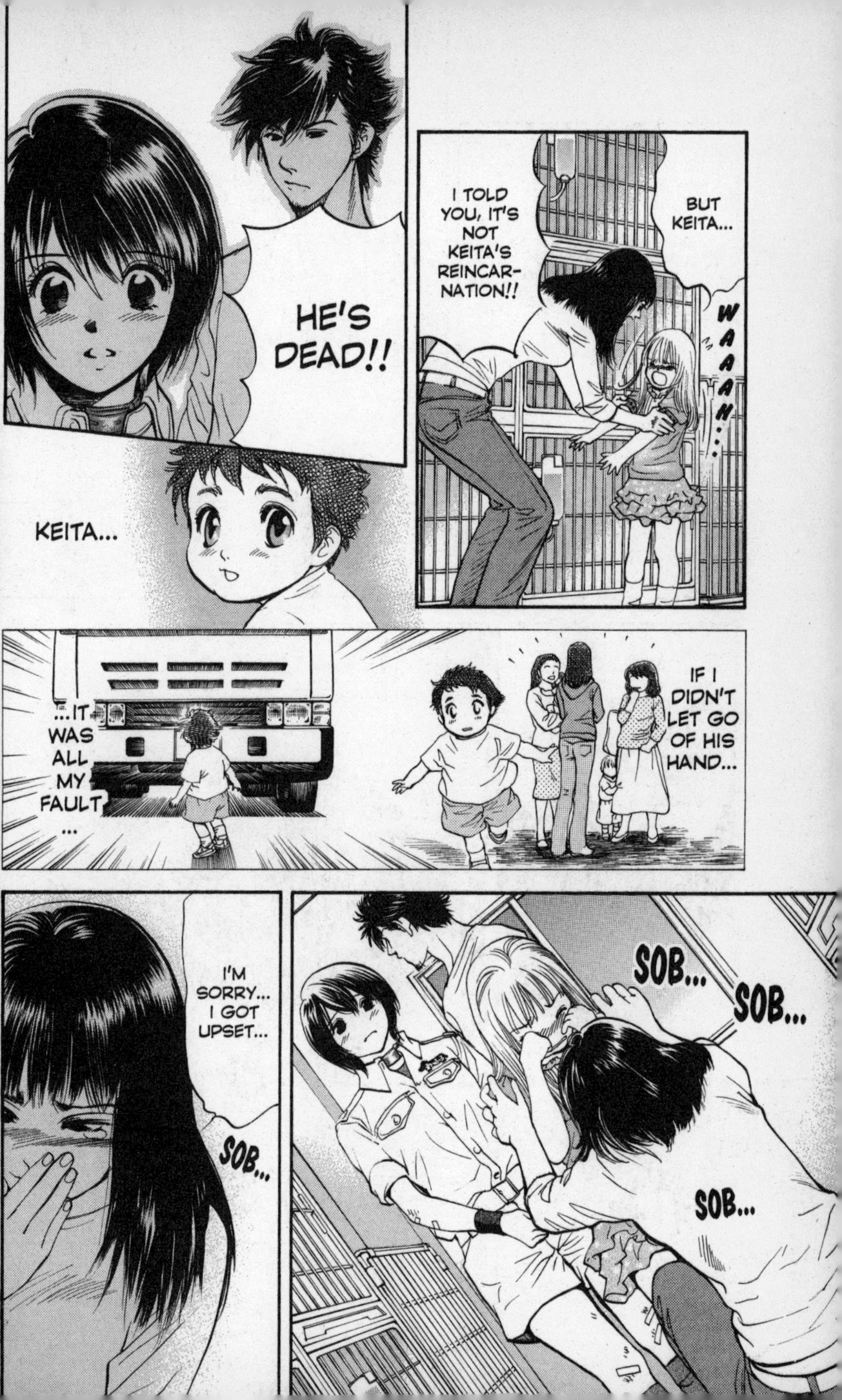
BUT KEITA...
I TOLD YOU, IT'S NOT KEITA'S REINCARNATION!!
WAAAAH...
HE'S DEAD!!
KEITA...
IF I DIDN'T LET GO OF HIS HAND...
...IT WAS ALL MY FAULT...
SOB...
SOB...
SOB...
I'M SORRY... I GOT UPSET...
SOB...

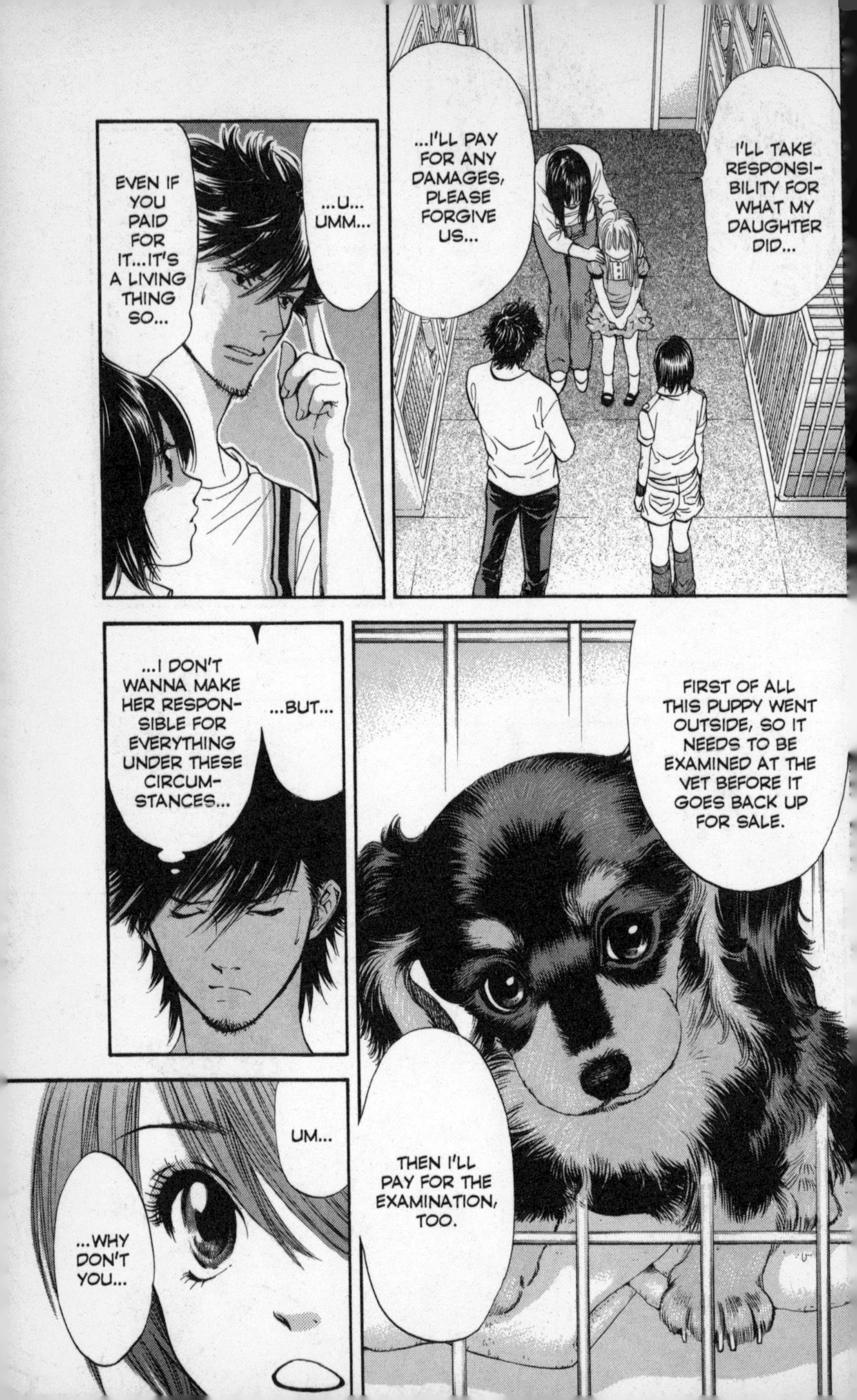
I'LL TAKE RESPONSIBILITY FOR WHAT MY DAUGHTER DID...
...I'LL PAY FOR ANY DAMAGES, PLEASE FORGIVE US...
...U... UMM...
EVEN IF YOU PAID FOR IT...IT'S A LIVING THING SO...
FIRST OF ALL THIS PUPPY WENT OUTSIDE, SO IT NEEDS TO BE EXAMINED AT THE VET BEFORE IT GOES BACK UP FOR SALE.
THEN I'LL PAY FOR THE EXAMINATION, TOO.
...BUT...
...I DON'T WANNA MAKE HER RESPONSIBLE FOR EVERYTHING UNDER THESE CIRCUMSTANCES...
UM...
...WHY DON'T YOU...

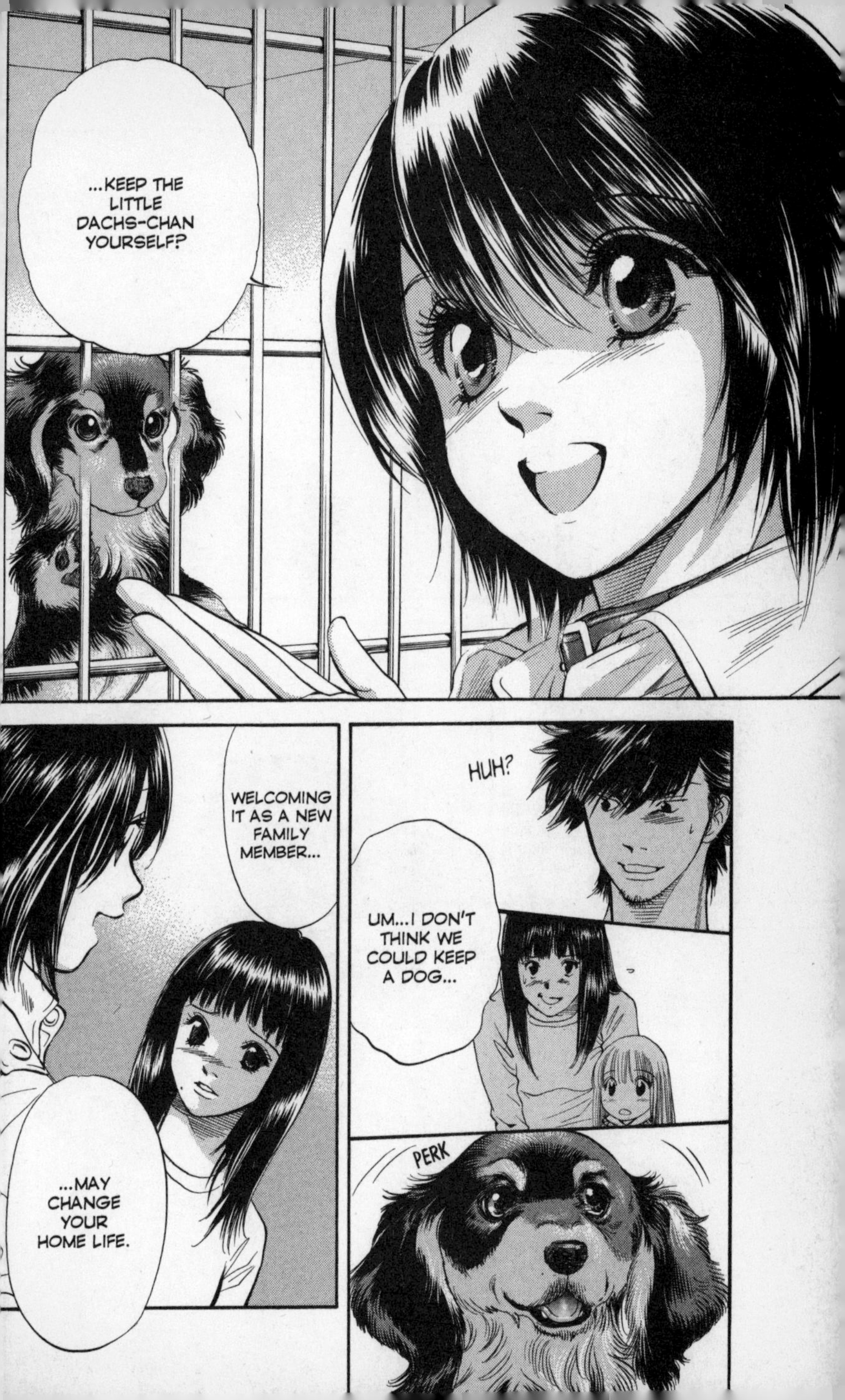
...KEEP THE LITTLE DACHS-CHAN YOURSELF?
HUH?
UM...I DON'T THINK WE COULD KEEP A DOG...
PERK
WELCOMING IT AS A NEW FAMILY MEMBER...
...MAY CHANGE YOUR HOME LIFE.

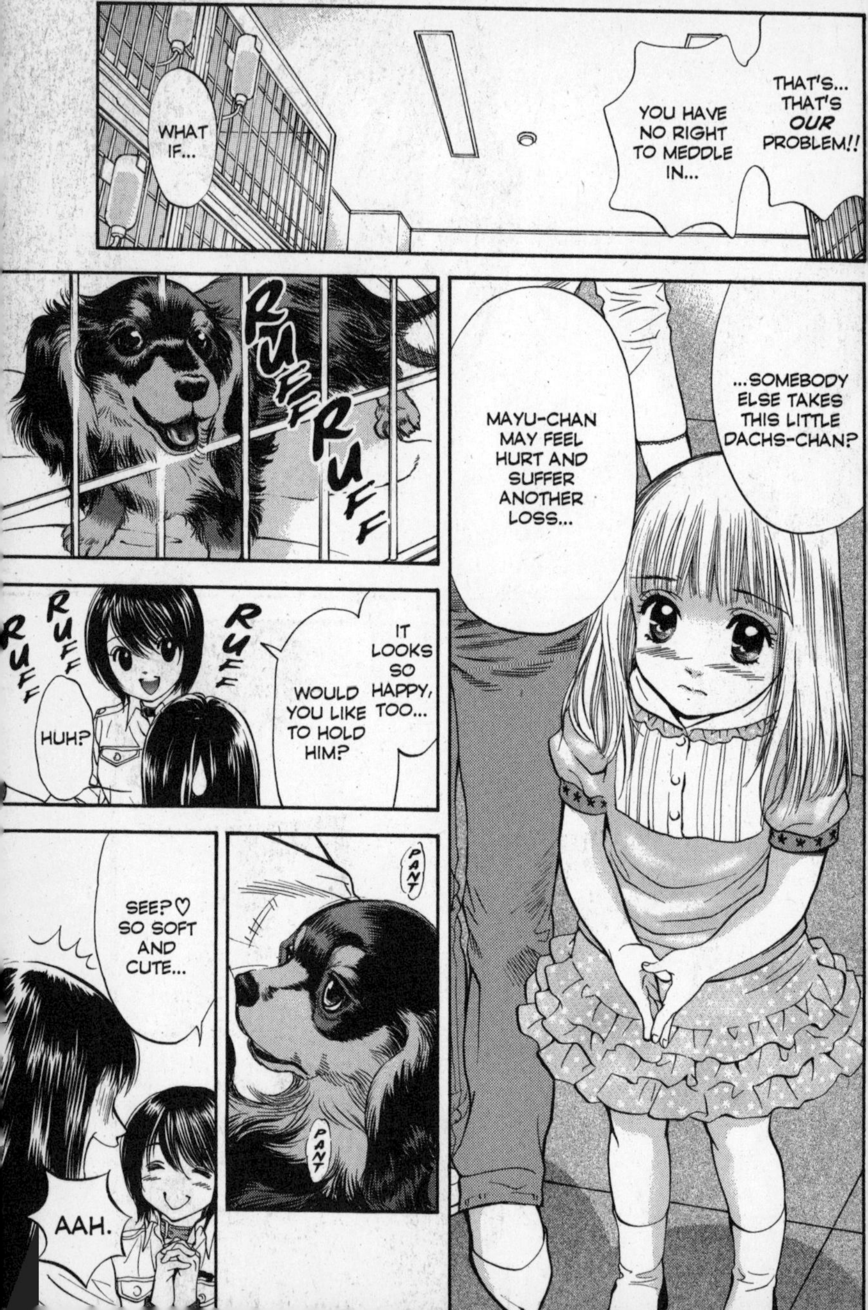
THAT'S... THAT'S *OUR* PROBLEM!!
YOU HAVE NO RIGHT TO MEDDLE IN...
WHAT IF...
...SOMEBODY ELSE TAKES THIS LITTLE DACHS-CHAN?
MAYU-CHAN MAY FEEL HURT AND SUFFER ANOTHER LOSS...
RUFF RUFF RUFF
IT LOOKS SO HAPPY, TOO...
WOULD YOU LIKE TO HOLD HIM?
RUFF
RUFF
HUH?
RUFF
PANT
PANT
SEE? ♡ SO SOFT AND CUTE...
AAH.

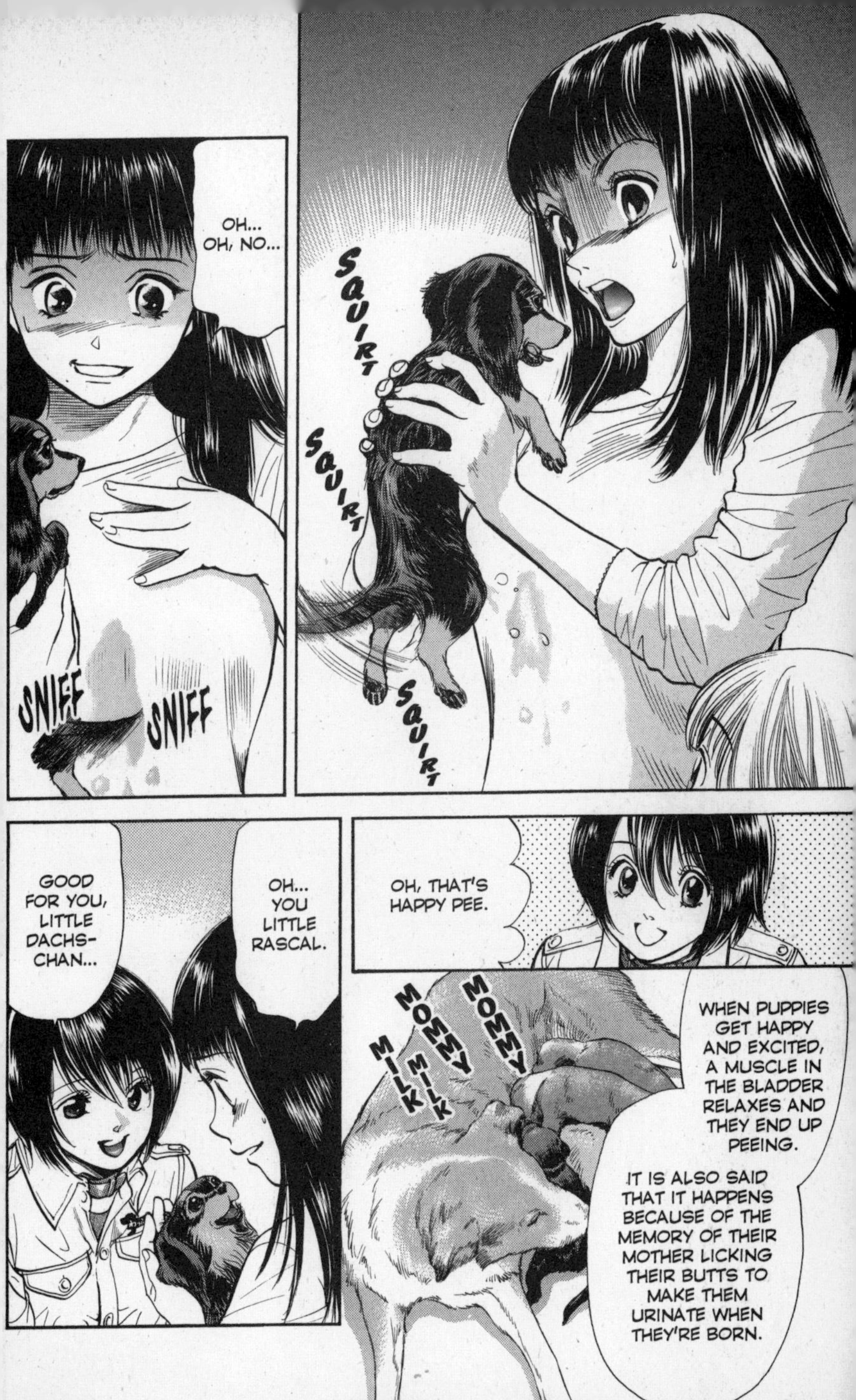
SQUIRT
SQUIRT
SQUIRT
OH... OH, NO...
SNIFF
SNIFF
OH, THAT'S HAPPY PEE.
MOMMY
MOMMY
MILK
MILK
WHEN PUPPIES GET HAPPY AND EXCITED, A MUSCLE IN THE BLADDER RELAXES AND THEY END UP PEEING.
IT IS ALSO SAID THAT IT HAPPENS BECAUSE OF THE MEMORY OF THEIR MOTHER LICKING THEIR BUTTS TO MAKE THEM URINATE WHEN THEY'RE BORN.
OH... YOU LITTLE RASCAL.
GOOD FOR YOU, LITTLE DACHS-CHAN...

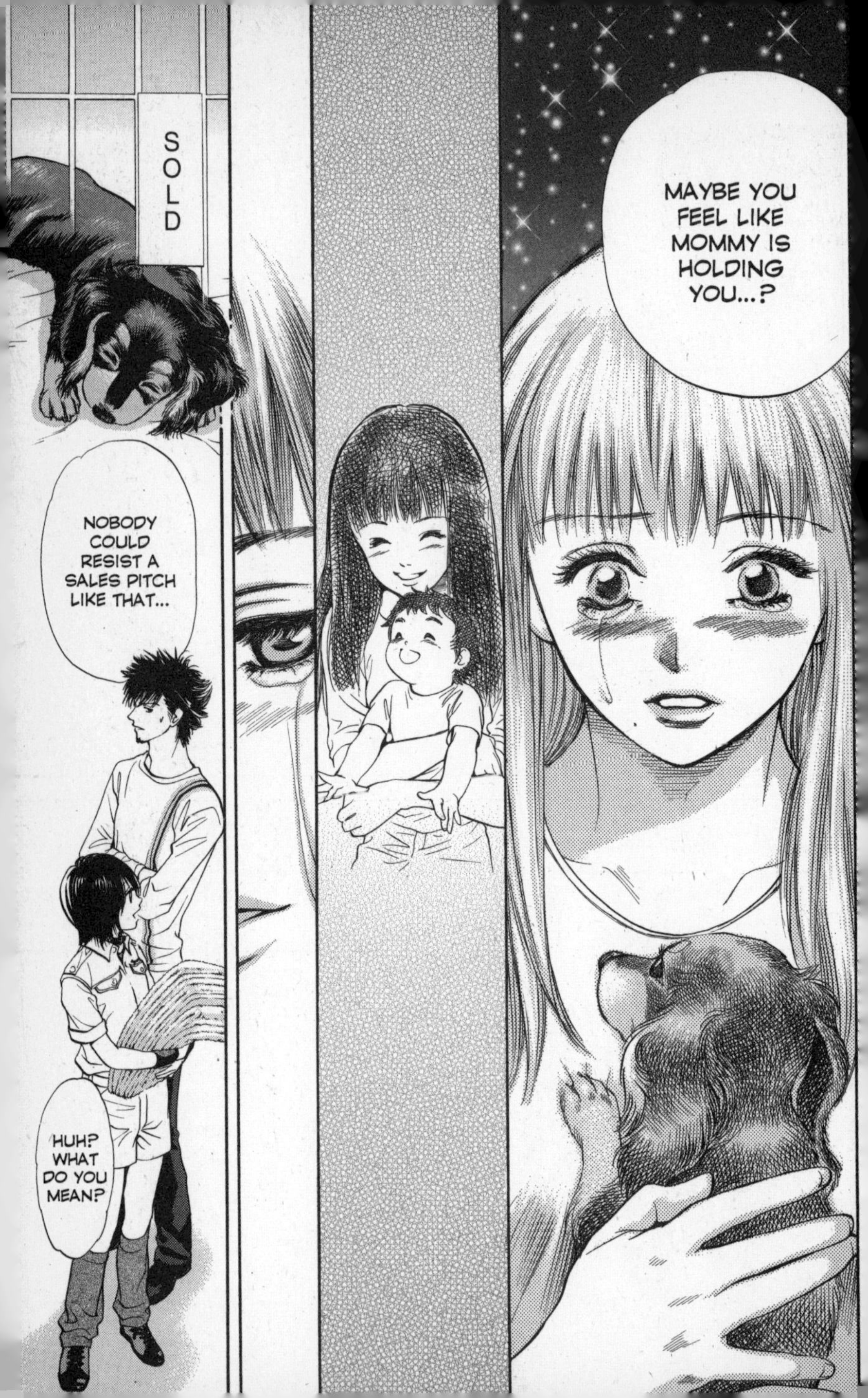
MAYBE YOU FEEL LIKE MOMMY IS HOLDING YOU...?
SOLD
NOBODY COULD RESIST A SALES PITCH LIKE THAT...
HUH? WHAT DO YOU MEAN?

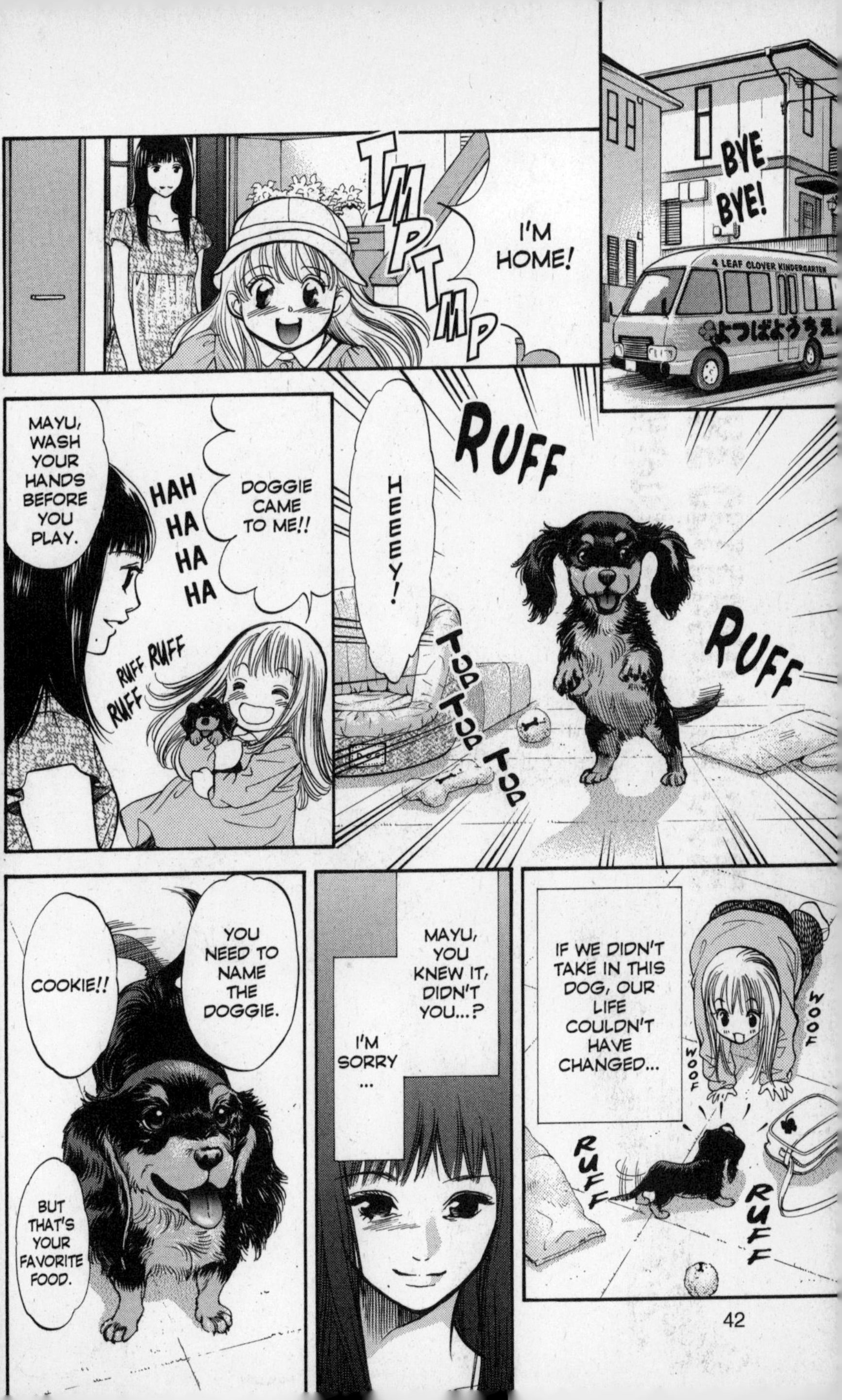

BYE BYE!
4 LEAF CLOVER KINDERGARTEN
よつばようちえ
TMP TMP
I'M HOME!
RUFF
HEEEY!
RUFF
TUP TUP TUP
DOGGIE CAME TO ME!!
HAH HA HA HA
MAYU, WASH YOUR HANDS BEFORE YOU PLAY.
RUFF RUFF RUFF
IF WE DIDN'T TAKE IN THIS DOG, OUR LIFE COULDN'T HAVE CHANGED...
WOOF
WOOF
RUFF
RUFF
MAYU, YOU KNEW IT, DIDN'T YOU...?
I'M SORRY ...
YOU NEED TO NAME THE DOGGIE.
COOKIE!!
BUT THAT'S YOUR FAVORITE FOOD.

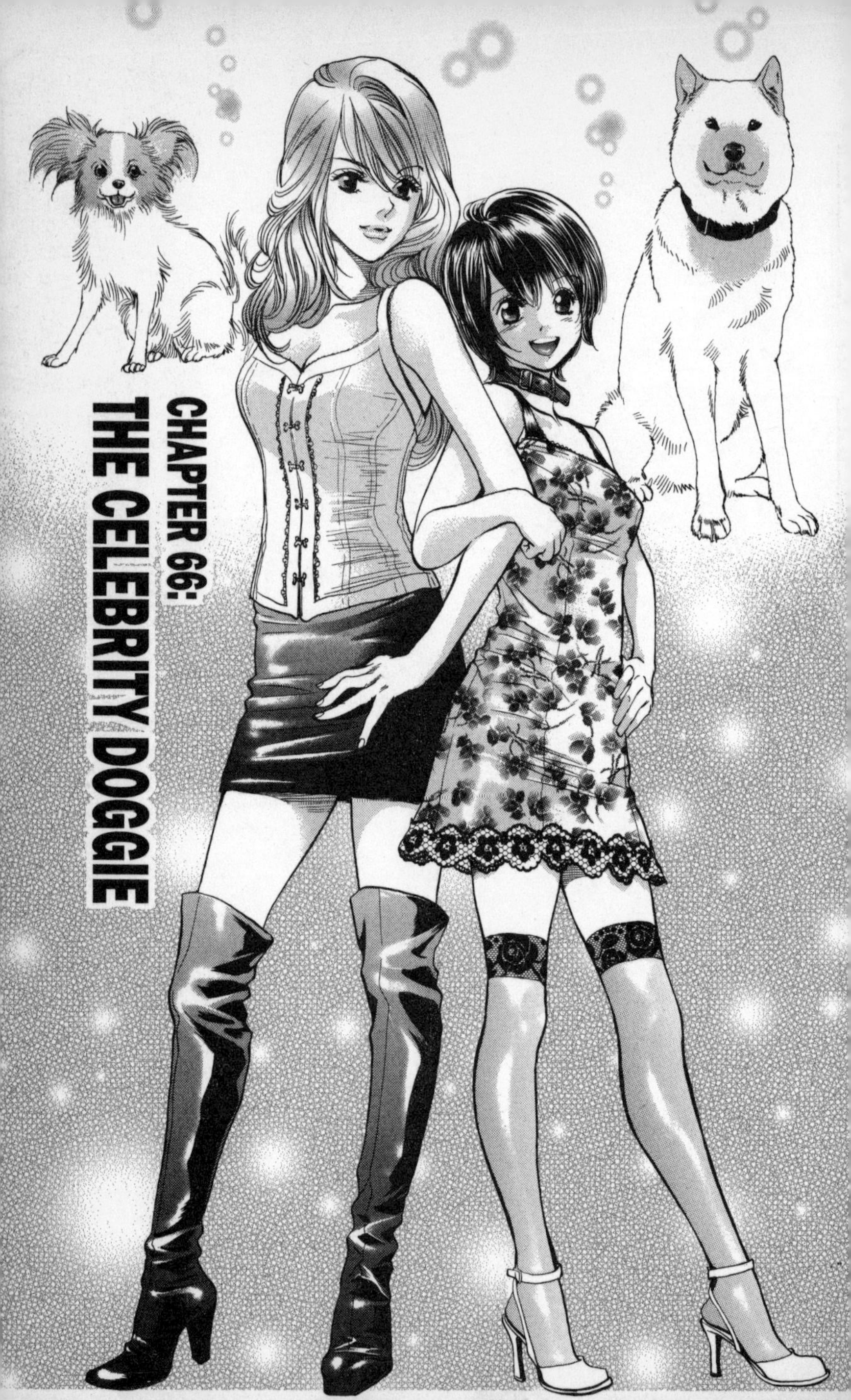
CHAPTER 66:
THE CELEBRITY DOGGIE

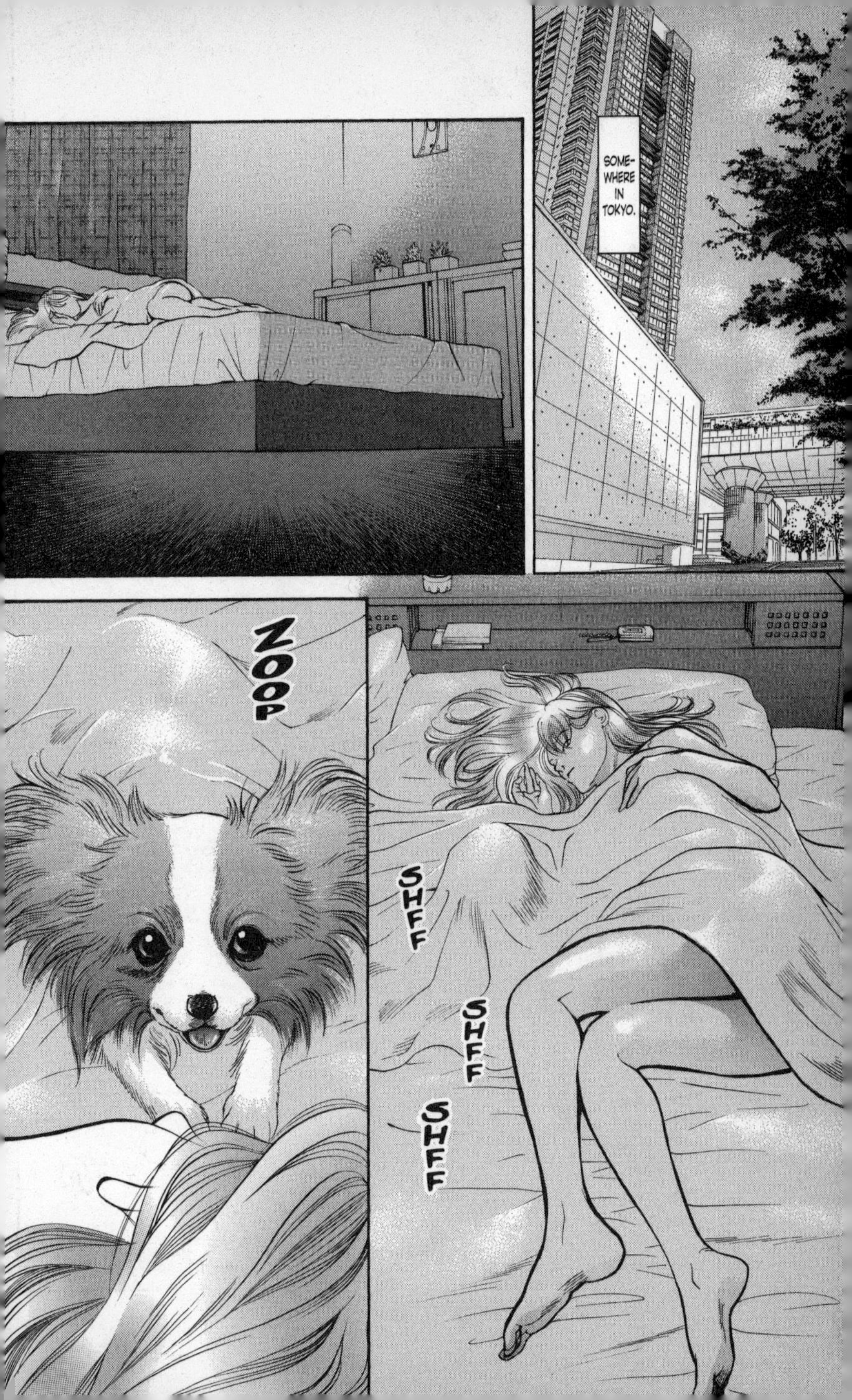
SOME-WHERE IN TOKYO.
SHFF
SHFF
SHFF
ZOOP

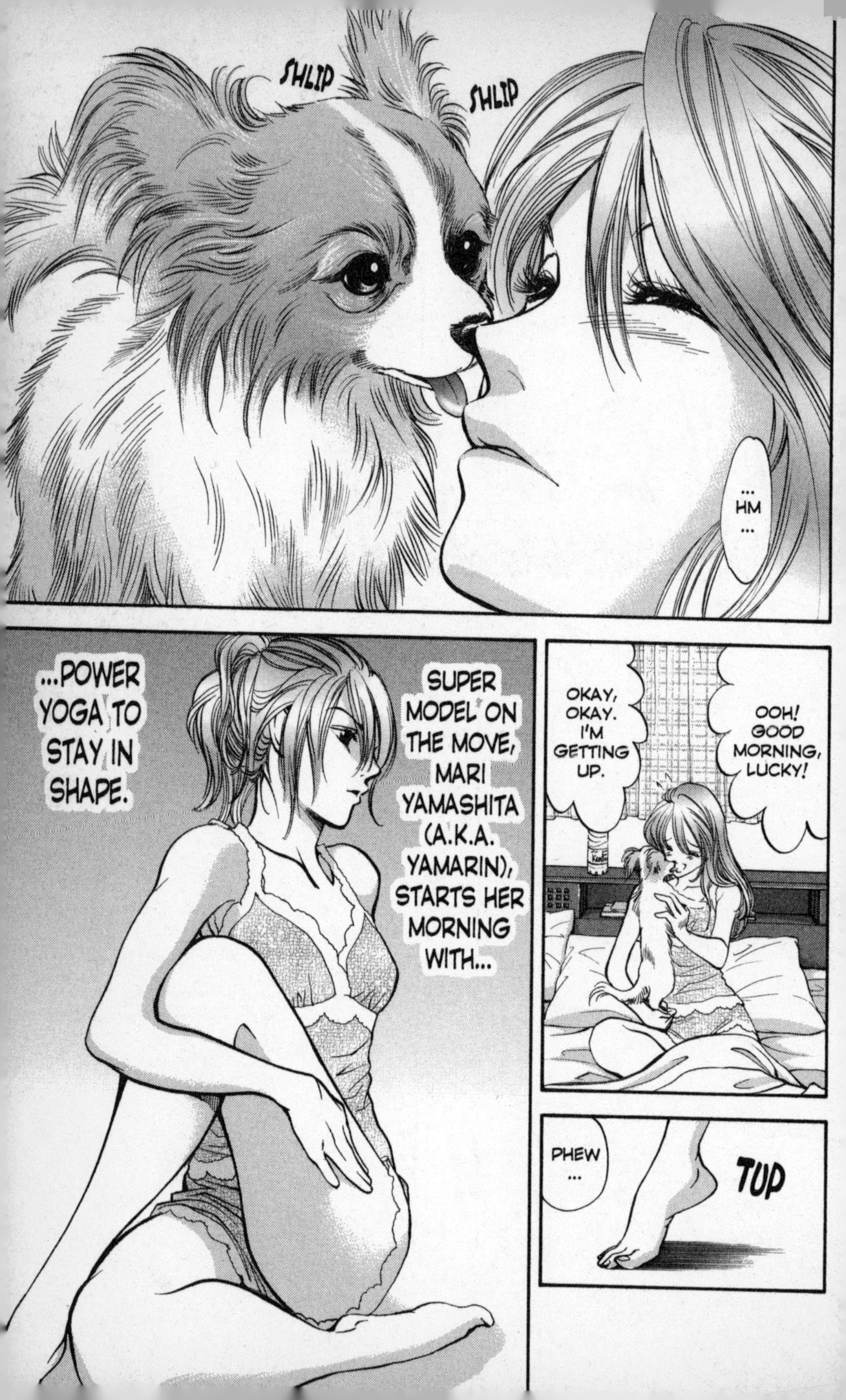
SHLIP
SHLIP
...HM...
OOH! GOOD MORNING, LUCKY!
OKAY, OKAY. I'M GETTING UP.
TUP
PHEW...
SUPER MODEL ON THE MOVE, MARI YAMASHITA (A.K.A. YAMARIN), STARTS HER MORNING WITH...
...POWER YOGA TO STAY IN SHAPE.

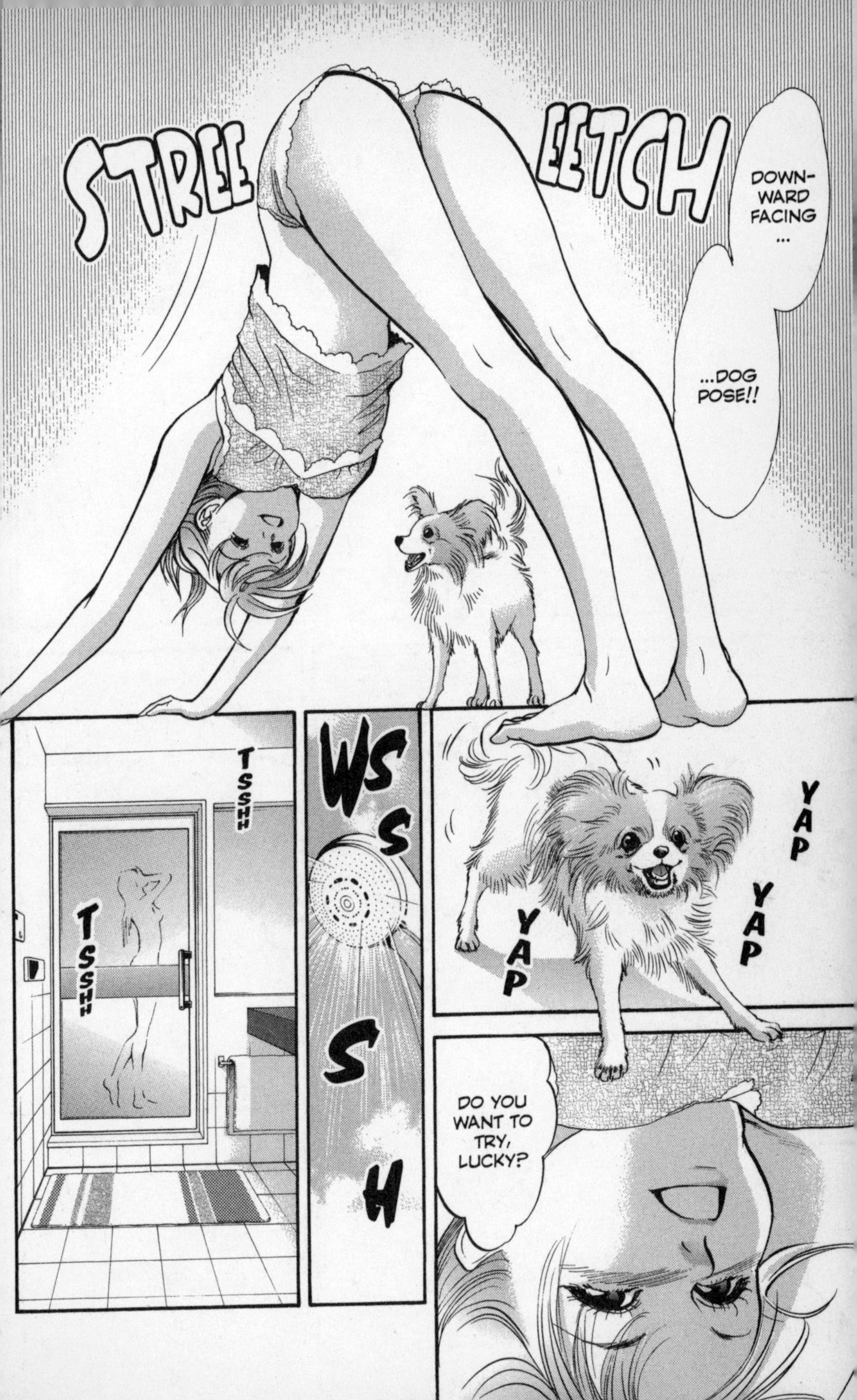
DOWN-WARD FACING ...
...DOG POSE!!
STREEEETCH
YAP YAP YAP
DO YOU WANT TO TRY, LUCKY?
WSSSH
TSSHH
TSSHH

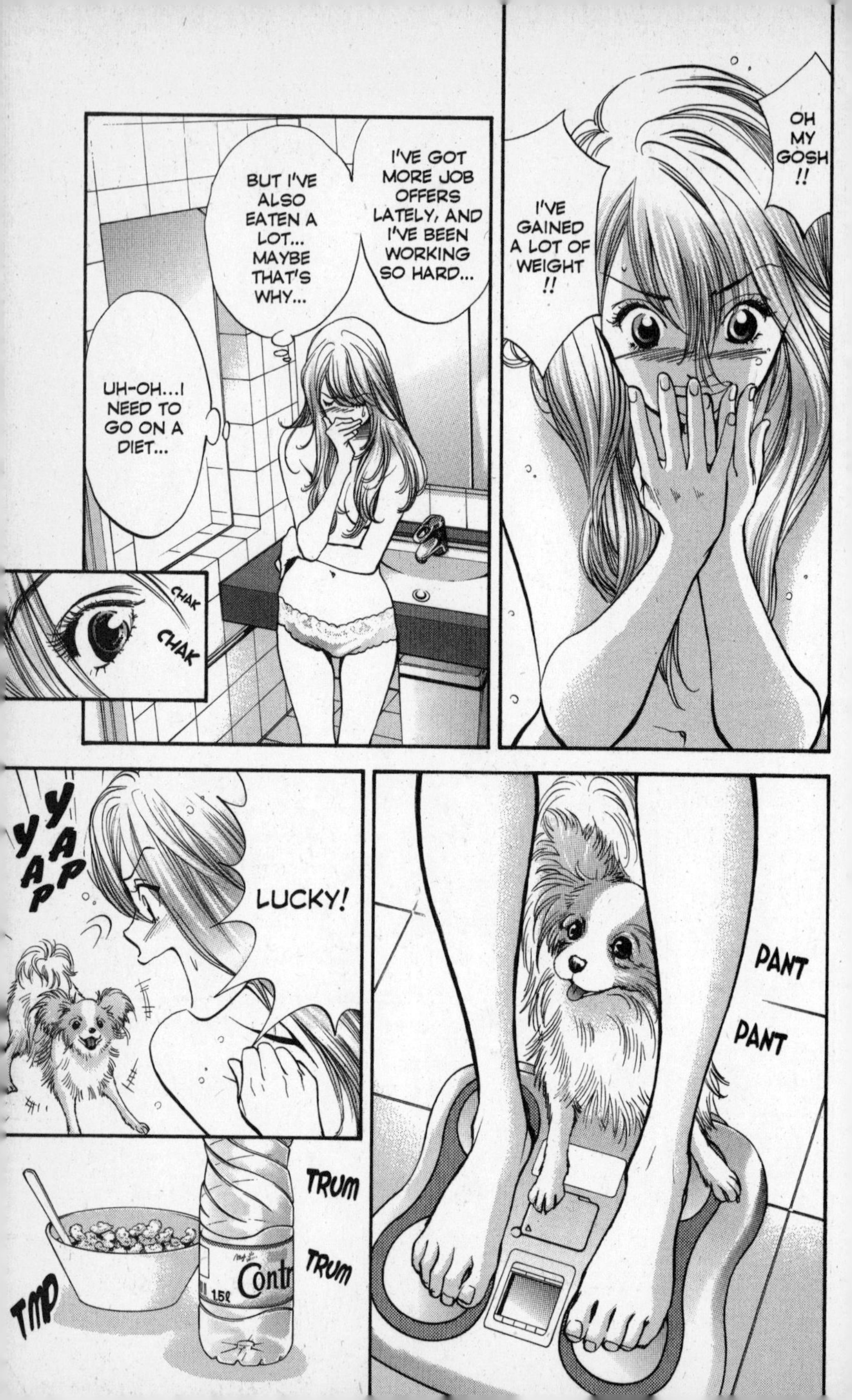
OH MY GOSH!!
I'VE GAINED A LOT OF WEIGHT!!
I'VE GOT MORE JOB OFFERS LATELY, AND I'VE BEEN WORKING SO HARD...
BUT I'VE ALSO EATEN A LOT... MAYBE THAT'S WHY...
UH-OH...I NEED TO GO ON A DIET...
CHAK
CHAK
LUCKY!
YAP YAP
YAP
PANT
PANT
TRUM
TRUM
TMP
1.5ℓ
Contr

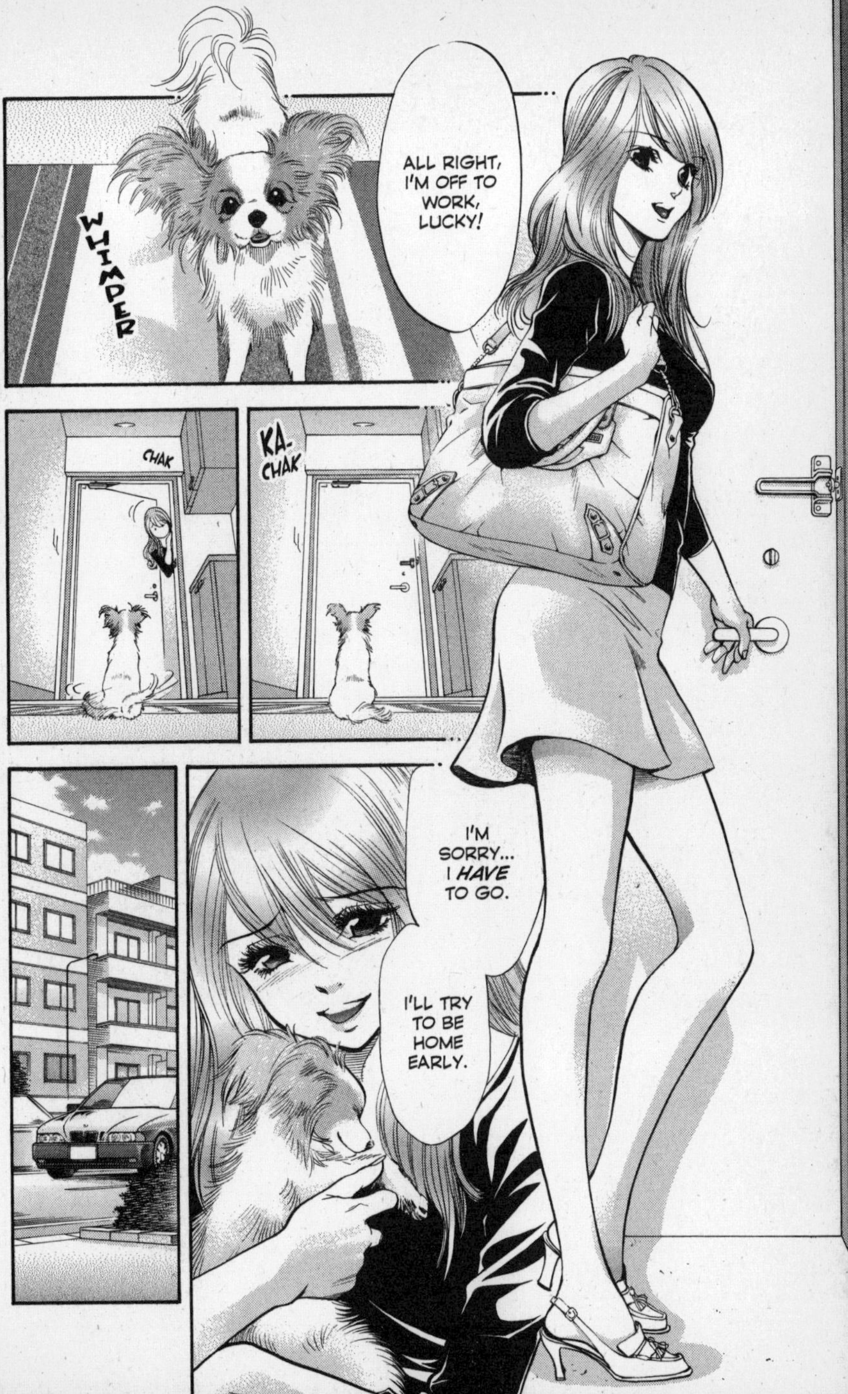
ALL RIGHT, I'M OFF TO WORK, LUCKY!
WHIMPER
CHAK
KA-CHAK
I'M SORRY... I HAVE TO GO.
I'LL TRY TO BE HOME EARLY.

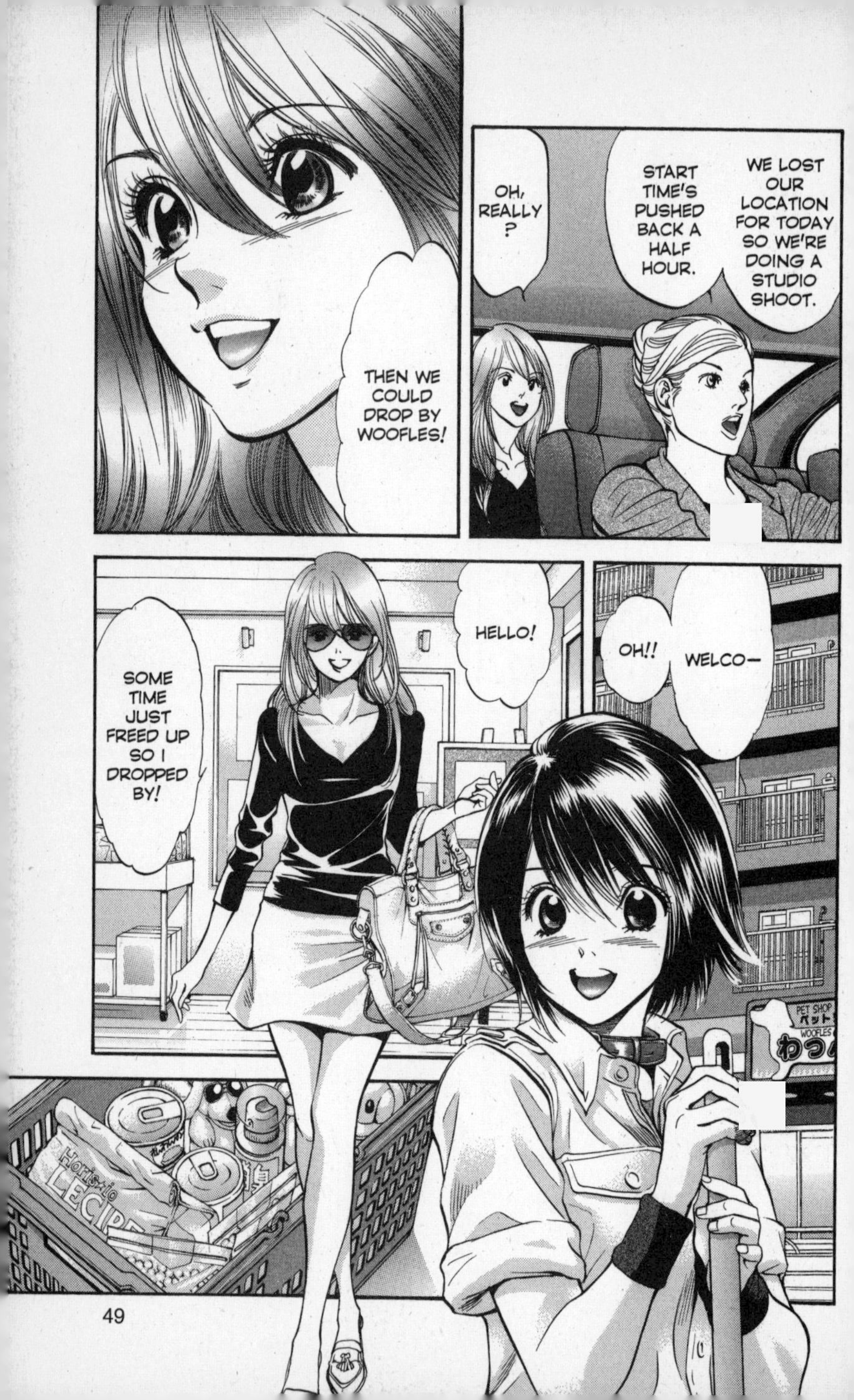
WE LOST OUR LOCATION FOR TODAY SO WE'RE DOING A STUDIO SHOOT.
START TIME'S PUSHED BACK A HALF HOUR.
OH, REALLY?
THEN WE COULD DROP BY WOOFLES!
WELCO—
OH!!
PET SHOP
WOOFLES
HELLO!
SOME TIME JUST FREED UP SO I DROPPED BY!

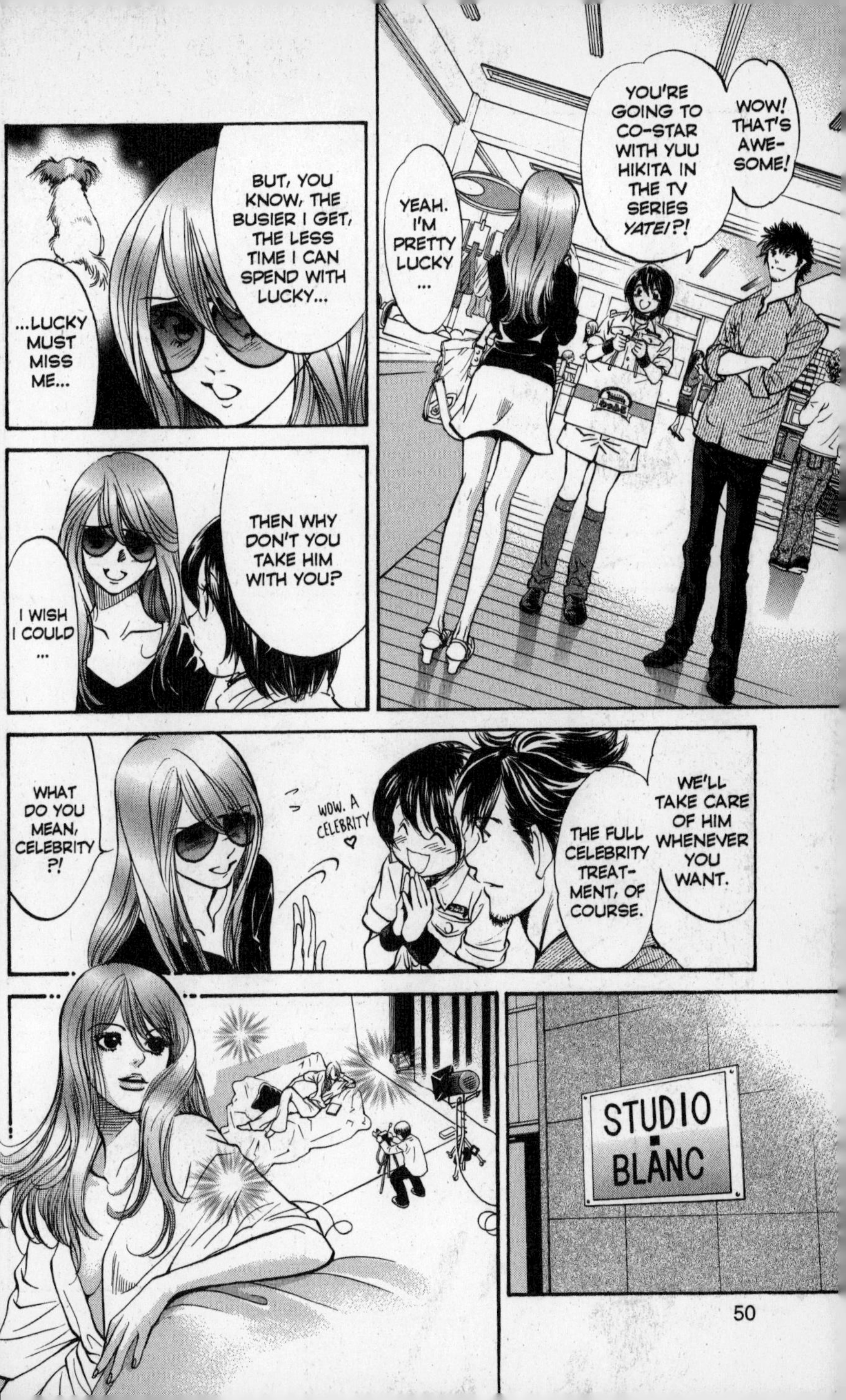
WOW! THAT'S AWE-SOME!
YOU'RE GOING TO CO-STAR WITH YUU HIKITA IN THE TV SERIES *YATEI*?!
YEAH. I'M PRETTY LUCKY ...
BUT, YOU KNOW, THE BUSIER I GET, THE LESS TIME I CAN SPEND WITH LUCKY...
...LUCKY MUST MISS ME...
THEN WHY DON'T YOU TAKE HIM WITH YOU?
I WISH I COULD ...
WE'LL TAKE CARE OF HIM WHENEVER YOU WANT.
THE FULL CELEBRITY TREAT-MENT, OF COURSE.
WOW. A CELEBRITY ♥
WHAT DO YOU MEAN, CELEBRITY?!
STUDIO BLANC

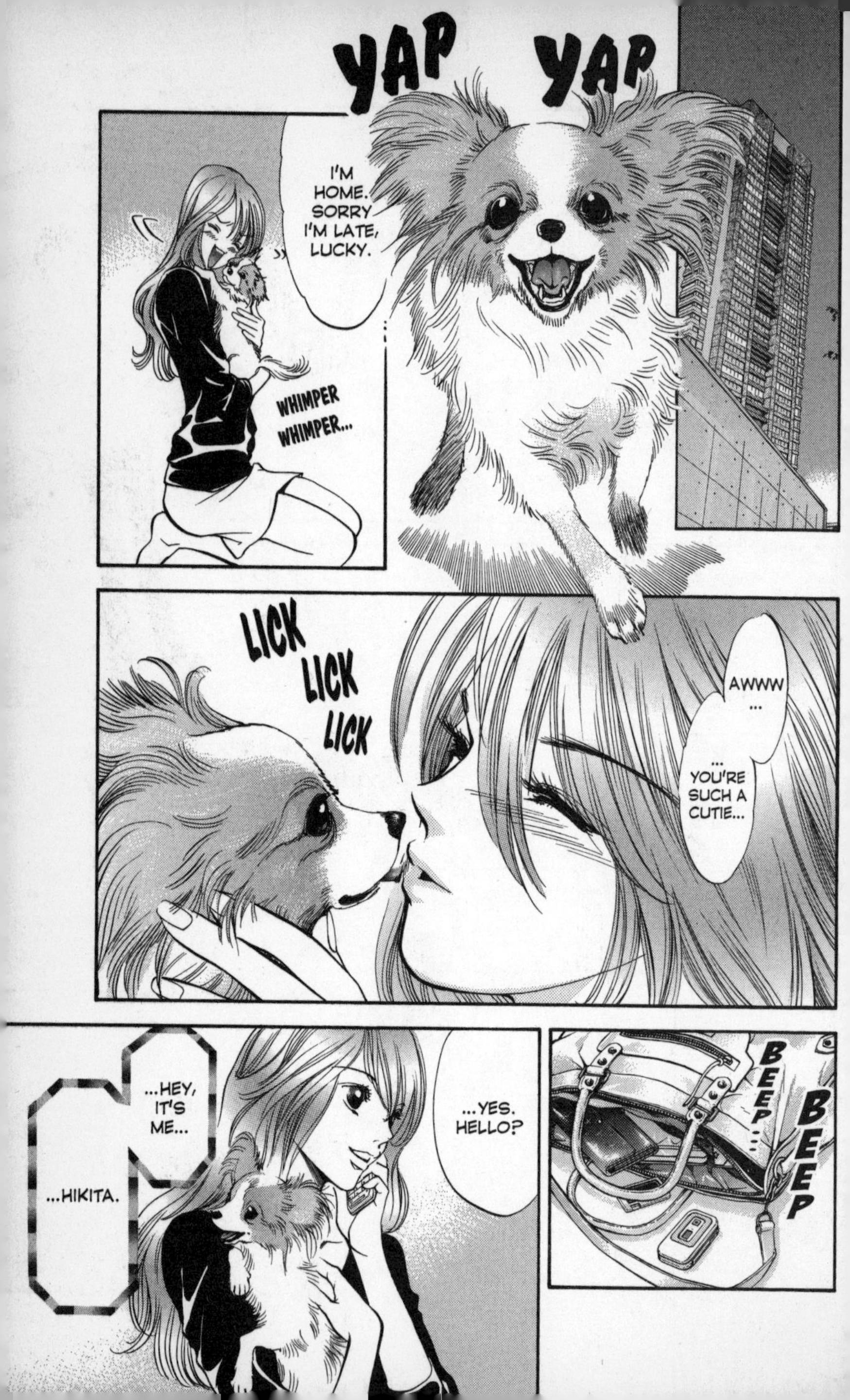
YAP YAP
I'M HOME. SORRY I'M LATE, LUCKY.
WHIMPER WHIMPER...
AWWW...
...YOU'RE SUCH A CUTIE...
LICK LICK LICK
BEEP... BEEP BEEP
...YES. HELLO?
...HEY, IT'S ME...
...HIKITA.

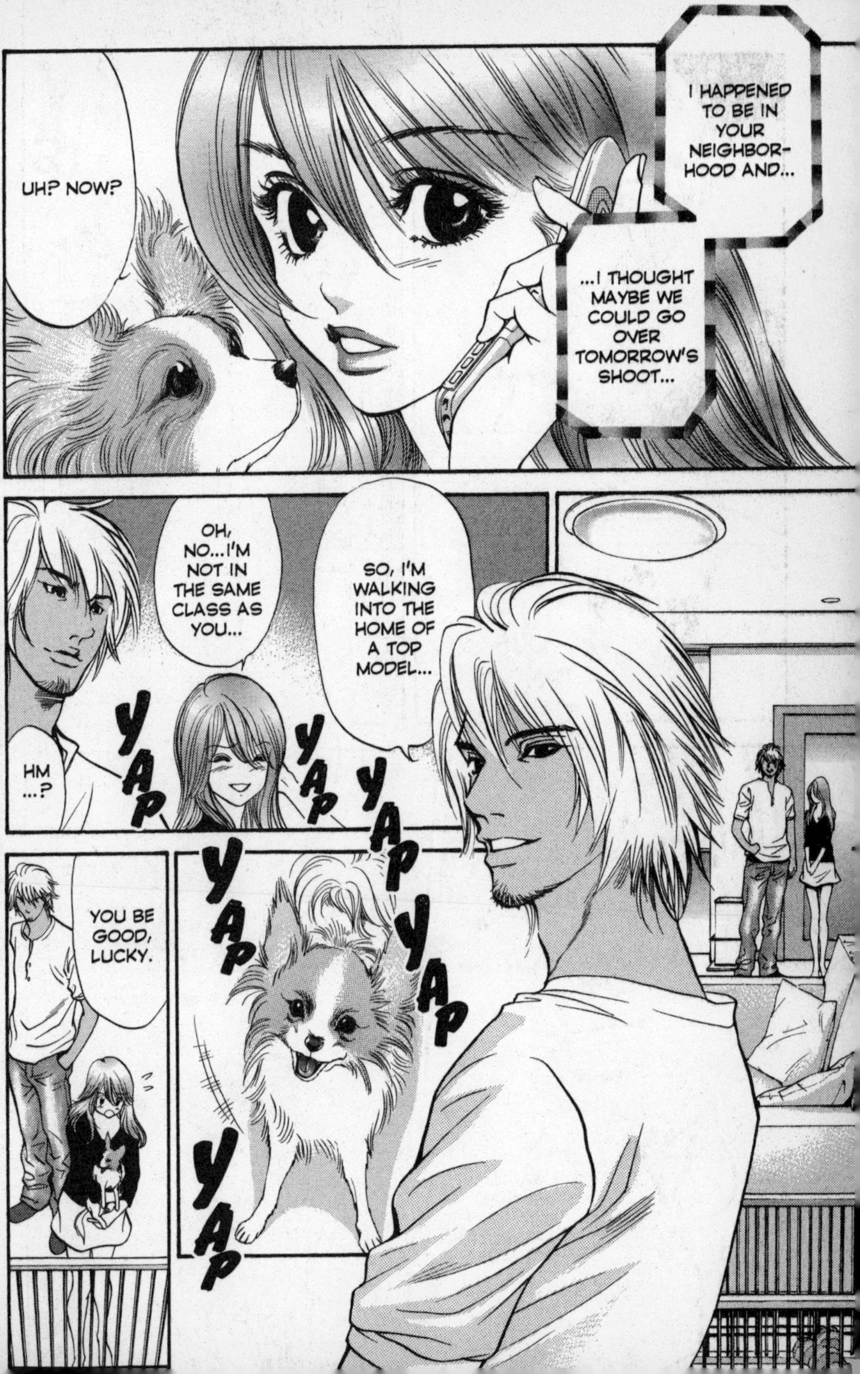
I HAPPENED TO BE IN YOUR NEIGHBOR-HOOD AND...
...I THOUGHT MAYBE WE COULD GO OVER TOMORROW'S SHOOT...
UH? NOW?
SO, I'M WALKING INTO THE HOME OF A TOP MODEL...
OH, NO...I'M NOT IN THE SAME CLASS AS YOU...
YAP YAP
HM ...?
YAP YAP
YAP YAP
YAP YAP
YOU BE GOOD, LUCKY.

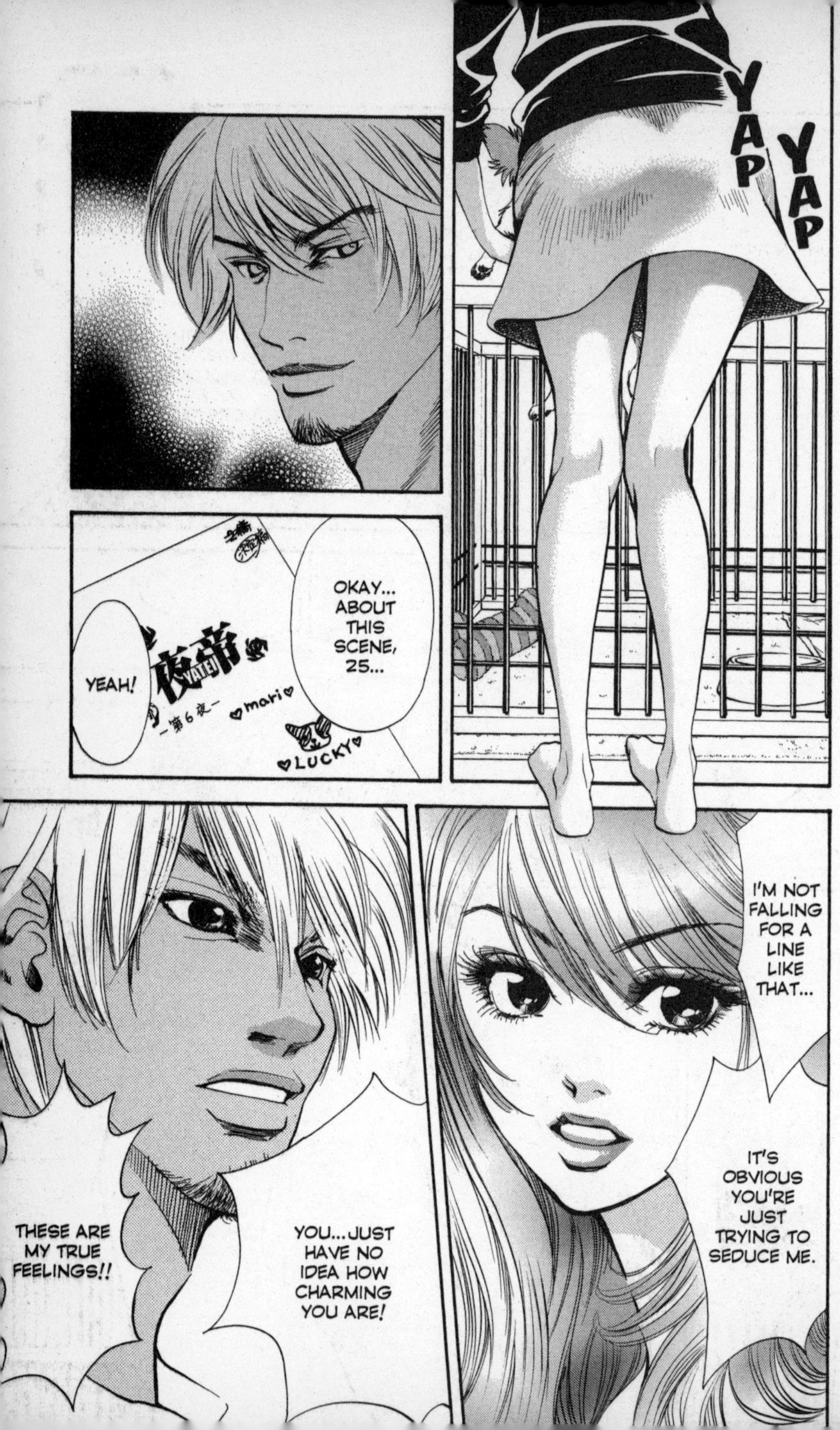
YAP YAP
YAP YAP
OKAY... ABOUT THIS SCENE, 25...
YEAH!
夜帝
YATEI
—第6夜—
♥mari♥
♥LUCKY♥
I'M NOT FALLING FOR A LINE LIKE THAT...
IT'S OBVIOUS YOU'RE JUST TRYING TO SEDUCE ME.
YOU...JUST HAVE NO IDEA HOW CHARMING YOU ARE!
THESE ARE MY TRUE FEELINGS!!

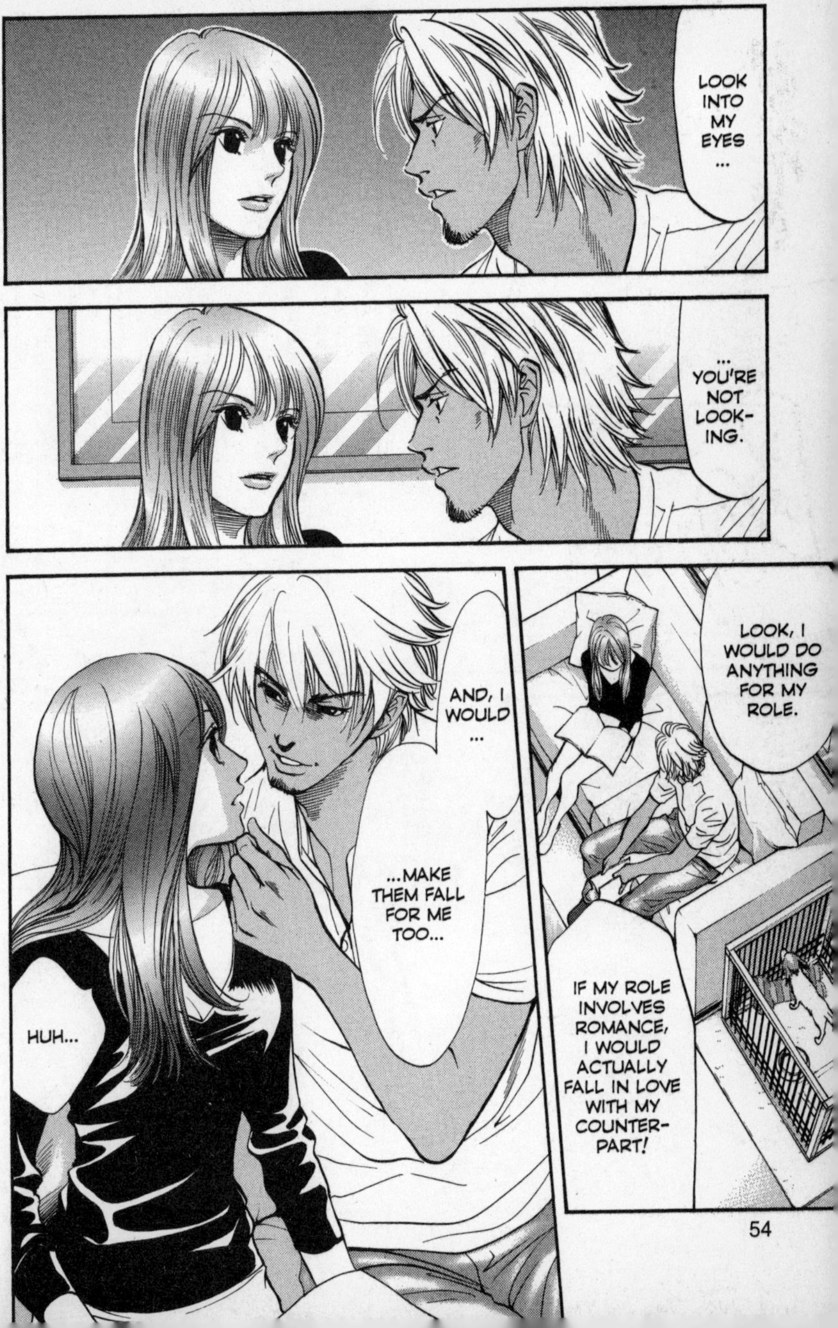
LOOK INTO MY EYES ...
... YOU'RE NOT LOOK-ING.
LOOK, I WOULD DO ANYTHING FOR MY ROLE.
IF MY ROLE INVOLVES ROMANCE, I WOULD ACTUALLY FALL IN LOVE WITH MY COUNTER-PART!
AND, I WOULD ...
...MAKE THEM FALL FOR ME TOO...
HUH...

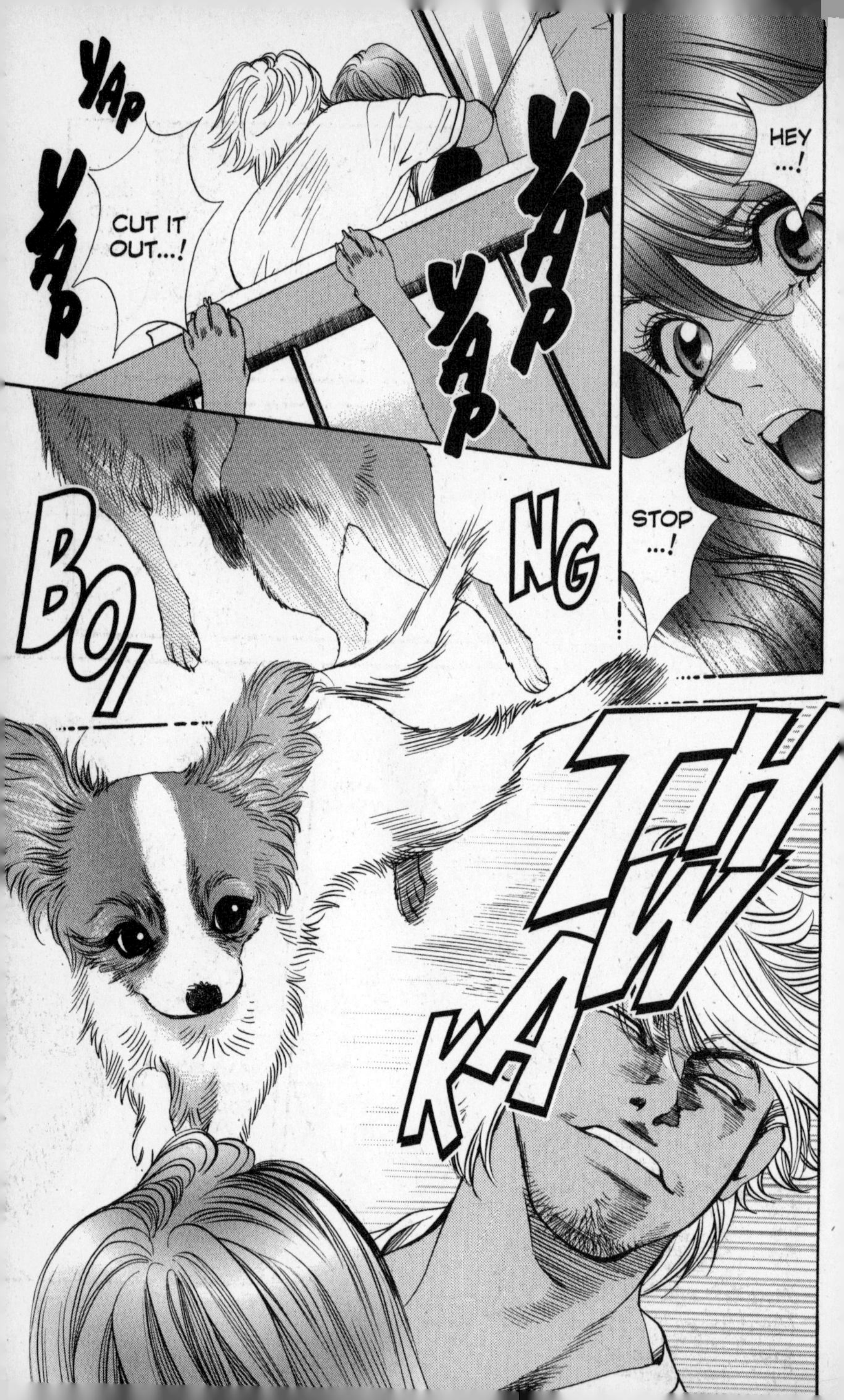
HEY ...!
STOP ...!
YAP YAP
YAP
CUT IT OUT...!
YAP
NG
BOI
THWAK

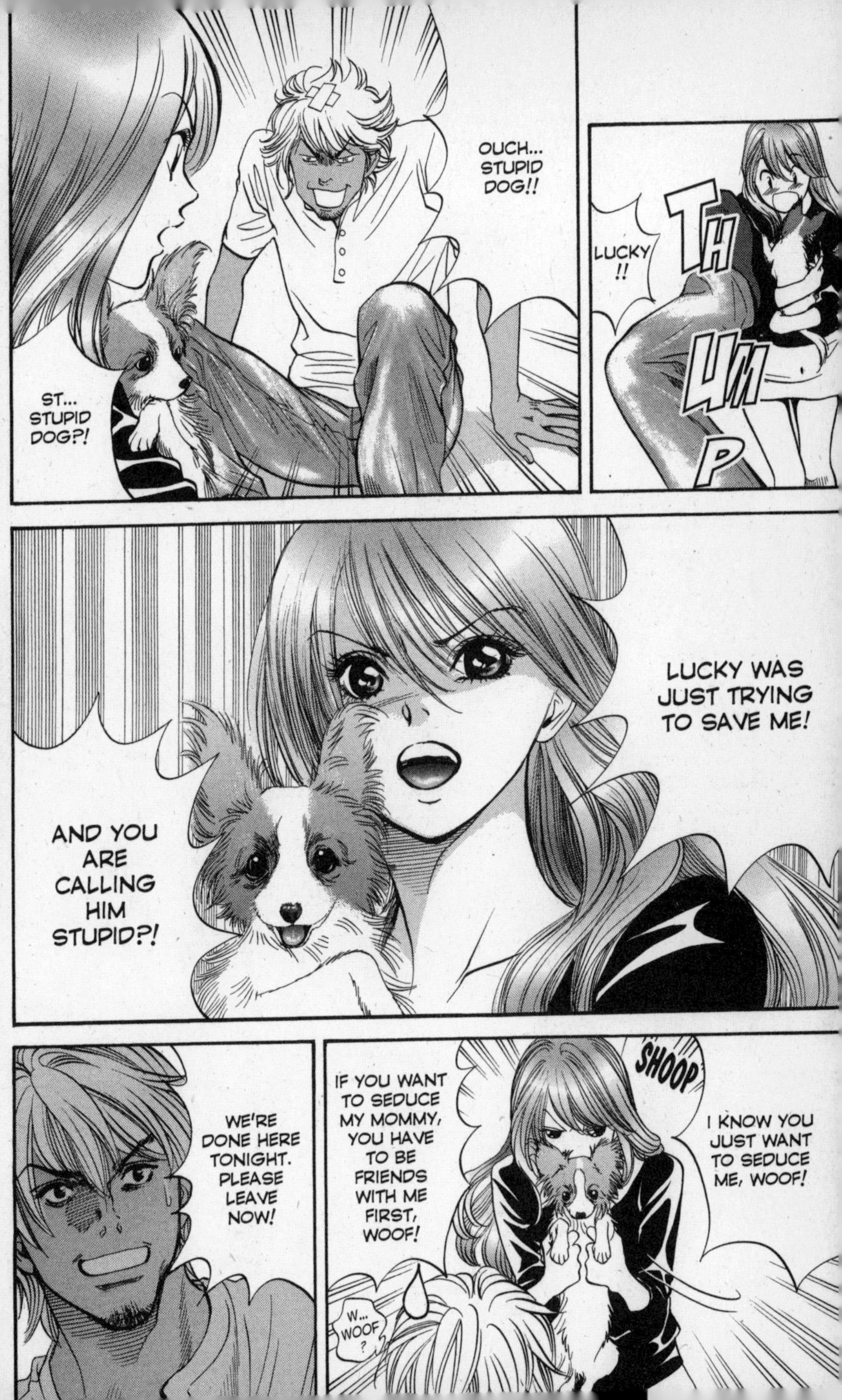
LUCKY!!
THUMP
OUCH... STUPID DOG!!
ST... STUPID DOG?!
LUCKY WAS JUST TRYING TO SAVE ME!
AND YOU ARE CALLING HIM STUPID?!
SHOOP
I KNOW YOU JUST WANT TO SEDUCE ME, WOOF!
IF YOU WANT TO SEDUCE MY MOMMY, YOU HAVE TO BE FRIENDS WITH ME FIRST, WOOF!
W... WOOF?
WE'RE DONE HERE TONIGHT. PLEASE LEAVE NOW!

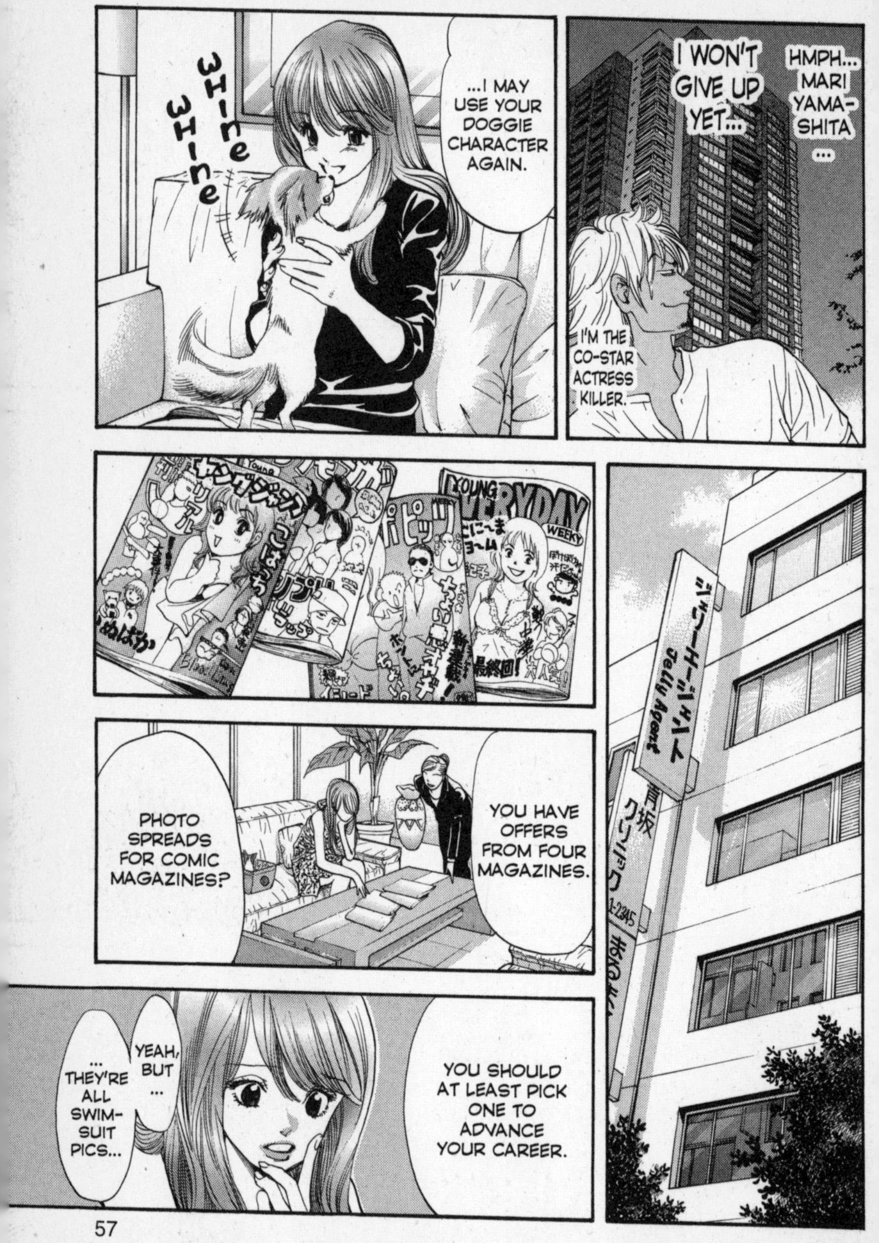
HMPH... MARI YAMA-SHITA ...
I WON'T GIVE UP YET...
I'M THE CO-STAR ACTRESS KILLER.
...I MAY USE YOUR DOGGIE CHARACTER AGAIN.
WHINE WHINE
Jelly Agent
YOUNG EVERYDAY WEEKY
YOU HAVE OFFERS FROM FOUR MAGAZINES.
PHOTO SPREADS FOR COMIC MAGAZINES?
YOU SHOULD AT LEAST PICK ONE TO ADVANCE YOUR CAREER.
YEAH, BUT ...
... THEY'RE ALL SWIM-SUIT PICS...

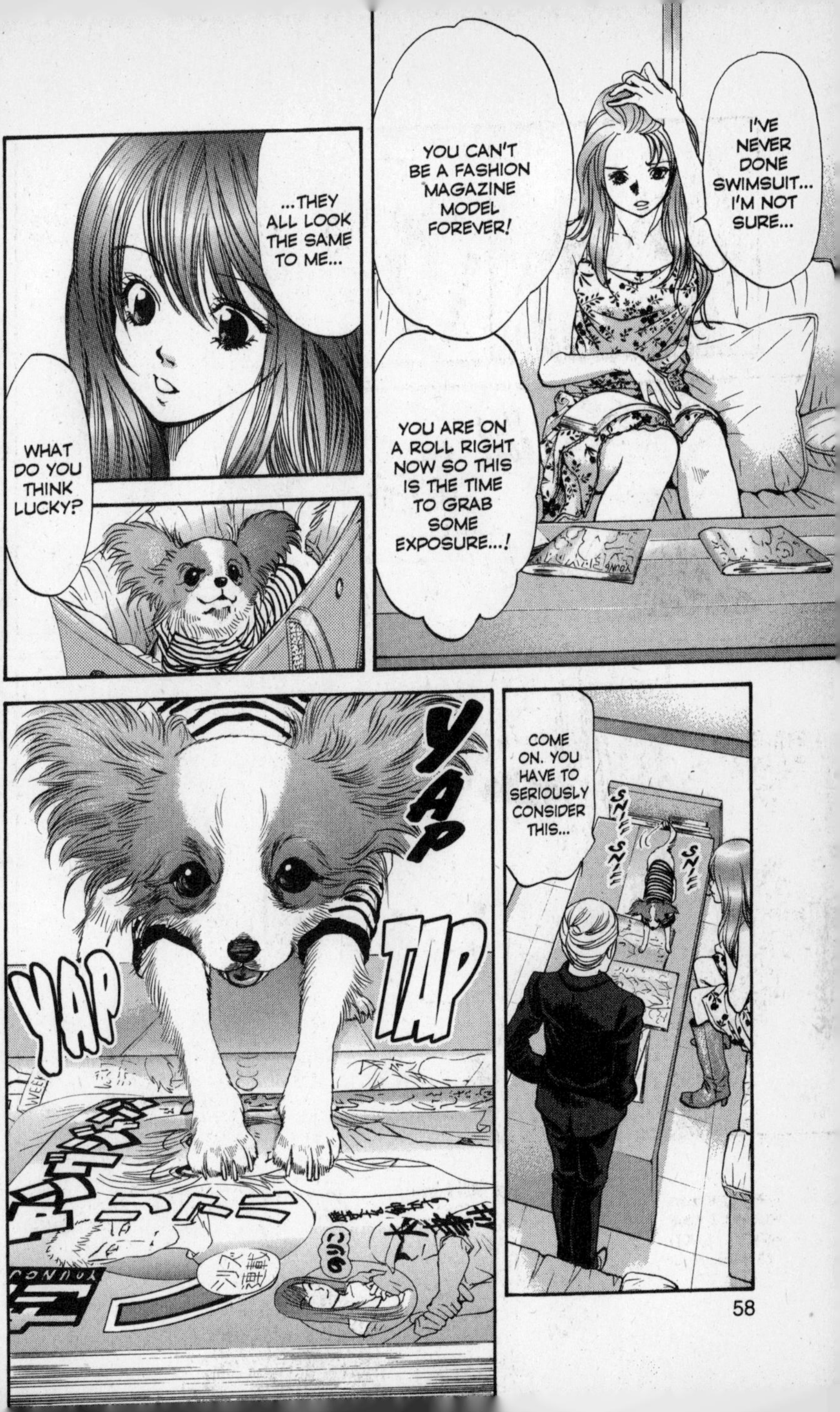
I'VE NEVER DONE SWIMSUIT... I'M NOT SURE...
YOU CAN'T BE A FASHION MAGAZINE MODEL FOREVER!
YOU ARE ON A ROLL RIGHT NOW SO THIS IS THE TIME TO GRAB SOME EXPOSURE...!
...THEY ALL LOOK THE SAME TO ME...
WHAT DO YOU THINK LUCKY?
COME ON. YOU HAVE TO SERIOUSLY CONSIDER THIS...
SNIFF SNIFF
SNIFF
YAP
YAP
TAP

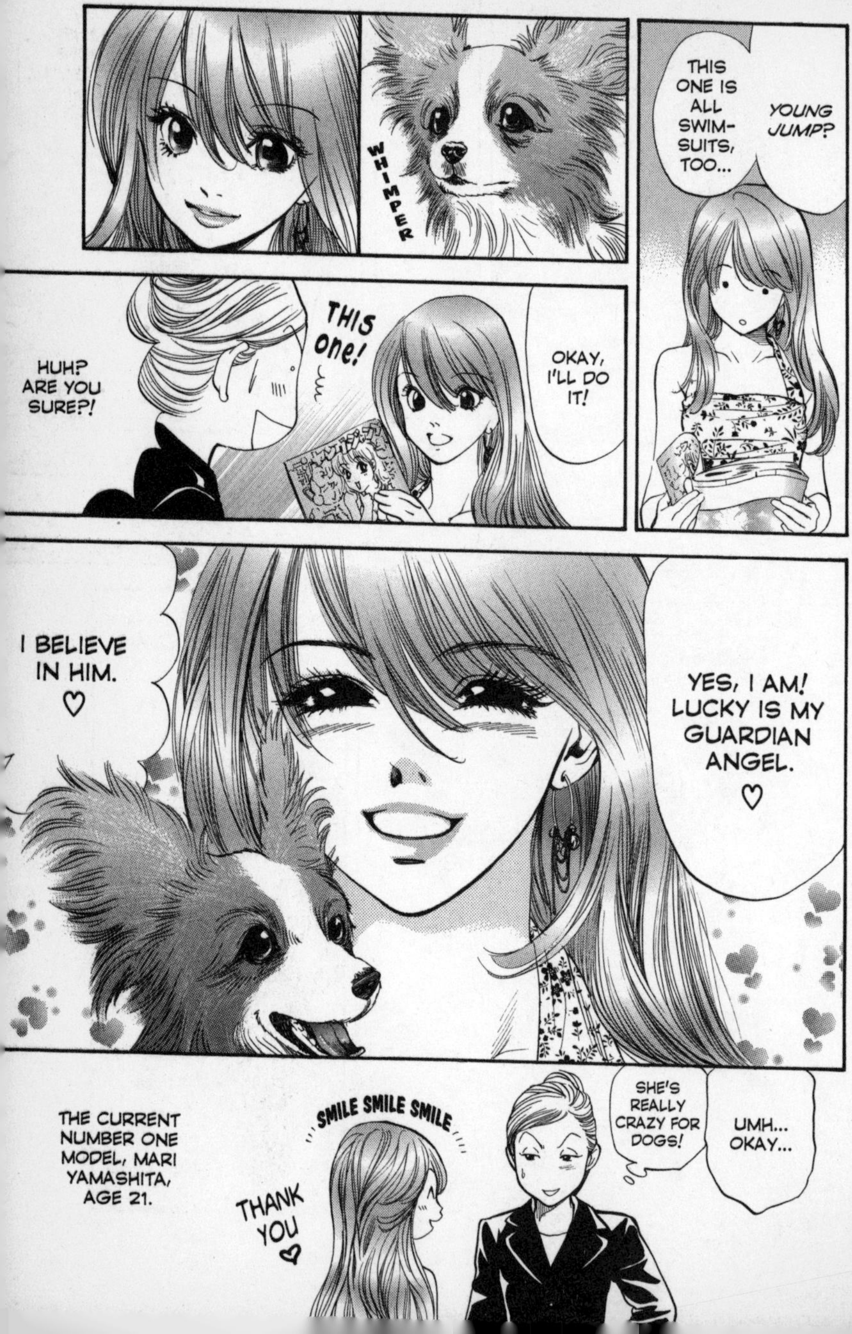
YOUNG JUMP?
THIS ONE IS ALL SWIM-SUITS, TOO...
WHIMPER
OKAY, I'LL DO IT!
THIS one!
HUH? ARE YOU SURE?!
YES, I AM! LUCKY IS MY GUARDIAN ANGEL. ♡
I BELIEVE IN HIM. ♡
UMH... OKAY...
SHE'S REALLY CRAZY FOR DOGS!
SMILE SMILE SMILE
THANK YOU ♡
THE CURRENT NUMBER ONE MODEL, MARI YAMASHITA, AGE 21.

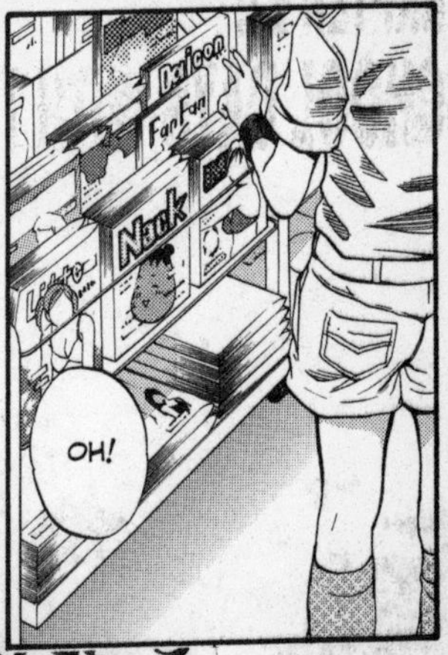
Daicon
Fan Fan
Nack
OH!

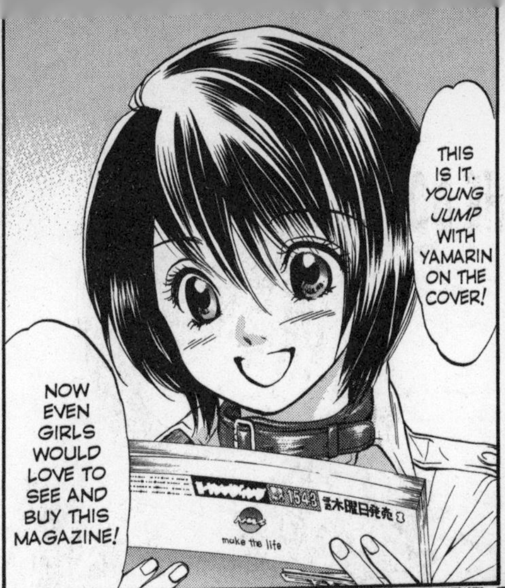
THIS IS IT. YOUNG JUMP WITH YAMARIN ON THE COVER!
NOW EVEN GIRLS WOULD LOVE TO SEE AND BUY THIS MAGAZINE!
make the life

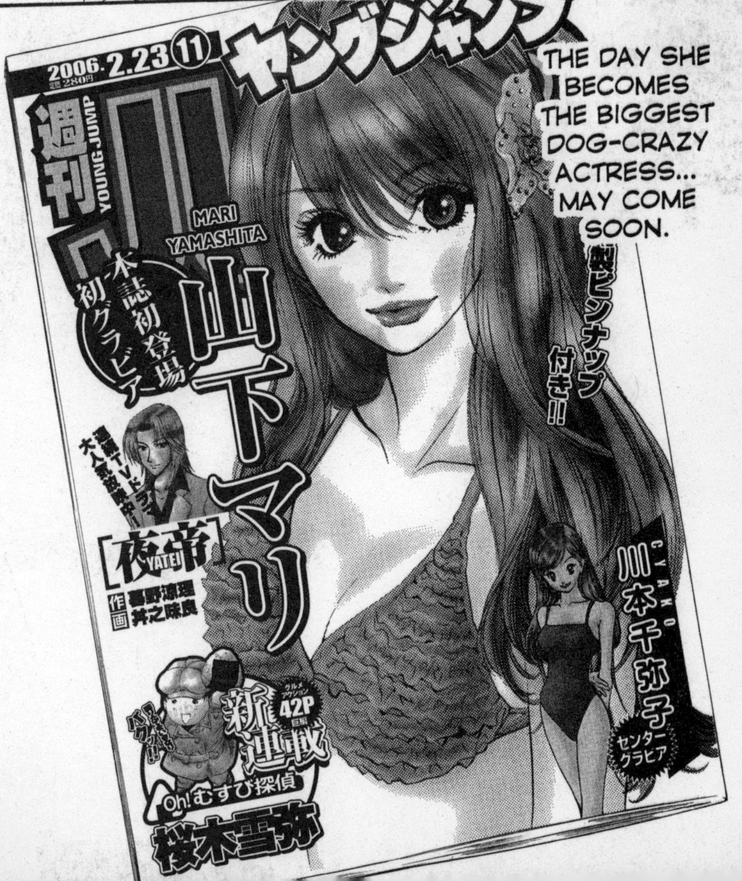
ヤングジャンプ
2006.2.23 11
週刊 YOUNG JUMP
THE DAY SHE BECOMES THE BIGGEST DOG-CRAZY ACTRESS... MAY COME SOON.
MARI YAMASHITA
本誌初登場 初グラビア
山下マリ
ピンナップ付き!!
夜帝 YATEI
川本千弥子
センターグラビア
新連載
42P
Oh!むすび探偵
桜木雪弥

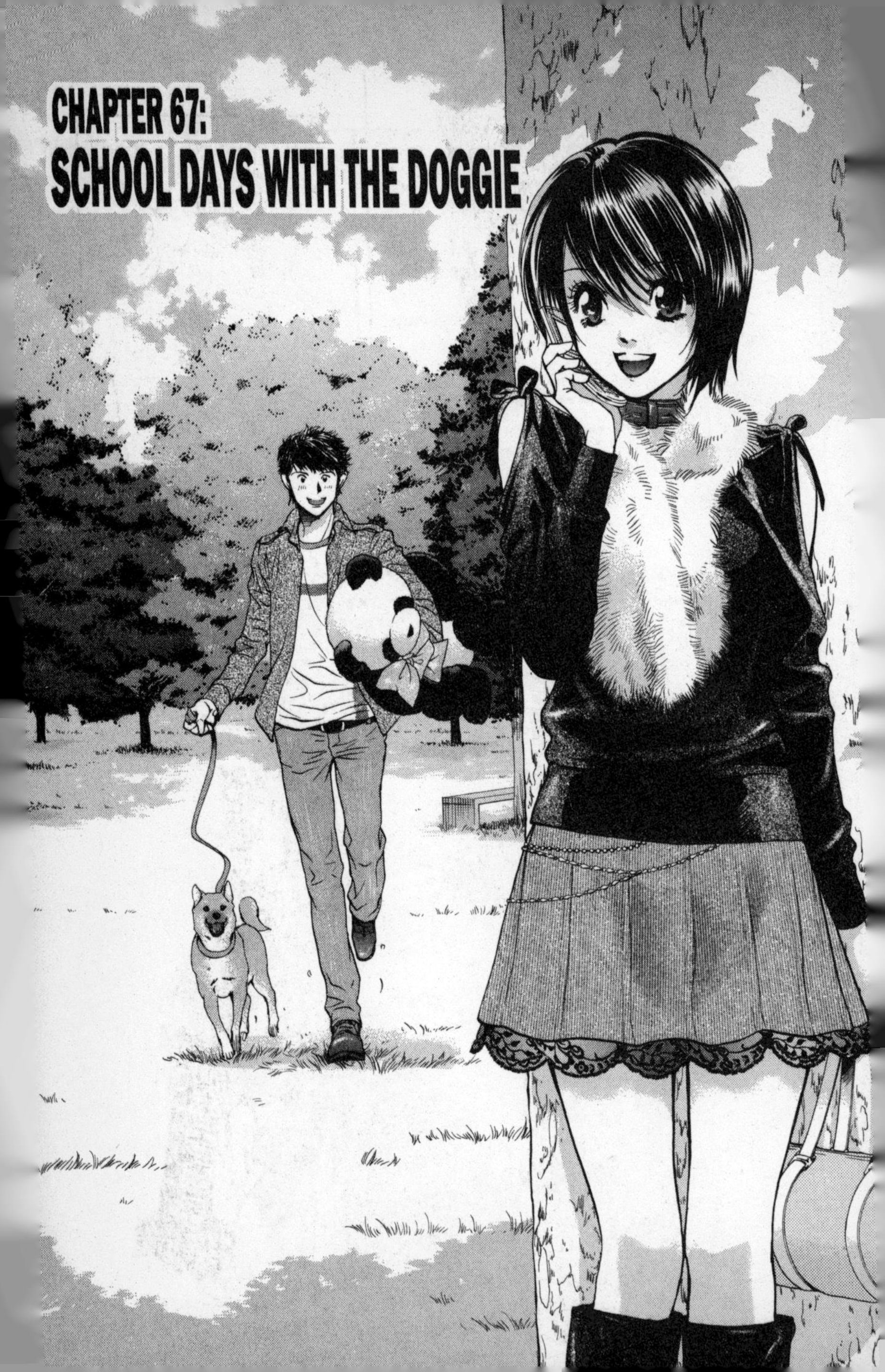
CHAPTER 67:
SCHOOL DAYS WITH THE DOGGIE

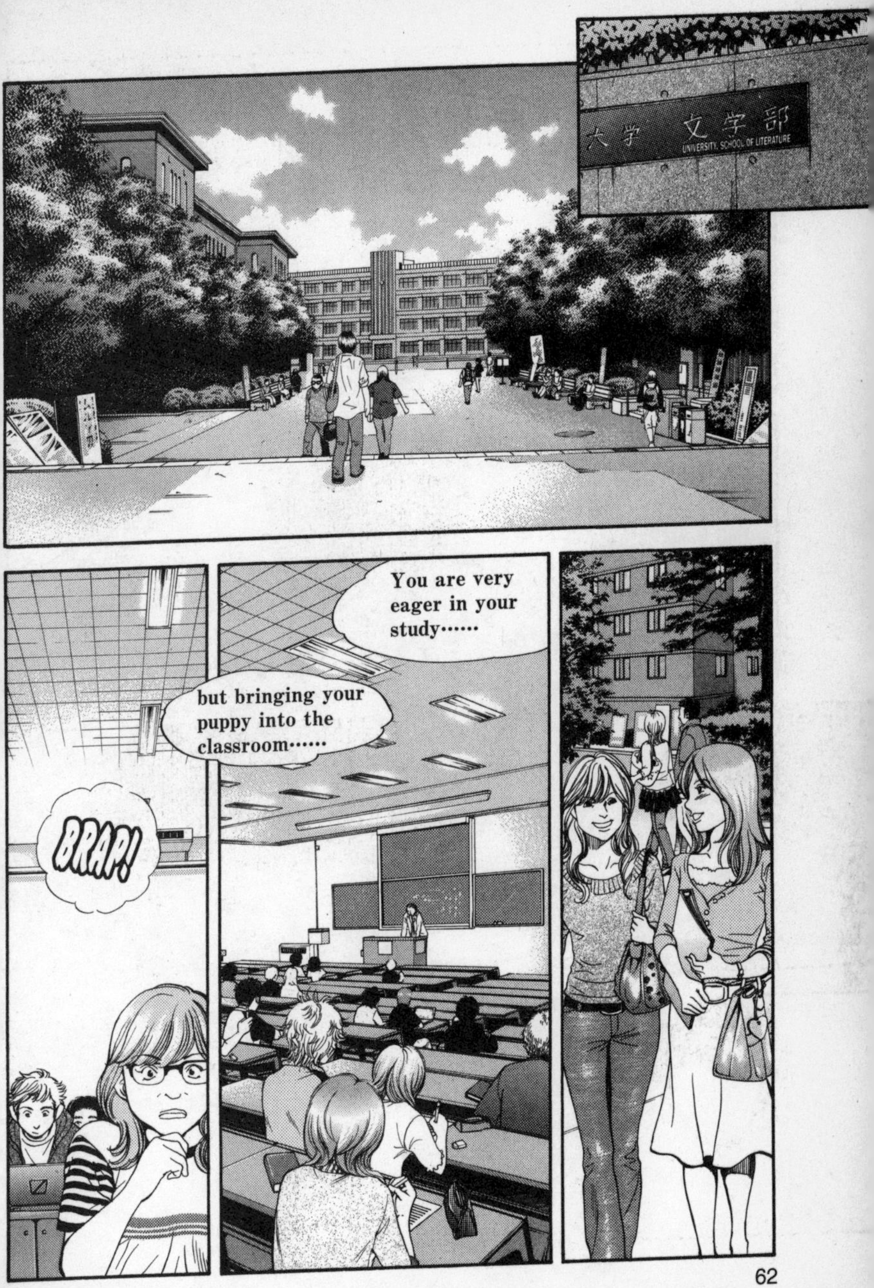
大学 文学部
UNIVERSITY, SCHOOL OF LITERATURE
You are very eager in your study……
but bringing your puppy into the classroom……
BRAP!

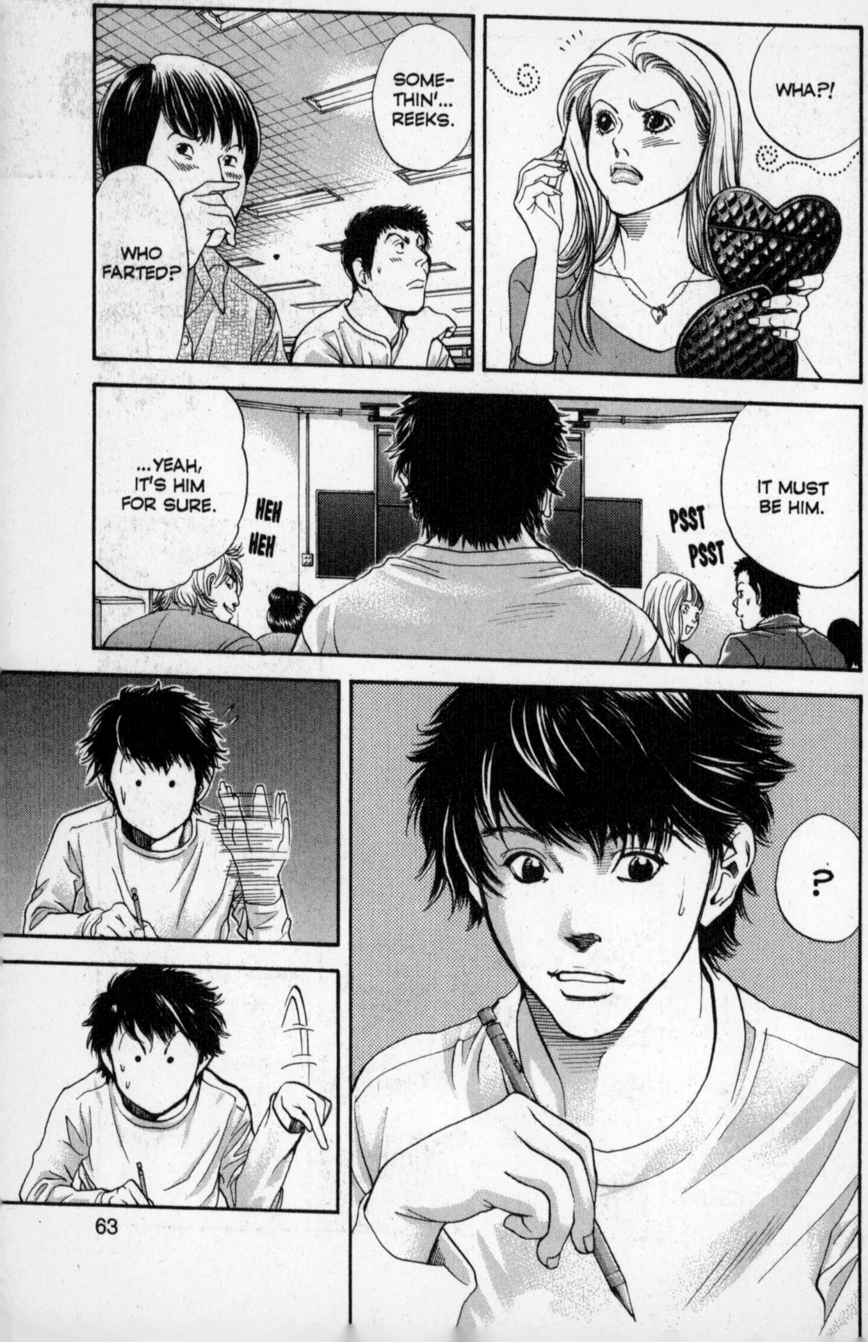
WHA?!
SOME-THIN'... REEKS.
WHO FARTED?
IT MUST BE HIM.
PSST PSST
HEH HEH
...YEAH, IT'S HIM FOR SURE.
?

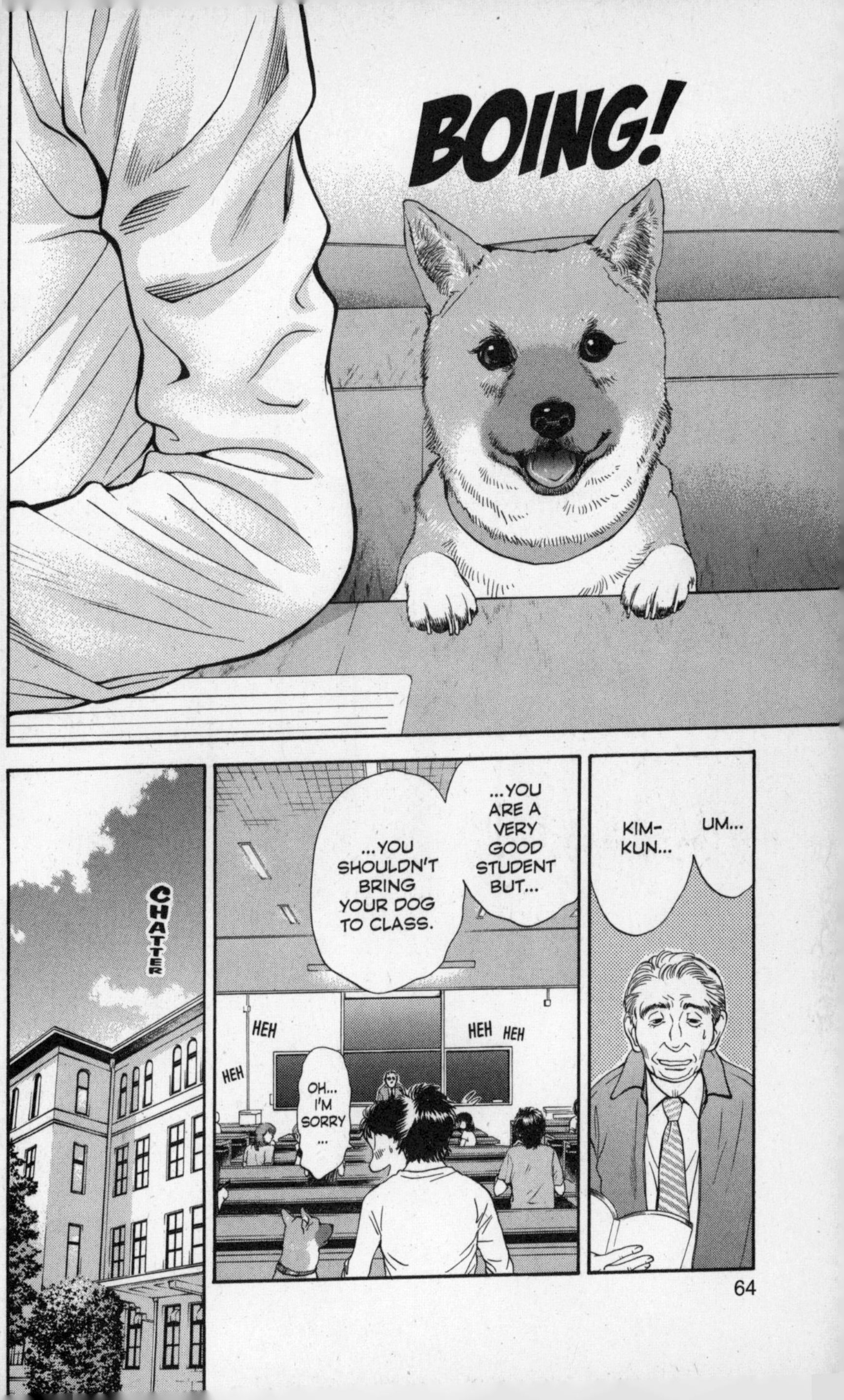
BOING!
UM...
KIM-KUN...
...YOU ARE A VERY GOOD STUDENT BUT...
...YOU SHOULDN'T BRING YOUR DOG TO CLASS.
HEH HEH
HEH
HEH
OH... I'M SORRY ...
CHATTER

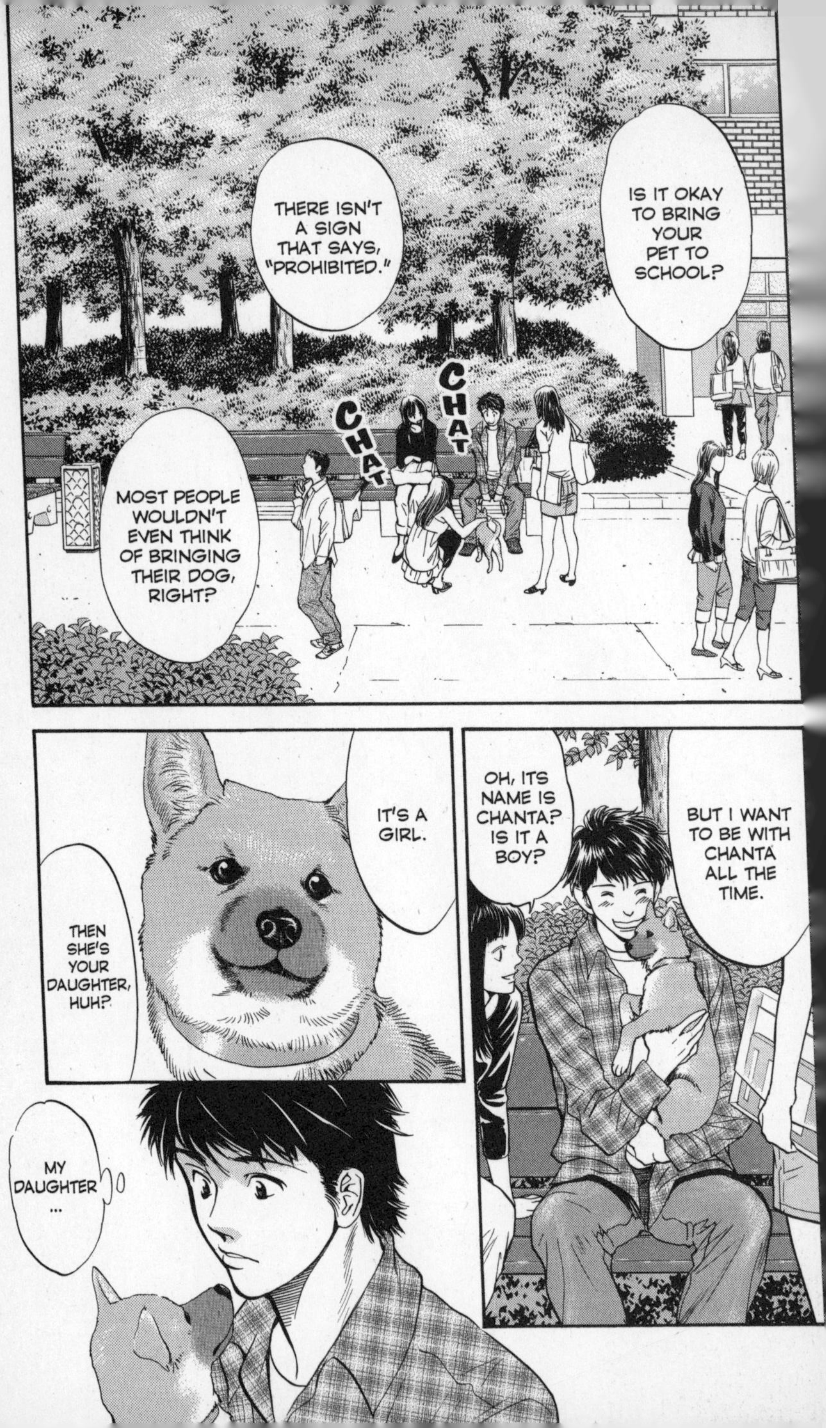
IS IT OKAY TO BRING YOUR PET TO SCHOOL?
THERE ISN'T A SIGN THAT SAYS, "PROHIBITED."
CHAT
CHAT
MOST PEOPLE WOULDN'T EVEN THINK OF BRINGING THEIR DOG, RIGHT?
BUT I WANT TO BE WITH CHANTA ALL THE TIME.
OH, ITS NAME IS CHANTA? IS IT A BOY?
IT'S A GIRL.
THEN SHE'S YOUR DAUGHTER, HUH?
MY DAUGHTER ...

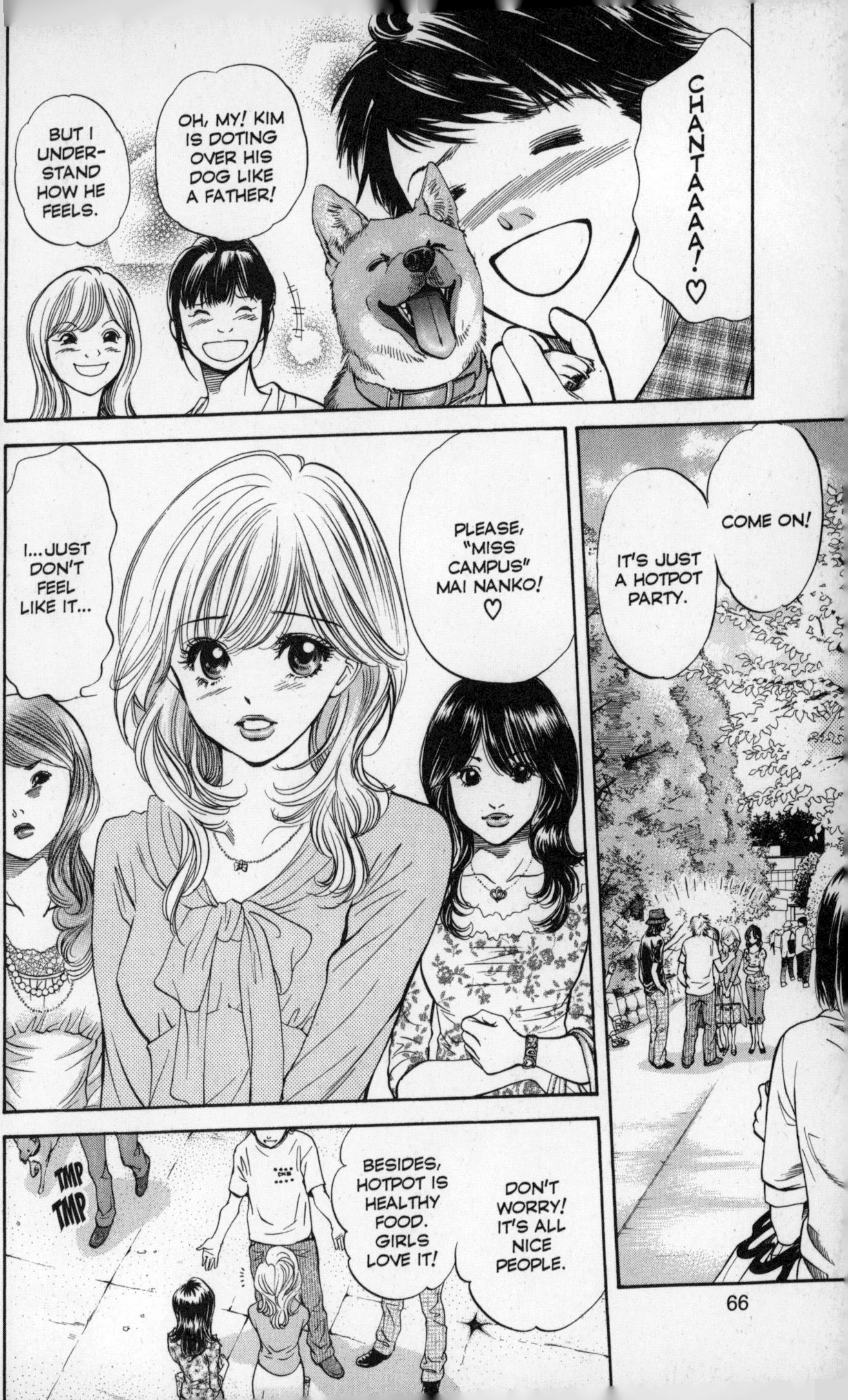
CHANTAAAA! ♡
OH, MY! KIM IS DOTING OVER HIS DOG LIKE A FATHER!
BUT I UNDER-STAND HOW HE FEELS.
COME ON!
IT'S JUST A HOTPOT PARTY.
PLEASE, "MISS CAMPUS" MAI NANKO! ♡
I...JUST DON'T FEEL LIKE IT...
DON'T WORRY! IT'S ALL NICE PEOPLE.
BESIDES, HOTPOT IS HEALTHY FOOD. GIRLS LOVE IT!
TMP TMP

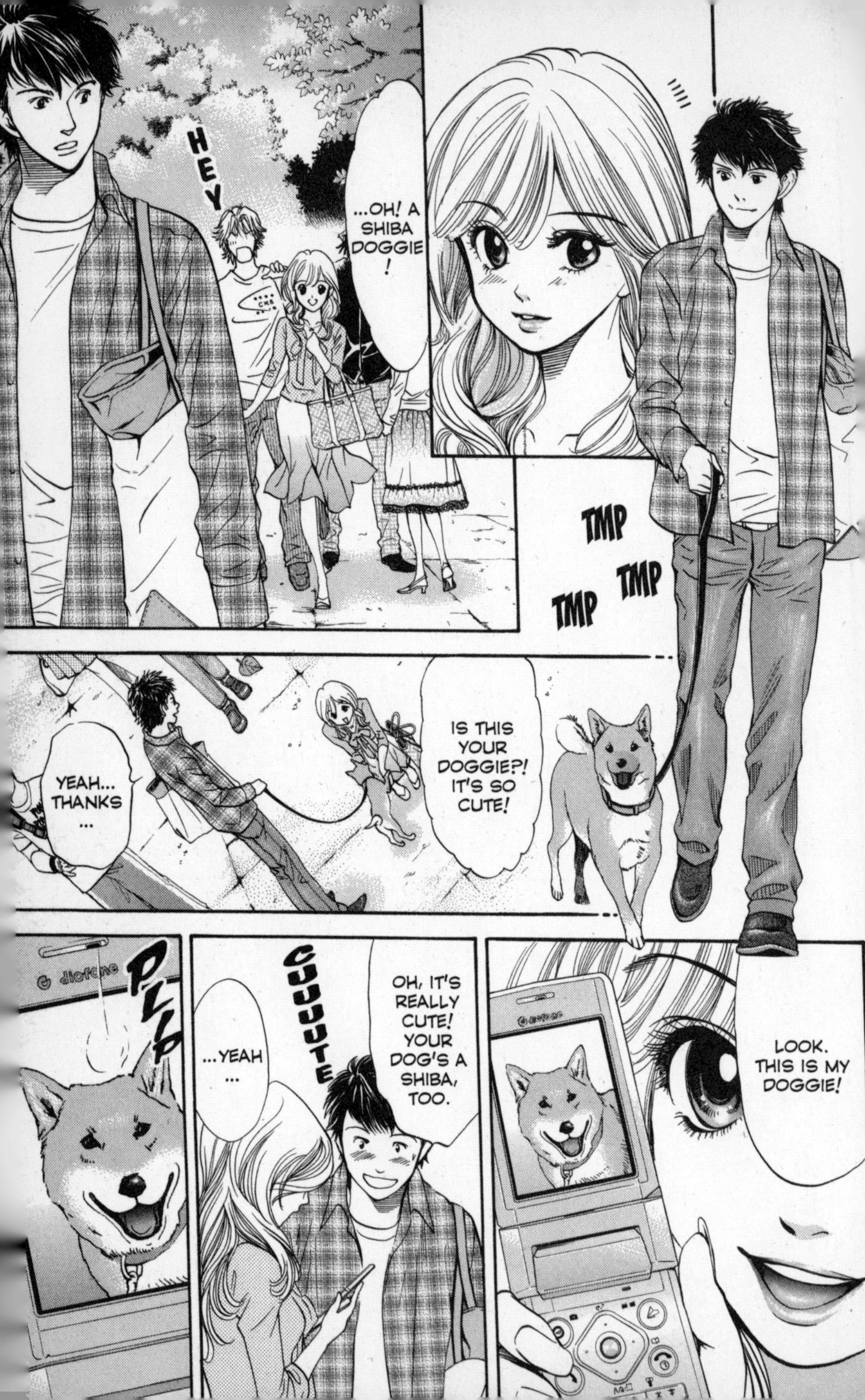
...OH! A SHIBA DOGGIE!
HEY
TMP TMP TMP
IS THIS YOUR DOGGIE?! IT'S SO CUTE!
YEAH... THANKS ...
LOOK. THIS IS MY DOGGIE!
OH, IT'S REALLY CUTE! YOUR DOG'S A SHIBA, TOO.
CUUUUTE
...YEAH ...
PLIP

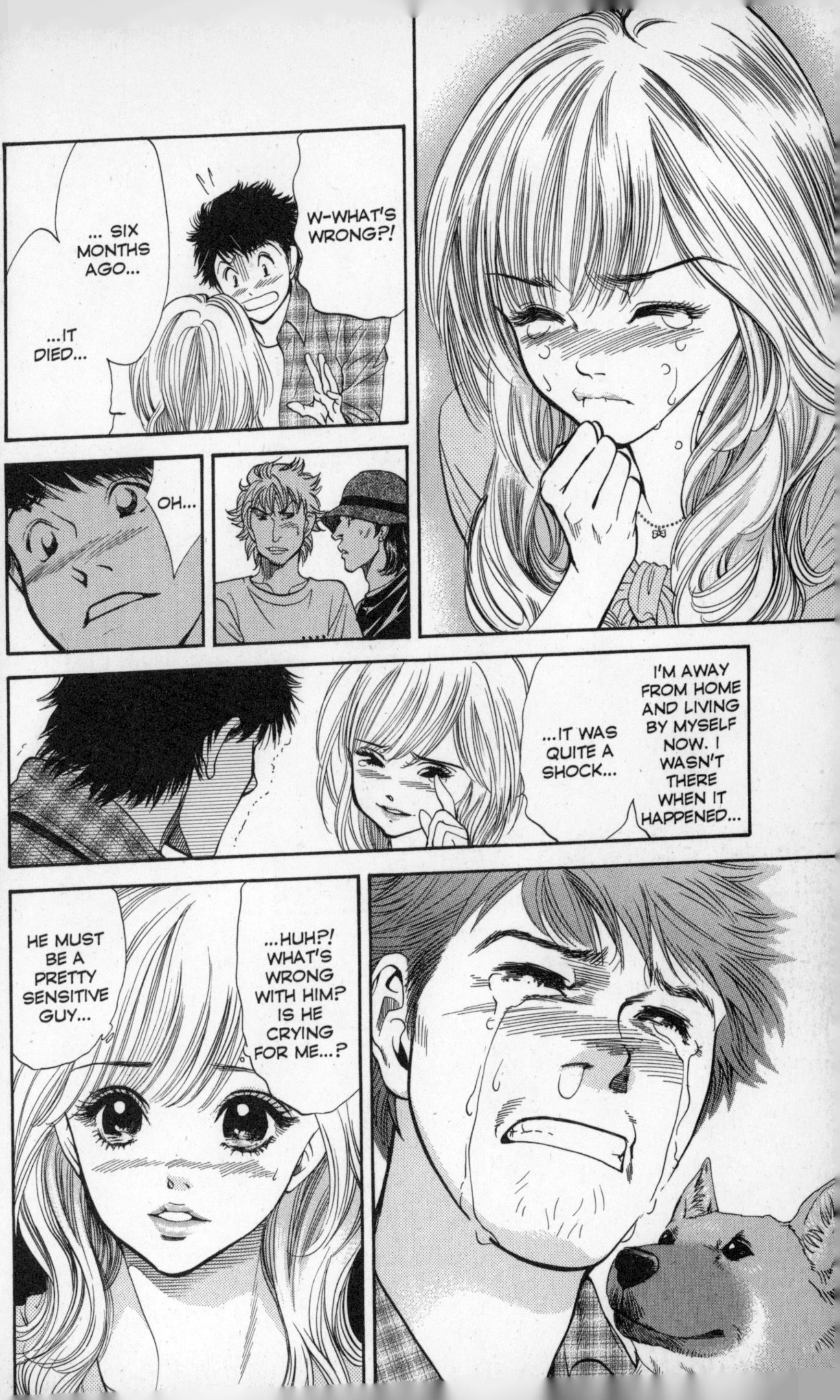
W-WHAT'S WRONG?!
... SIX MONTHS AGO...
...IT DIED...
OH...
I'M AWAY FROM HOME AND LIVING BY MYSELF NOW. I WASN'T THERE WHEN IT HAPPENED...
...IT WAS QUITE A SHOCK...
...HUH?! WHAT'S WRONG WITH HIM? IS HE CRYING FOR ME...?
HE MUST BE A PRETTY SENSITIVE GUY...

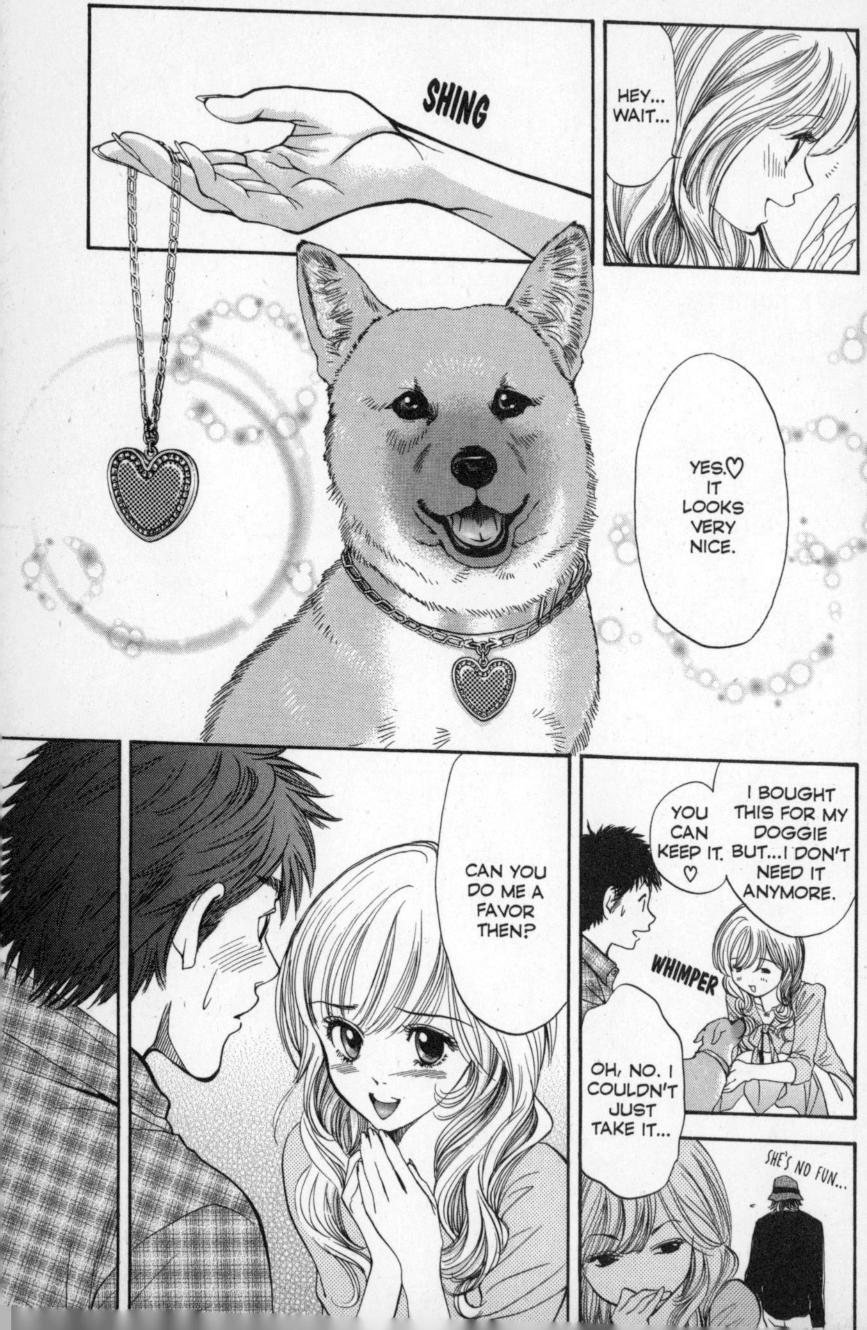
HEY... WAIT...
SHING
YES.♡ IT LOOKS VERY NICE.
I BOUGHT THIS FOR MY DOGGIE BUT...I DON'T NEED IT ANYMORE.
YOU CAN KEEP IT. ♡
WHIMPER
OH, NO. I COULDN'T JUST TAKE IT...
SHE'S NO FUN...
CAN YOU DO ME A FAVOR THEN?

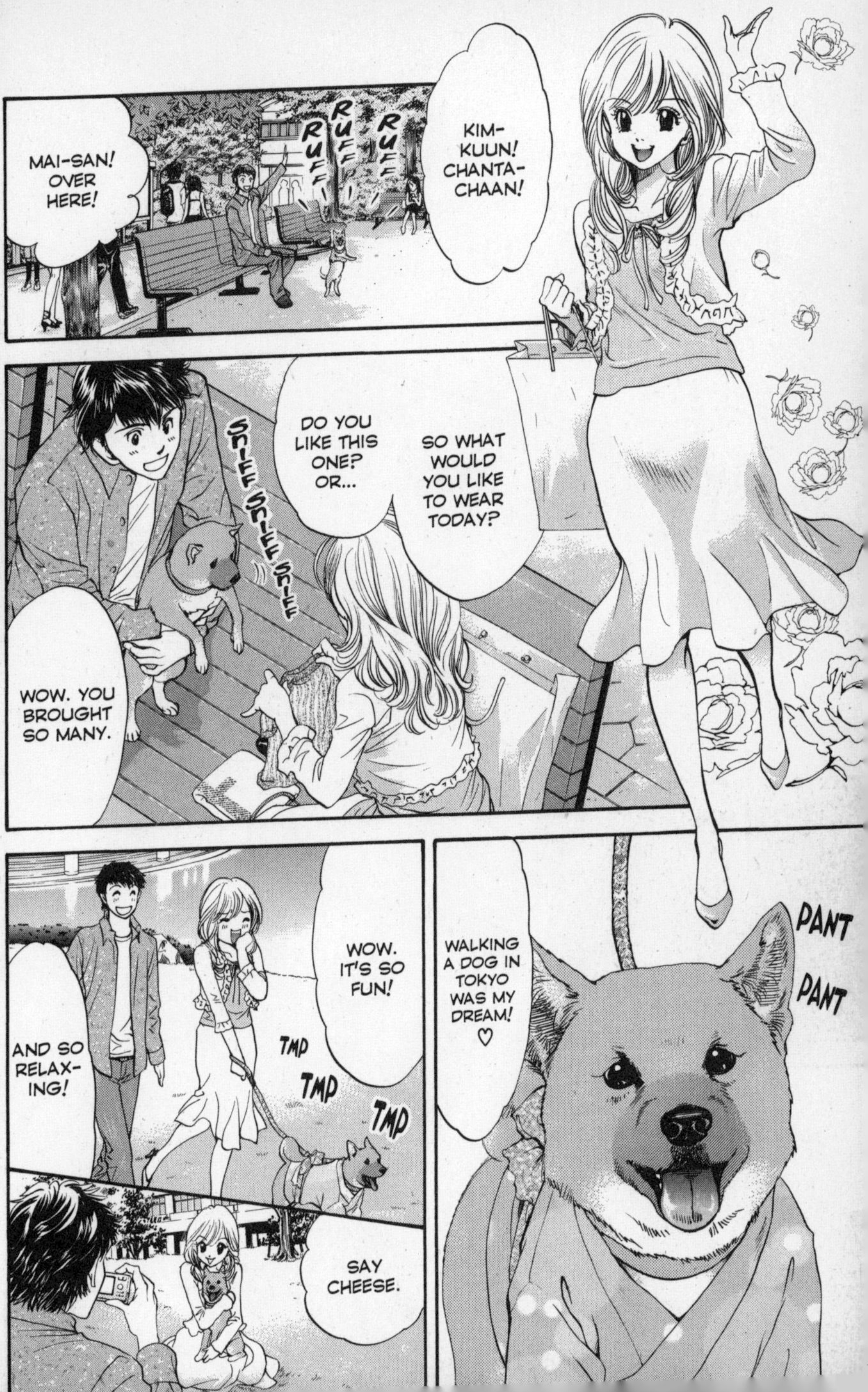
KIM-KUUN! CHANTA-CHAAN!
RUFF RUFF RUFF
MAI-SAN! OVER HERE!
SO WHAT WOULD YOU LIKE TO WEAR TODAY?
DO YOU LIKE THIS ONE? OR...
SNIFF SNIFF SNIFF
WOW. YOU BROUGHT SO MANY.
PANT PANT
WALKING A DOG IN TOKYO WAS MY DREAM! ♡
WOW. IT'S SO FUN!
TMP TMP TMP
AND SO RELAXING!
SAY CHEESE.

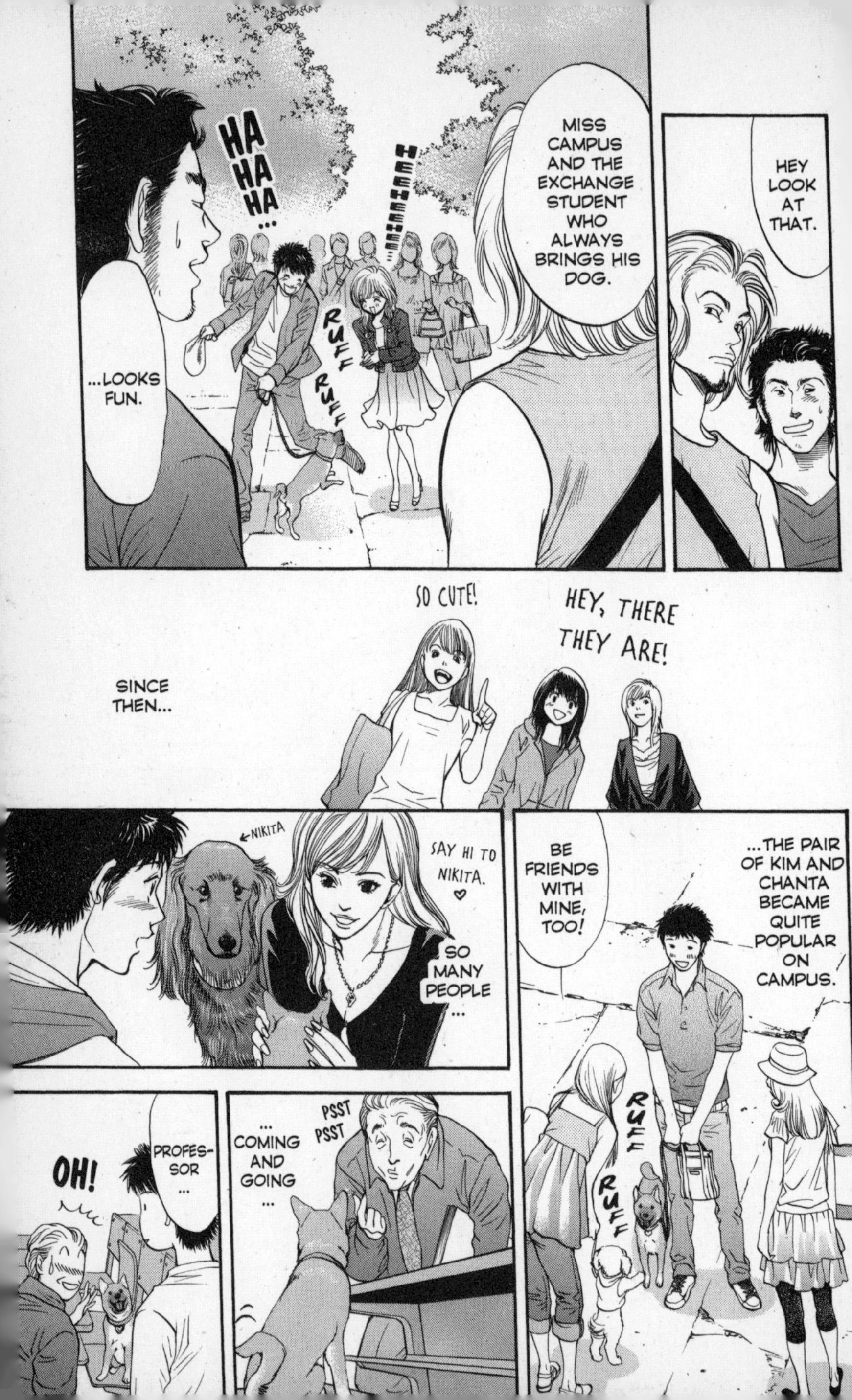
HEY LOOK AT THAT.
MISS CAMPUS AND THE EXCHANGE STUDENT WHO ALWAYS BRINGS HIS DOG.
HEEHEEHEE...
HA HA HA...
RUFF RUFF
...LOOKS FUN.
HEY, THERE THEY ARE!
SO CUTE!
SINCE THEN...
...THE PAIR OF KIM AND CHANTA BECAME QUITE POPULAR ON CAMPUS.
BE FRIENDS WITH MINE, TOO!
RUFF RUFF
SAY HI TO NIKITA. ♡
←NIKITA
SO MANY PEOPLE...
PSST PSST
...COMING AND GOING...
PROFES-SOR...
OH!

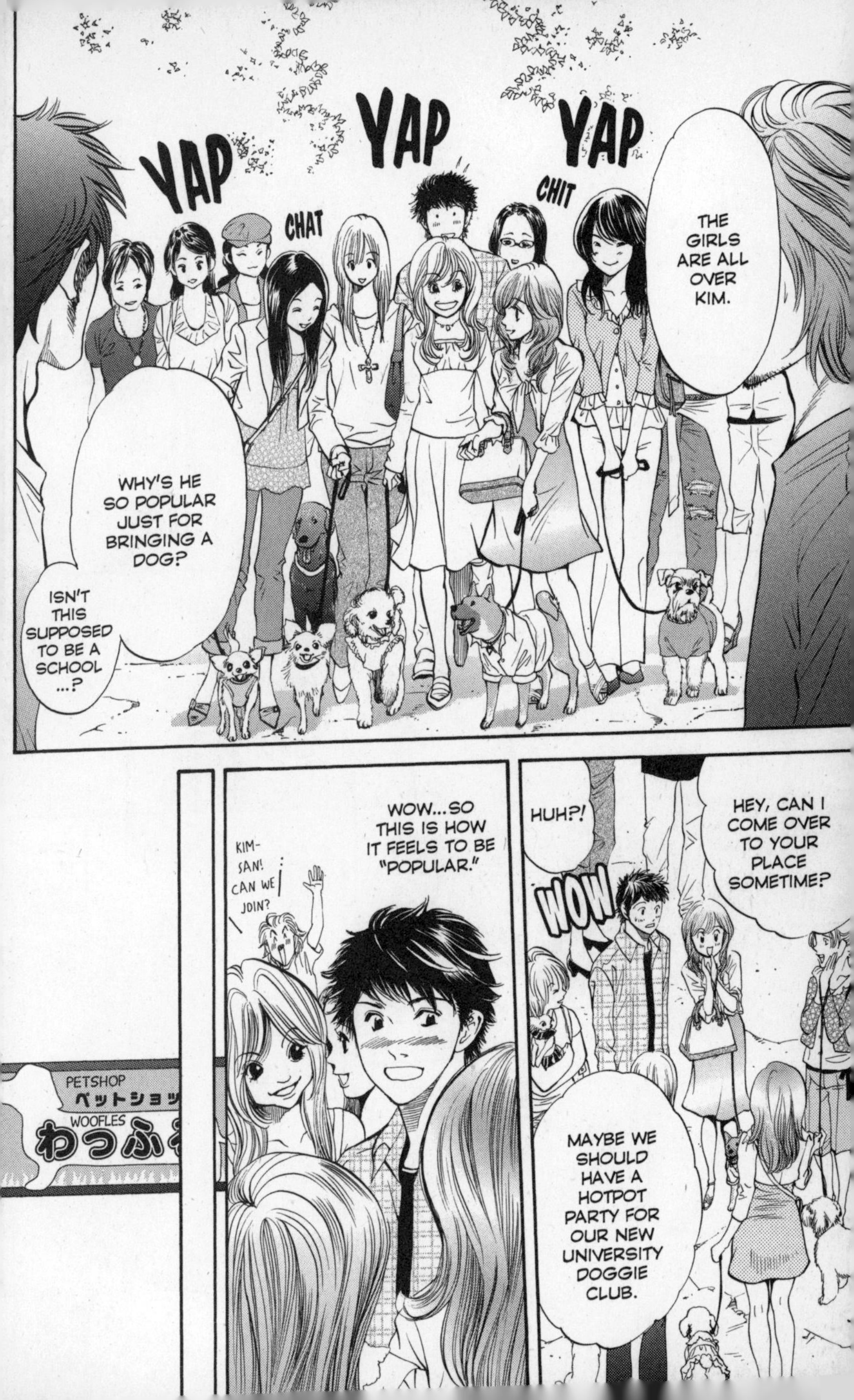
THE GIRLS ARE ALL OVER KIM.
YAP
CHIT
YAP
CHAT
YAP
WHY'S HE SO POPULAR JUST FOR BRINGING A DOG?
ISN'T THIS SUPPOSED TO BE A SCHOOL ...?
HEY, CAN I COME OVER TO YOUR PLACE SOMETIME?
HUH?!
WOW
MAYBE WE SHOULD HAVE A HOTPOT PARTY FOR OUR NEW UNIVERSITY DOGGIE CLUB.
WOW...SO THIS IS HOW IT FEELS TO BE "POPULAR."
KIM-SAN! CAN WE JOIN?
PETSHOP
WOOFLES

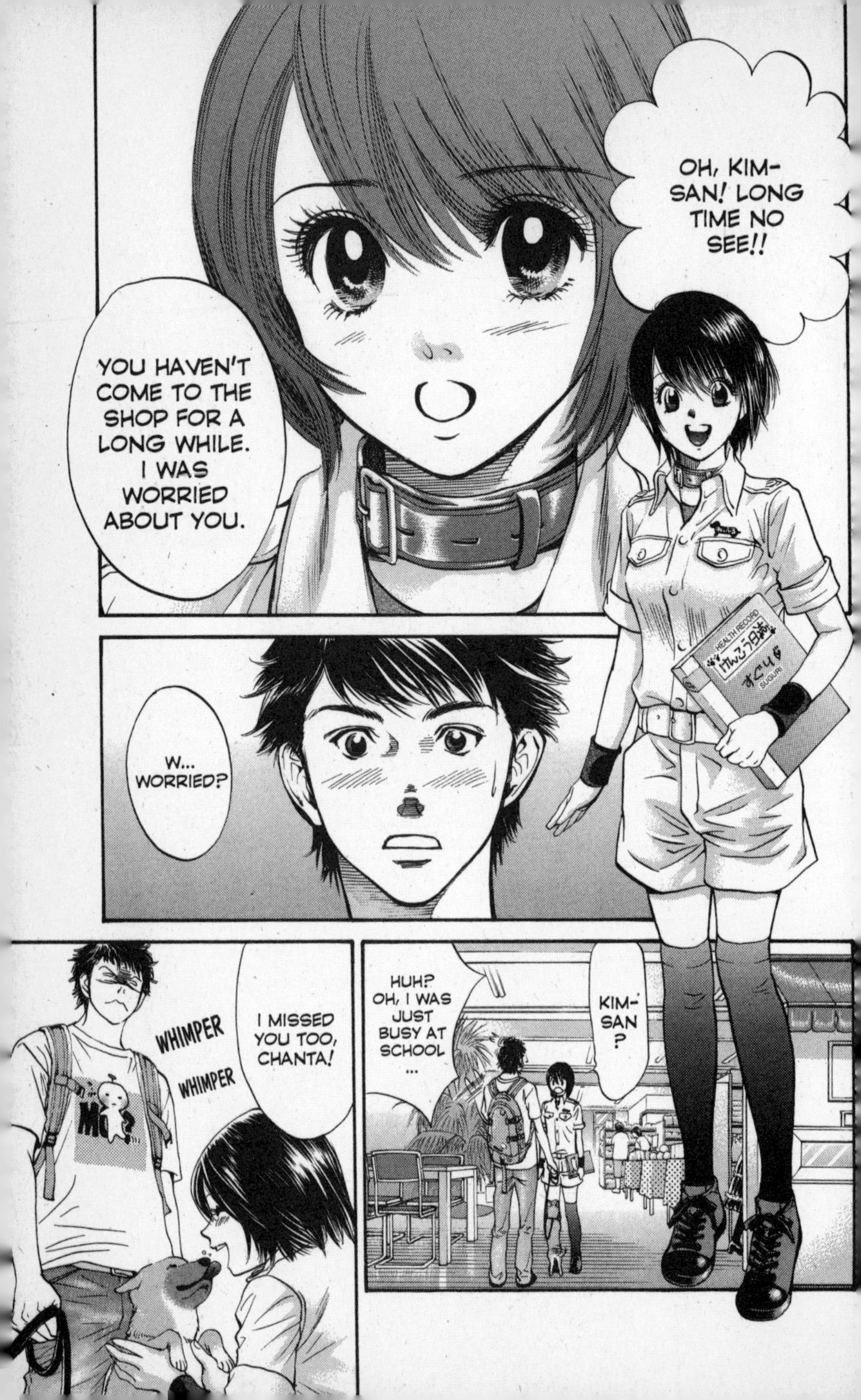
OH, KIM-SAN! LONG TIME NO SEE!!
YOU HAVEN'T COME TO THE SHOP FOR A LONG WHILE. I WAS WORRIED ABOUT YOU.
W... WORRIED?
KIM-SAN?
HUH? OH, I WAS JUST BUSY AT SCHOOL...
I MISSED YOU TOO, CHANTA!
WHIMPER
WHIMPER

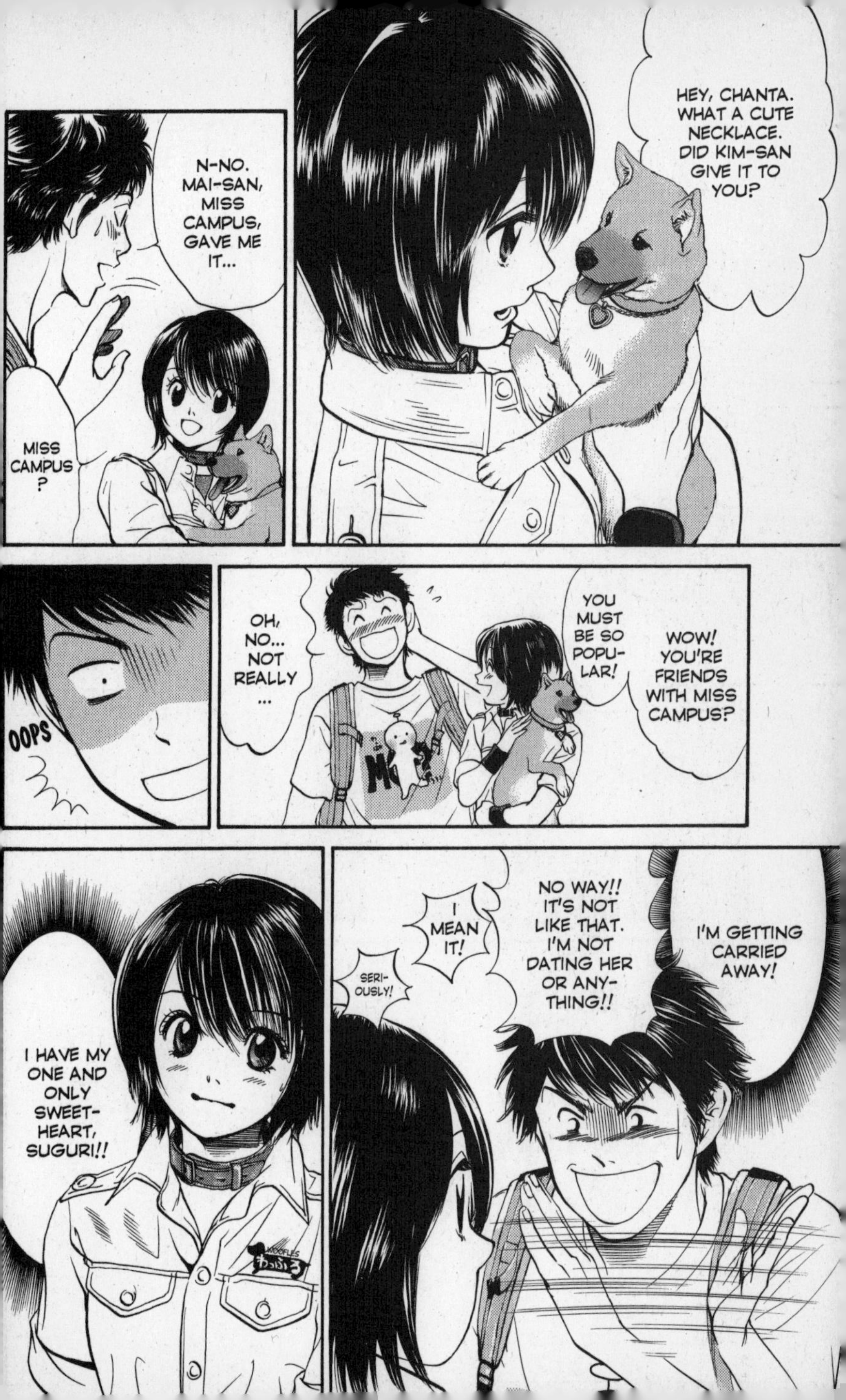
HEY, CHANTA. WHAT A CUTE NECKLACE. DID KIM-SAN GIVE IT TO YOU?
N-NO. MAI-SAN, MISS CAMPUS, GAVE ME IT...
MISS CAMPUS ?
WOW! YOU'RE FRIENDS WITH MISS CAMPUS?
YOU MUST BE SO POPU-LAR!
OH, NO... NOT REALLY ...
OOPS
I'M GETTING CARRIED AWAY!
NO WAY!! IT'S NOT LIKE THAT. I'M NOT DATING HER OR ANY-THING!!
I MEAN IT!
SERI-OUSLY!
I HAVE MY ONE AND ONLY SWEET-HEART, SUGURI!!

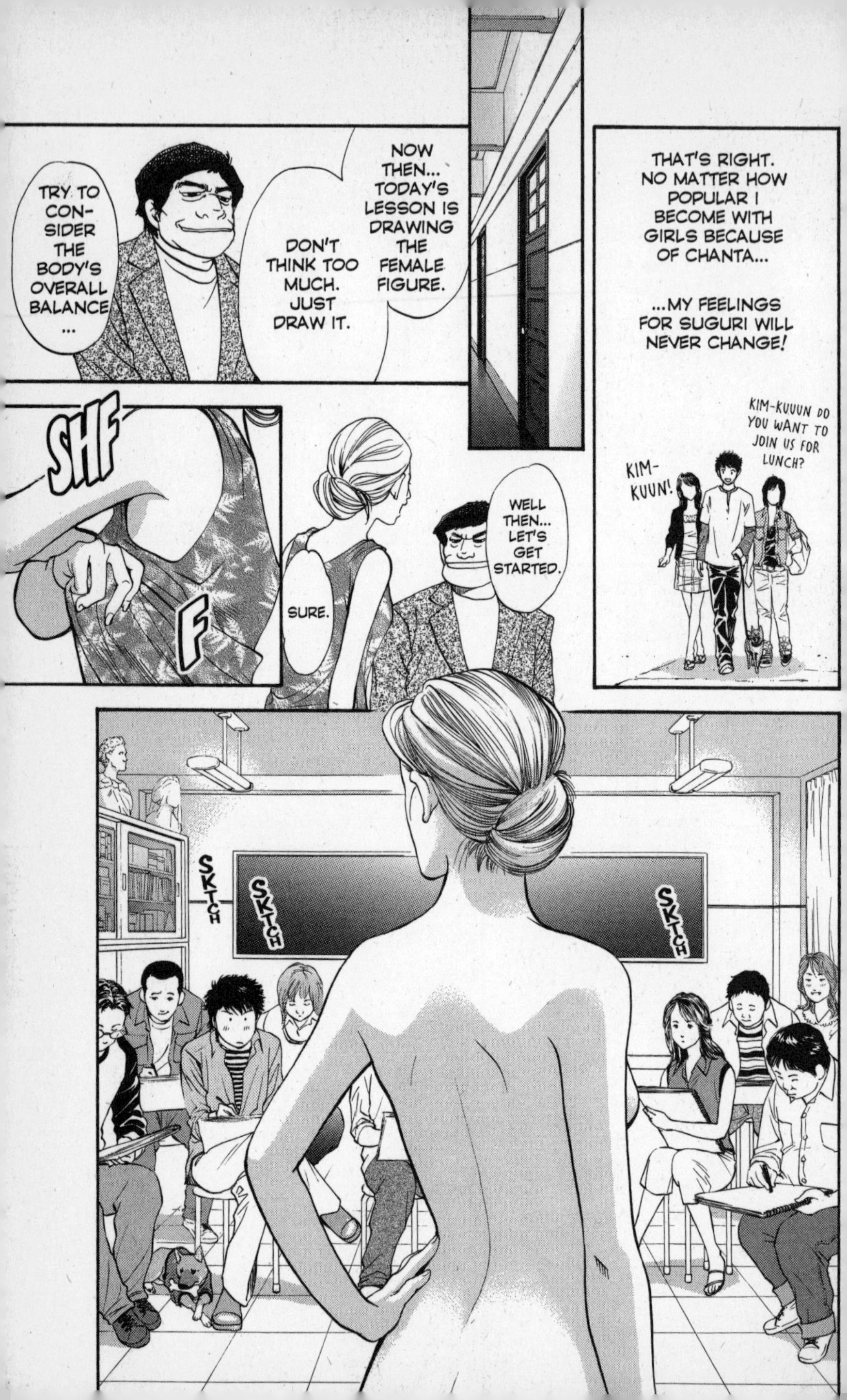
THAT'S RIGHT. NO MATTER HOW POPULAR I BECOME WITH GIRLS BECAUSE OF CHANTA...
...MY FEELINGS FOR SUGURI WILL NEVER CHANGE!
KIM-KUUUN DO YOU WANT TO JOIN US FOR LUNCH?
KIM-KUUN!
NOW THEN... TODAY'S LESSON IS DRAWING THE FEMALE FIGURE.
DON'T THINK TOO MUCH. JUST DRAW IT.
TRY TO CONSIDER THE BODY'S OVERALL BALANCE...
WELL THEN... LET'S GET STARTED.
SURE.
SHF
F
SKTCH
SKTCH
SKTCH

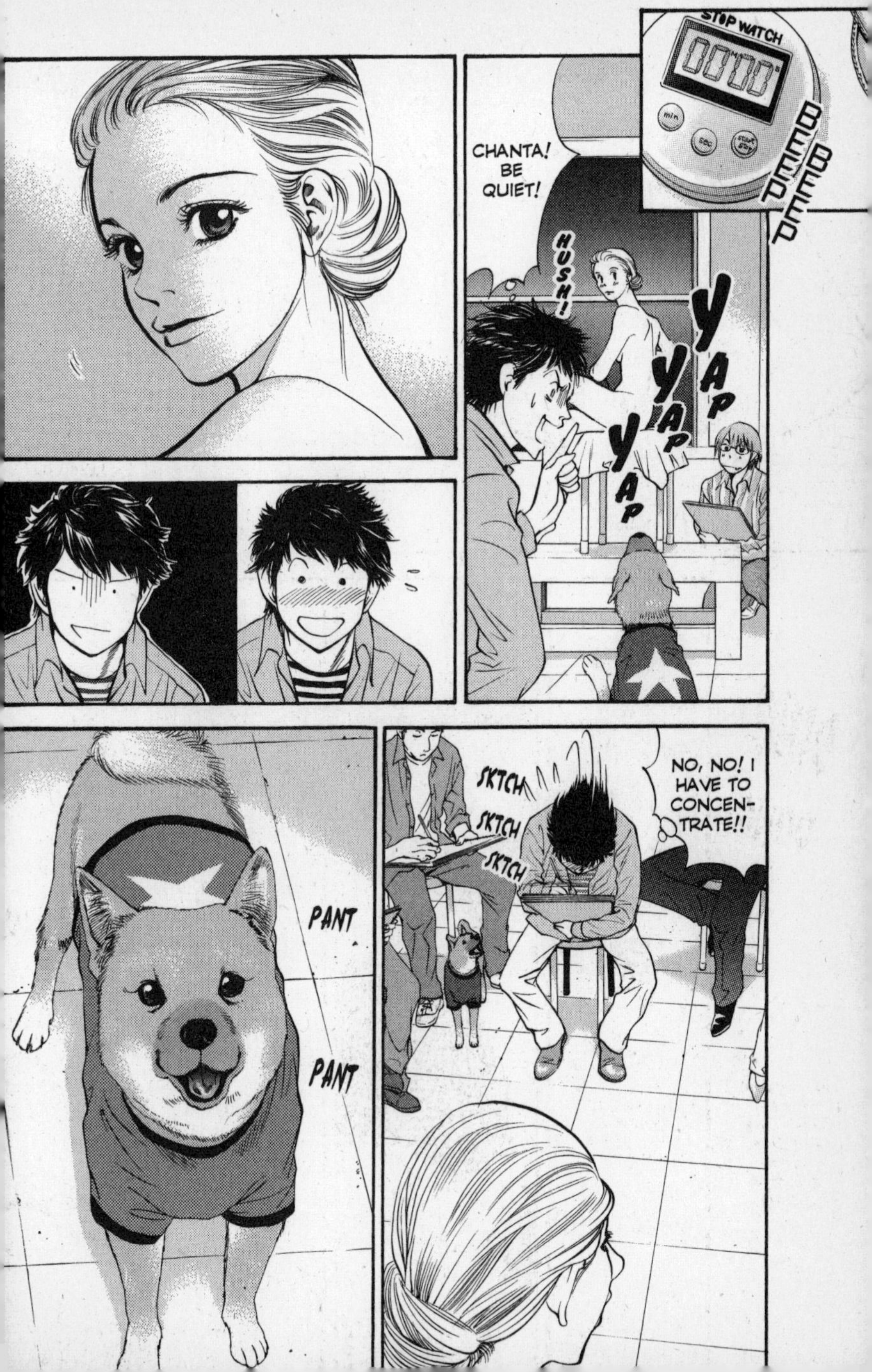
STOP WATCH
BEEP
BEEP
CHANTA! BE QUIET!
HUSH!
YAP
YAP
YAP
YAP
NO, NO! I HAVE TO CONCEN-TRATE!!
SKTCH
SKTCH
SKTCH
PANT
PANT

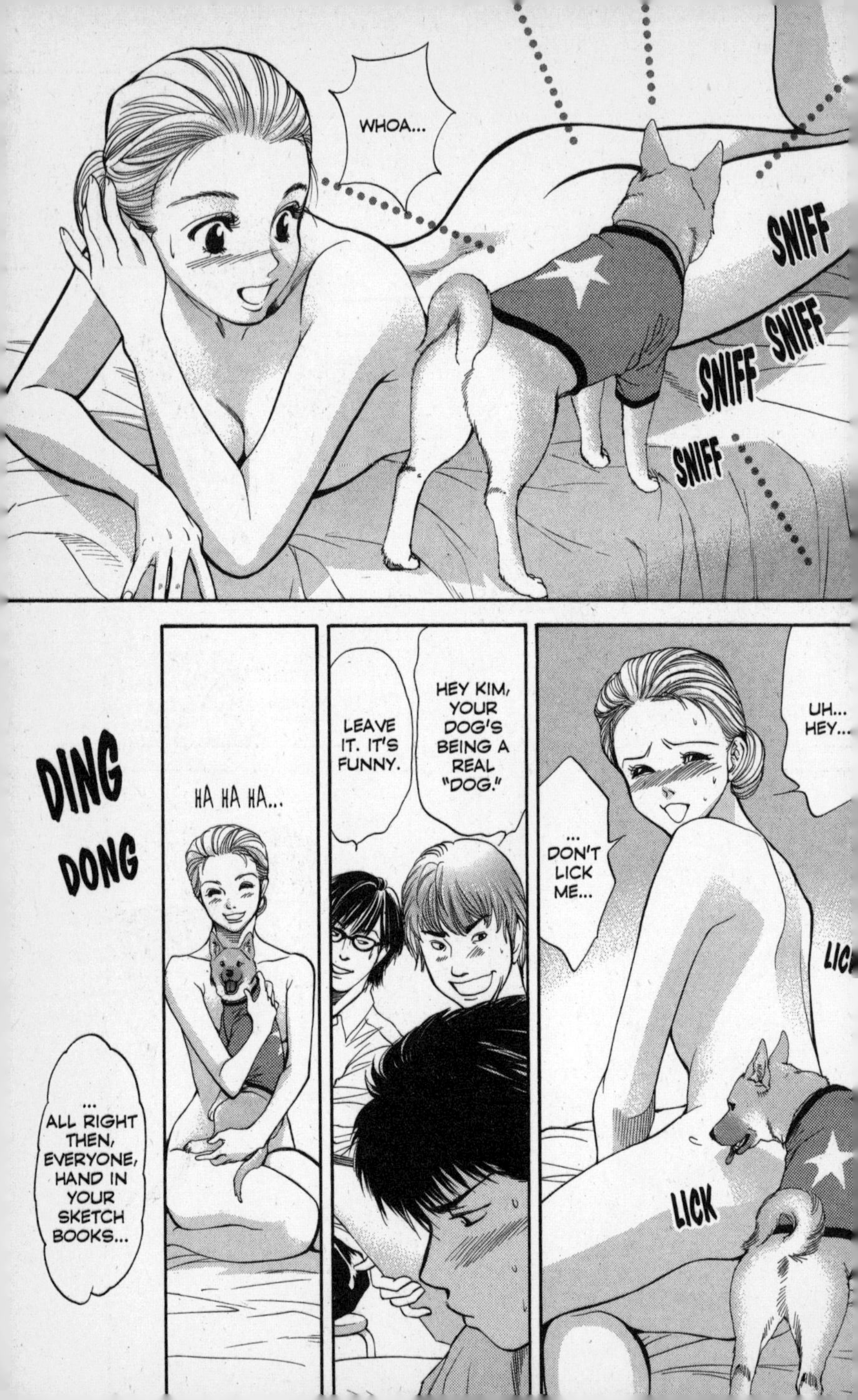
WHOA...
SNIFF
SNIFF
SNIFF
SNIFF
UH... HEY...
... DON'T LICK ME...
LICK
HEY KIM, YOUR DOG'S BEING A REAL "DOG."
LEAVE IT. IT'S FUNNY.
HA HA HA...
DING
DONG
... ALL RIGHT THEN, EVERYONE, HAND IN YOUR SKETCH BOOKS...

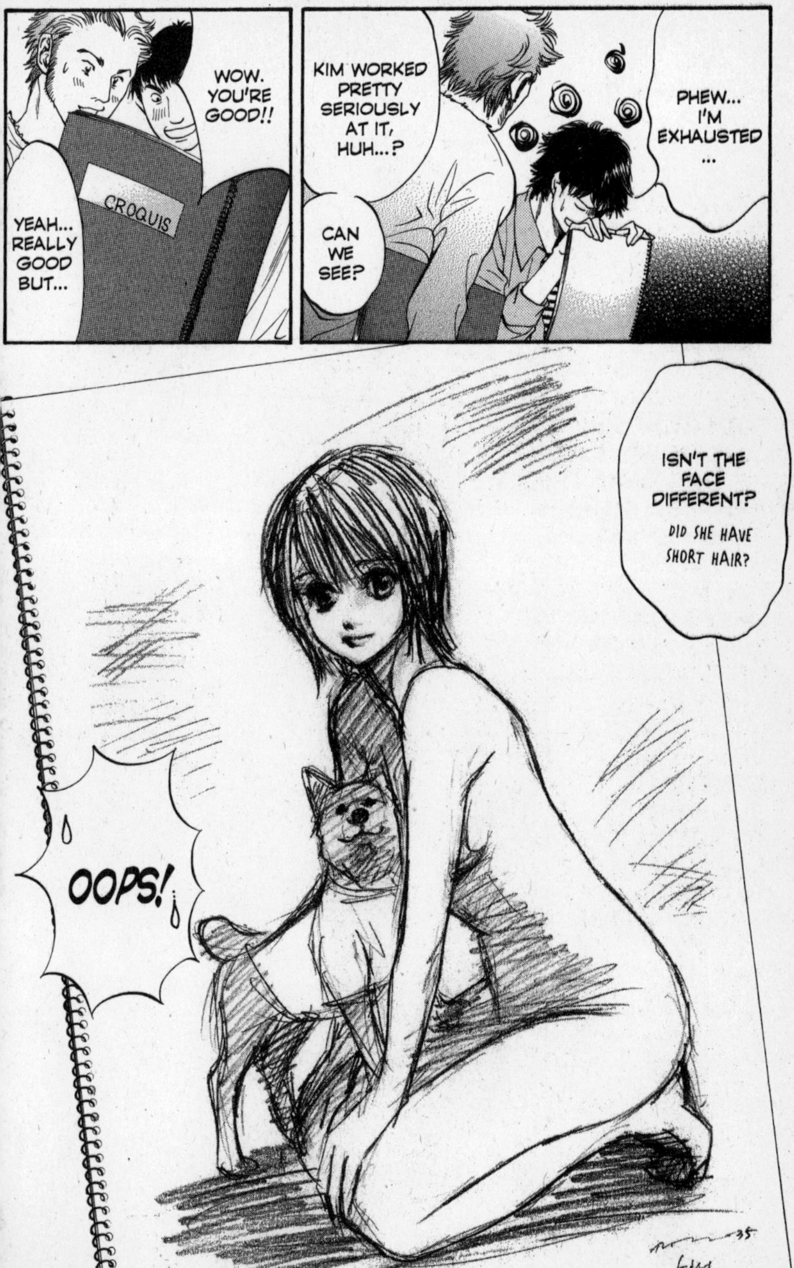
PHEW... I'M EXHAUSTED ...
KIM WORKED PRETTY SERIOUSLY AT IT, HUH...?
CAN WE SEE?
WOW. YOU'RE GOOD!!
CROQUIS
YEAH... REALLY GOOD BUT...
ISN'T THE FACE DIFFERENT?
DID SHE HAVE SHORT HAIR?
OOPS!
KIM

HELLO EVERYONE!
INUBAKA ALREADY HAS SEVEN VOLUMES RELEASED. THANKS YOU VERY MUCH FOR READING IT.
THERE ARE SO MANY HAPPY DOGS LIVING WITH PEOPLE BUT, AS MANY HAPPY DOGS AS THERE ARE, THERE ARE ALSO DOGS IN HARSH SITUATIONS...
WHEN I THINK ABOUT THE FACT THAT IN MOST CASES HUMANS ARE THE CAUSE OF THAT, I FEEL VERY SAD...
I WISH THAT REALITY WOULD DISAPPEAR SOMEDAY...
BUT WE HAVE TO ACT TO MAKE THAT HAPPEN...
I THINK ABOUT THIS A LOT RECENTLY...

SEE YOU IN VOLUME 8

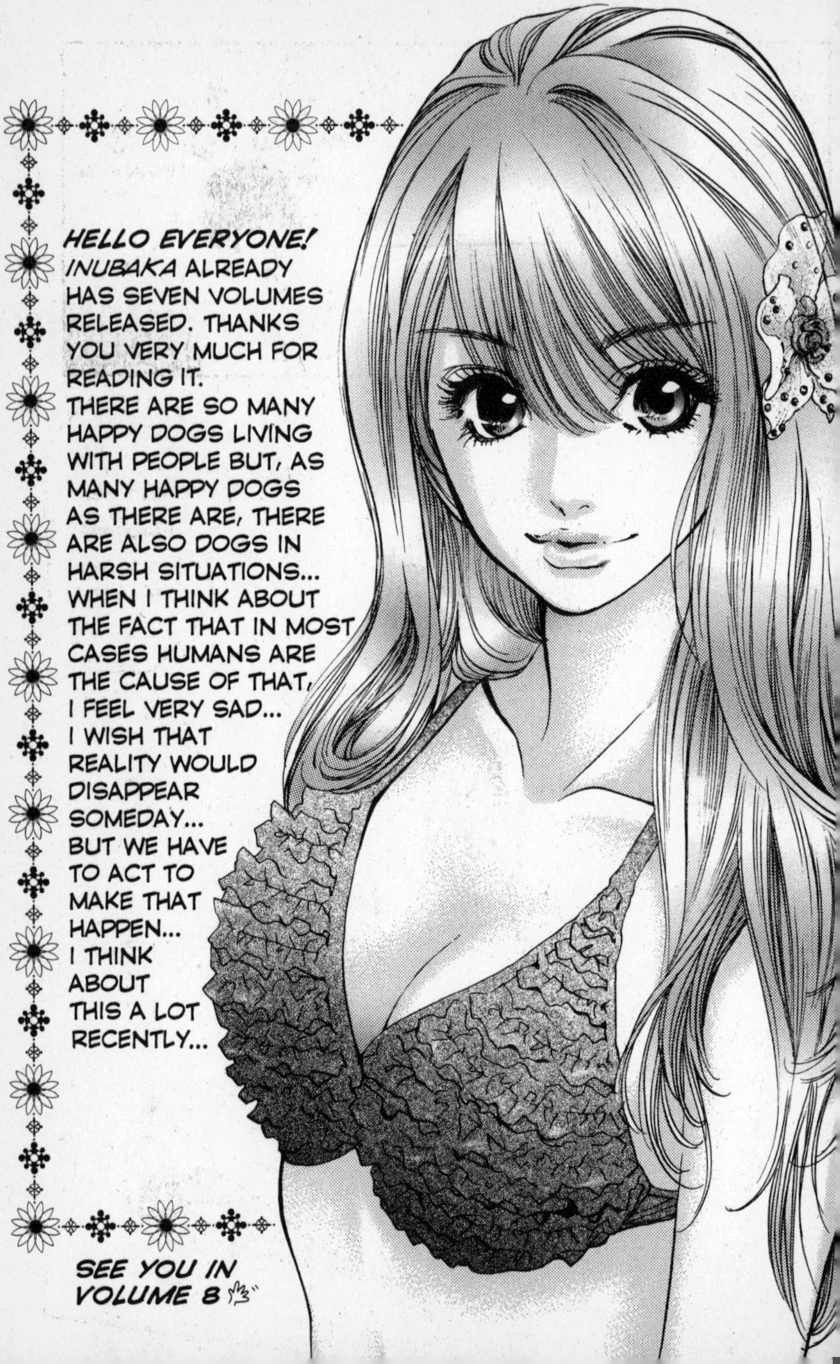

CHAPTER 68:
THE SCISSORHANDS

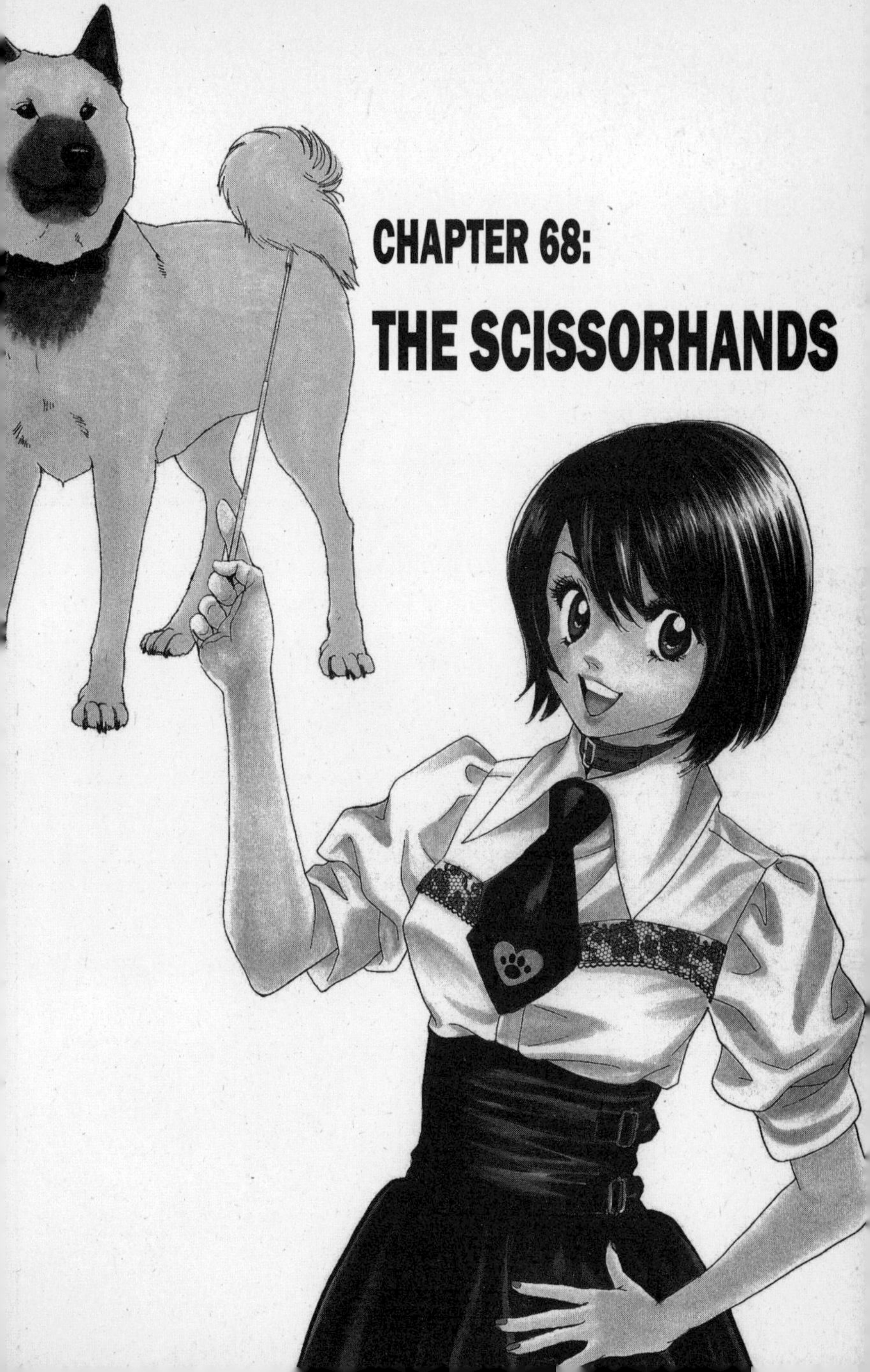

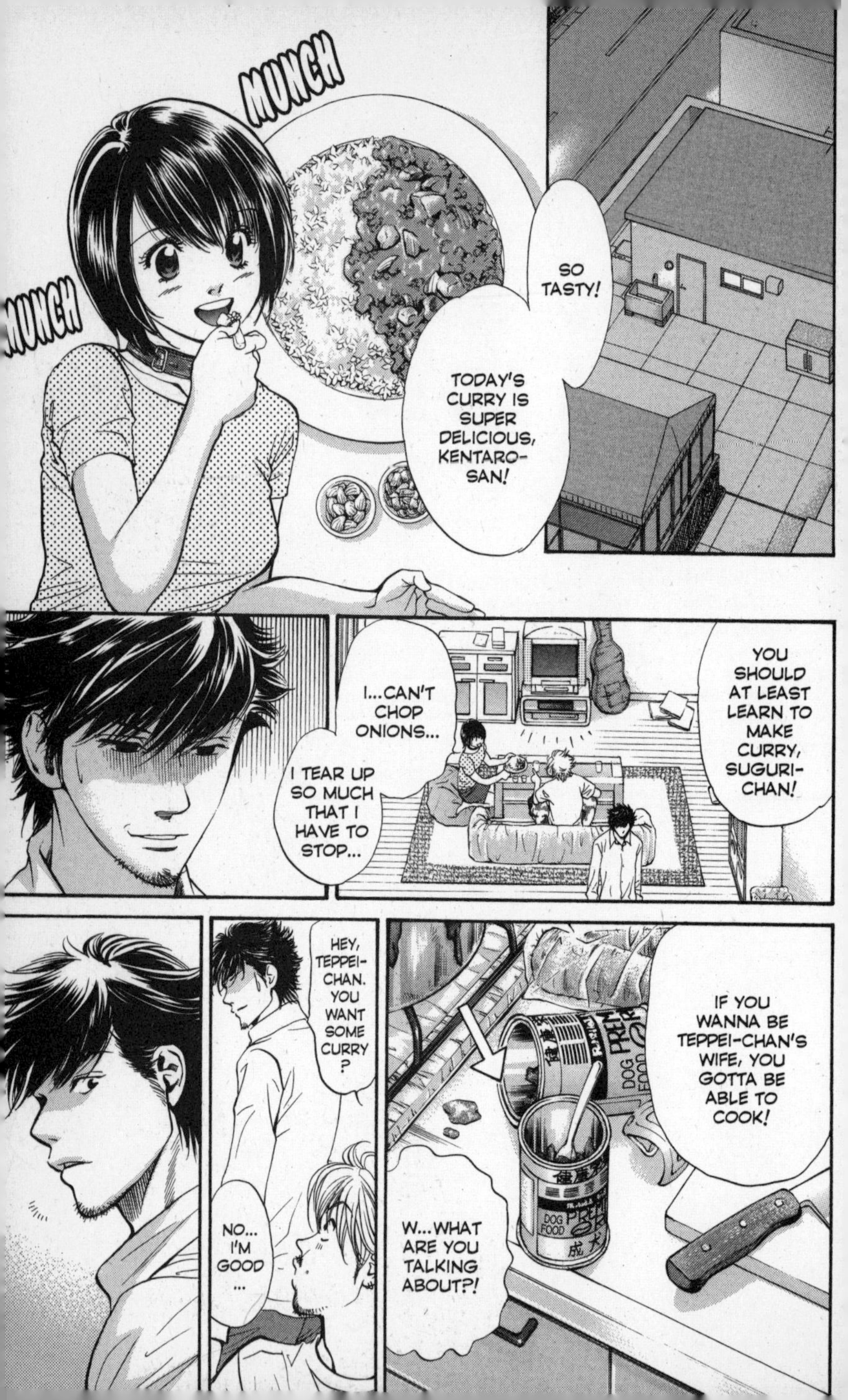
SO TASTY!
TODAY'S CURRY IS SUPER DELICIOUS, KENTARO-SAN!
MUNCH
MUNCH
YOU SHOULD AT LEAST LEARN TO MAKE CURRY, SUGURI-CHAN!
I...CAN'T CHOP ONIONS...
I TEAR UP SO MUCH THAT I HAVE TO STOP...
IF YOU WANNA BE TEPPEI-CHAN'S WIFE, YOU GOTTA BE ABLE TO COOK!
W...WHAT ARE YOU TALKING ABOUT?!
HEY, TEPPEI-CHAN. YOU WANT SOME CURRY?
NO... I'M GOOD ...

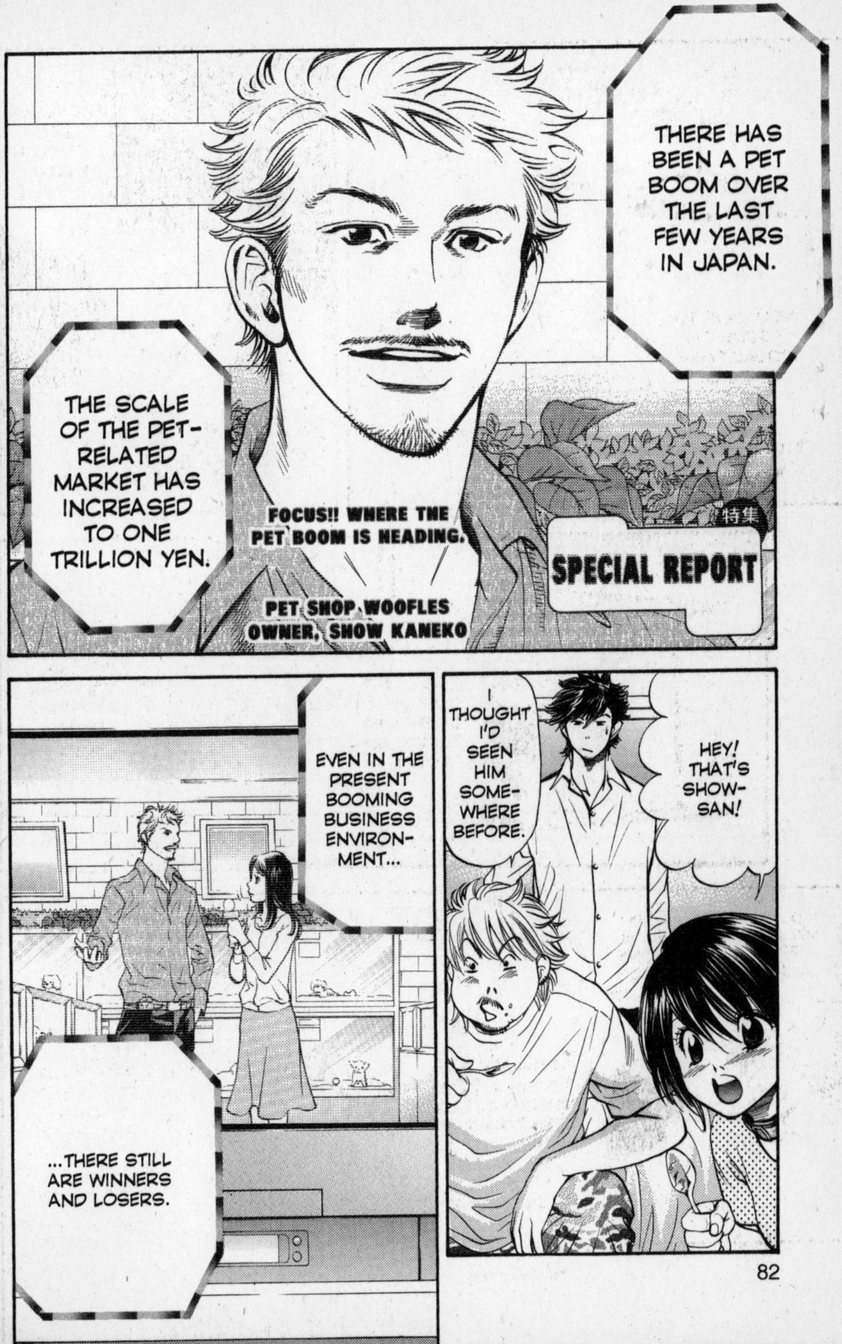
THERE HAS BEEN A PET BOOM OVER THE LAST FEW YEARS IN JAPAN.
THE SCALE OF THE PET-RELATED MARKET HAS INCREASED TO ONE TRILLION YEN.
特集
SPECIAL REPORT
FOCUS!! WHERE THE PET BOOM IS HEADING.
PET SHOP WOOFLES OWNER, SHOW KANEKO
HEY! THAT'S SHOW-SAN!
I THOUGHT I'D SEEN HIM SOMEWHERE BEFORE.
EVEN IN THE PRESENT BOOMING BUSINESS ENVIRONMENT...
...THERE STILL ARE WINNERS AND LOSERS.

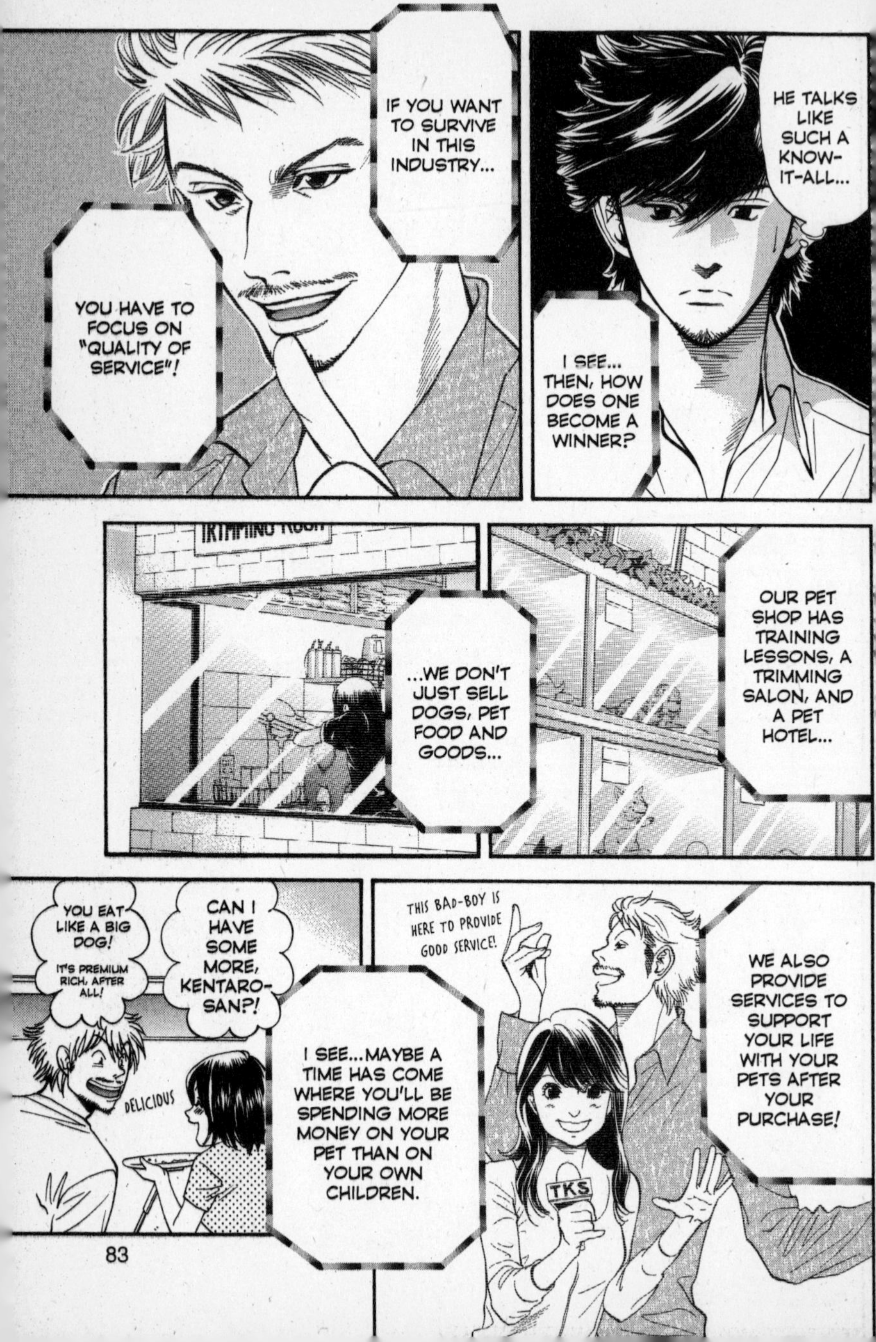
HE TALKS LIKE SUCH A KNOW-IT-ALL...
I SEE... THEN, HOW DOES ONE BECOME A WINNER?
IF YOU WANT TO SURVIVE IN THIS INDUSTRY...
YOU HAVE TO FOCUS ON "QUALITY OF SERVICE"!
OUR PET SHOP HAS TRAINING LESSONS, A TRIMMING SALON, AND A PET HOTEL...
...WE DON'T JUST SELL DOGS, PET FOOD AND GOODS...
WE ALSO PROVIDE SERVICES TO SUPPORT YOUR LIFE WITH YOUR PETS AFTER YOUR PURCHASE!
THIS BAD-BOY IS HERE TO PROVIDE GOOD SERVICE!
TKS
I SEE...MAYBE A TIME HAS COME WHERE YOU'LL BE SPENDING MORE MONEY ON YOUR PET THAN ON YOUR OWN CHILDREN.
CAN I HAVE SOME MORE, KENTARO-SAN?!
YOU EAT LIKE A BIG DOG!
IT'S PREMIUM RICH, AFTER ALL!
DELICIOUS

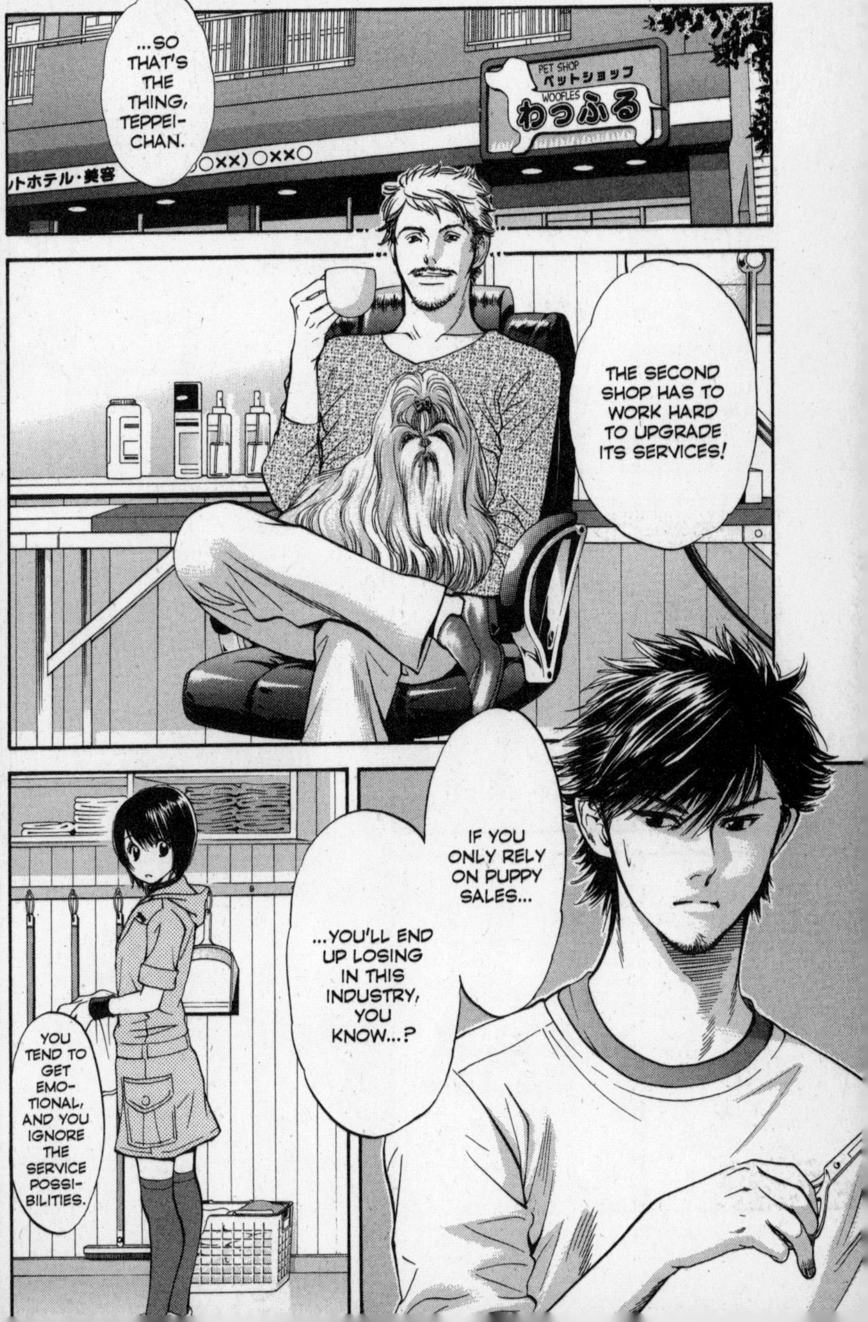
PET SHOP
ペットショップ
WOOFLES
わっふる
ットホテル・美容
...SO THAT'S THE THING, TEPPEI-CHAN.
THE SECOND SHOP HAS TO WORK HARD TO UPGRADE ITS SERVICES!
IF YOU ONLY RELY ON PUPPY SALES...
...YOU'LL END UP LOSING IN THIS INDUSTRY, YOU KNOW...?
YOU TEND TO GET EMO-TIONAL, AND YOU IGNORE THE SERVICE POSSI-BILITIES.

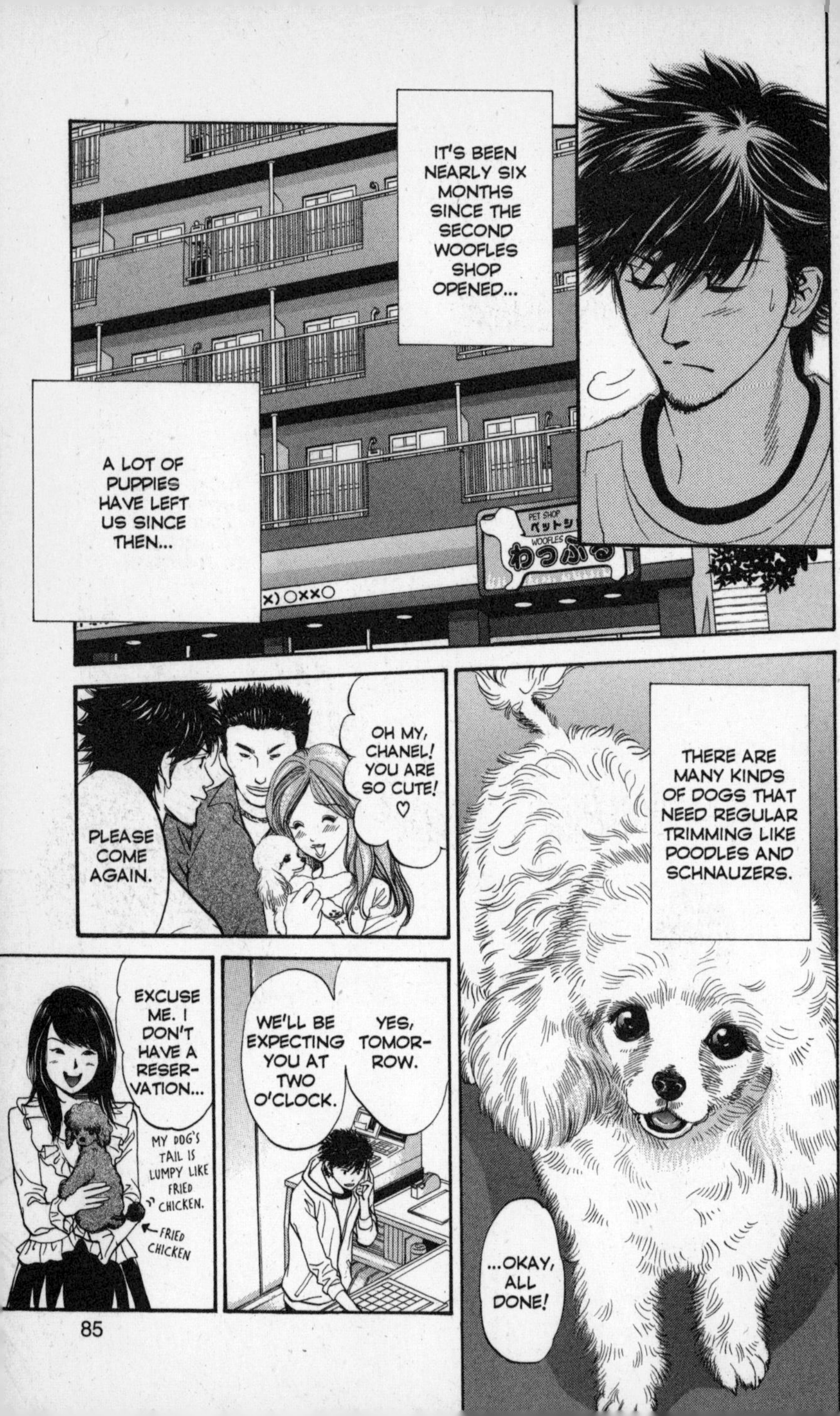
IT'S BEEN NEARLY SIX MONTHS SINCE THE SECOND WOOFLES SHOP OPENED...
A LOT OF PUPPIES HAVE LEFT US SINCE THEN...
PET SHOP
WOOFLES
THERE ARE MANY KINDS OF DOGS THAT NEED REGULAR TRIMMING LIKE POODLES AND SCHNAUZERS.
...OKAY, ALL DONE!
OH MY, CHANEL! YOU ARE SO CUTE! ♡
PLEASE COME AGAIN.
YES, TOMORROW.
WE'LL BE EXPECTING YOU AT TWO O'CLOCK.
EXCUSE ME. I DON'T HAVE A RESERVATION...
MY DOG'S TAIL IS LUMPY LIKE FRIED CHICKEN.
FRIED CHICKEN

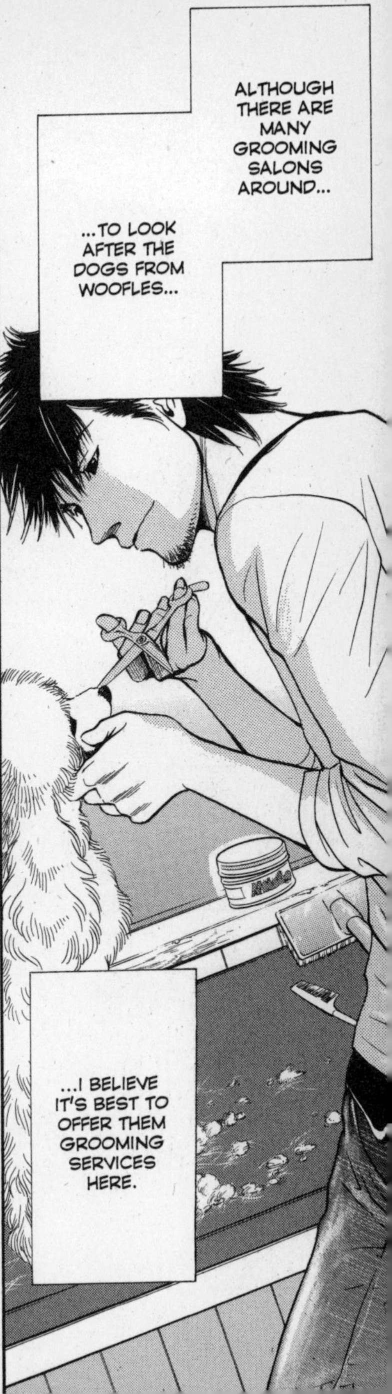
ALTHOUGH THERE ARE MANY GROOMING SALONS AROUND...
...TO LOOK AFTER THE DOGS FROM WOOFLES...
...I BELIEVE IT'S BEST TO OFFER THEM GROOMING SERVICES HERE.

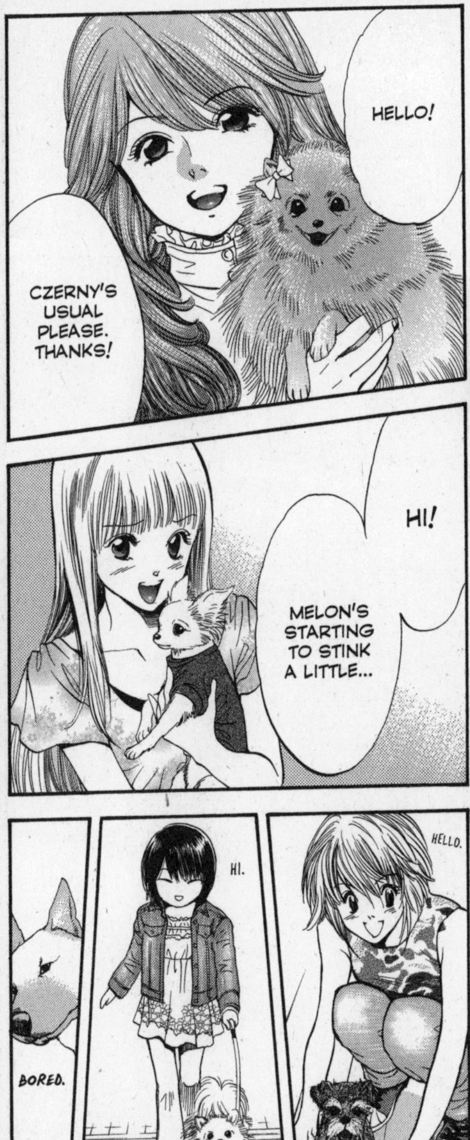
HELLO!
CZERNY'S USUAL PLEASE. THANKS!
HI!
MELON'S STARTING TO STINK A LITTLE...
HELLO.
HI.
BORED.

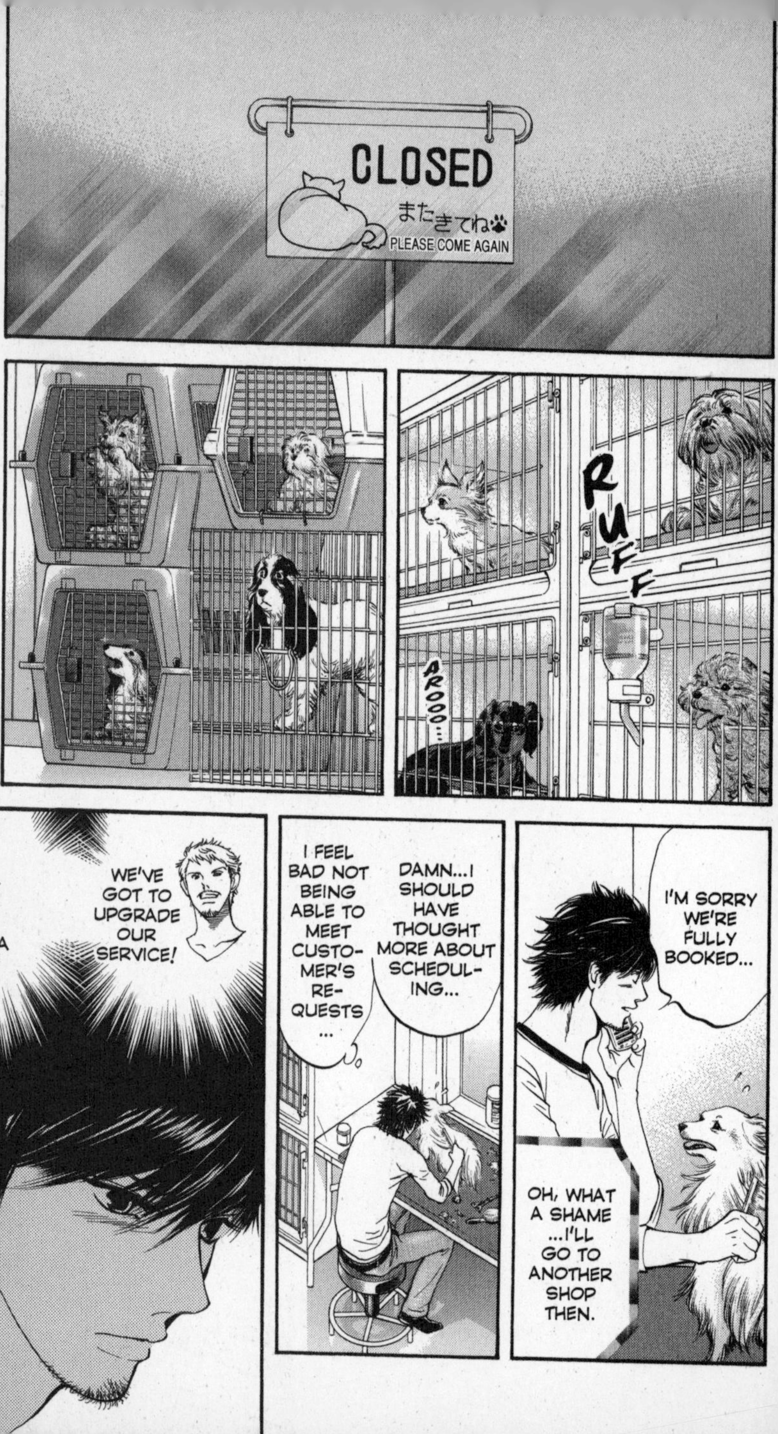
CLOSED
またきてね
PLEASE COME AGAIN
RUFF RUFF
AROOO...
I'M SORRY WE'RE FULLY BOOKED...
OH, WHAT A SHAME ...I'LL GO TO ANOTHER SHOP THEN.
DAMN...I SHOULD HAVE THOUGHT MORE ABOUT SCHEDULING...
I FEEL BAD NOT BEING ABLE TO MEET CUSTOMER'S REQUESTS...
WE'VE GOT TO UPGRADE OUR SERVICE!
OTHERWISE YOU'LL END UP A LOSER!

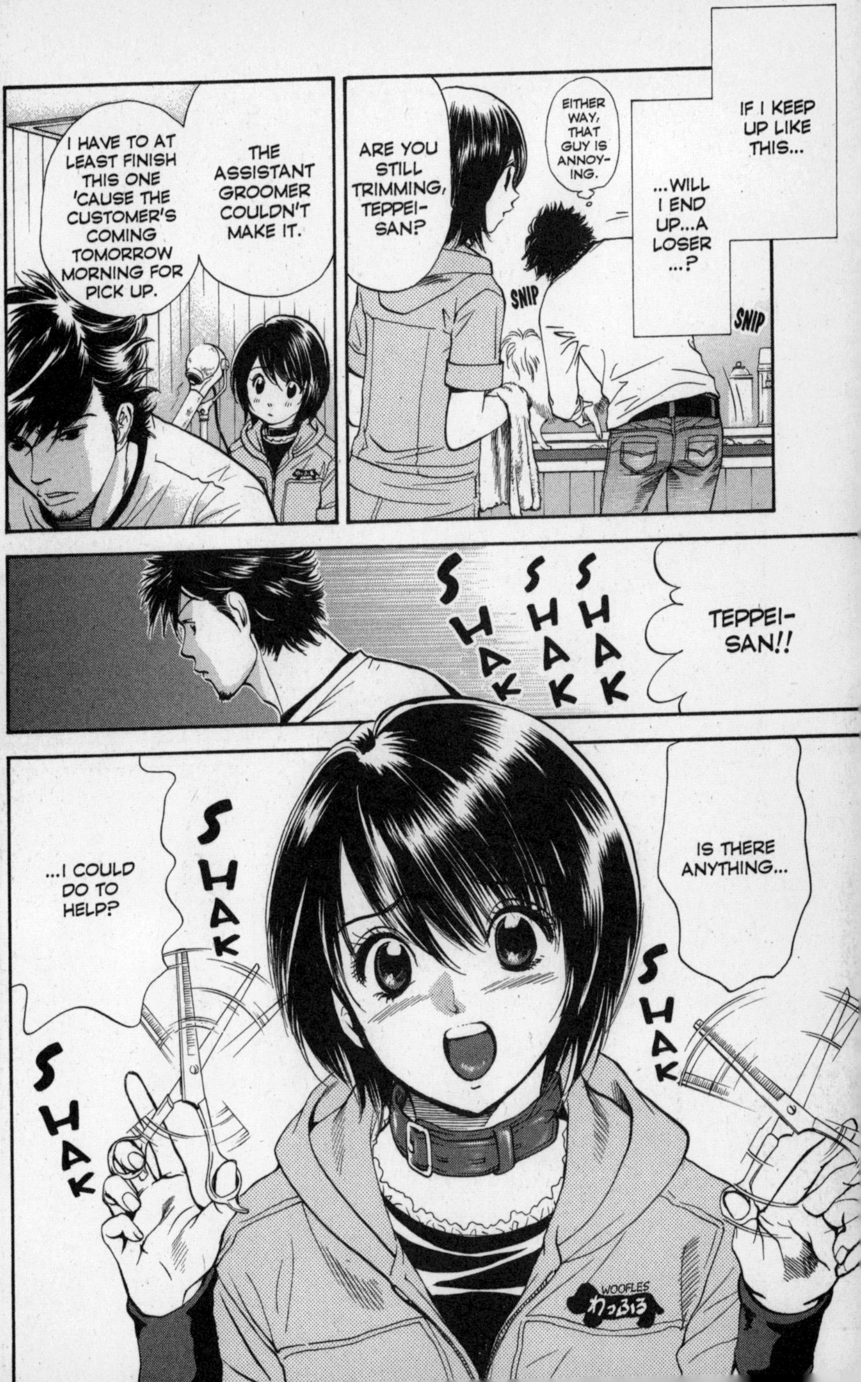

IF I KEEP UP LIKE THIS...
...WILL I END UP...A LOSER ...?
EITHER WAY, THAT GUY IS ANNOYING.
ARE YOU STILL TRIMMING, TEPPEI-SAN?
SNIP
SNIP
THE ASSISTANT GROOMER COULDN'T MAKE IT.
I HAVE TO AT LEAST FINISH THIS ONE 'CAUSE THE CUSTOMER'S COMING TOMORROW MORNING FOR PICK UP.
TEPPEI-SAN!!
SHAK
SHAK
SHAK
IS THERE ANYTHING...
SHAK
SHAK
...I COULD DO TO HELP?
SHAK
WOOFLES
わっふる

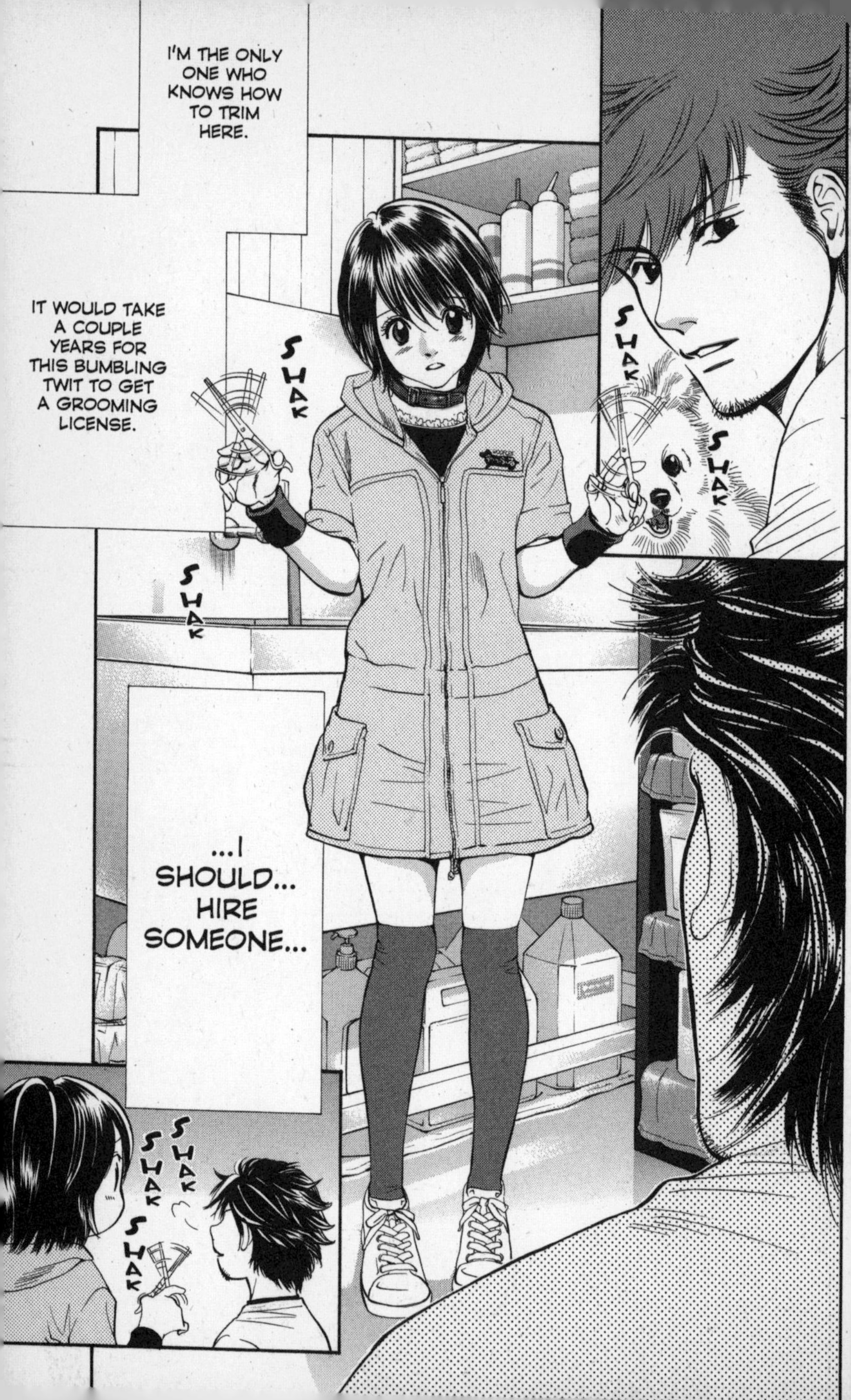
SHAK
SHAK
I'M THE ONLY ONE WHO KNOWS HOW TO TRIM HERE.
IT WOULD TAKE A COUPLE YEARS FOR THIS BUMBLING TWIT TO GET A GROOMING LICENSE.
SHAK
SHAK
...I SHOULD... HIRE SOMEONE...
SHAK
SHAK
SHAK

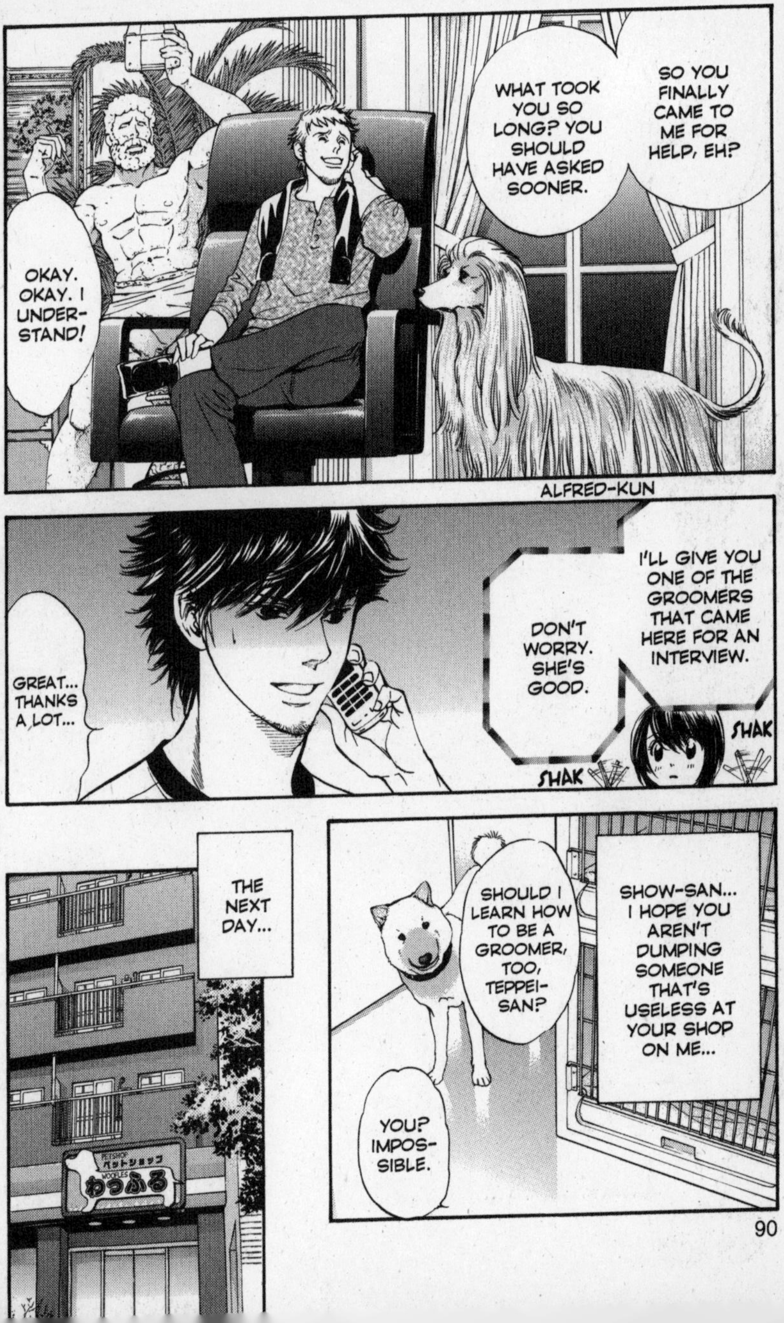
SO YOU FINALLY CAME TO ME FOR HELP, EH?
WHAT TOOK YOU SO LONG? YOU SHOULD HAVE ASKED SOONER.
OKAY. OKAY. I UNDERSTAND!
ALFRED-KUN
I'LL GIVE YOU ONE OF THE GROOMERS THAT CAME HERE FOR AN INTERVIEW.
DON'T WORRY. SHE'S GOOD.
SHAK
SHAK
GREAT... THANKS A LOT...
SHOW-SAN... I HOPE YOU AREN'T DUMPING SOMEONE THAT'S USELESS AT YOUR SHOP ON ME...
SHOULD I LEARN HOW TO BE A GROOMER, TOO, TEPPEI-SAN?
YOU? IMPOSSIBLE.
THE NEXT DAY...
PETSHOP
ペットショップ
WOOFLES
わっふる

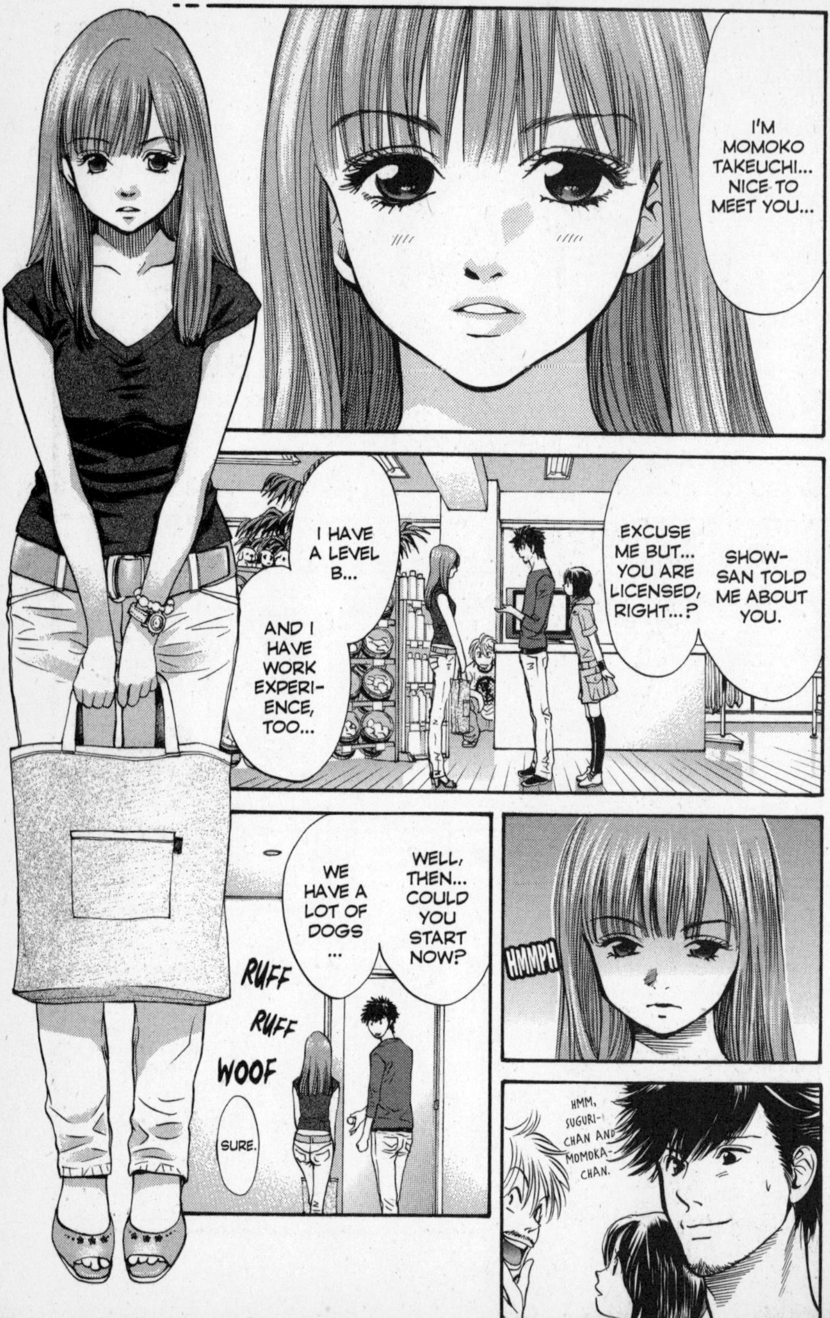
I'M MOMOKO TAKEUCHI... NICE TO MEET YOU...
SHOW-SAN TOLD ME ABOUT YOU.
EXCUSE ME BUT... YOU ARE LICENSED, RIGHT...?
I HAVE A LEVEL B...
AND I HAVE WORK EXPERIENCE, TOO...
HMMPH
WELL, THEN... COULD YOU START NOW?
WE HAVE A LOT OF DOGS ...
RUFF
RUFF
WOOF
SURE.
HMM, SUGURI-CHAN AND MOMOKA-CHAN.

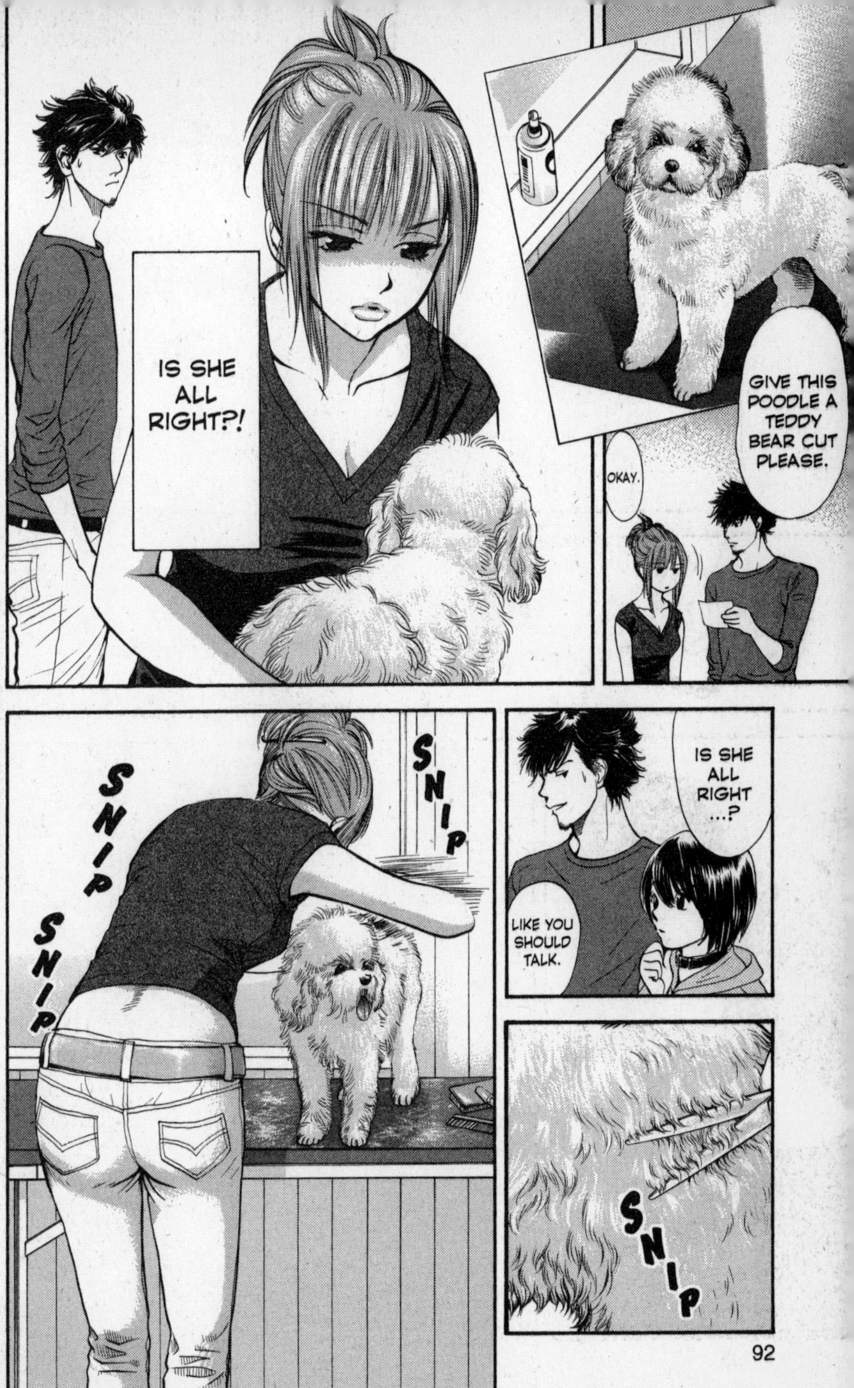
GIVE THIS POODLE A TEDDY BEAR CUT PLEASE.
OKAY.
IS SHE ALL RIGHT?!
IS SHE ALL RIGHT ...?
LIKE YOU SHOULD TALK.
SNIP
SNIP
SNIP
SNIP

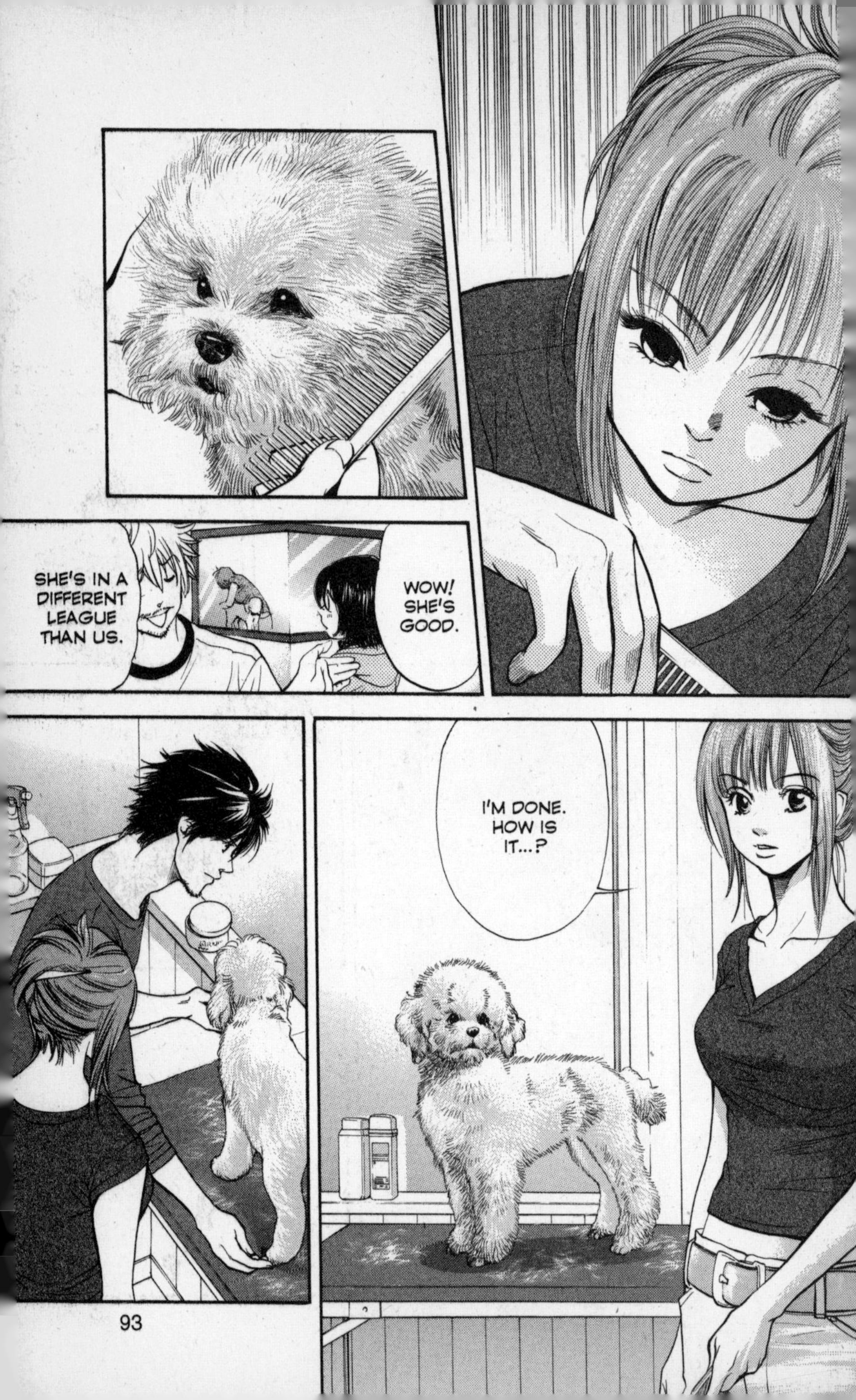
WOW! SHE'S GOOD.
SHE'S IN A DIFFERENT LEAGUE THAN US.
I'M DONE. HOW IS IT...?

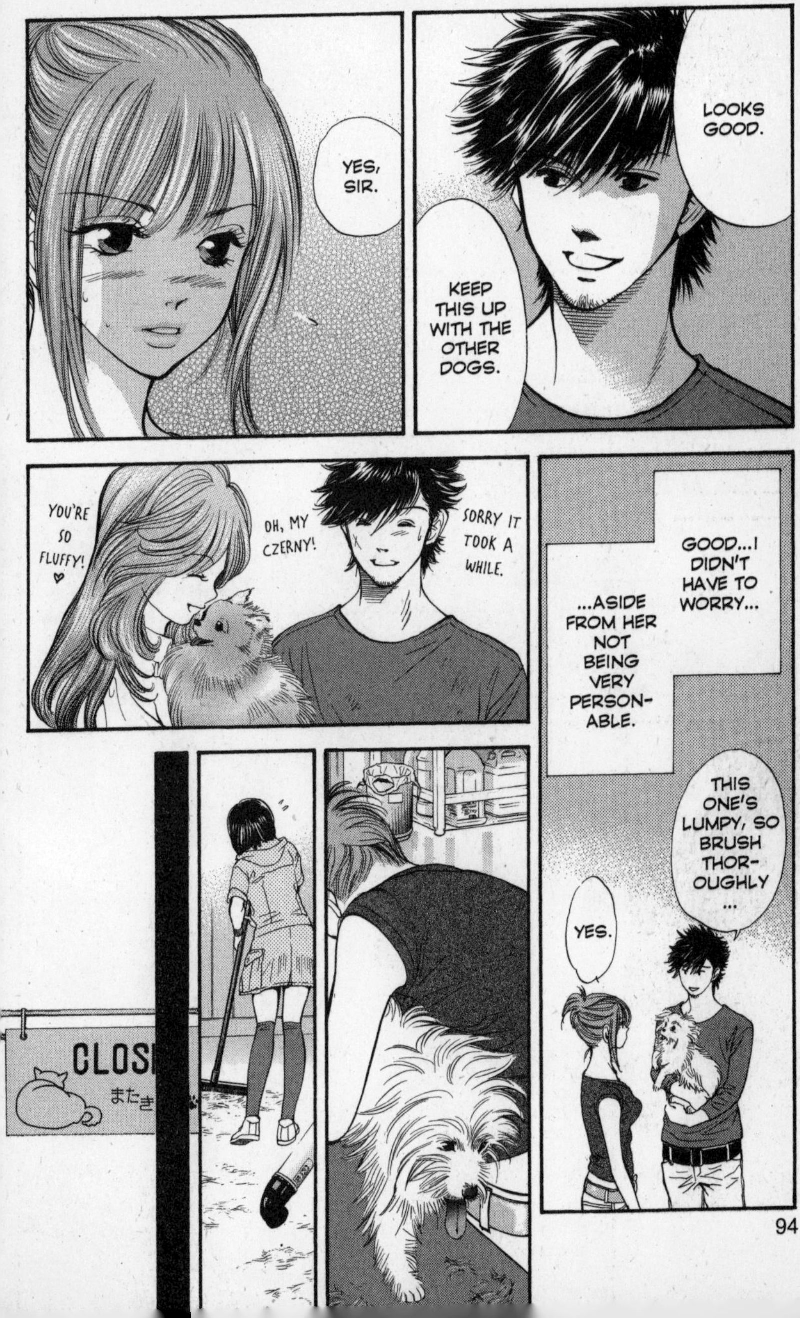
LOOKS GOOD.
KEEP THIS UP WITH THE OTHER DOGS.
YES, SIR.
GOOD...I DIDN'T HAVE TO WORRY...
...ASIDE FROM HER NOT BEING VERY PERSON-ABLE.
THIS ONE'S LUMPY, SO BRUSH THOR-OUGHLY ...
YES.
SORRY IT TOOK A WHILE.
OH, MY CZERNY!
YOU'RE SO FLUFFY! ♡

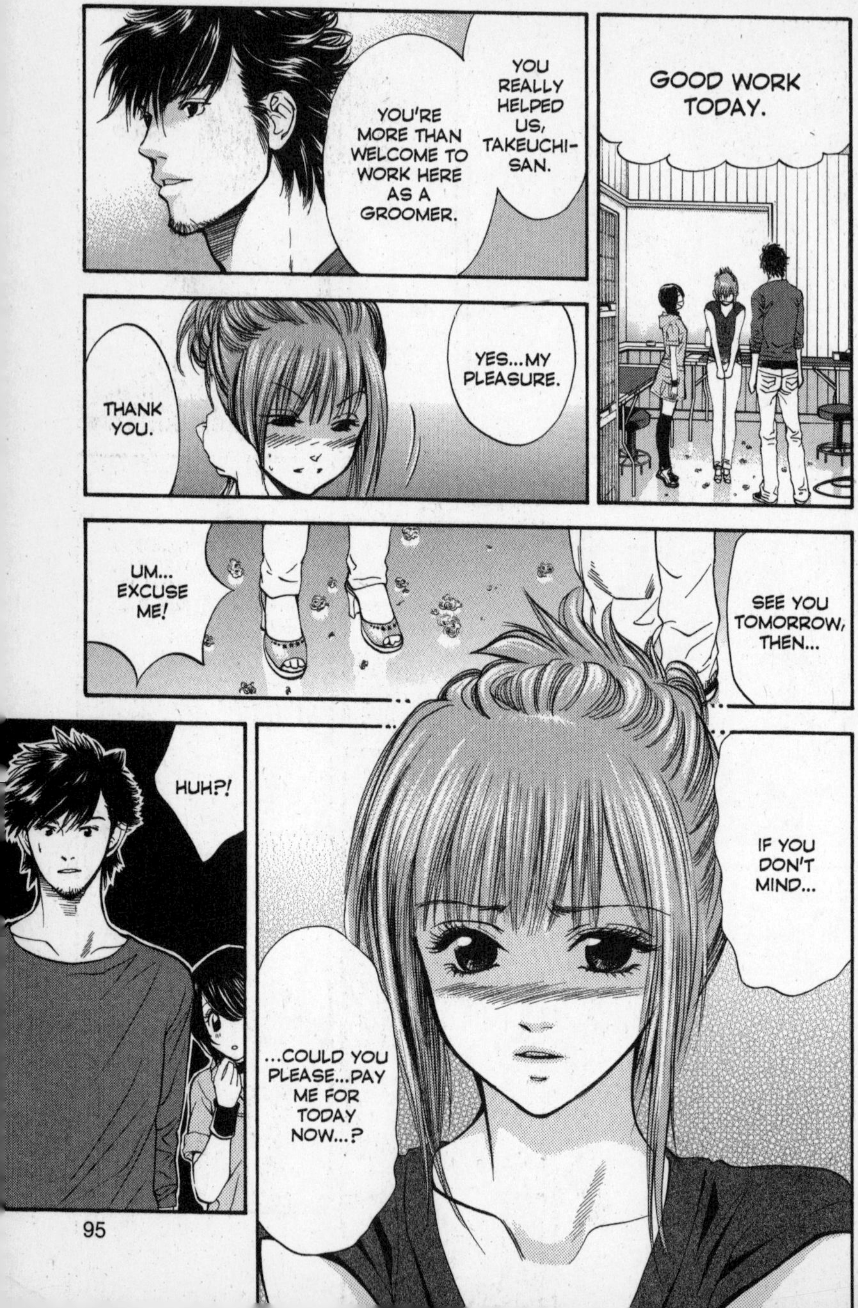
GOOD WORK TODAY.
YOU REALLY HELPED US, TAKEUCHI-SAN.
YOU'RE MORE THAN WELCOME TO WORK HERE AS A GROOMER.
YES...MY PLEASURE.
THANK YOU.
SEE YOU TOMORROW, THEN...
UM... EXCUSE ME!
IF YOU DON'T MIND...
...COULD YOU PLEASE...PAY ME FOR TODAY NOW...?
HUH?!

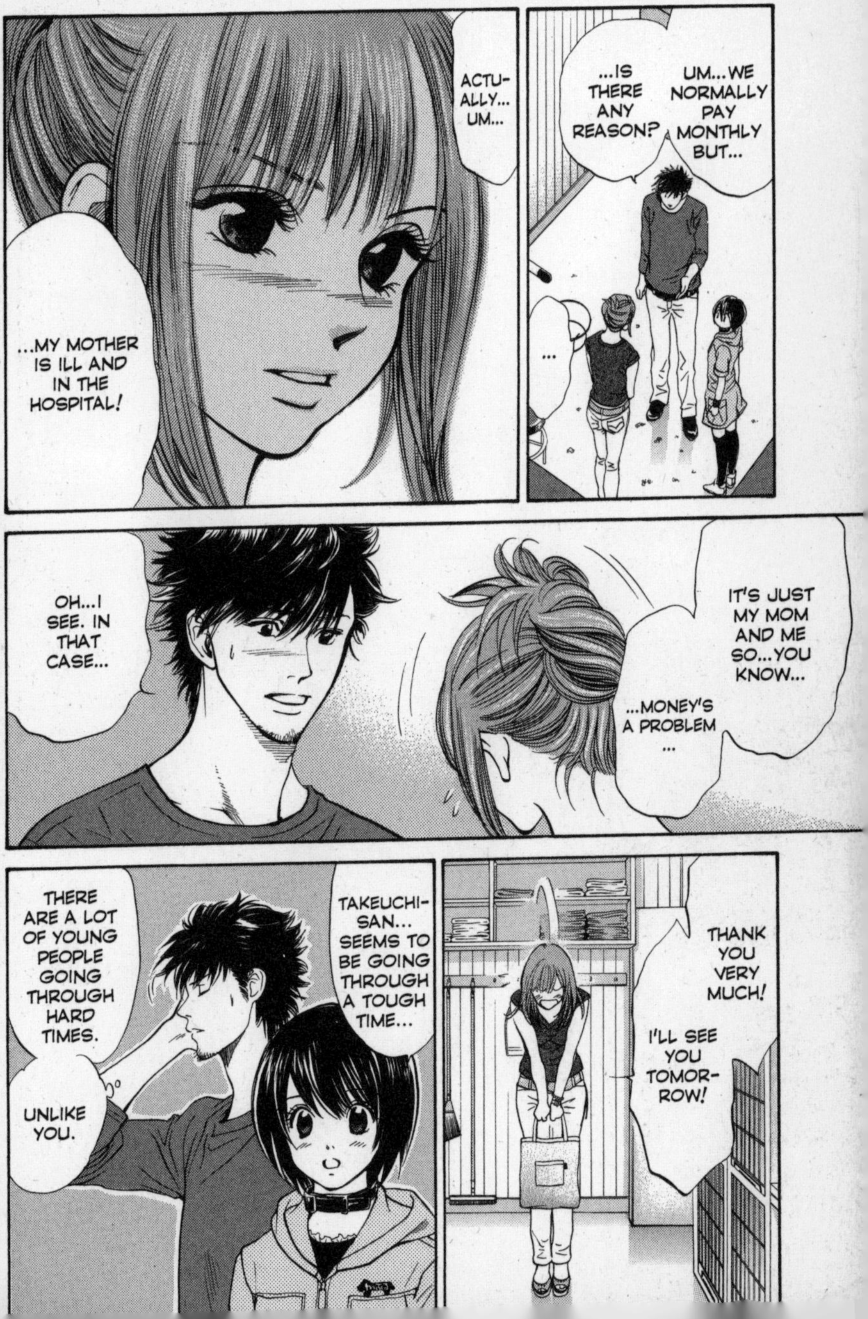
UM...WE NORMALLY PAY MONTHLY BUT...
...IS THERE ANY REASON?
...
ACTU-ALLY... UM...
...MY MOTHER IS ILL AND IN THE HOSPITAL!
IT'S JUST MY MOM AND ME SO...YOU KNOW...
...MONEY'S A PROBLEM ...
OH...I SEE. IN THAT CASE...
THANK YOU VERY MUCH!
I'LL SEE YOU TOMOR-ROW!
TAKEUCHI-SAN... SEEMS TO BE GOING THROUGH A TOUGH TIME...
THERE ARE A LOT OF YOUNG PEOPLE GOING THROUGH HARD TIMES.
UNLIKE YOU.

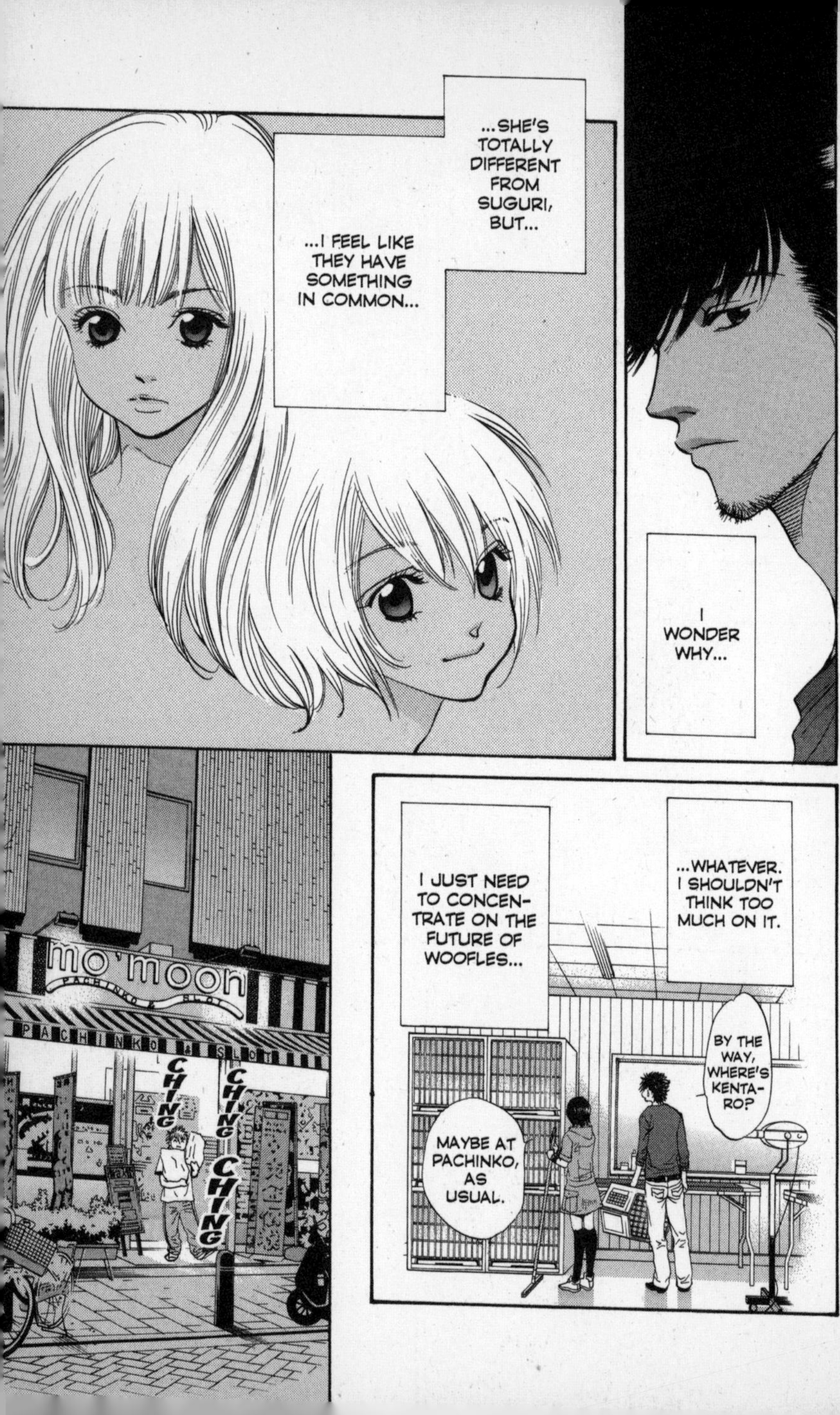
...SHE'S TOTALLY DIFFERENT FROM SUGURI, BUT...
...I FEEL LIKE THEY HAVE SOMETHING IN COMMON...
I WONDER WHY...
...WHATEVER. I SHOULDN'T THINK TOO MUCH ON IT.
I JUST NEED TO CONCEN-TRATE ON THE FUTURE OF WOOFLES...
BY THE WAY, WHERE'S KENTA-RO?
MAYBE AT PACHINKO, AS USUAL.
mo'moon
PACHINKO & SLOT
PACHINKO & SLOT
CHING
CHING
CHING

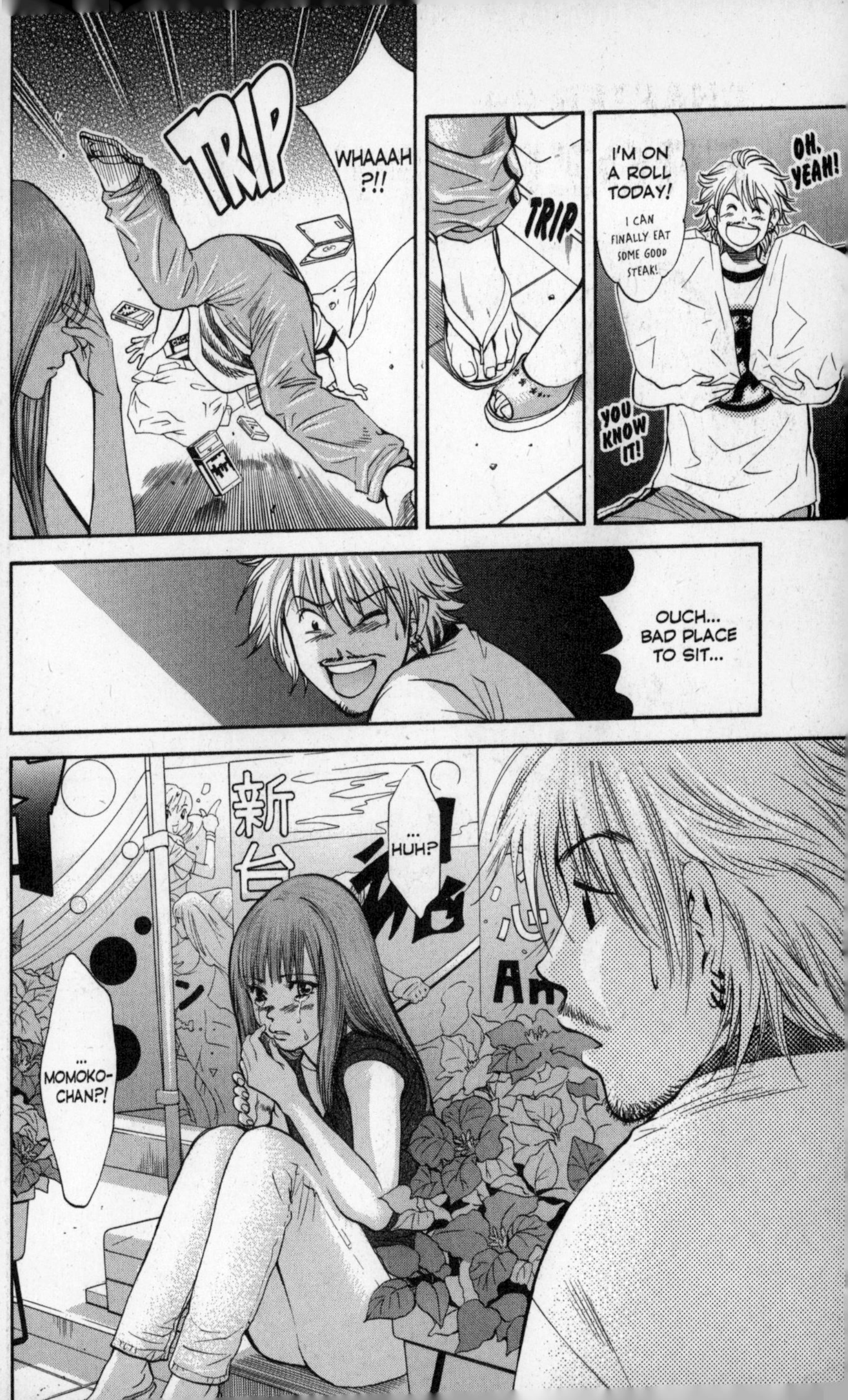
OH, YEAH!
I'M ON A ROLL TODAY!
I CAN FINALLY EAT SOME GOOD STEAK!
YOU KNOW IT!
TRIP
WHAAAH?!!
TRIP
OUCH... BAD PLACE TO SIT...
新台
...HUH?
...MOMOKO-CHAN?!

CHAPTER 69: FROZEN PEACH

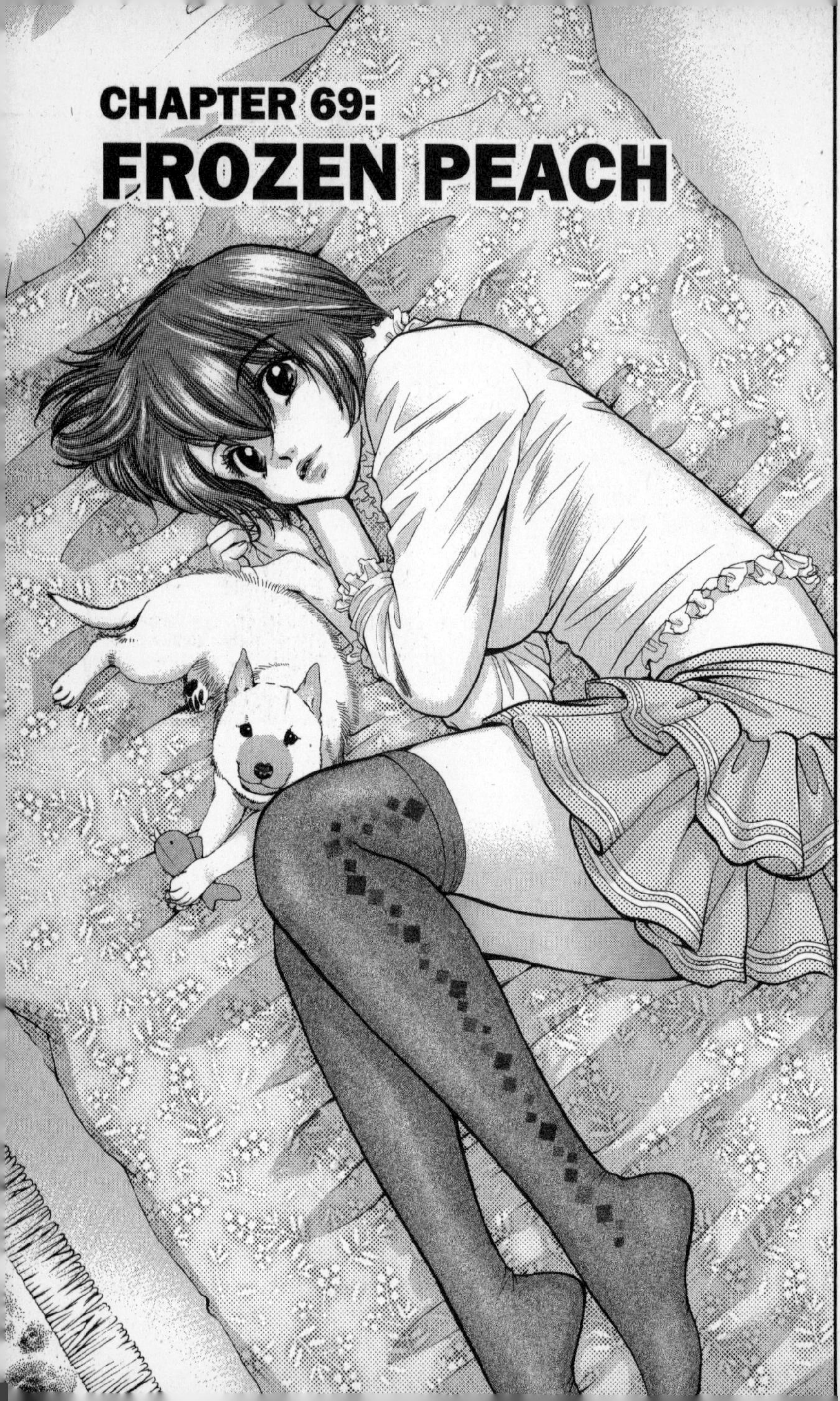

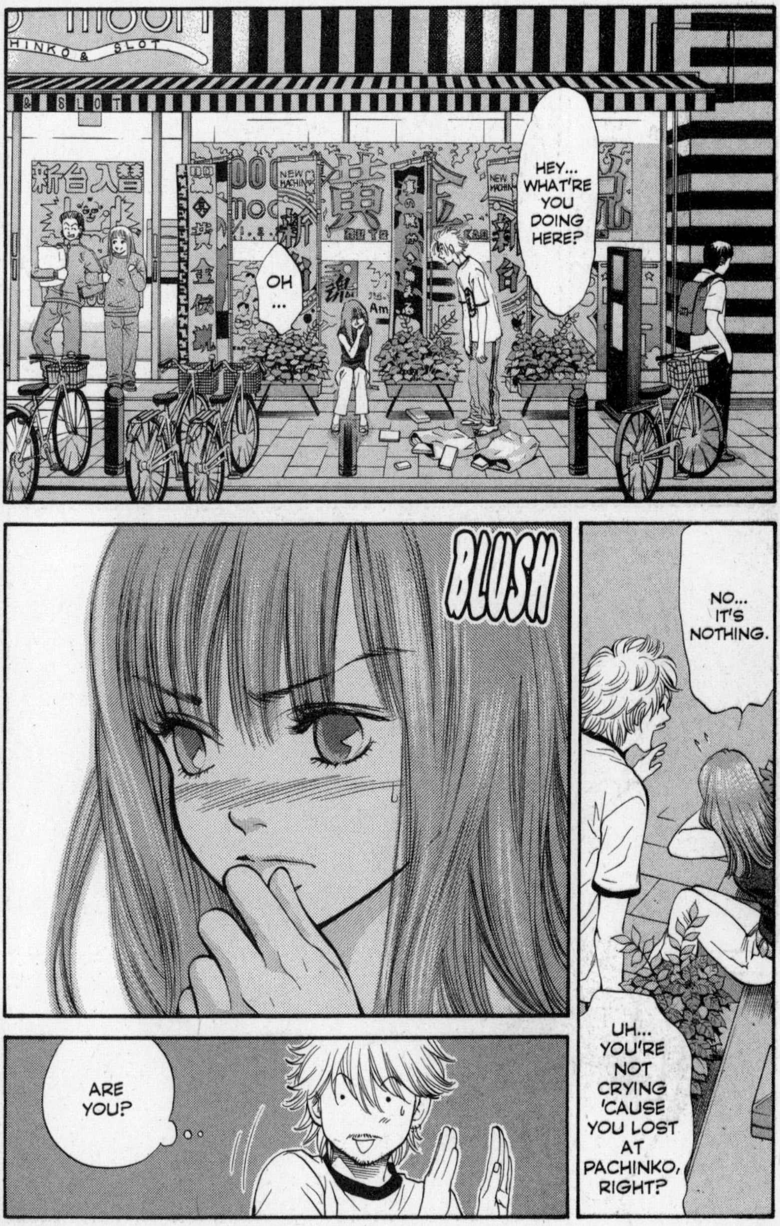
HEY... WHAT'RE YOU DOING HERE?
OH ...
NO... IT'S NOTHING.
UH... YOU'RE NOT CRYING 'CAUSE YOU LOST AT PACHINKO, RIGHT?
BLUSH
ARE YOU?

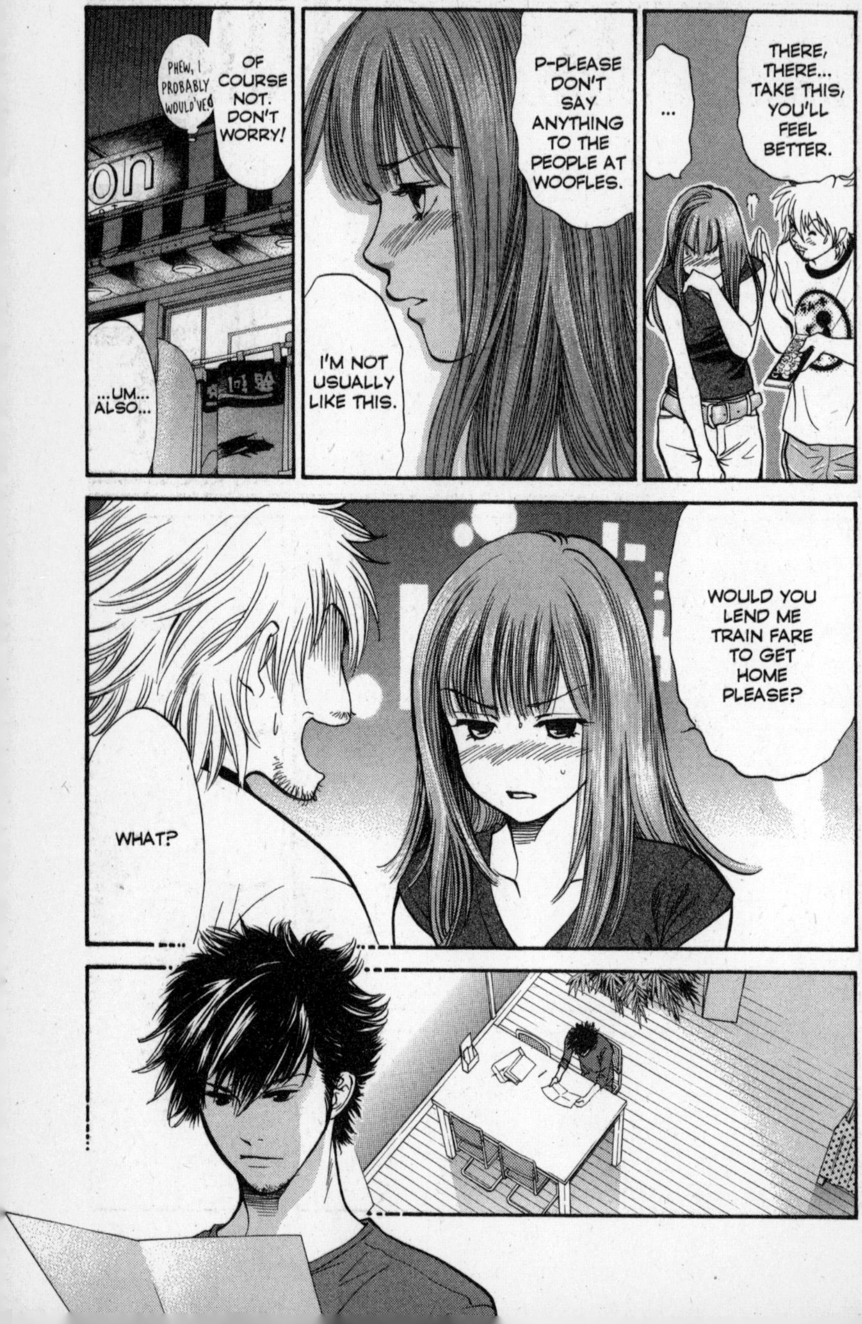
THERE, THERE... TAKE THIS, YOU'LL FEEL BETTER.
...
P-PLEASE DON'T SAY ANYTHING TO THE PEOPLE AT WOOFLES.
I'M NOT USUALLY LIKE THIS.
OF COURSE NOT. DON'T WORRY!
PHEW, I PROBABLY WOULD'VE
...UM... ALSO...
WOULD YOU LEND ME TRAIN FARE TO GET HOME PLEASE?
WHAT?

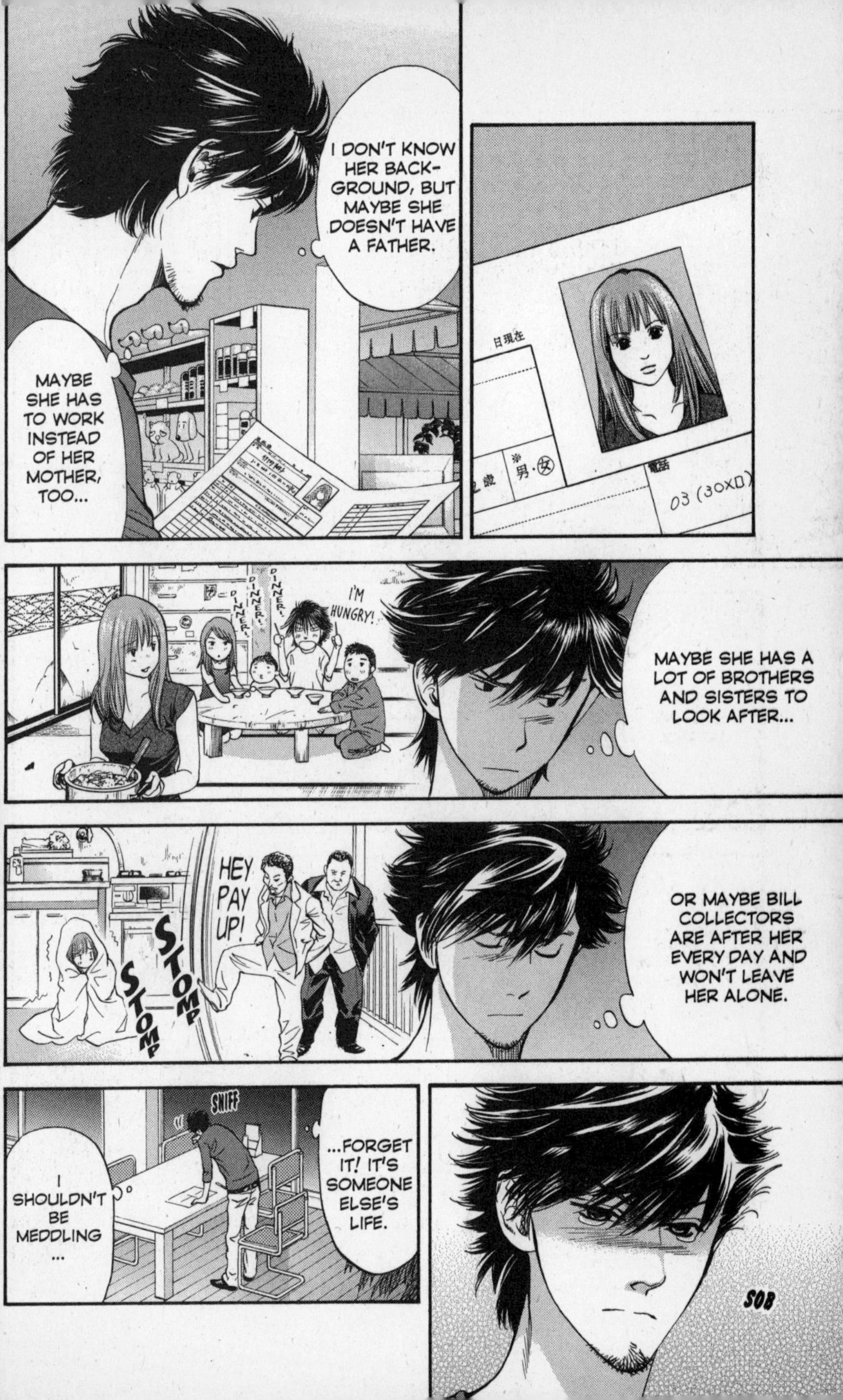

日現在
男・女
電話
I DON'T KNOW HER BACK-GROUND, BUT MAYBE SHE DOESN'T HAVE A FATHER.
MAYBE SHE HAS TO WORK INSTEAD OF HER MOTHER, TOO...
MAYBE SHE HAS A LOT OF BROTHERS AND SISTERS TO LOOK AFTER...
I'M HUNGRY!
DINNER!
DINNER!
OR MAYBE BILL COLLECTORS ARE AFTER HER EVERY DAY AND WON'T LEAVE HER ALONE.
HEY PAY UP!
STOMP
STOMP
SOB
...FORGET IT! IT'S SOMEONE ELSE'S LIFE.
SNIFF
I SHOULDN'T BE MEDDLING ...

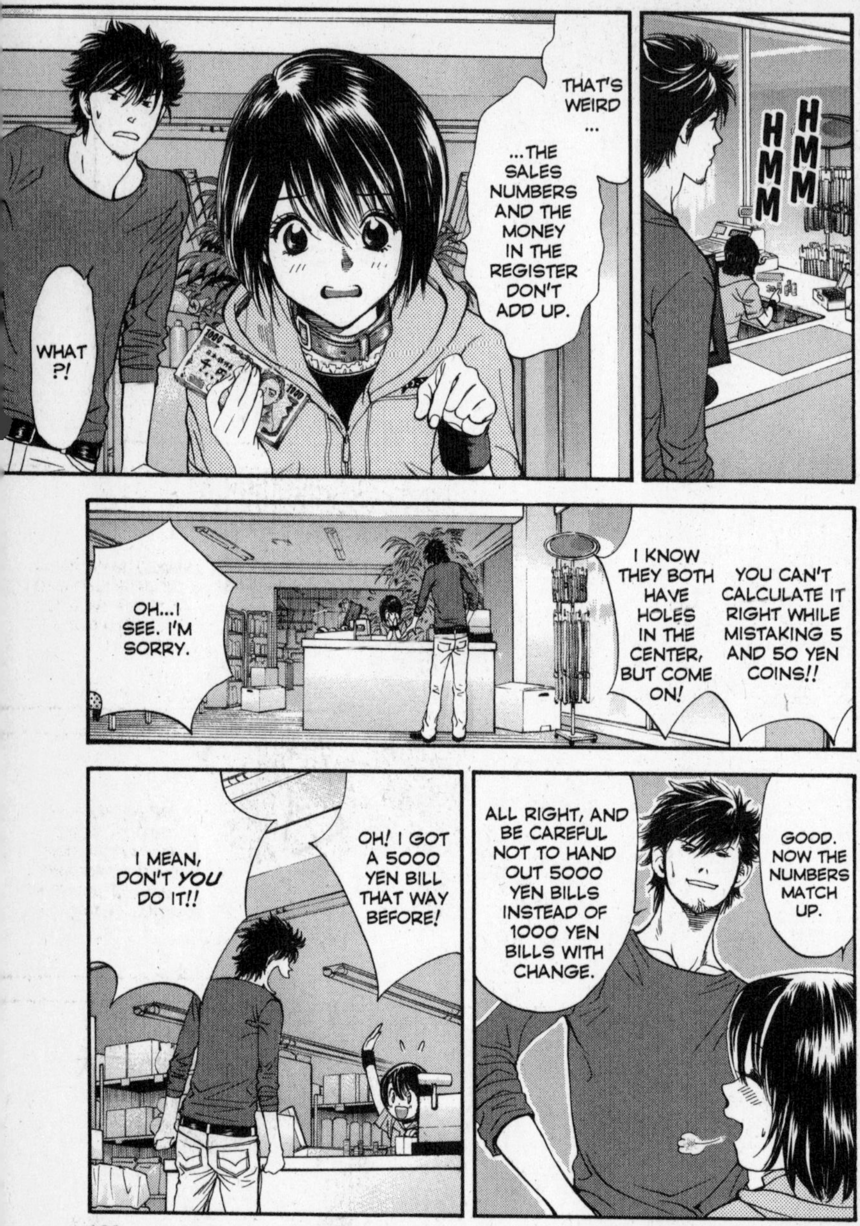
HMM HMM
THAT'S WEIRD...
...THE SALES NUMBERS AND THE MONEY IN THE REGISTER DON'T ADD UP.
WHAT ?!
I KNOW THEY BOTH HAVE HOLES IN THE CENTER, BUT COME ON! YOU CAN'T CALCULATE IT RIGHT WHILE MISTAKING 5 AND 50 YEN COINS!!
OH...I SEE. I'M SORRY.
GOOD. NOW THE NUMBERS MATCH UP.
ALL RIGHT, AND BE CAREFUL NOT TO HAND OUT 5000 YEN BILLS INSTEAD OF 1000 YEN BILLS WITH CHANGE.
OH! I GOT A 5000 YEN BILL THAT WAY BEFORE!
I MEAN, DON'T *YOU* DO IT!!

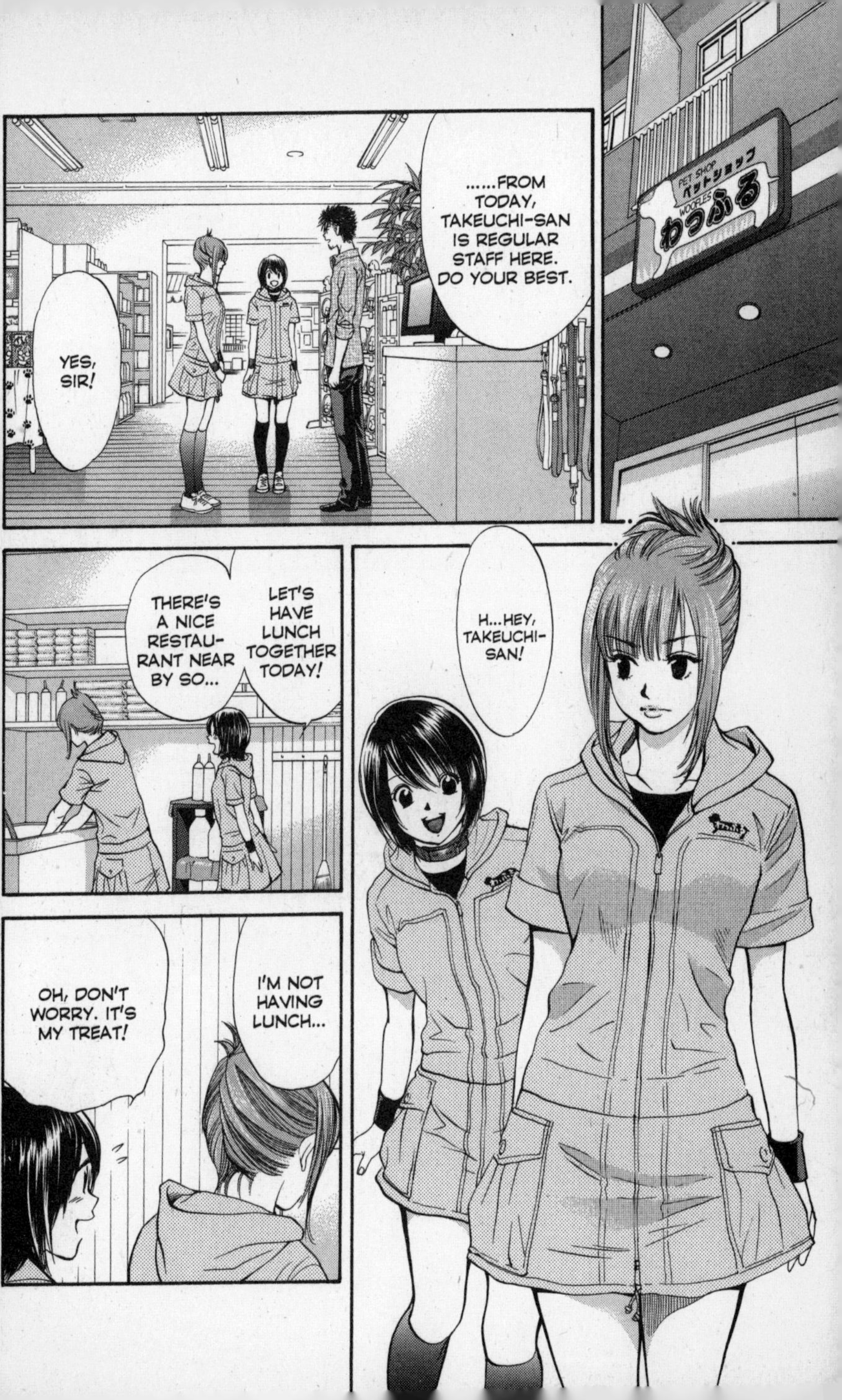
PET SHOP ペットショップ
WOOFLES わっふる
......FROM TODAY, TAKEUCHI-SAN IS REGULAR STAFF HERE. DO YOUR BEST.
YES, SIR!
H...HEY, TAKEUCHI-SAN!
LET'S HAVE LUNCH TOGETHER TODAY!
THERE'S A NICE RESTAU-RANT NEAR BY SO...
I'M NOT HAVING LUNCH...
OH, DON'T WORRY. IT'S MY TREAT!

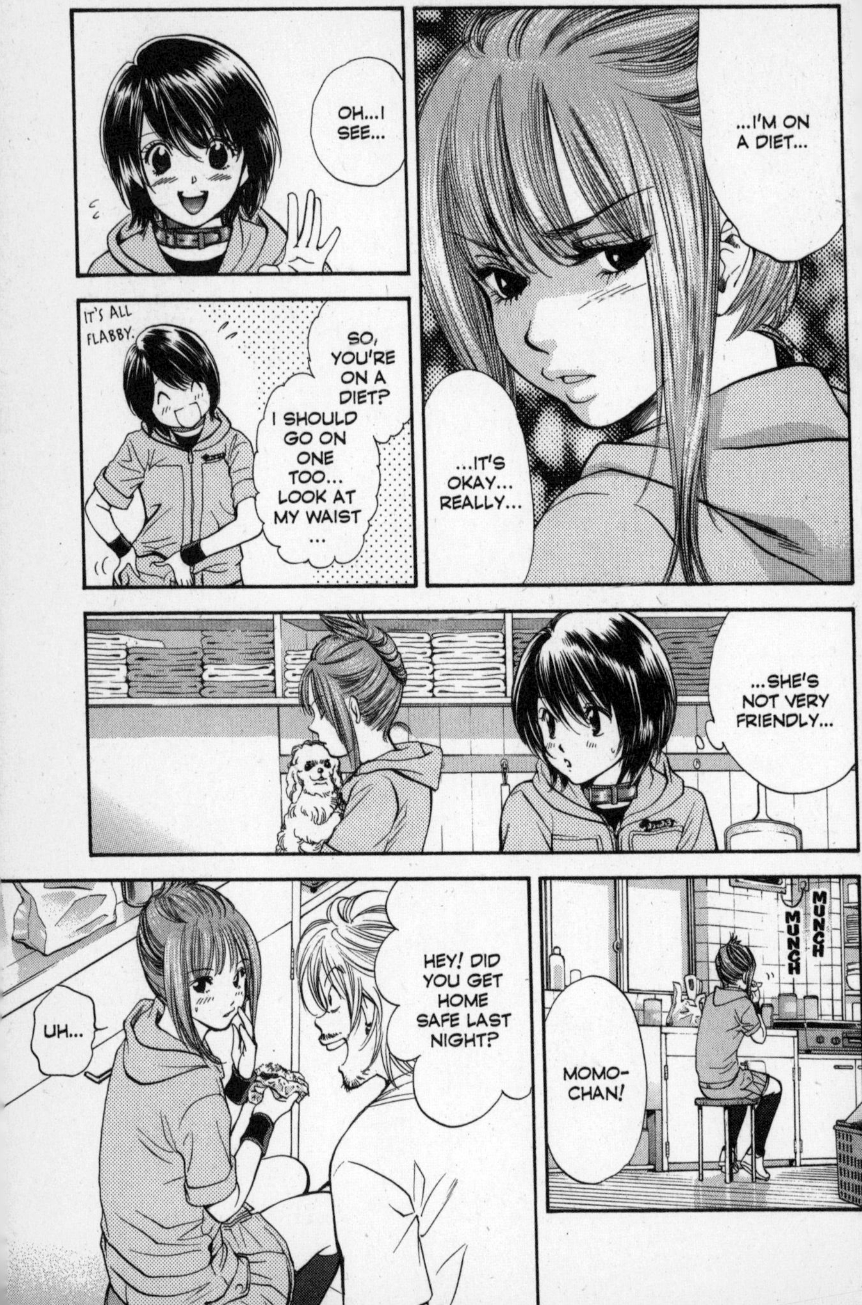
...I'M ON A DIET...
...IT'S OKAY... REALLY...
OH...I SEE...
SO, YOU'RE ON A DIET? I SHOULD GO ON ONE TOO... LOOK AT MY WAIST ...
IT'S ALL FLABBY.
...SHE'S NOT VERY FRIENDLY...
MUNCH
MUNCH
MOMO-CHAN!
HEY! DID YOU GET HOME SAFE LAST NIGHT?
UH...

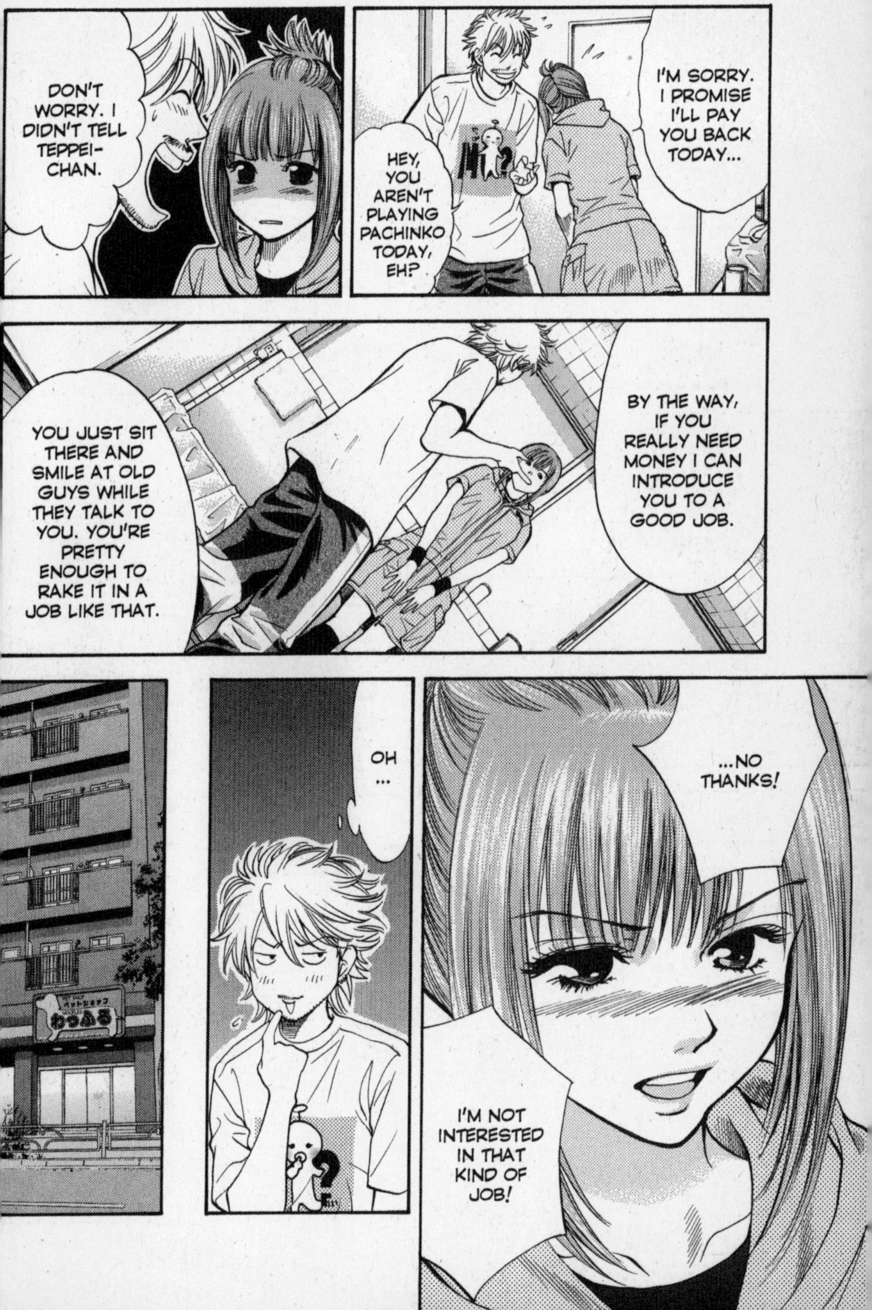
I'M SORRY. I PROMISE I'LL PAY YOU BACK TODAY...
HEY, YOU AREN'T PLAYING PACHINKO TODAY, EH?
DON'T WORRY. I DIDN'T TELL TEPPEI-CHAN.
BY THE WAY, IF YOU REALLY NEED MONEY I CAN INTRODUCE YOU TO A GOOD JOB.
YOU JUST SIT THERE AND SMILE AT OLD GUYS WHILE THEY TALK TO YOU. YOU'RE PRETTY ENOUGH TO RAKE IT IN A JOB LIKE THAT.
...NO THANKS!
I'M NOT INTERESTED IN THAT KIND OF JOB!
OH ...

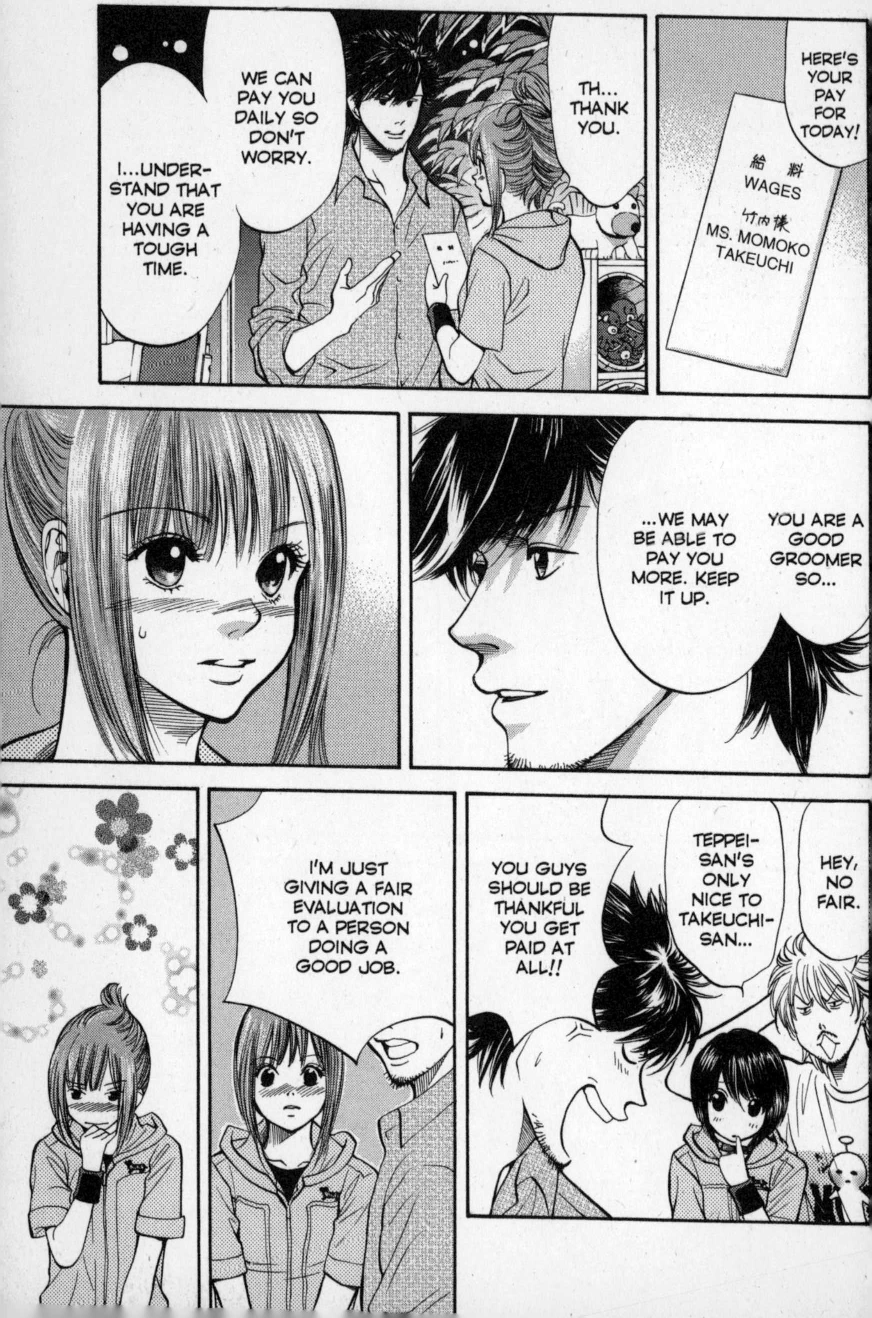
HERE'S YOUR PAY FOR TODAY!
給料
WAGES
竹内様
MS. MOMOKO TAKEUCHI
TH... THANK YOU.
WE CAN PAY YOU DAILY SO DON'T WORRY.
I...UNDER-STAND THAT YOU ARE HAVING A TOUGH TIME.
YOU ARE A GOOD GROOMER SO...
...WE MAY BE ABLE TO PAY YOU MORE. KEEP IT UP.
HEY, NO FAIR.
TEPPEI-SAN'S ONLY NICE TO TAKEUCHI-SAN...
YOU GUYS SHOULD BE THANKFUL YOU GET PAID AT ALL!!
I'M JUST GIVING A FAIR EVALUATION TO A PERSON DOING A GOOD JOB.

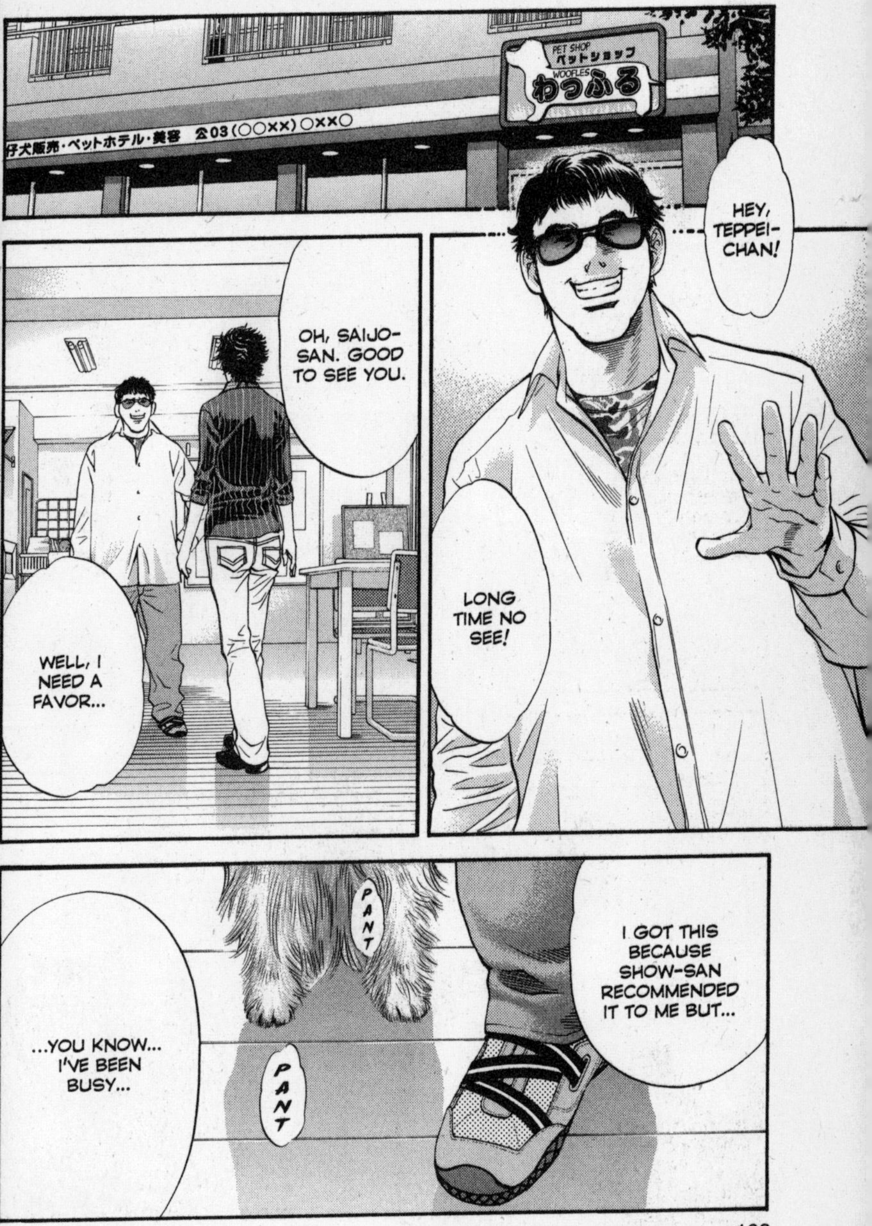
PET SHOP
ペットショップ
WOOFLES
わっふる
仔犬販売・ペットホテル・美容 ☎03(○○××)○××○
HEY, TEPPEI-CHAN!
LONG TIME NO SEE!
OH, SAIJO-SAN. GOOD TO SEE YOU.
WELL, I NEED A FAVOR...
I GOT THIS BECAUSE SHOW-SAN RECOMMENDED IT TO ME BUT...
PANT
PANT
...YOU KNOW... I'VE BEEN BUSY...

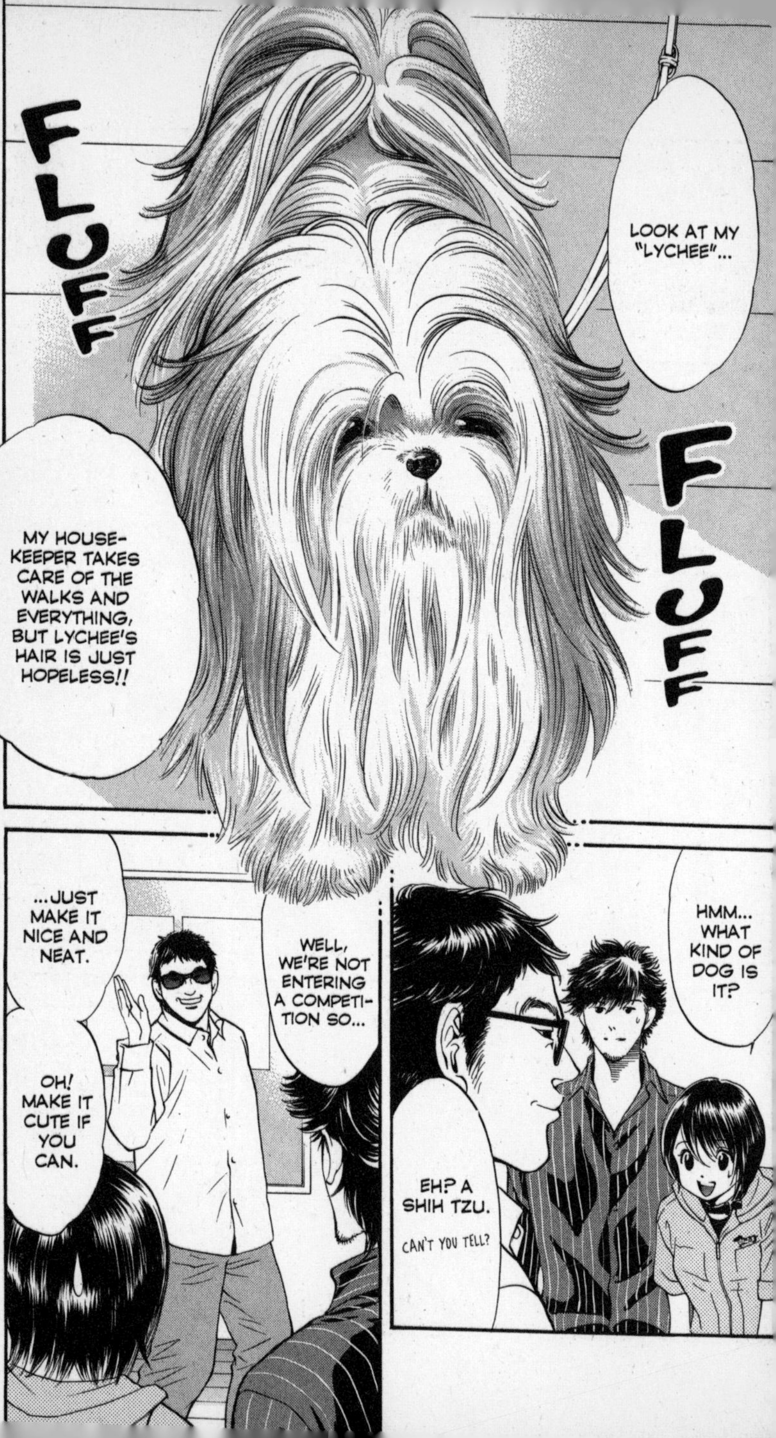
LOOK AT MY "LYCHEE"...
FLUFF
FLUFF
MY HOUSE-KEEPER TAKES CARE OF THE WALKS AND EVERYTHING, BUT LYCHEE'S HAIR IS JUST HOPELESS!!
HMM... WHAT KIND OF DOG IS IT?
EH? A SHIH TZU.
CAN'T YOU TELL?
WELL, WE'RE NOT ENTERING A COMPETITION SO...
...JUST MAKE IT NICE AND NEAT.
OH! MAKE IT CUTE IF YOU CAN.

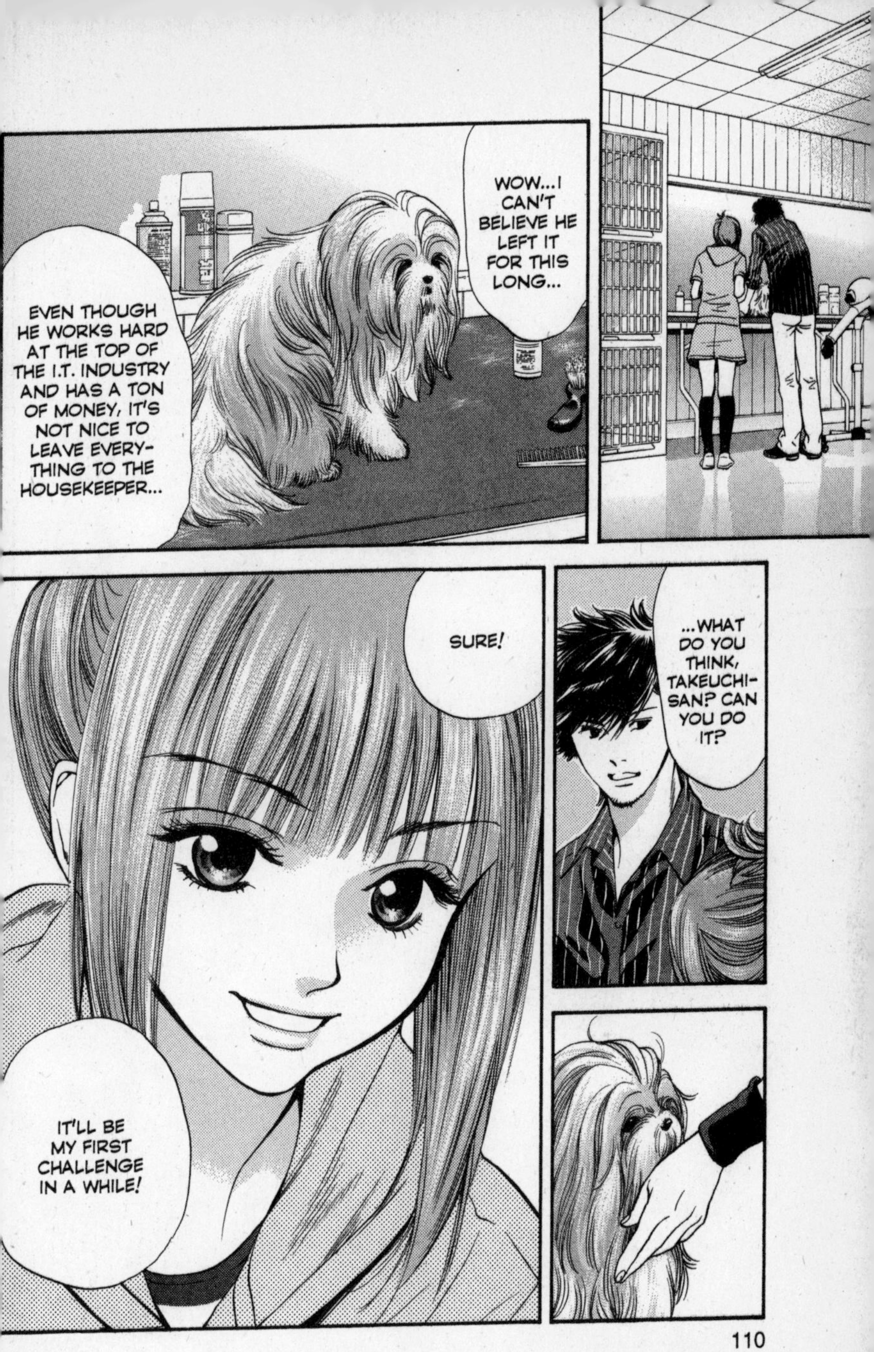
WOW...I CAN'T BELIEVE HE LEFT IT FOR THIS LONG...
EVEN THOUGH HE WORKS HARD AT THE TOP OF THE I.T. INDUSTRY AND HAS A TON OF MONEY, IT'S NOT NICE TO LEAVE EVERY-THING TO THE HOUSEKEEPER...
...WHAT DO YOU THINK, TAKEUCHI-SAN? CAN YOU DO IT?
SURE!
IT'LL BE MY FIRST CHALLENGE IN A WHILE!

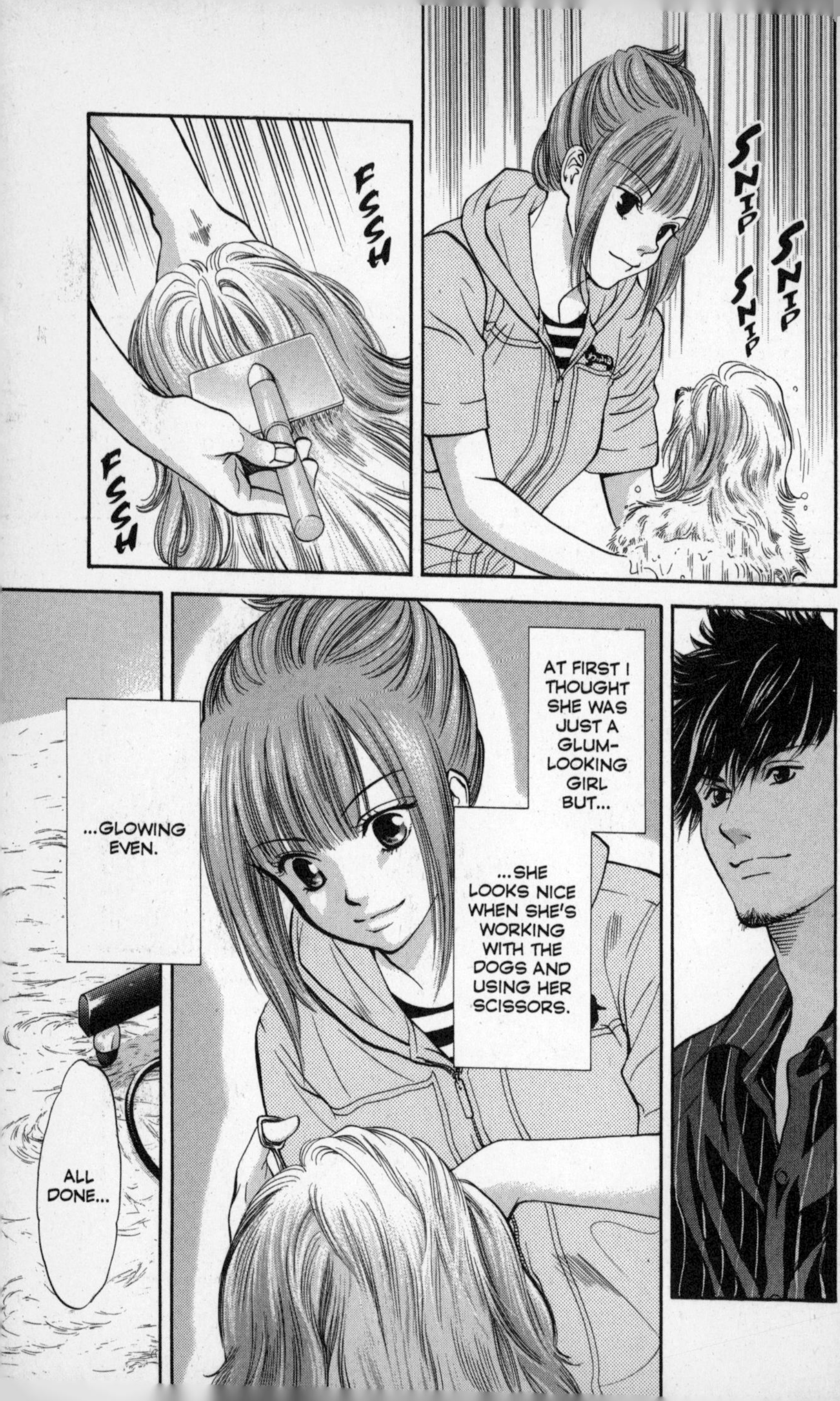
SNIP
SNIP SNIP
FSSH
FSSH
AT FIRST I THOUGHT SHE WAS JUST A GLUM-LOOKING GIRL BUT...
...SHE LOOKS NICE WHEN SHE'S WORKING WITH THE DOGS AND USING HER SCISSORS.
...GLOWING EVEN.
ALL DONE...

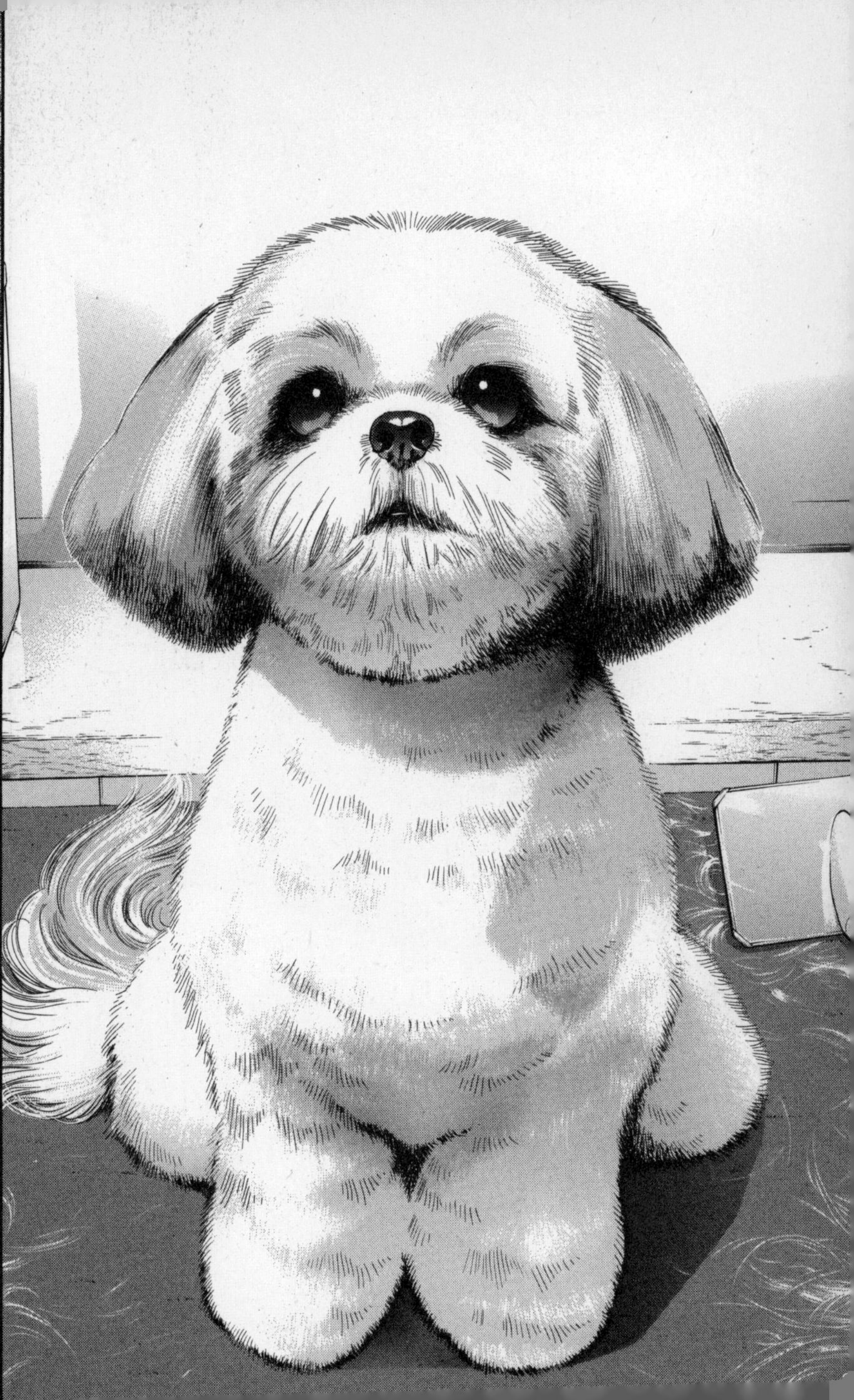

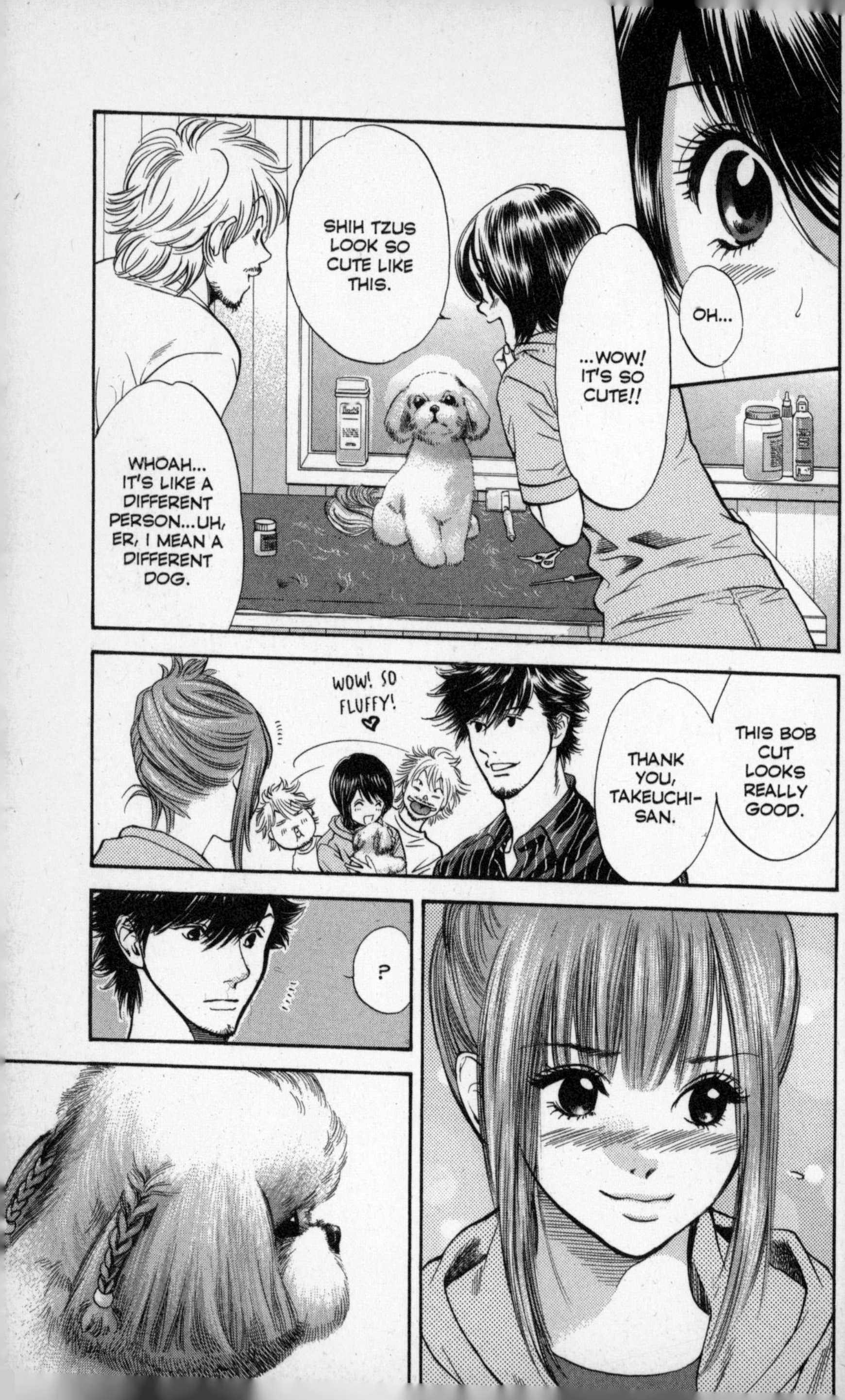
OH...
...WOW! IT'S SO CUTE!!
SHIH TZUS LOOK SO CUTE LIKE THIS.
WHOAH... IT'S LIKE A DIFFERENT PERSON...UH, ER, I MEAN A DIFFERENT DOG.
THIS BOB CUT LOOKS REALLY GOOD.
THANK YOU, TAKEUCHI-SAN.
WOW! SO FLUFFY!
?

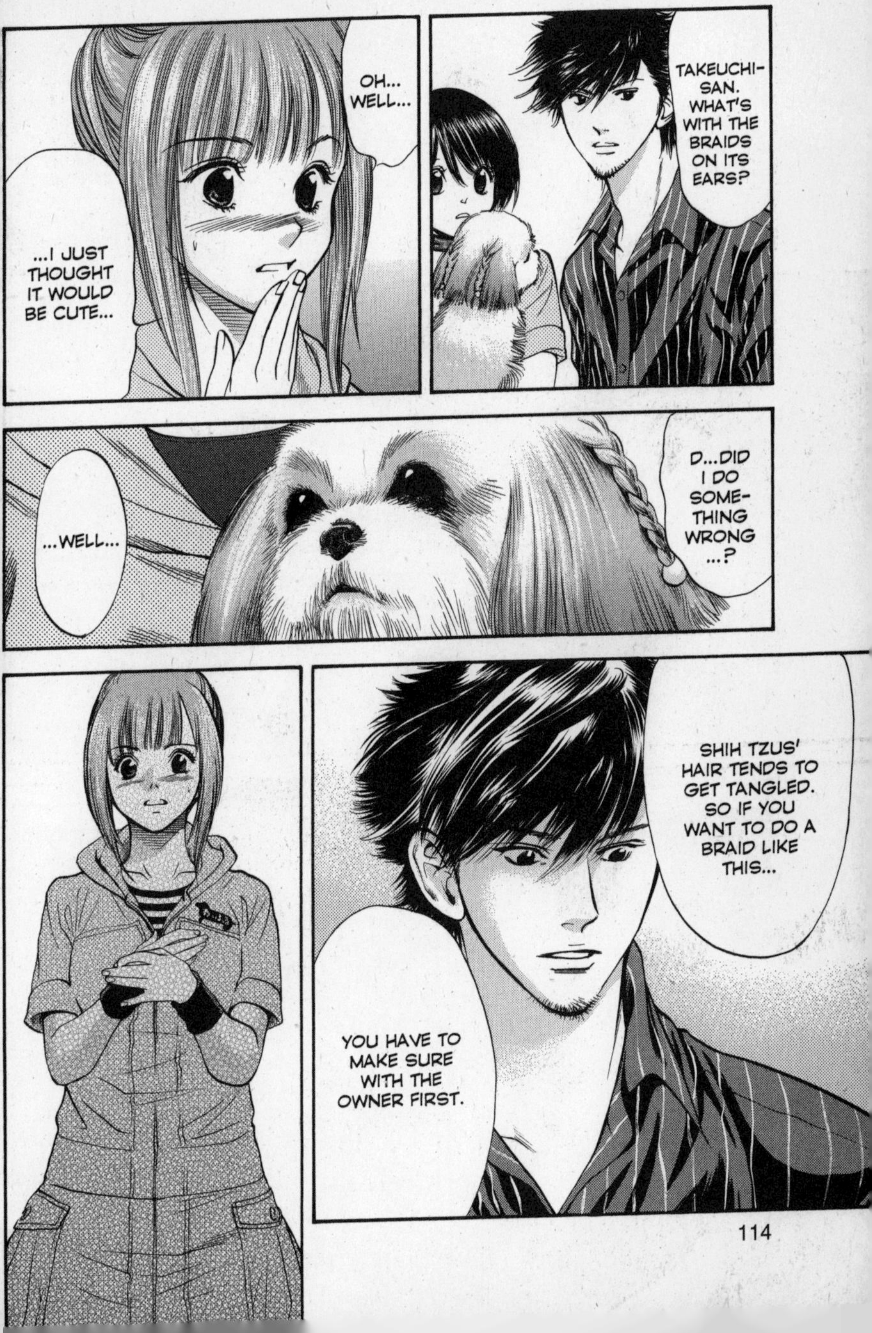
TAKEUCHI-SAN. WHAT'S WITH THE BRAIDS ON ITS EARS?
OH... WELL...
...I JUST THOUGHT IT WOULD BE CUTE...
D...DID I DO SOME-THING WRONG ...?
...WELL...
SHIH TZUS' HAIR TENDS TO GET TANGLED. SO IF YOU WANT TO DO A BRAID LIKE THIS...
YOU HAVE TO MAKE SURE WITH THE OWNER FIRST.

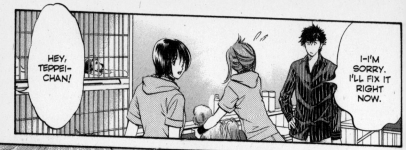

HEY, TEPPEI-CHAN!

I-I'M SORRY. I'LL FIX IT RIGHT NOW.

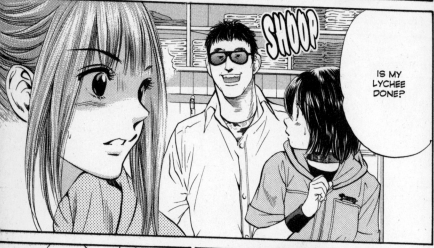

IS MY LYCHEE DONE?

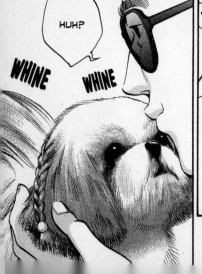

HUH?

WHINE WHINE

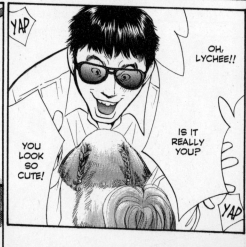

OH, LYCHEE!!

YOU LOOK SO CUTE!

IS IT REALLY YOU?

YAP

YAP

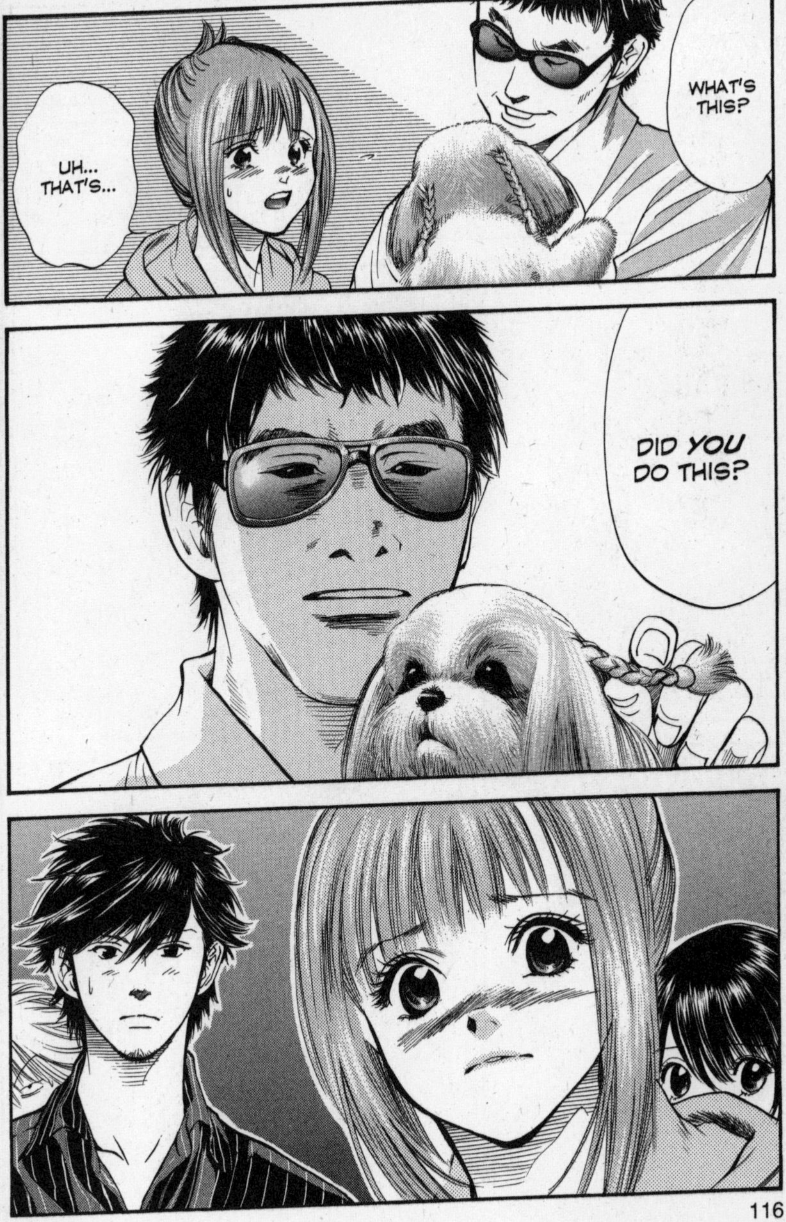
WHAT'S THIS?
UH... THAT'S...
DID YOU DO THIS?

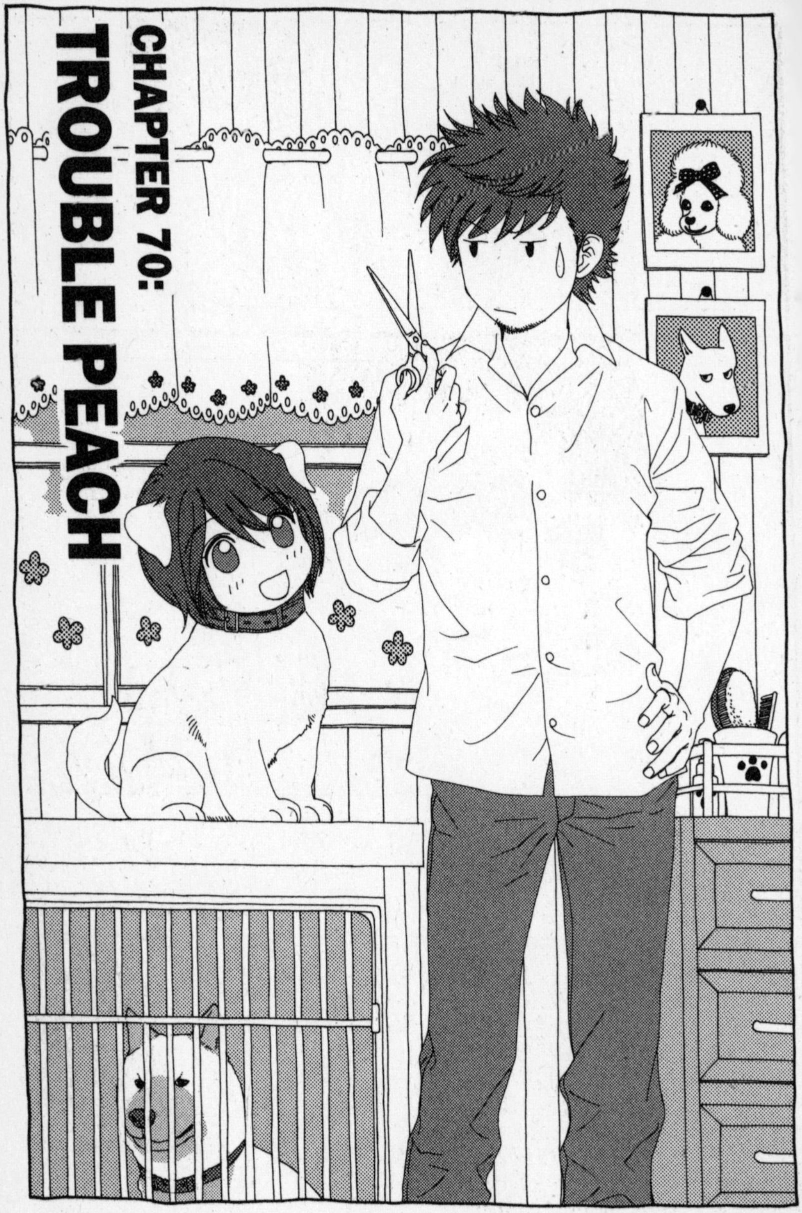
CHAPTER 70:
TROUBLE PEACH

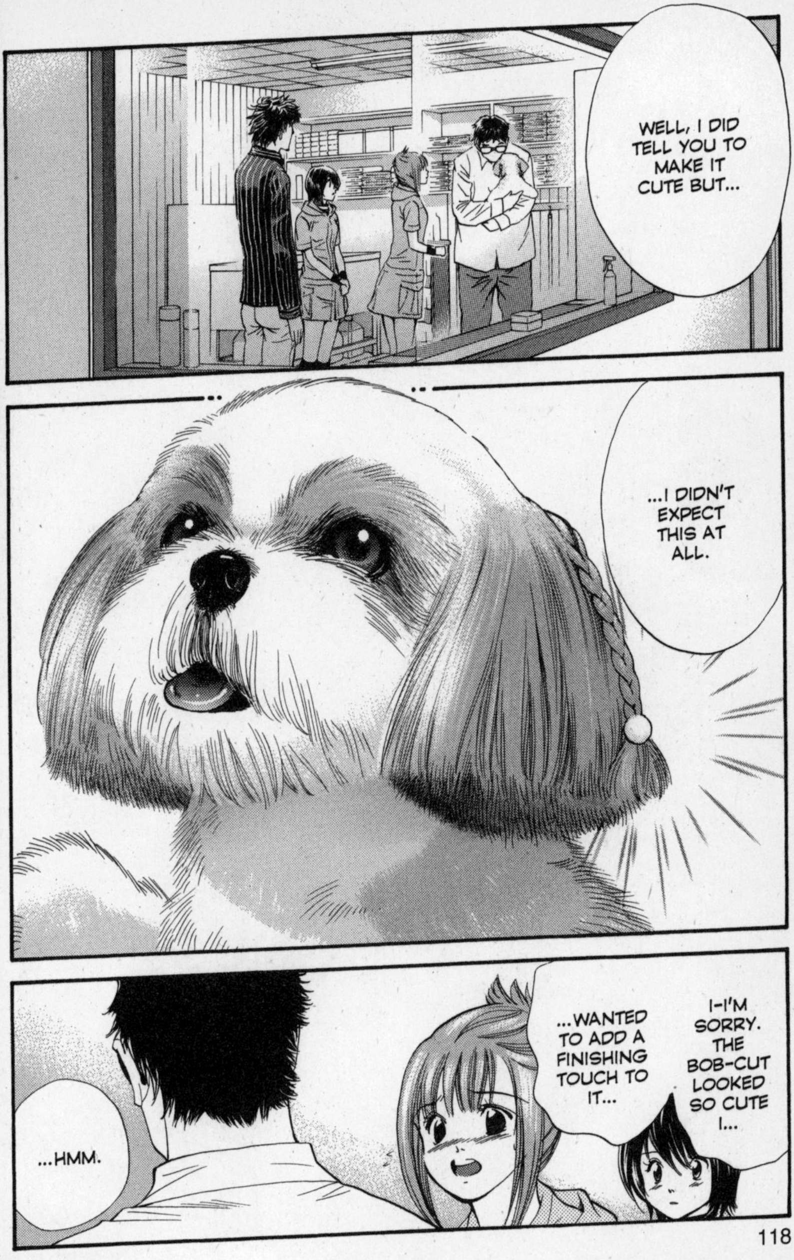
WELL, I DID TELL YOU TO MAKE IT CUTE BUT...
...I DIDN'T EXPECT THIS AT ALL.
I-I'M SORRY. THE BOB-CUT LOOKED SO CUTE I...
...WANTED TO ADD A FINISHING TOUCH TO IT...
...HMM.

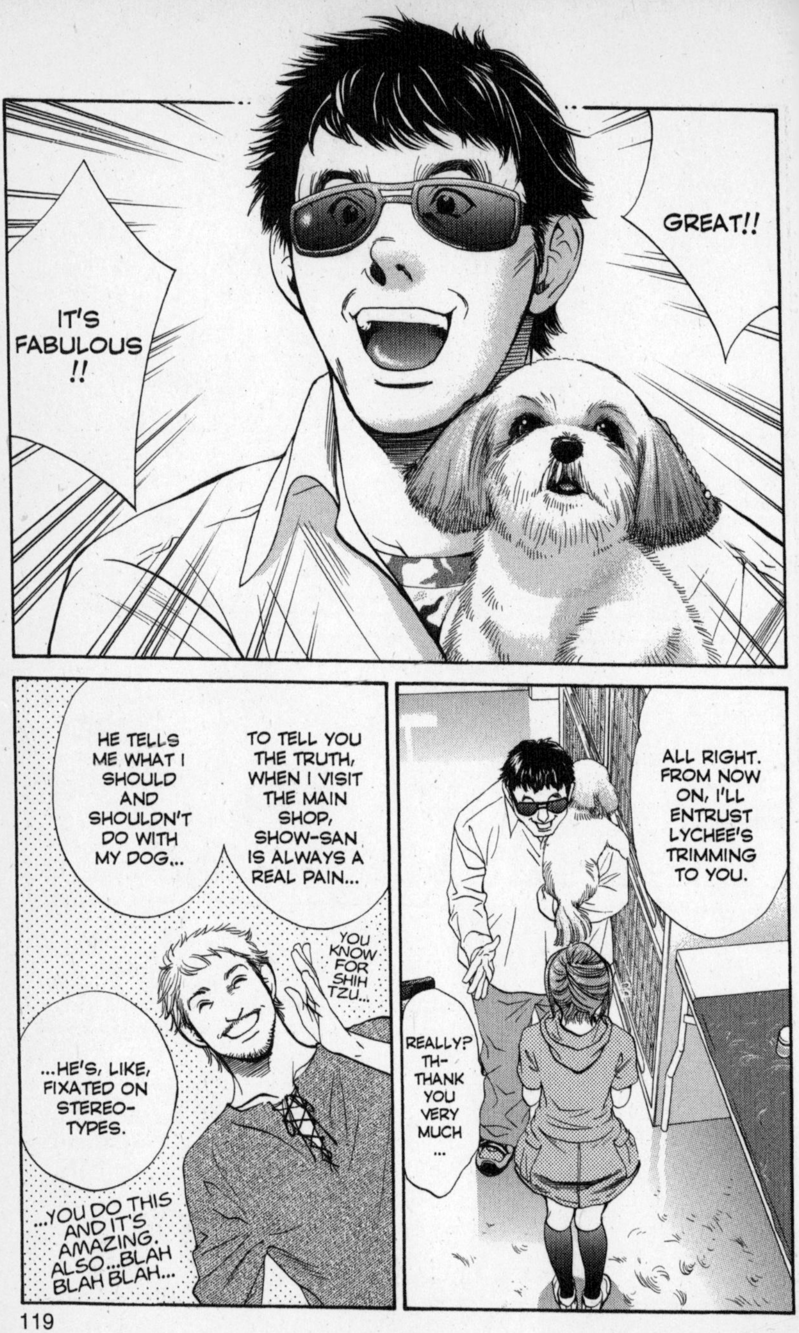
GREAT!!
IT'S FABULOUS!!
ALL RIGHT. FROM NOW ON, I'LL ENTRUST LYCHEE'S TRIMMING TO YOU.
REALLY? TH-THANK YOU VERY MUCH...
TO TELL YOU THE TRUTH, WHEN I VISIT THE MAIN SHOP, SHOW-SAN IS ALWAYS A REAL PAIN...
HE TELLS ME WHAT I SHOULD AND SHOULDN'T DO WITH MY DOG...
YOU KNOW FOR SHIH TZU...
...HE'S, LIKE, FIXATED ON STEREO-TYPES.
...YOU DO THIS AND IT'S AMAZING. ALSO...BLAH BLAH BLAH...

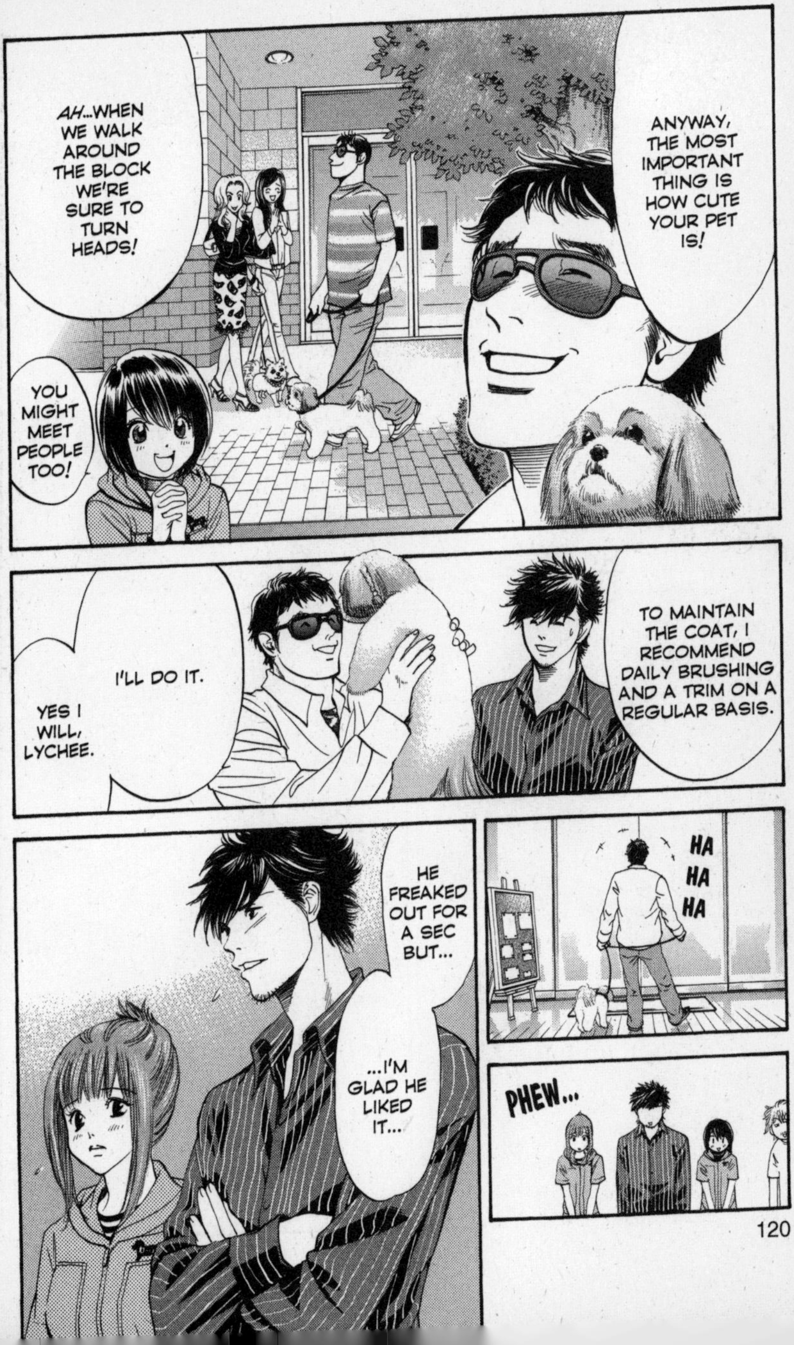
ANYWAY, THE MOST IMPORTANT THING IS HOW CUTE YOUR PET IS!
AH...WHEN WE WALK AROUND THE BLOCK WE'RE SURE TO TURN HEADS!
YOU MIGHT MEET PEOPLE TOO!
TO MAINTAIN THE COAT, I RECOMMEND DAILY BRUSHING AND A TRIM ON A REGULAR BASIS.
I'LL DO IT.
YES I WILL, LYCHEE.
HA HA HA
PHEW...
HE FREAKED OUT FOR A SEC BUT...
...I'M GLAD HE LIKED IT...

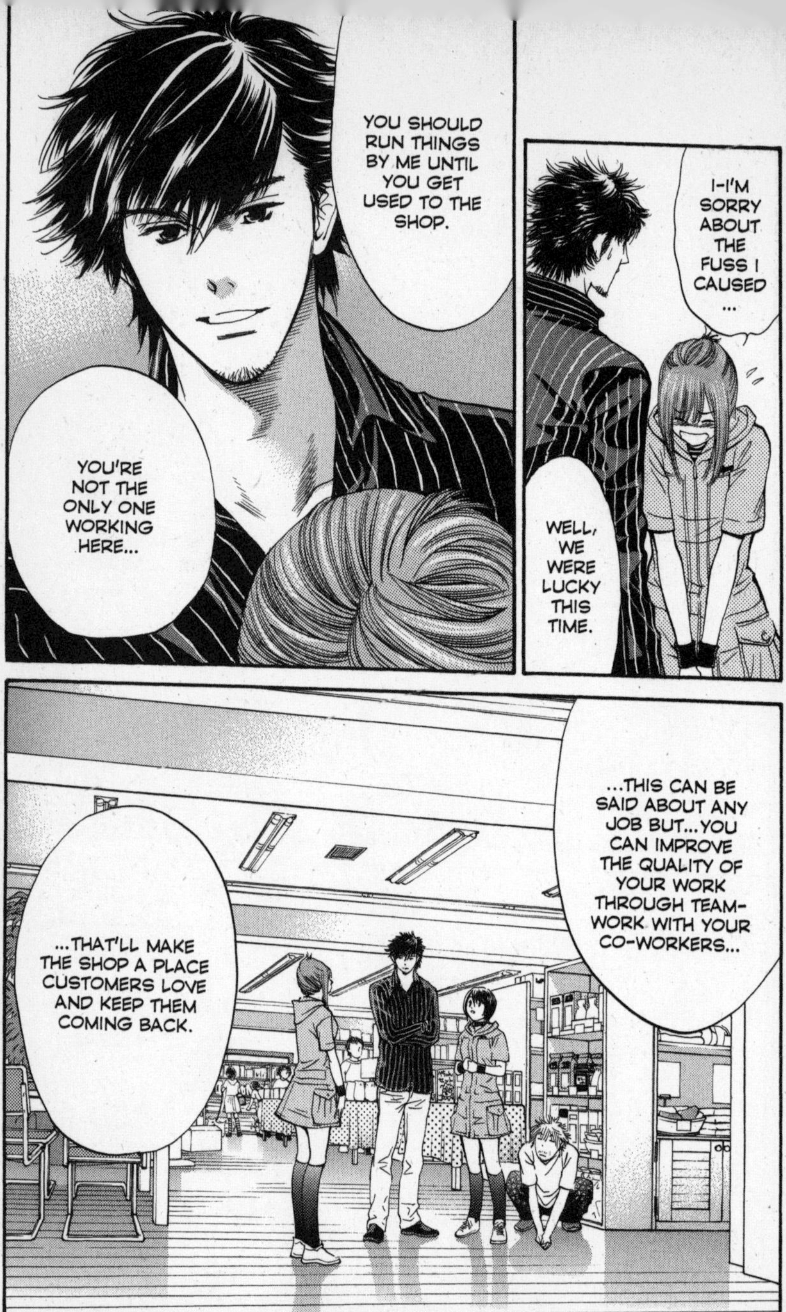
I-I'M SORRY ABOUT THE FUSS I CAUSED...
WELL, WE WERE LUCKY THIS TIME.
YOU SHOULD RUN THINGS BY ME UNTIL YOU GET USED TO THE SHOP.
YOU'RE NOT THE ONLY ONE WORKING HERE...
...THIS CAN BE SAID ABOUT ANY JOB BUT...YOU CAN IMPROVE THE QUALITY OF YOUR WORK THROUGH TEAM-WORK WITH YOUR CO-WORKERS...
...THAT'LL MAKE THE SHOP A PLACE CUSTOMERS LOVE AND KEEP THEM COMING BACK.

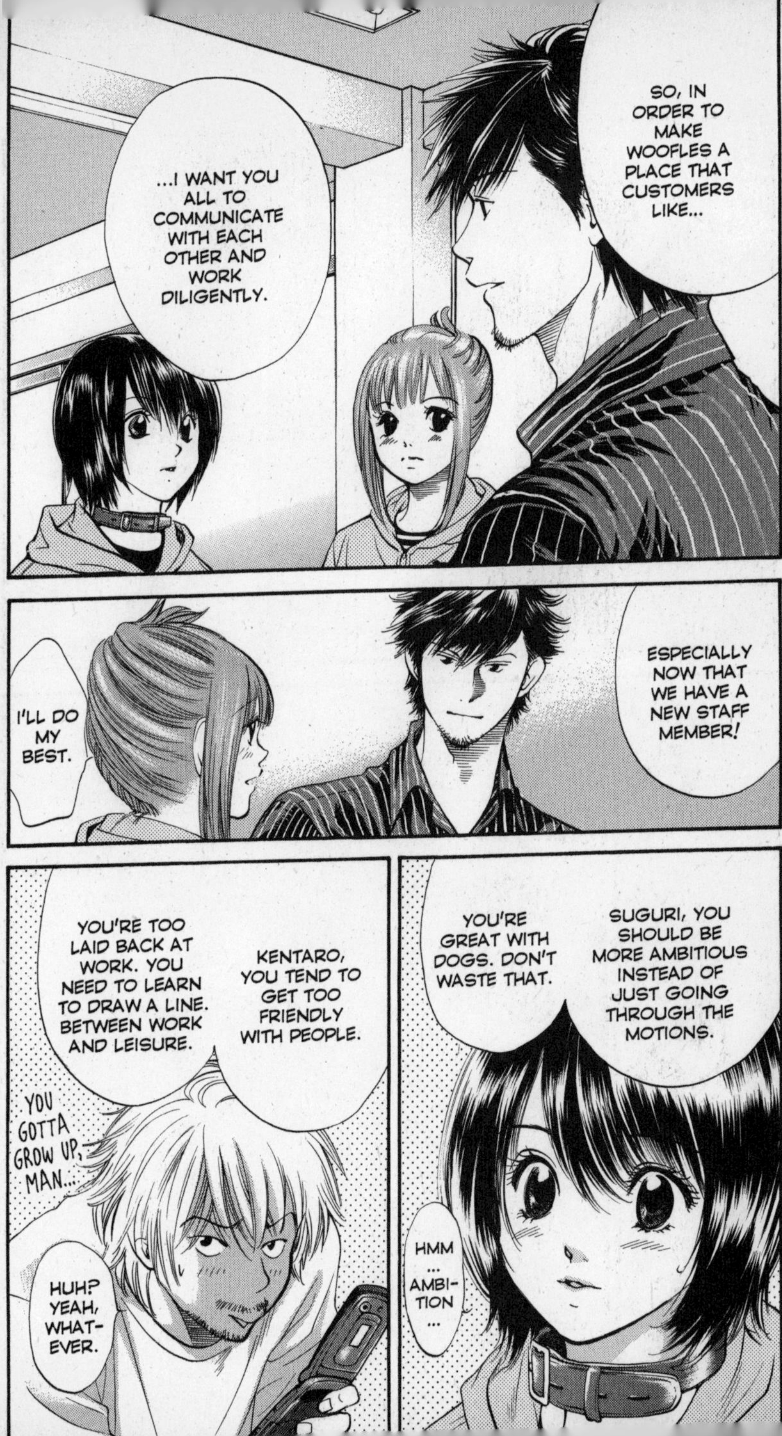
SO, IN ORDER TO MAKE WOOFLES A PLACE THAT CUSTOMERS LIKE...
...I WANT YOU ALL TO COMMUNICATE WITH EACH OTHER AND WORK DILIGENTLY.
ESPECIALLY NOW THAT WE HAVE A NEW STAFF MEMBER!
I'LL DO MY BEST.
SUGURI, YOU SHOULD BE MORE AMBITIOUS INSTEAD OF JUST GOING THROUGH THE MOTIONS.
YOU'RE GREAT WITH DOGS. DON'T WASTE THAT.
HMM ... AMBITION ...
KENTARO, YOU TEND TO GET TOO FRIENDLY WITH PEOPLE.
YOU'RE TOO LAID BACK AT WORK. YOU NEED TO LEARN TO DRAW A LINE. BETWEEN WORK AND LEISURE.
YOU GOTTA GROW UP, MAN...
HUH? YEAH, WHATEVER.

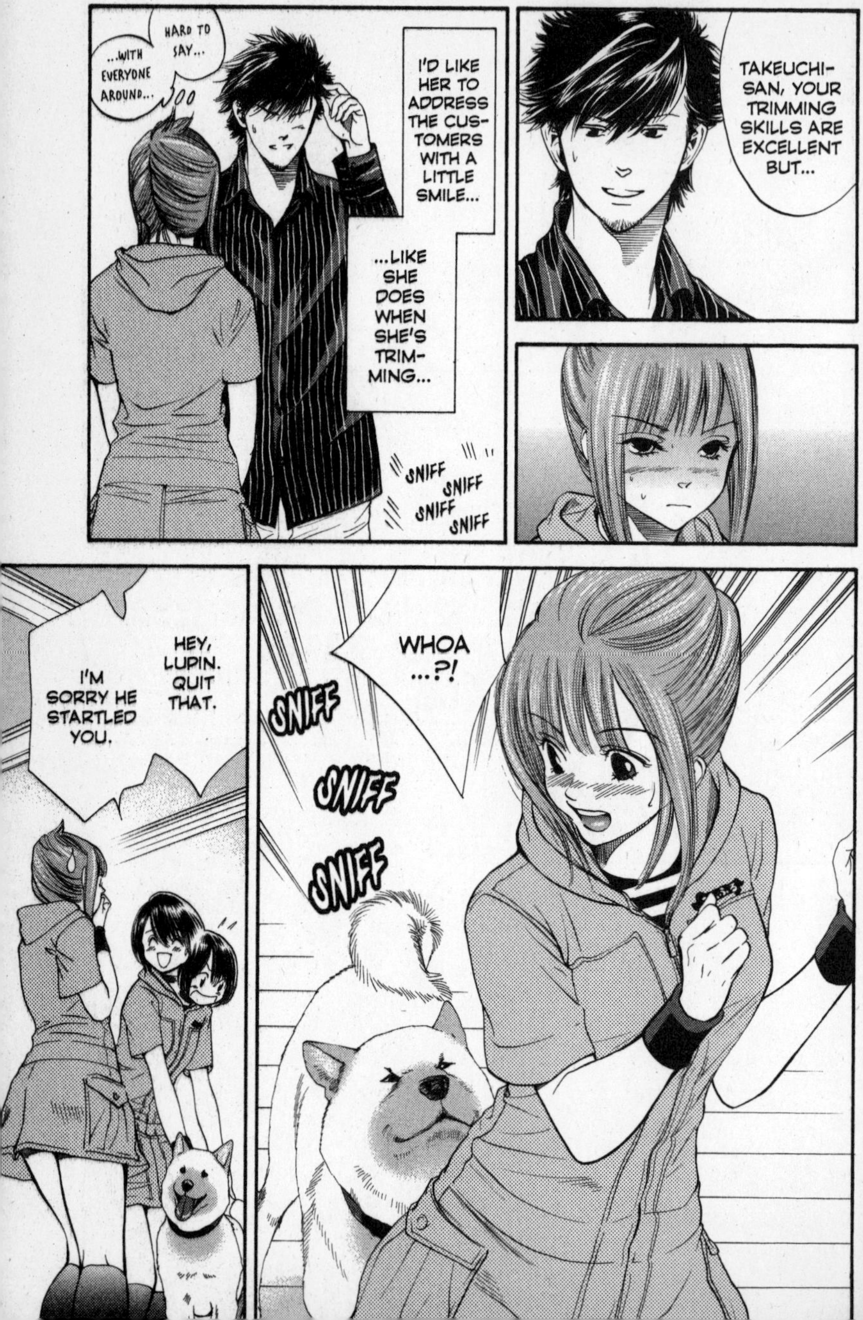
TAKEUCHI-SAN, YOUR TRIMMING SKILLS ARE EXCELLENT BUT...
I'D LIKE HER TO ADDRESS THE CUSTOMERS WITH A LITTLE SMILE...
...LIKE SHE DOES WHEN SHE'S TRIMMING...
HARD TO SAY...
...WITH EVERYONE AROUND...
SNIFF SNIFF SNIFF SNIFF
WHOA ...?!
SNIFF
SNIFF
SNIFF
HEY, LUPIN. QUIT THAT.
I'M SORRY HE STARTLED YOU.

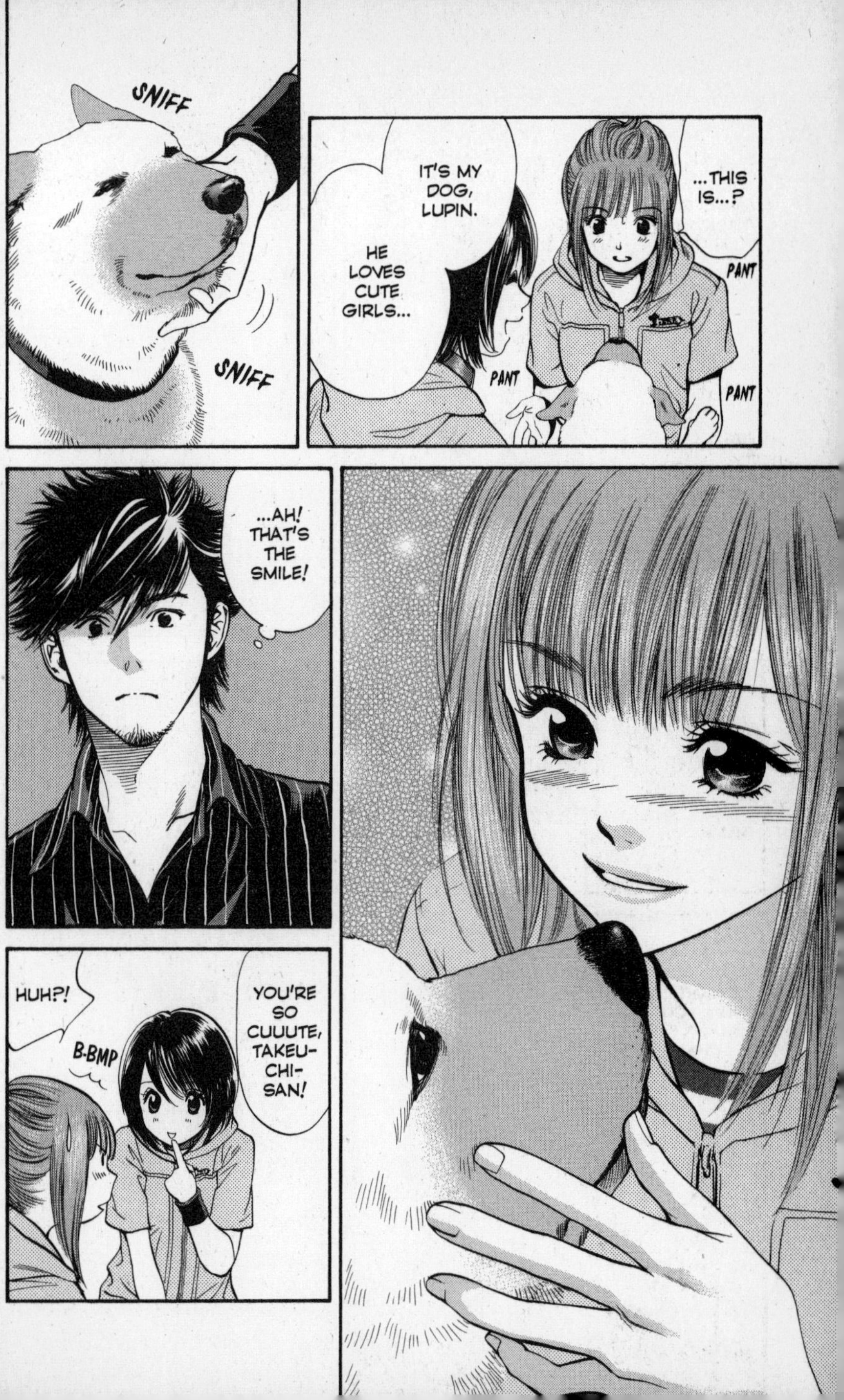
...THIS IS...?
PANT
IT'S MY DOG, LUPIN.
HE LOVES CUTE GIRLS...
PANT
PANT
SNIFF
SNIFF
...AH! THAT'S THE SMILE!
YOU'RE SO CUUUTE, TAKEUCHI-SAN!
HUH?!
B-BMP

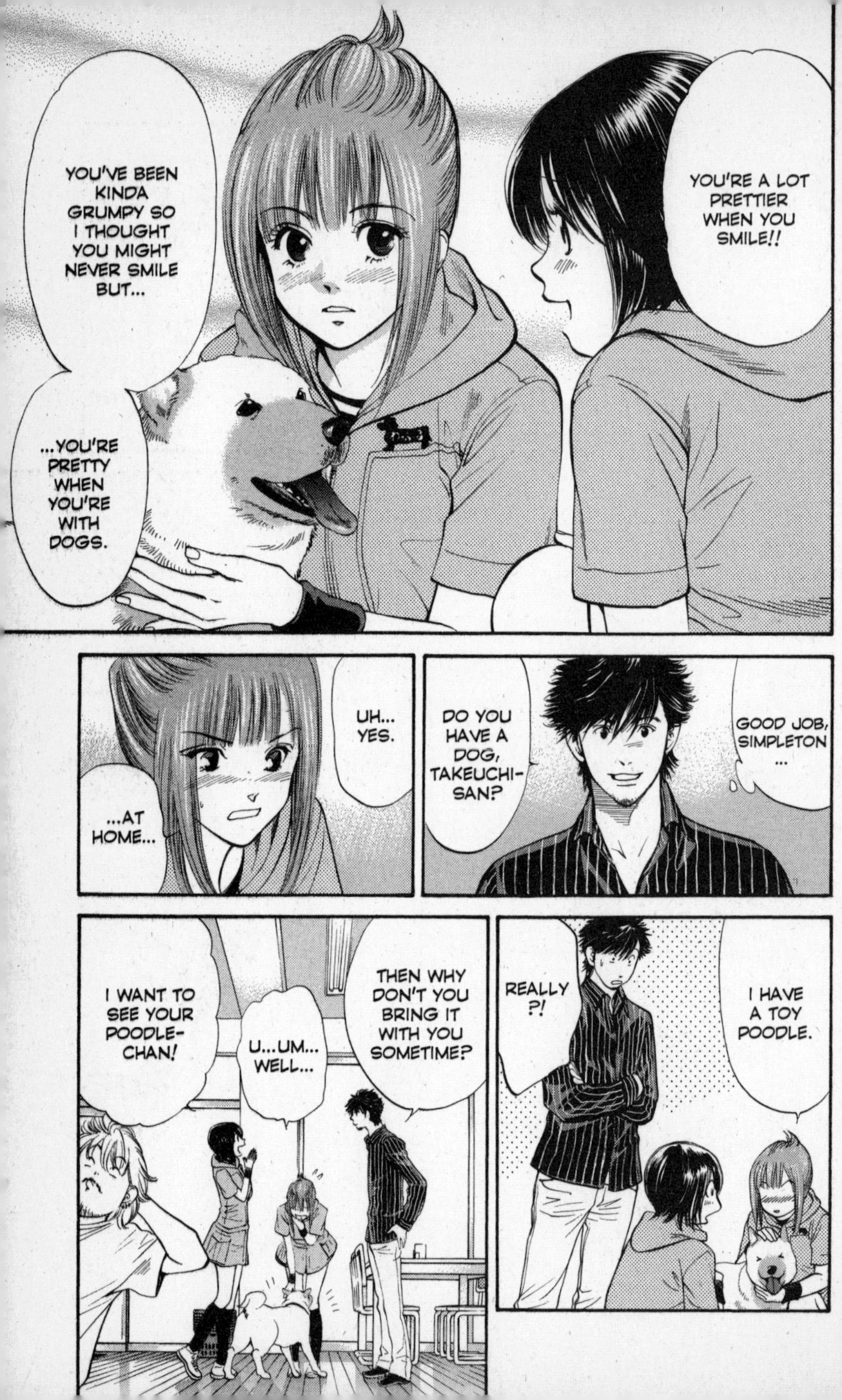
YOU'RE A LOT PRETTIER WHEN YOU SMILE!!
YOU'VE BEEN KINDA GRUMPY SO I THOUGHT YOU MIGHT NEVER SMILE BUT...
...YOU'RE PRETTY WHEN YOU'RE WITH DOGS.
GOOD JOB, SIMPLETON ...
DO YOU HAVE A DOG, TAKEUCHI-SAN?
UH... YES.
...AT HOME...
I HAVE A TOY POODLE.
REALLY ?!
THEN WHY DON'T YOU BRING IT WITH YOU SOMETIME?
I WANT TO SEE YOUR POODLE-CHAN!
U...UM... WELL...

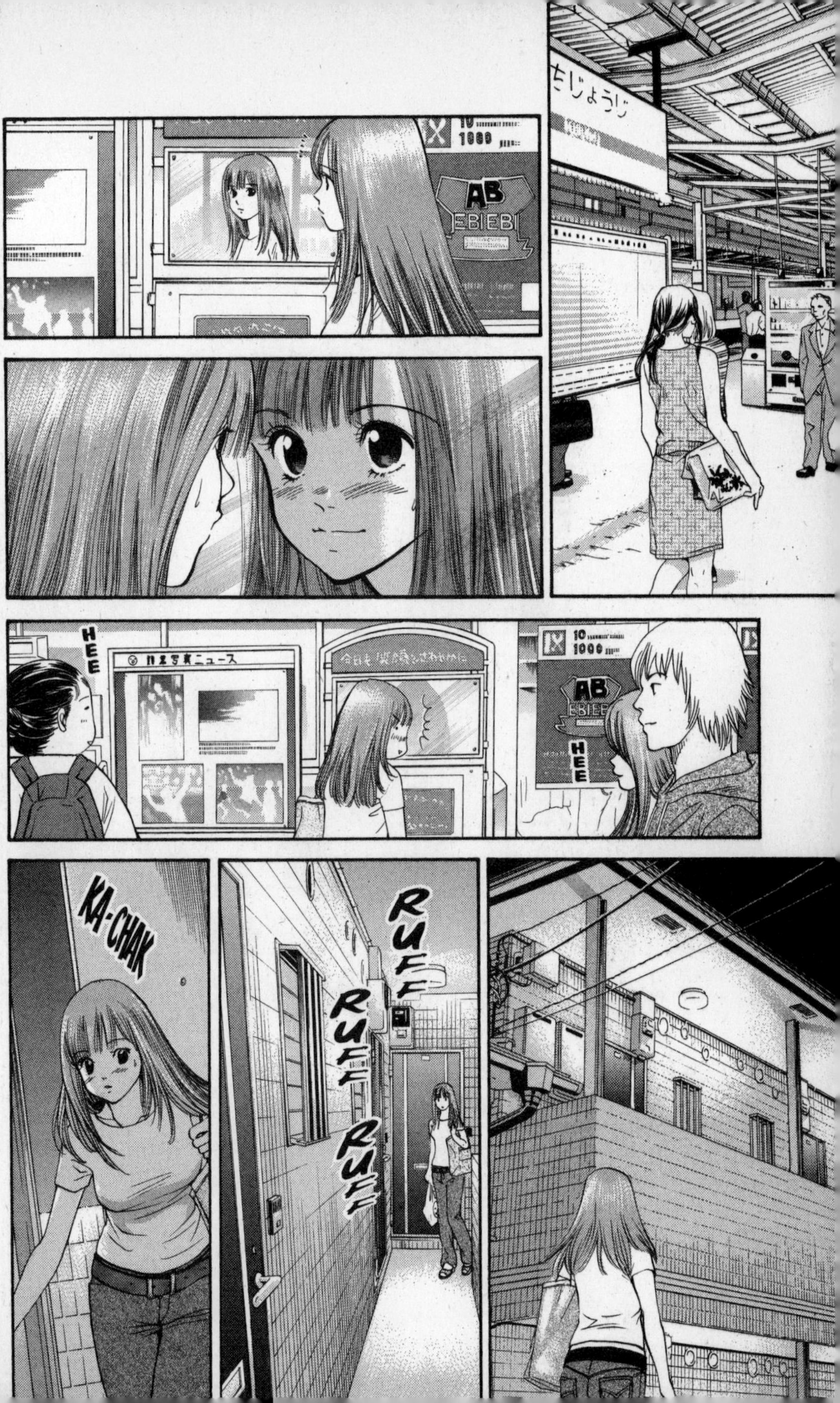
ちじょうじ
AB
EBIEBI
HEE
HEE
RUFF
RUFF
RUFF
KA-CHAK

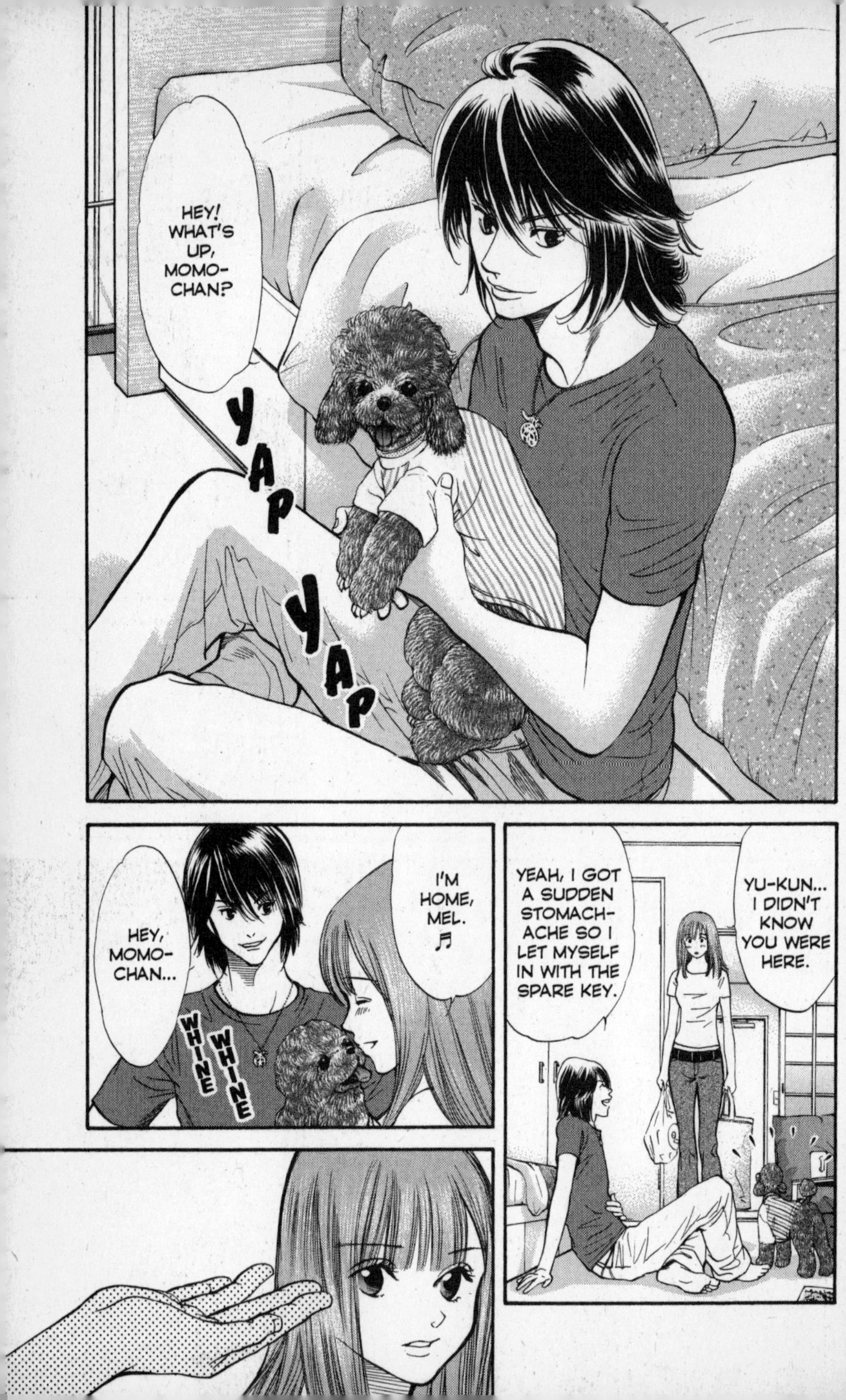
HEY! WHAT'S UP, MOMO-CHAN?
YAP YAP
YAP YAP
YU-KUN... I DIDN'T KNOW YOU WERE HERE.
YEAH, I GOT A SUDDEN STOMACH-ACHE SO I LET MYSELF IN WITH THE SPARE KEY.
I'M HOME, MEL. ♬
HEY, MOMO-CHAN...
WHINE WHINE

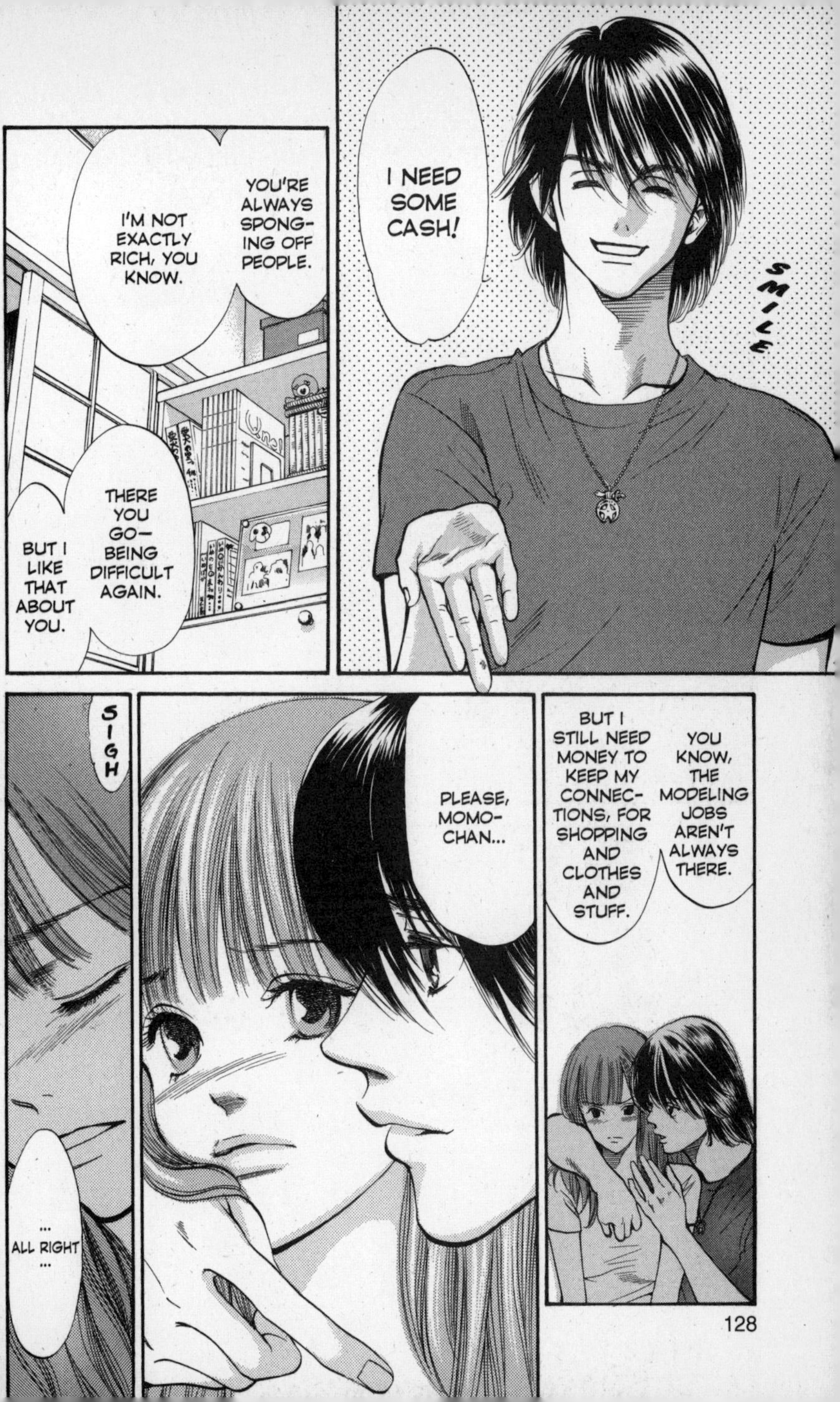
I NEED SOME CASH!
SMILE
YOU'RE ALWAYS SPONG-ING OFF PEOPLE.
I'M NOT EXACTLY RICH, YOU KNOW.
THERE YOU GO—BEING DIFFICULT AGAIN.
BUT I LIKE THAT ABOUT YOU.
YOU KNOW, THE MODELING JOBS AREN'T ALWAYS THERE.
BUT I STILL NEED MONEY TO KEEP MY CONNEC-TIONS, FOR SHOPPING AND CLOTHES AND STUFF.
PLEASE, MOMO-CHAN...
SIGH
... ALL RIGHT ...

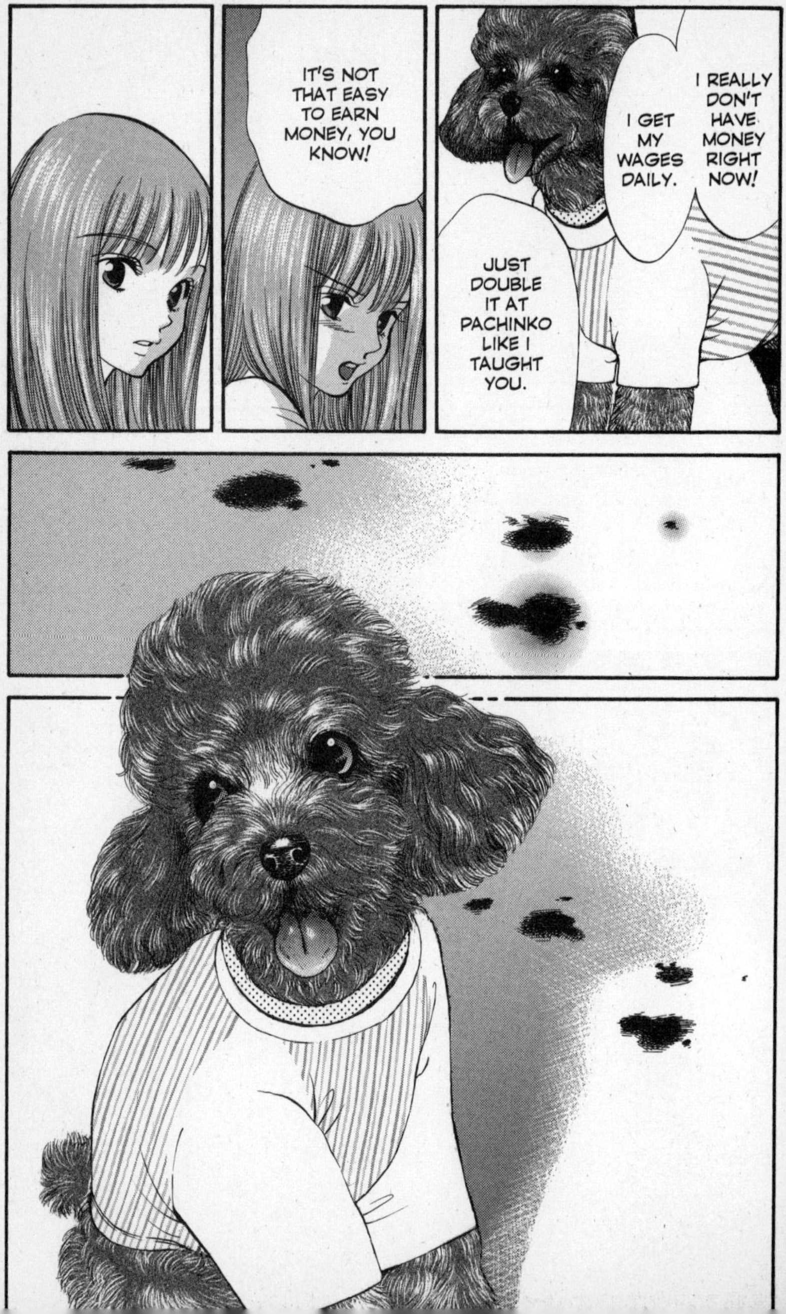
I REALLY DON'T HAVE MONEY RIGHT NOW!
I GET MY WAGES DAILY.
JUST DOUBLE IT AT PACHINKO LIKE I TAUGHT YOU.
IT'S NOT THAT EASY TO EARN MONEY, YOU KNOW!

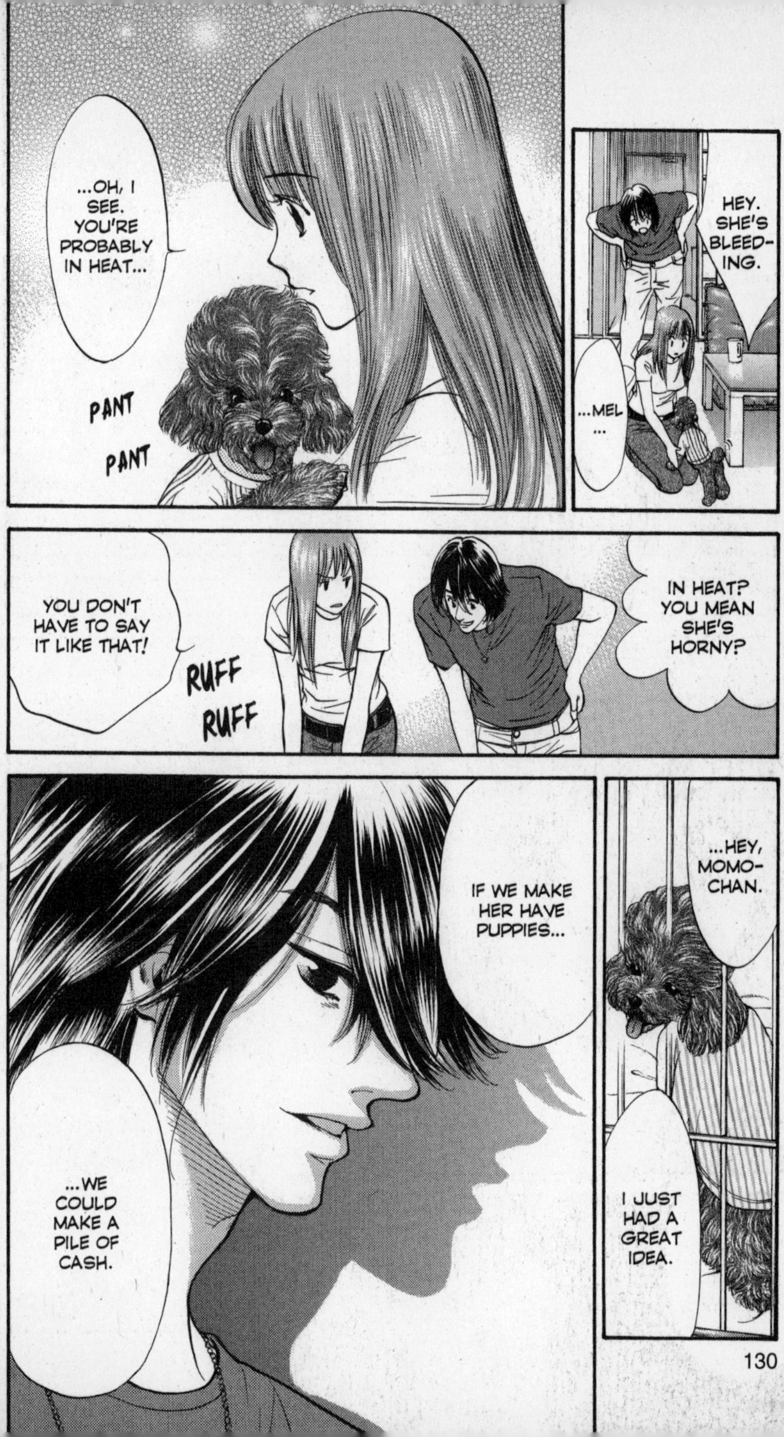
HEY. SHE'S BLEED-ING.
...MEL ...
...OH, I SEE. YOU'RE PROBABLY IN HEAT...
PANT
PANT
IN HEAT? YOU MEAN SHE'S HORNY?
YOU DON'T HAVE TO SAY IT LIKE THAT!
RUFF
RUFF
...HEY, MOMO-CHAN.
I JUST HAD A GREAT IDEA.
IF WE MAKE HER HAVE PUPPIES...
...WE COULD MAKE A PILE OF CASH.

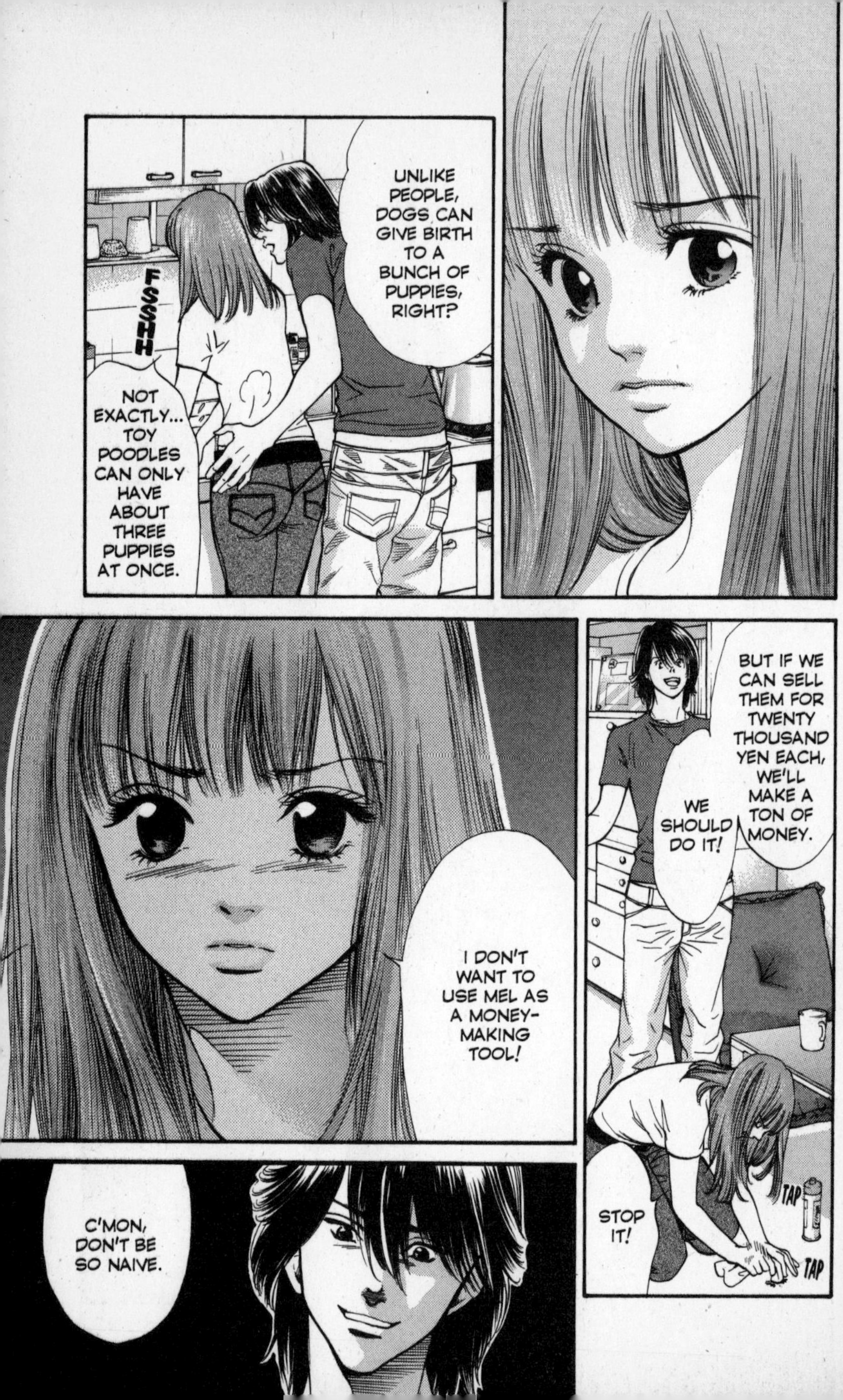
UNLIKE PEOPLE, DOGS CAN GIVE BIRTH TO A BUNCH OF PUPPIES, RIGHT?
FSSHH
NOT EXACTLY... TOY POODLES CAN ONLY HAVE ABOUT THREE PUPPIES AT ONCE.
BUT IF WE CAN SELL THEM FOR TWENTY THOUSAND YEN EACH, WE'LL MAKE A TON OF MONEY.
WE SHOULD DO IT!
STOP IT!
TAP
TAP
I DON'T WANT TO USE MEL AS A MONEY-MAKING TOOL!
C'MON, DON'T BE SO NAIVE.

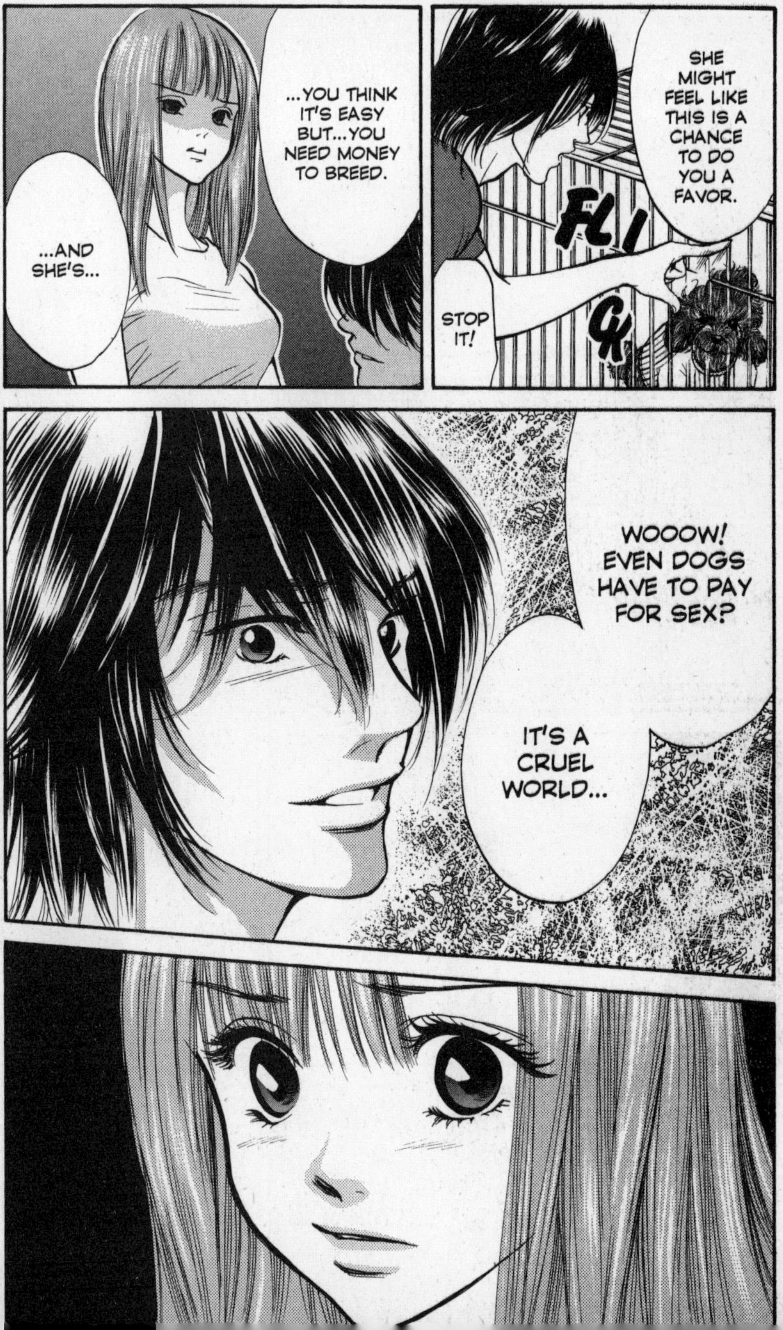
SHE MIGHT FEEL LIKE THIS IS A CHANCE TO DO YOU A FAVOR.
FLICK
STOP IT!
...YOU THINK IT'S EASY BUT...YOU NEED MONEY TO BREED.
...AND SHE'S...
WOOOW! EVEN DOGS HAVE TO PAY FOR SEX?
IT'S A CRUEL WORLD...

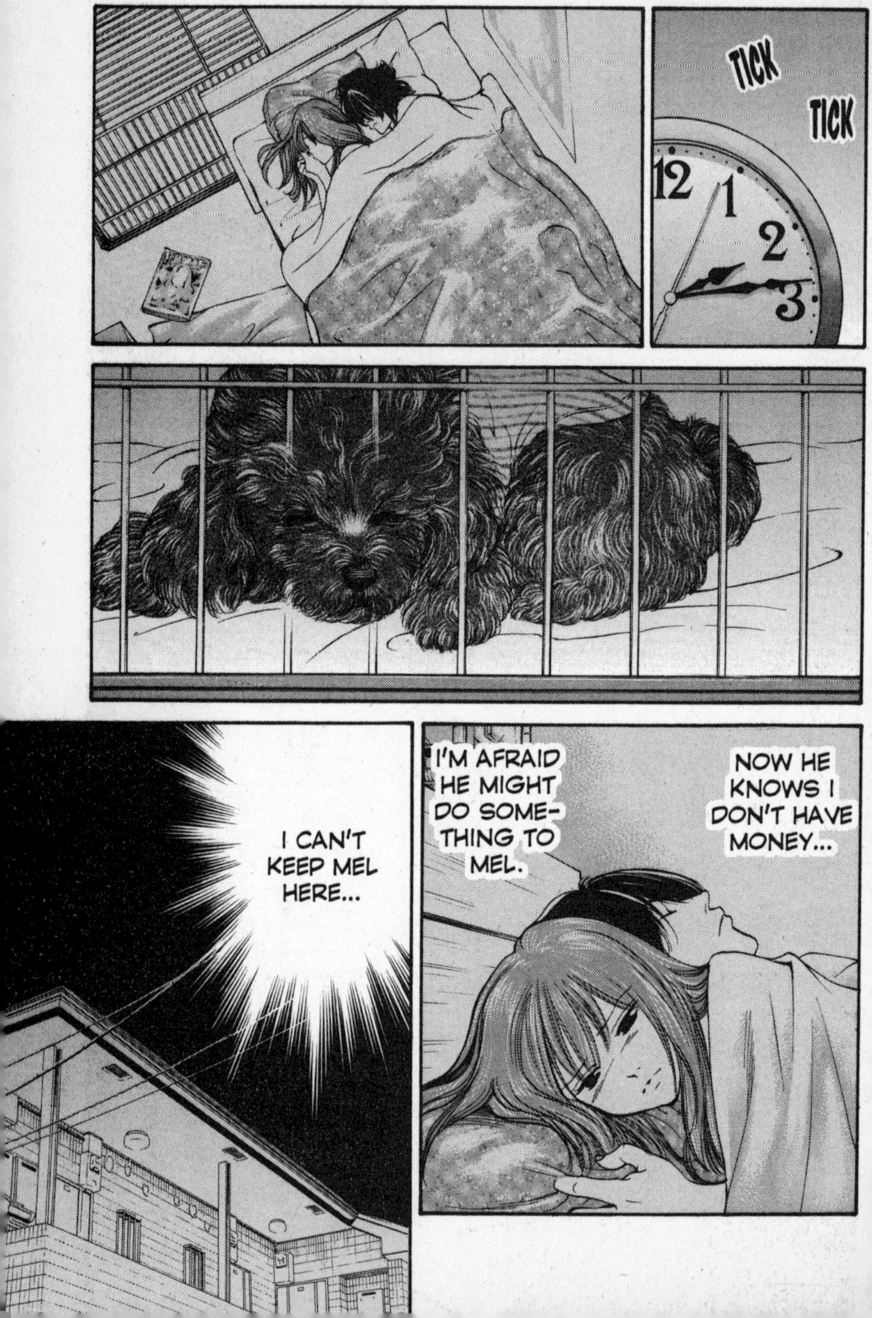
TICK
TICK
NOW HE KNOWS I DON'T HAVE MONEY...
I'M AFRAID HE MIGHT DO SOME-THING TO MEL.
I CAN'T KEEP MEL HERE...

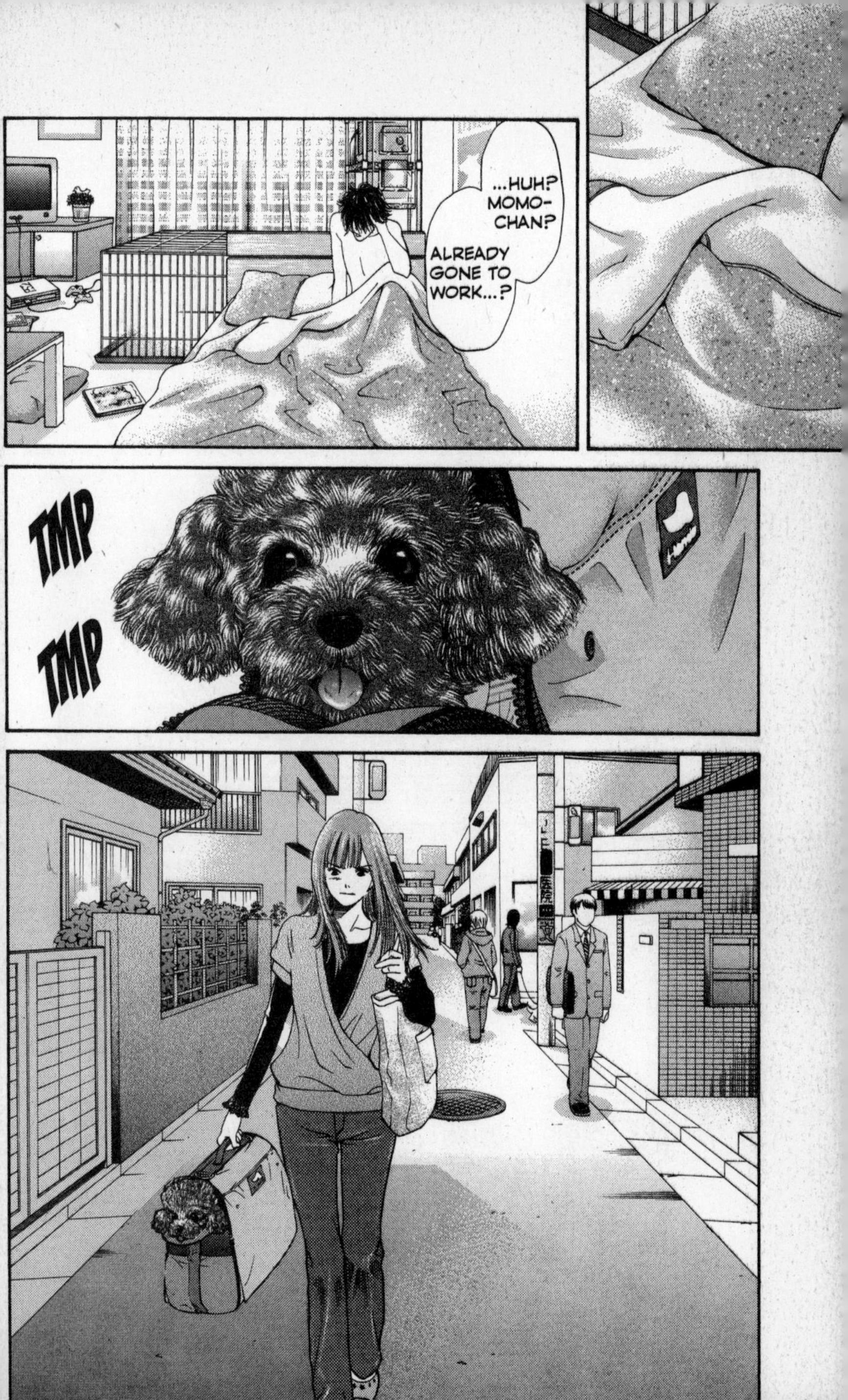
...HUH? MOMO-CHAN?
ALREADY GONE TO WORK...?
TMP
TMP

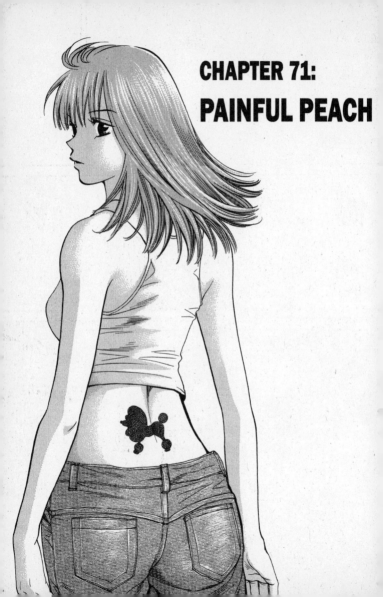

CHAPTER 71:
PAINFUL PEACH

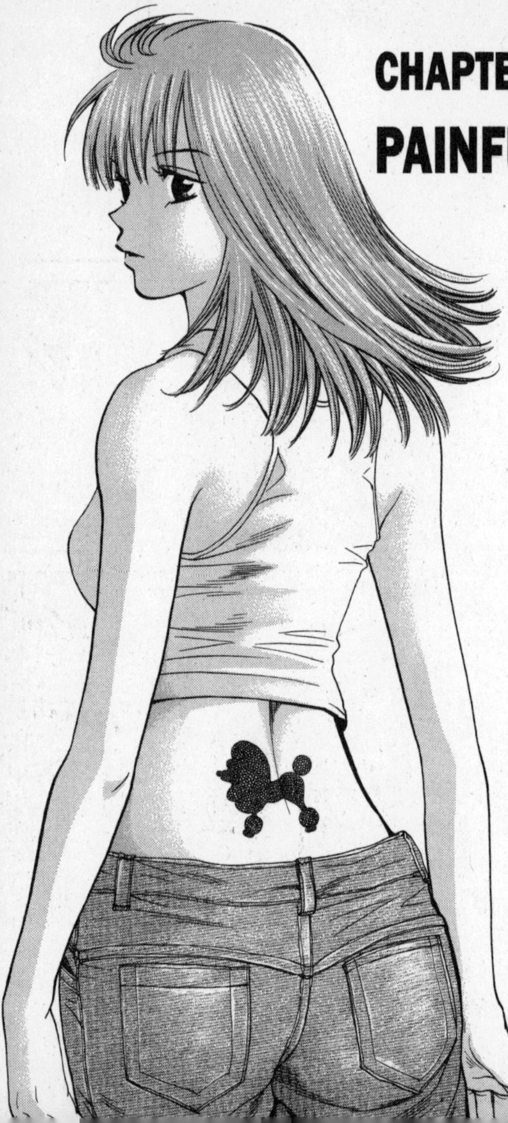

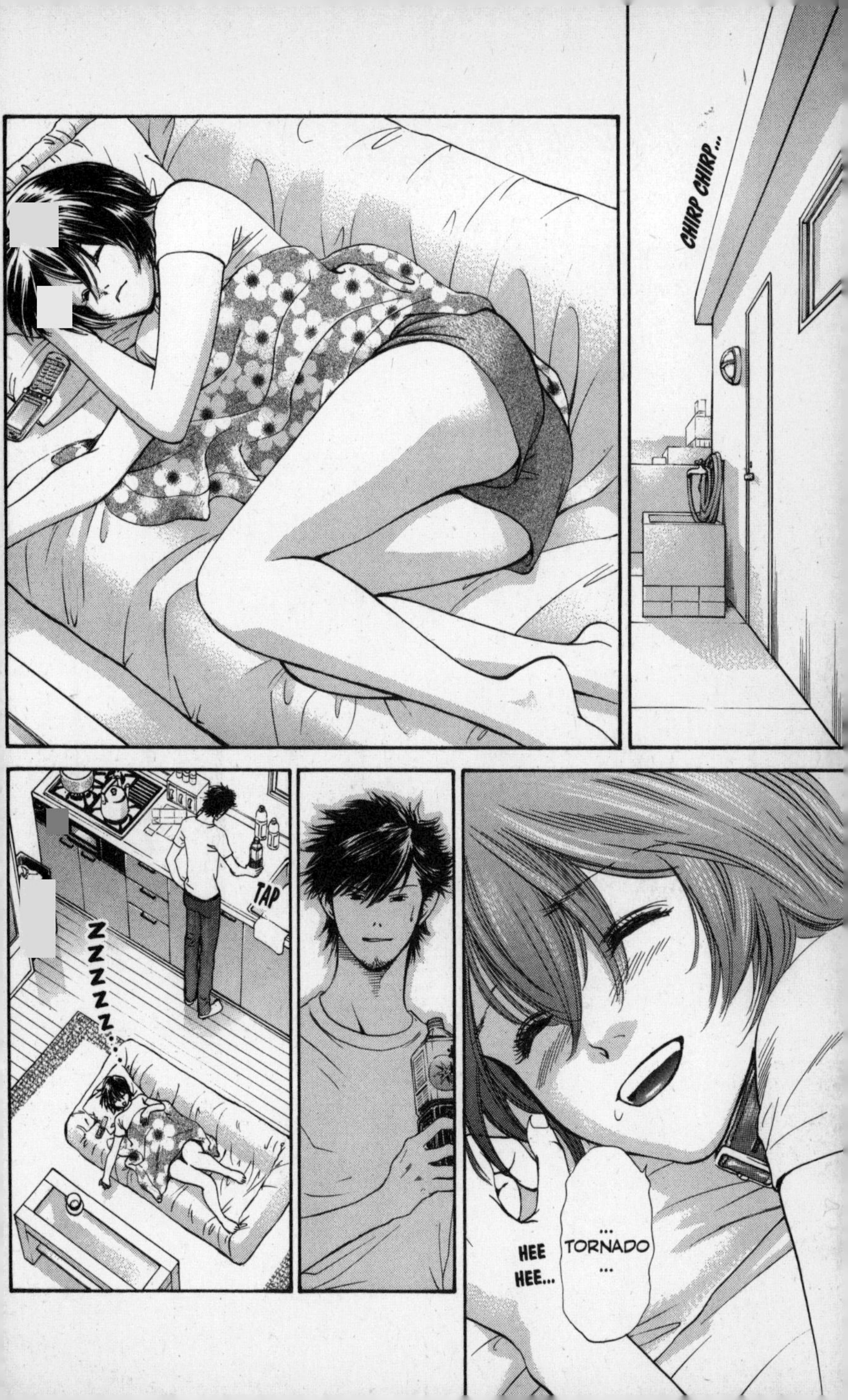
CHIRP CHIRP...
... TORNADO ...
HEE HEE...
TAP
ZZZZZ...

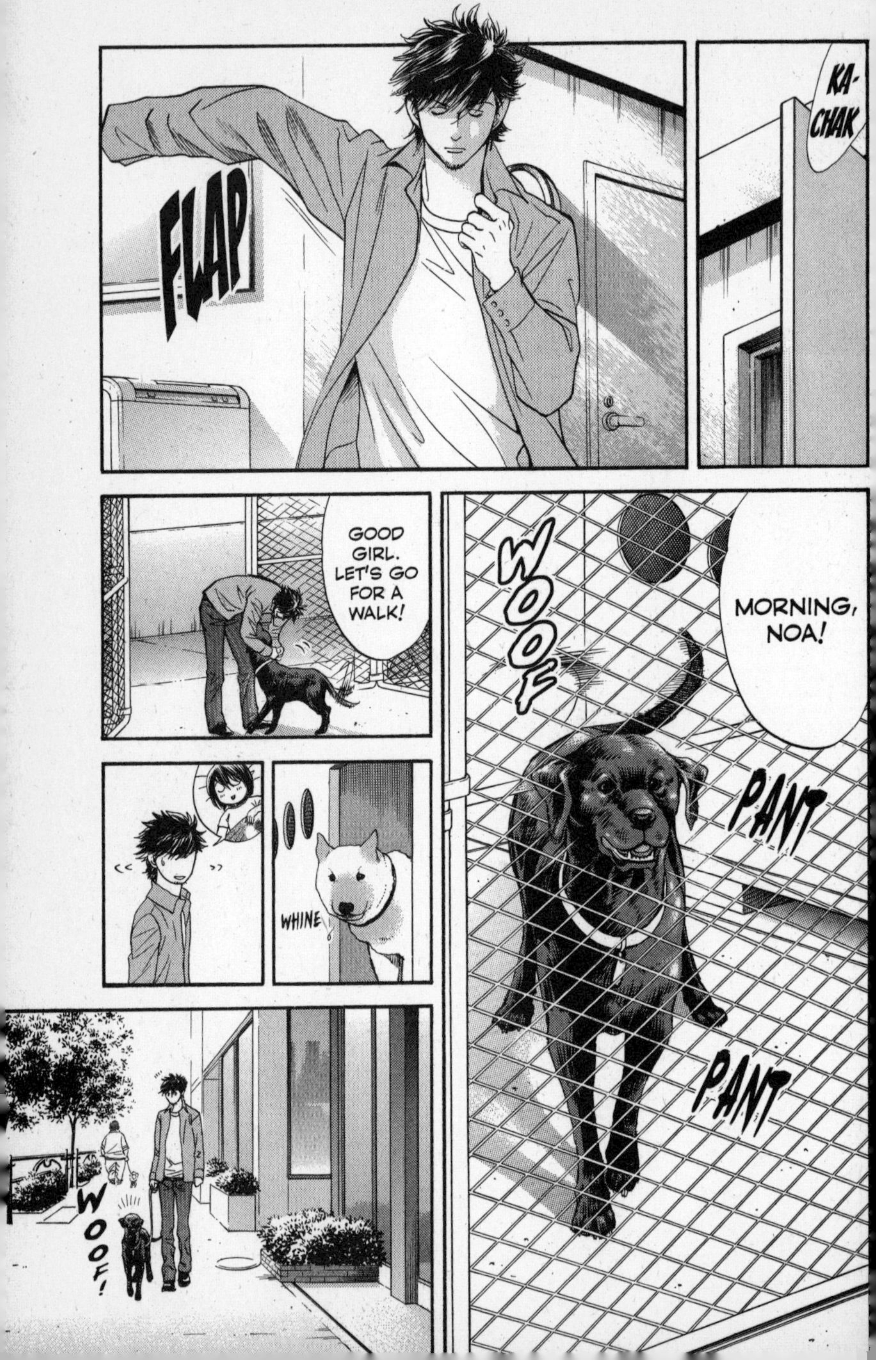
KA-CHAK
FLAP
MORNING, NOA!
WOOF
PANT
PANT
GOOD GIRL. LET'S GO FOR A WALK!
WHINE
WOOF WOOF!

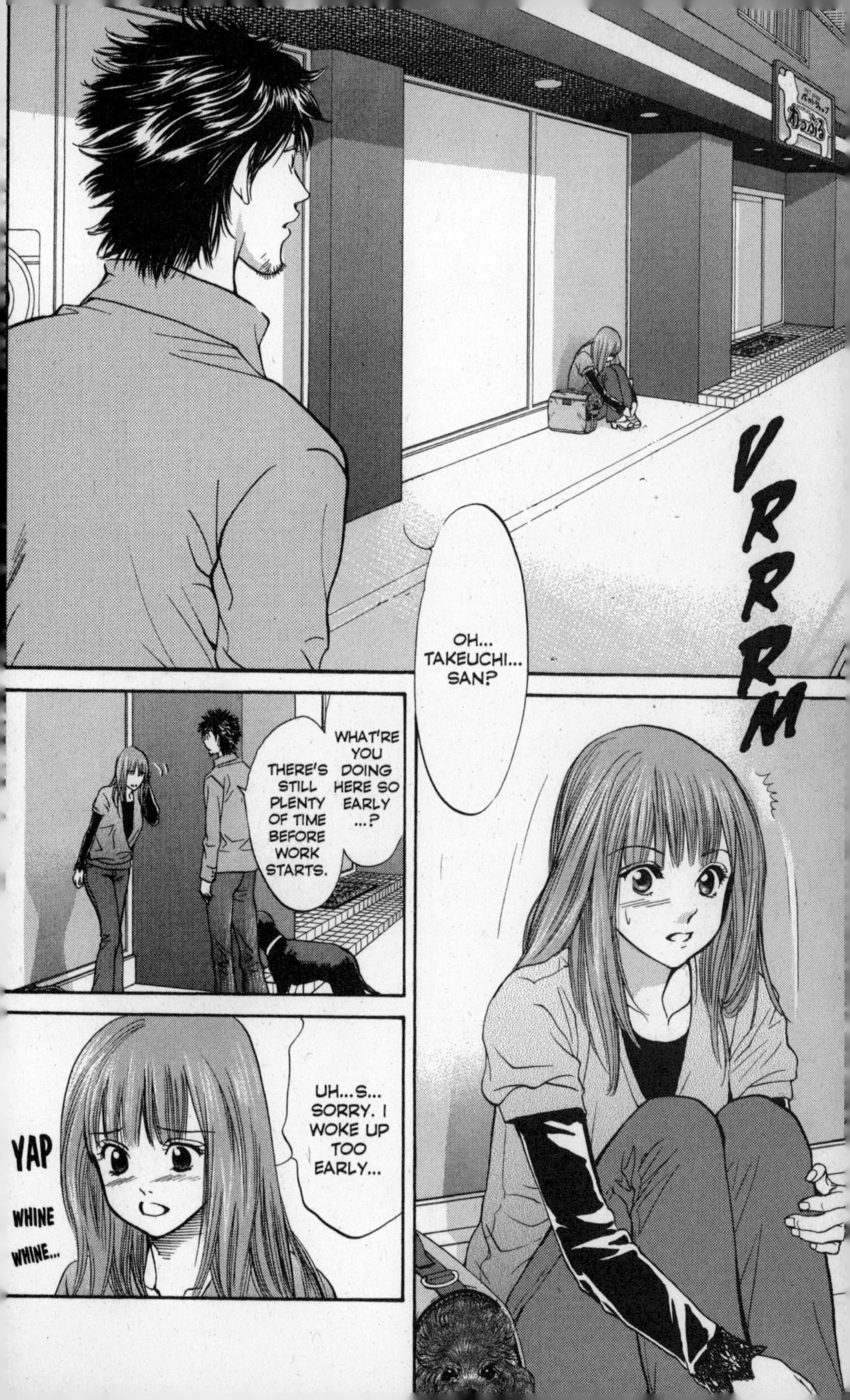
VRRRM
OH... TAKEUCHI... SAN?
WHAT'RE YOU DOING HERE SO EARLY ...?
THERE'S STILL PLENTY OF TIME BEFORE WORK STARTS.
UH... S... SORRY. I WOKE UP TOO EARLY...
YAP
WHINE WHINE...

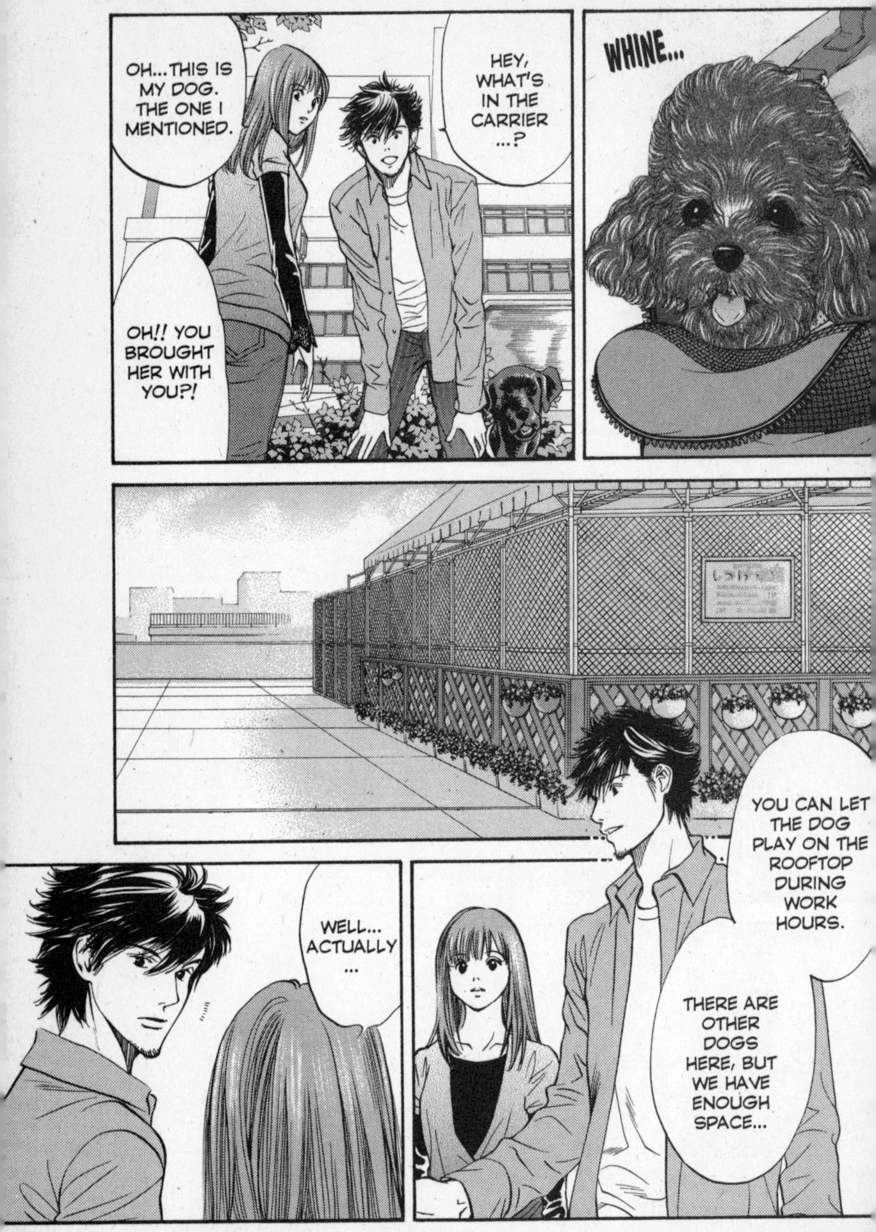
WHINE...
HEY, WHAT'S IN THE CARRIER ...?
OH...THIS IS MY DOG. THE ONE I MENTIONED.
OH!! YOU BROUGHT HER WITH YOU?!
YOU CAN LET THE DOG PLAY ON THE ROOFTOP DURING WORK HOURS.
THERE ARE OTHER DOGS HERE, BUT WE HAVE ENOUGH SPACE...
WELL... ACTUALLY ...

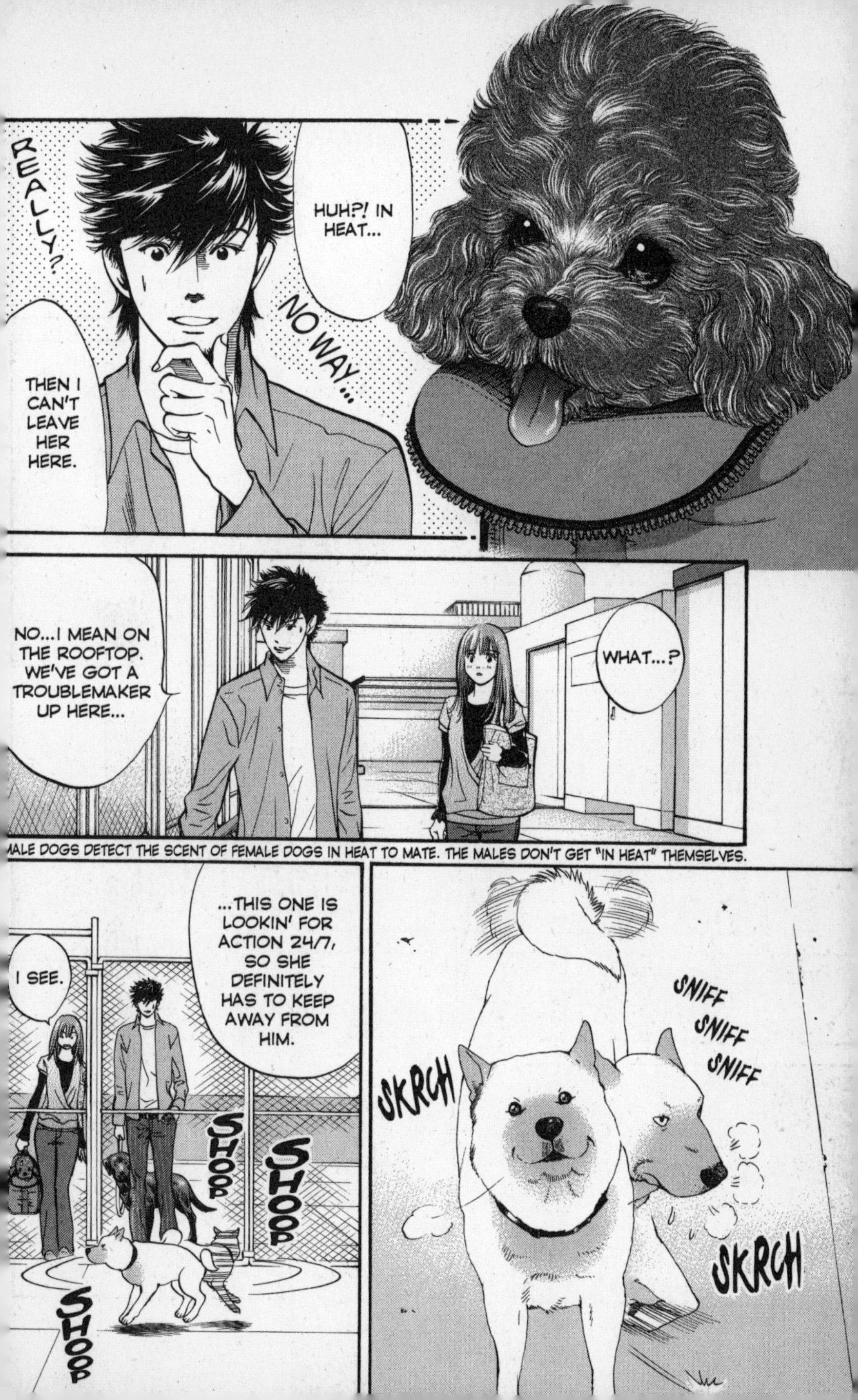
HUH?! IN HEAT...
NO WAY...
REALLY?
THEN I CAN'T LEAVE HER HERE.
WHAT...?
NO...I MEAN ON THE ROOFTOP. WE'VE GOT A TROUBLEMAKER UP HERE...
MALE DOGS DETECT THE SCENT OF FEMALE DOGS IN HEAT TO MATE. THE MALES DON'T GET "IN HEAT" THEMSELVES.
SNIFF SNIFF SNIFF
SKRCH
SKRCH
...THIS ONE IS LOOKIN' FOR ACTION 24/7, SO SHE DEFINITELY HAS TO KEEP AWAY FROM HIM.
I SEE.
SHOOP
SHOOP
SHOOP

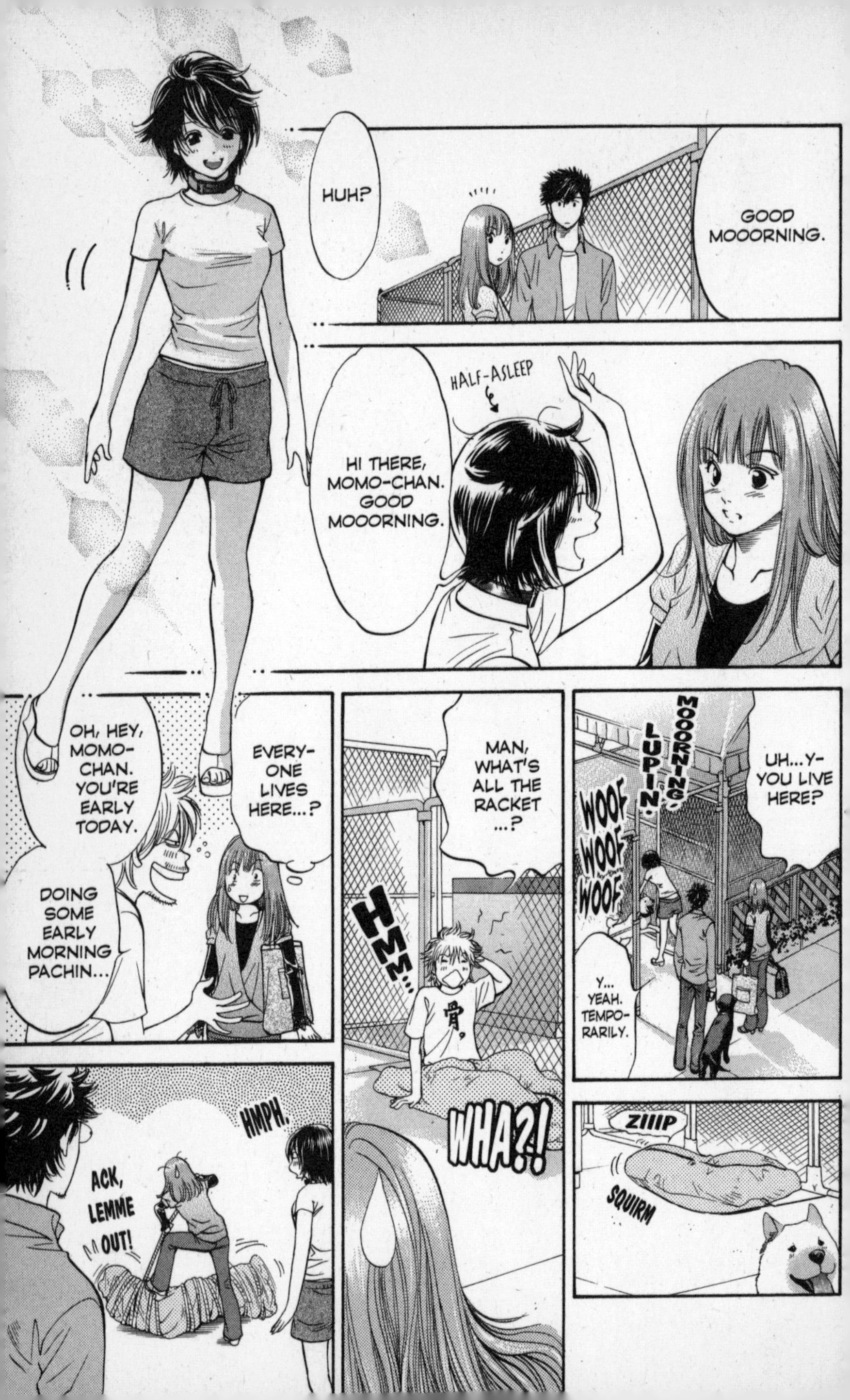
GOOD MOOORNING.
HUH?
HALF-ASLEEP
HI THERE, MOMO-CHAN. GOOD MOOORNING.
UH...Y-YOU LIVE HERE?
MOOORNING, LUPIN.
WOOF WOOF WOOF
Y... YEAH. TEMPORARILY.
ZIIIP
SQUIRM
MAN, WHAT'S ALL THE RACKET ...?
HMM...
WHA?!
OH, HEY, MOMO-CHAN. YOU'RE EARLY TODAY.
EVERY-ONE LIVES HERE...?
DOING SOME EARLY MORNING PACHIN...
HMPH.
ACK, LEMME OUT!

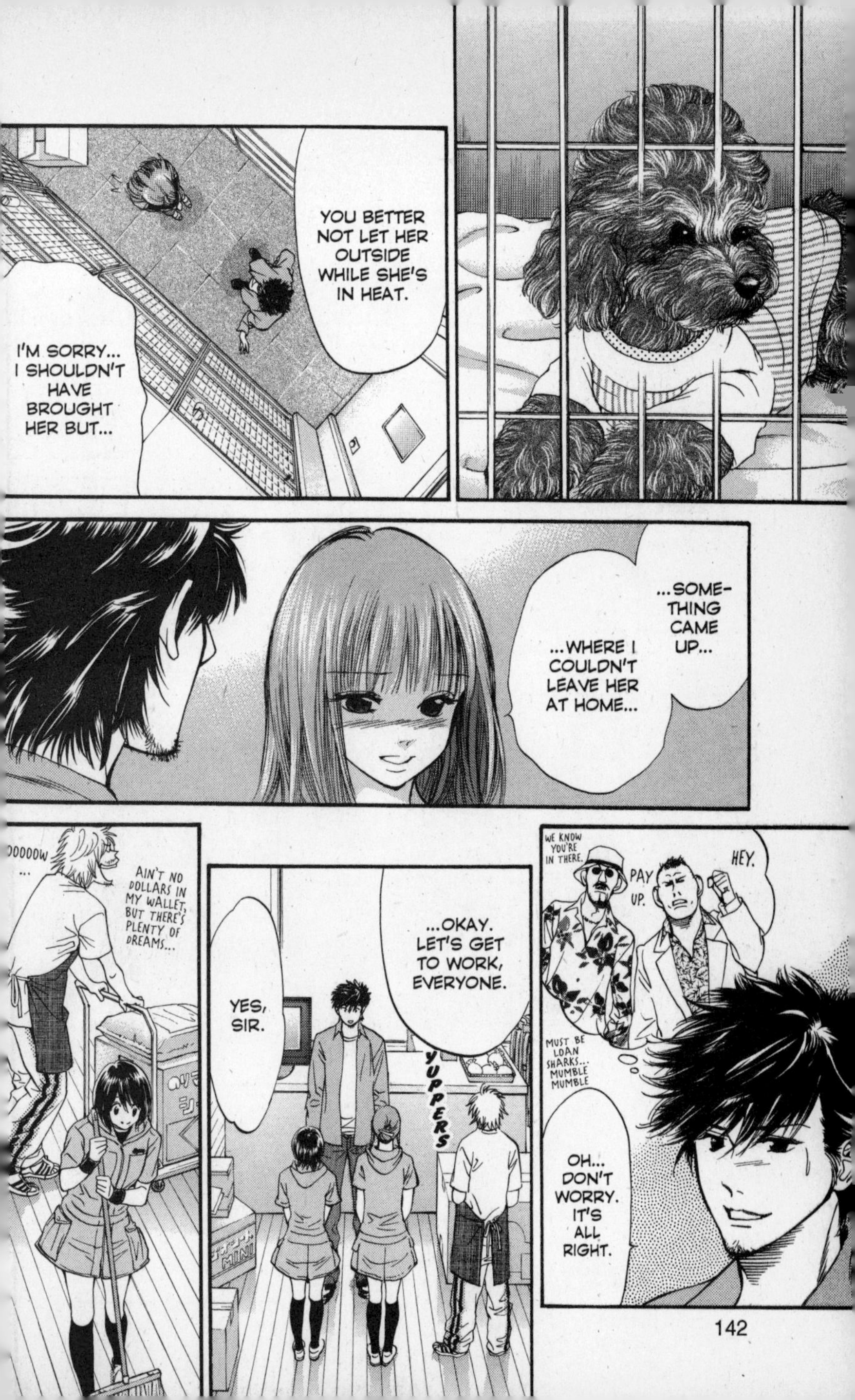
YOU BETTER NOT LET HER OUTSIDE WHILE SHE'S IN HEAT.
I'M SORRY... I SHOULDN'T HAVE BROUGHT HER BUT...
...SOME-THING CAME UP...
...WHERE I COULDN'T LEAVE HER AT HOME...
HEY.
PAY UP.
WE KNOW YOU'RE IN THERE.
MUST BE LOAN SHARKS... MUMBLE MUMBLE
OH... DON'T WORRY. IT'S ALL RIGHT.
...OKAY. LET'S GET TO WORK, EVERYONE.
YES, SIR.
YUPPERS
AIN'T NO DOLLARS IN MY WALLET, BUT THERE'S PLENTY OF DREAMS...

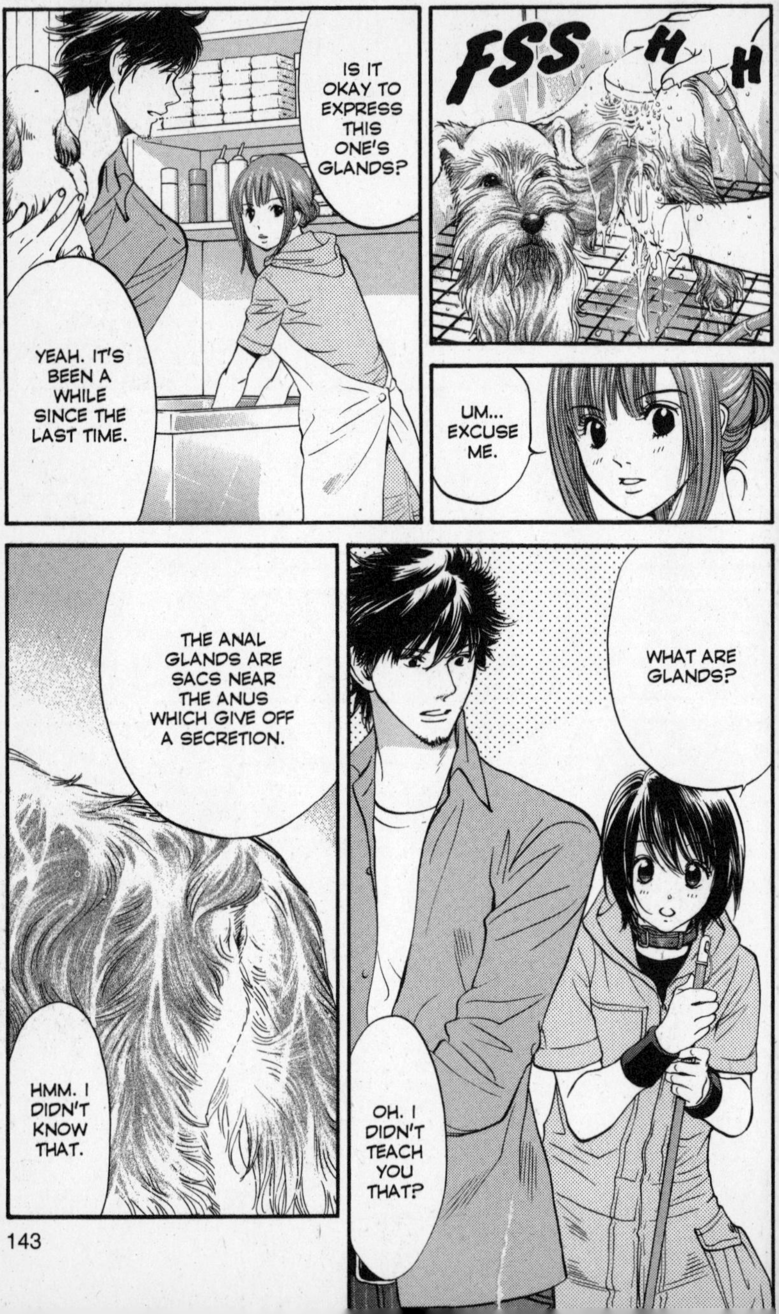
FSS
H H
UM... EXCUSE ME.
IS IT OKAY TO EXPRESS THIS ONE'S GLANDS?
YEAH. IT'S BEEN A WHILE SINCE THE LAST TIME.
WHAT ARE GLANDS?
OH. I DIDN'T TEACH YOU THAT?
THE ANAL GLANDS ARE SACS NEAR THE ANUS WHICH GIVE OFF A SECRETION.
HMM. I DIDN'T KNOW THAT.

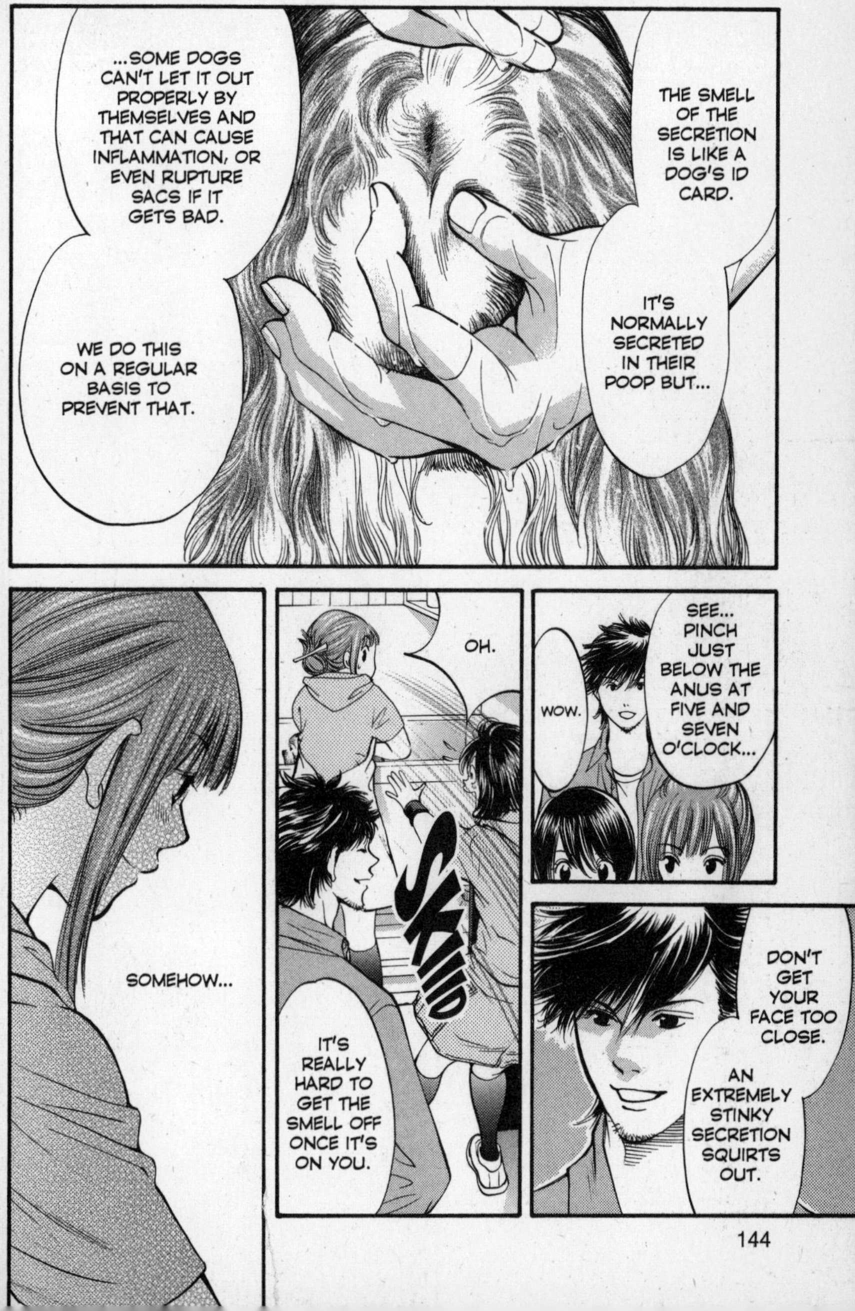
THE SMELL OF THE SECRETION IS LIKE A DOG'S ID CARD.
IT'S NORMALLY SECRETED IN THEIR POOP BUT...
...SOME DOGS CAN'T LET IT OUT PROPERLY BY THEMSELVES AND THAT CAN CAUSE INFLAMMATION, OR EVEN RUPTURE SACS IF IT GETS BAD.
WE DO THIS ON A REGULAR BASIS TO PREVENT THAT.
SEE... PINCH JUST BELOW THE ANUS AT FIVE AND SEVEN O'CLOCK...
WOW.
DON'T GET YOUR FACE TOO CLOSE.
AN EXTREMELY STINKY SECRETION SQUIRTS OUT.
OH.
SKIID
IT'S REALLY HARD TO GET THE SMELL OFF ONCE IT'S ON YOU.
SOMEHOW...

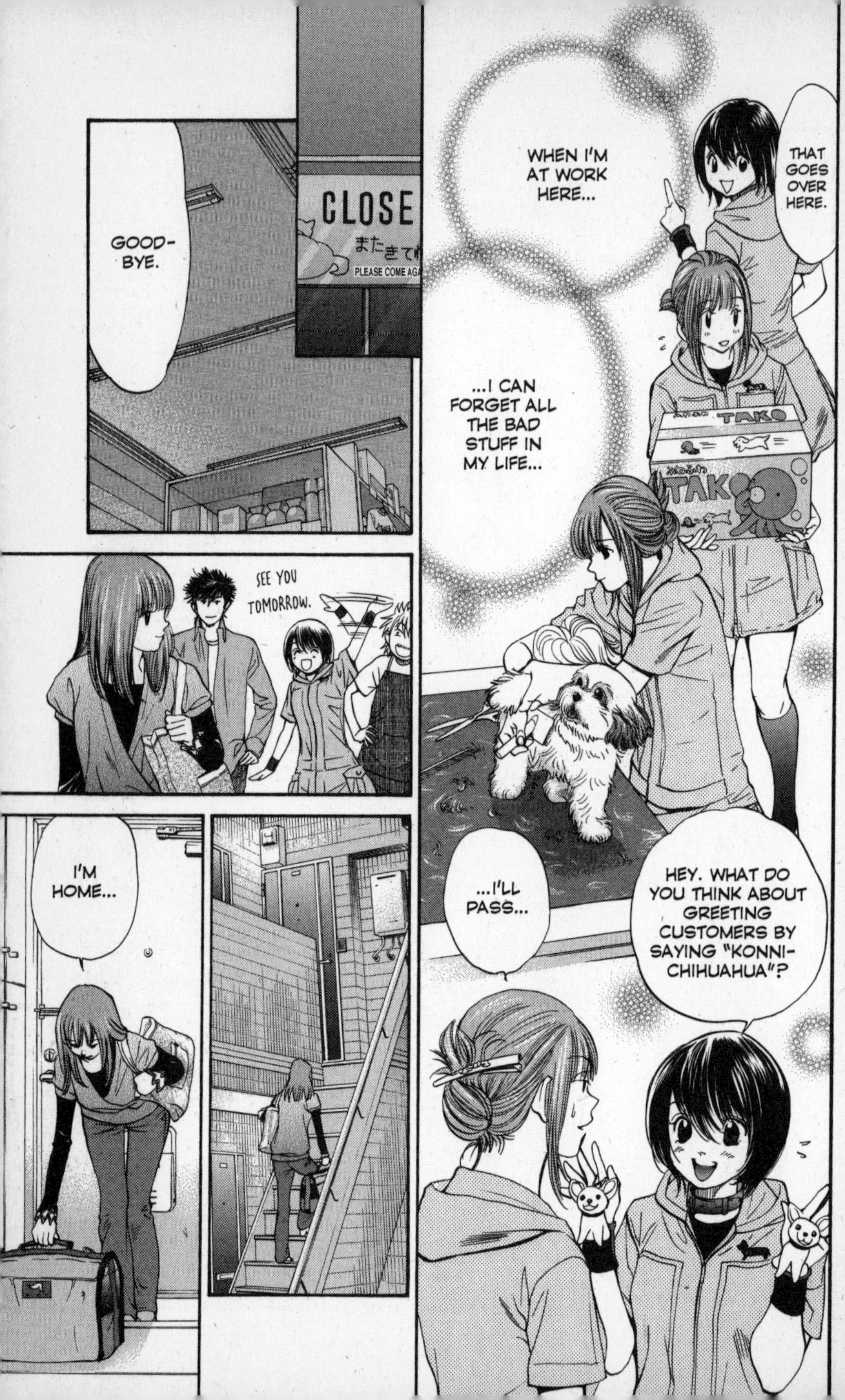
THAT GOES OVER HERE.
WHEN I'M AT WORK HERE...
...I CAN FORGET ALL THE BAD STUFF IN MY LIFE...
TAKO
HEY. WHAT DO YOU THINK ABOUT GREETING CUSTOMERS BY SAYING "KONNI-CHIHUAHUA"?
...I'LL PASS...
CLOSE
PLEASE COME AGA
GOOD-BYE.
SEE YOU TOMORROW.
I'M HOME...

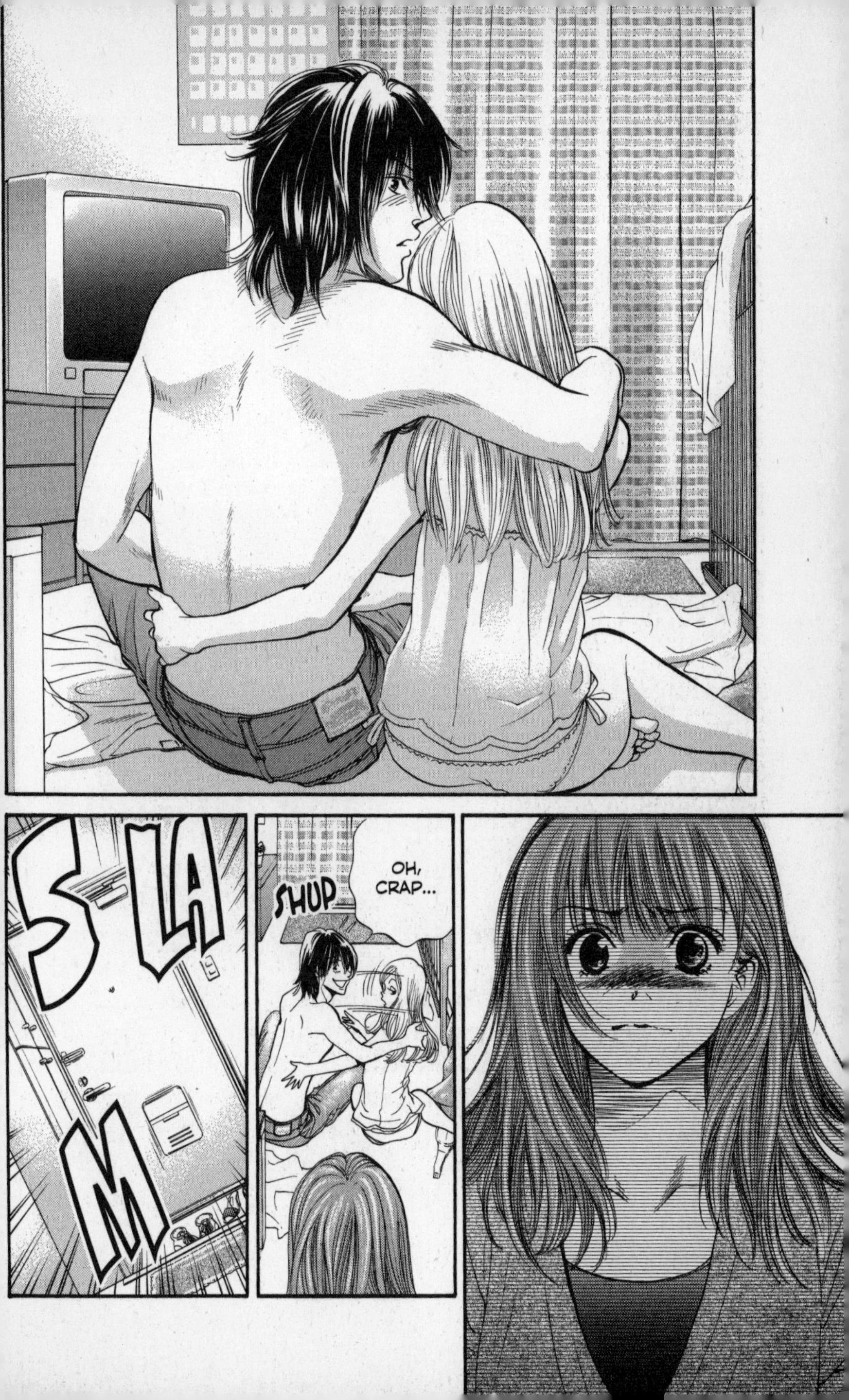
OH, CRAP...
SHUP
SLAM

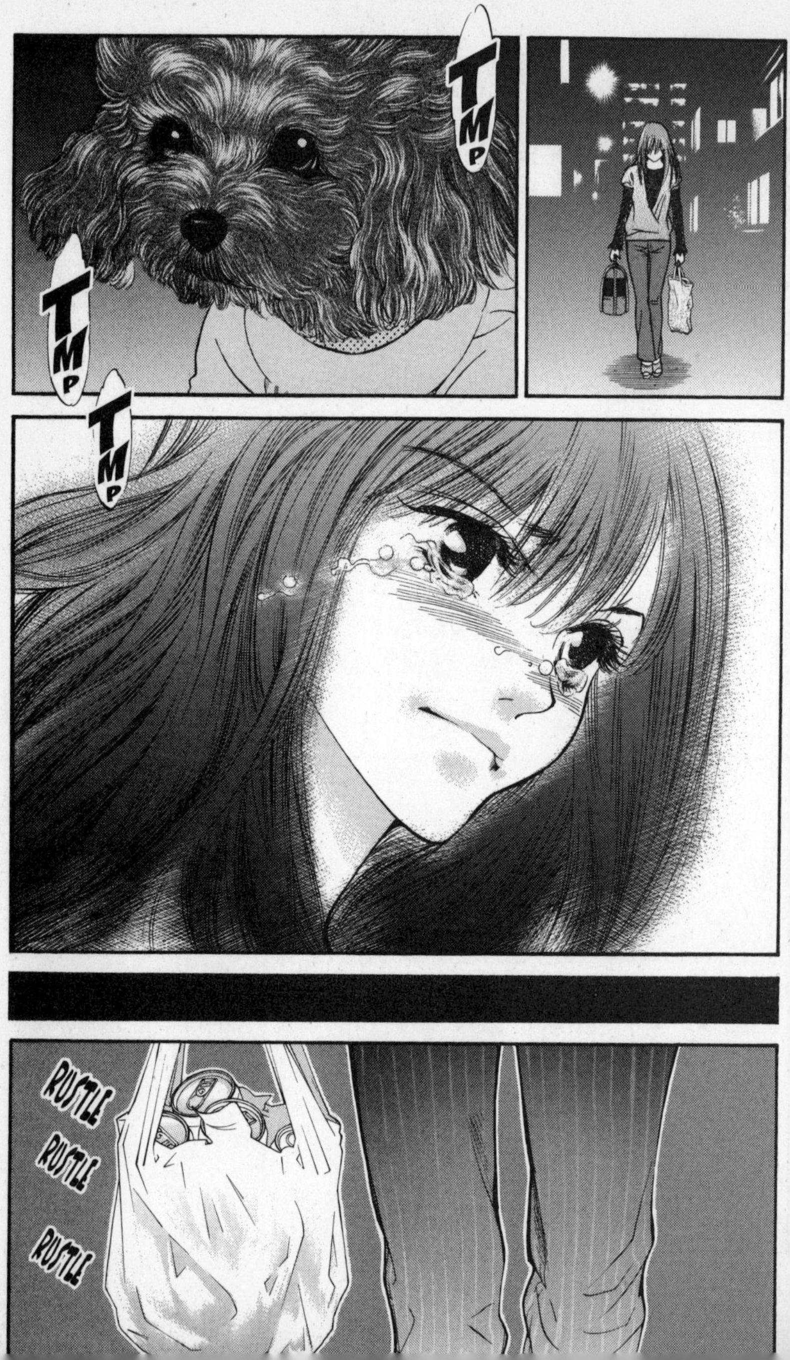
TMP
TMP
TMP
RUSTLE
RUSTLE
RUSTLE

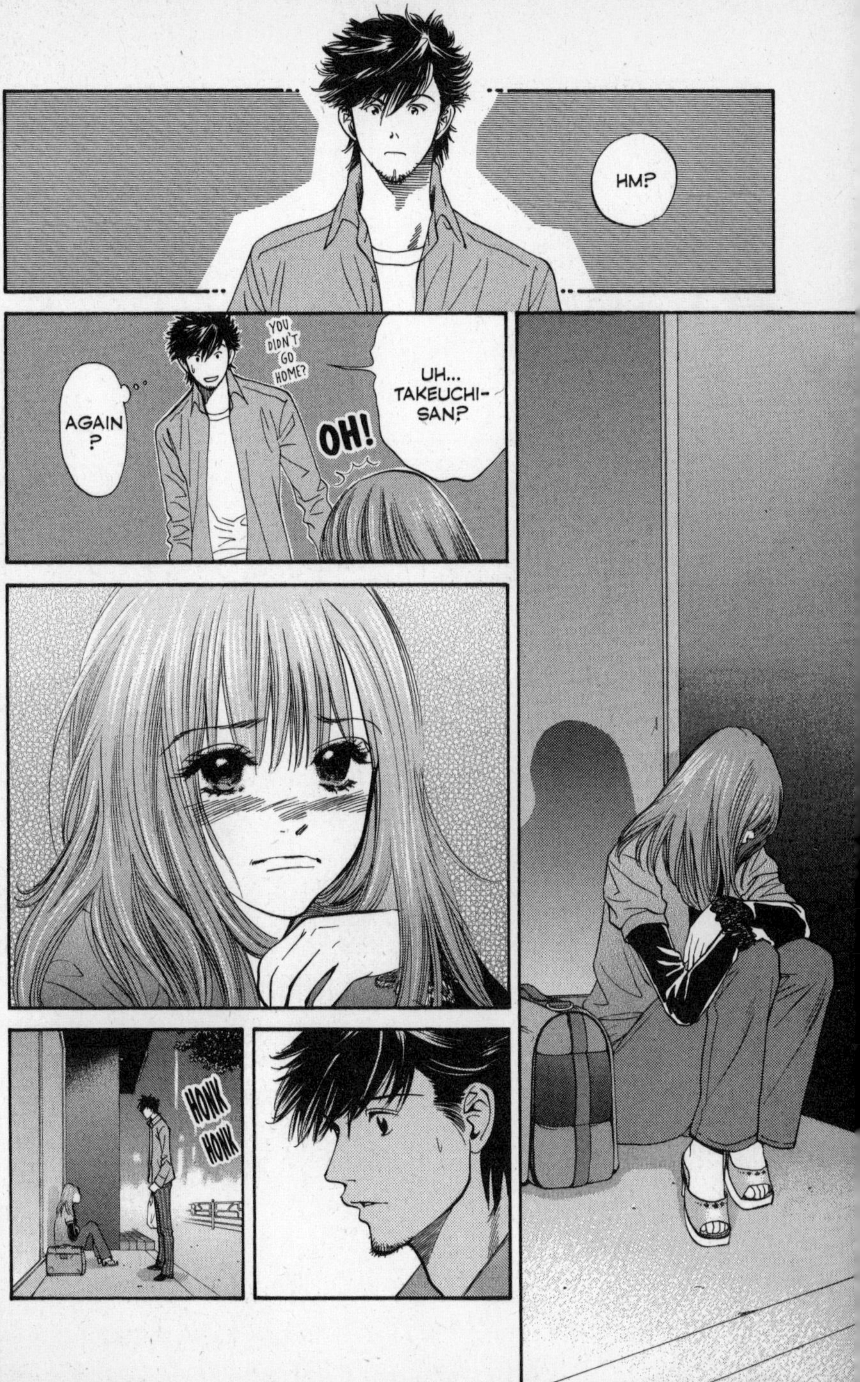
HM?
UH... TAKEUCHI-SAN?
YOU DIDN'T GO HOME?
OH!
AGAIN?
HONK HONK

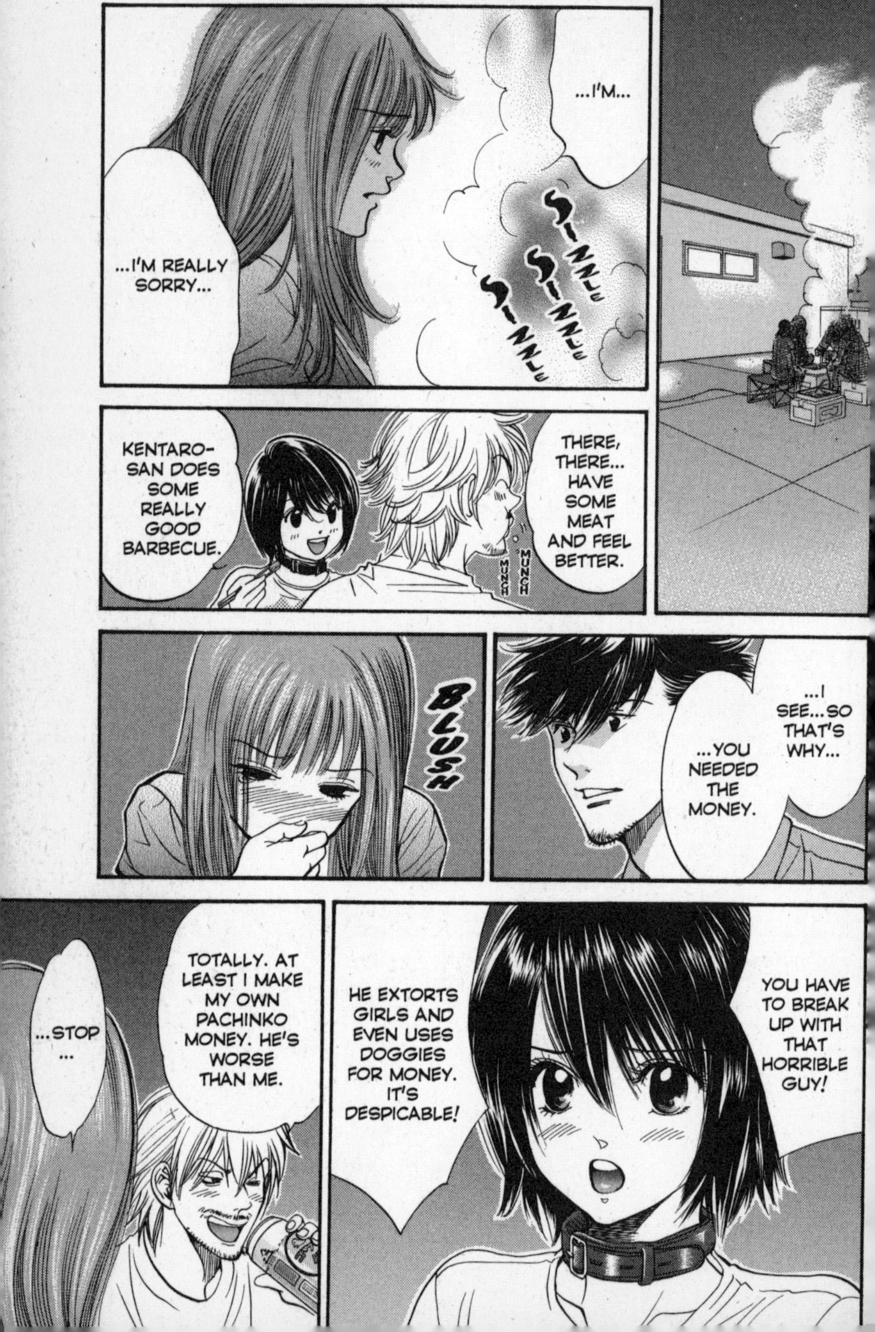
...I'M...
SIZZLE SIZZLE SIZZLE
...I'M REALLY SORRY...
THERE, THERE... HAVE SOME MEAT AND FEEL BETTER.
MUNCH MUNCH
KENTARO-SAN DOES SOME REALLY GOOD BARBECUE.
...I SEE... SO THAT'S WHY...
...YOU NEEDED THE MONEY.
BLUSH
YOU HAVE TO BREAK UP WITH THAT HORRIBLE GUY!
HE EXTORTS GIRLS AND EVEN USES DOGGIES FOR MONEY. IT'S DESPICABLE!
TOTALLY. AT LEAST I MAKE MY OWN PACHINKO MONEY. HE'S WORSE THAN ME.
...STOP ...

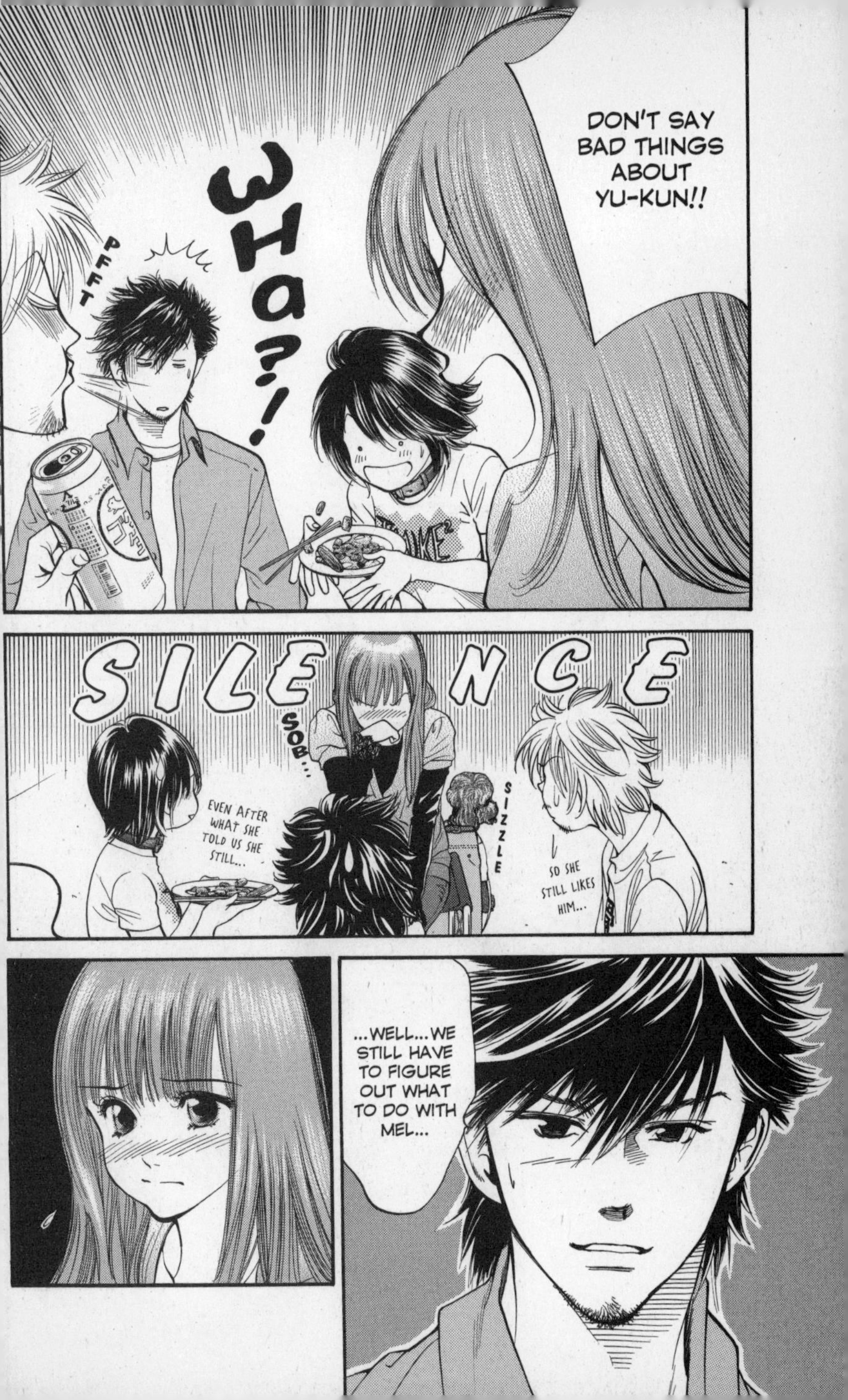
DON'T SAY BAD THINGS ABOUT YU-KUN!!
WHAT?!
PFFT
SILENCE
SIZZLE
SO SHE STILL LIKES HIM...
SOB...
EVEN AFTER WHAT SHE TOLD US SHE STILL...
...WELL...WE STILL HAVE TO FIGURE OUT WHAT TO DO WITH MEL...

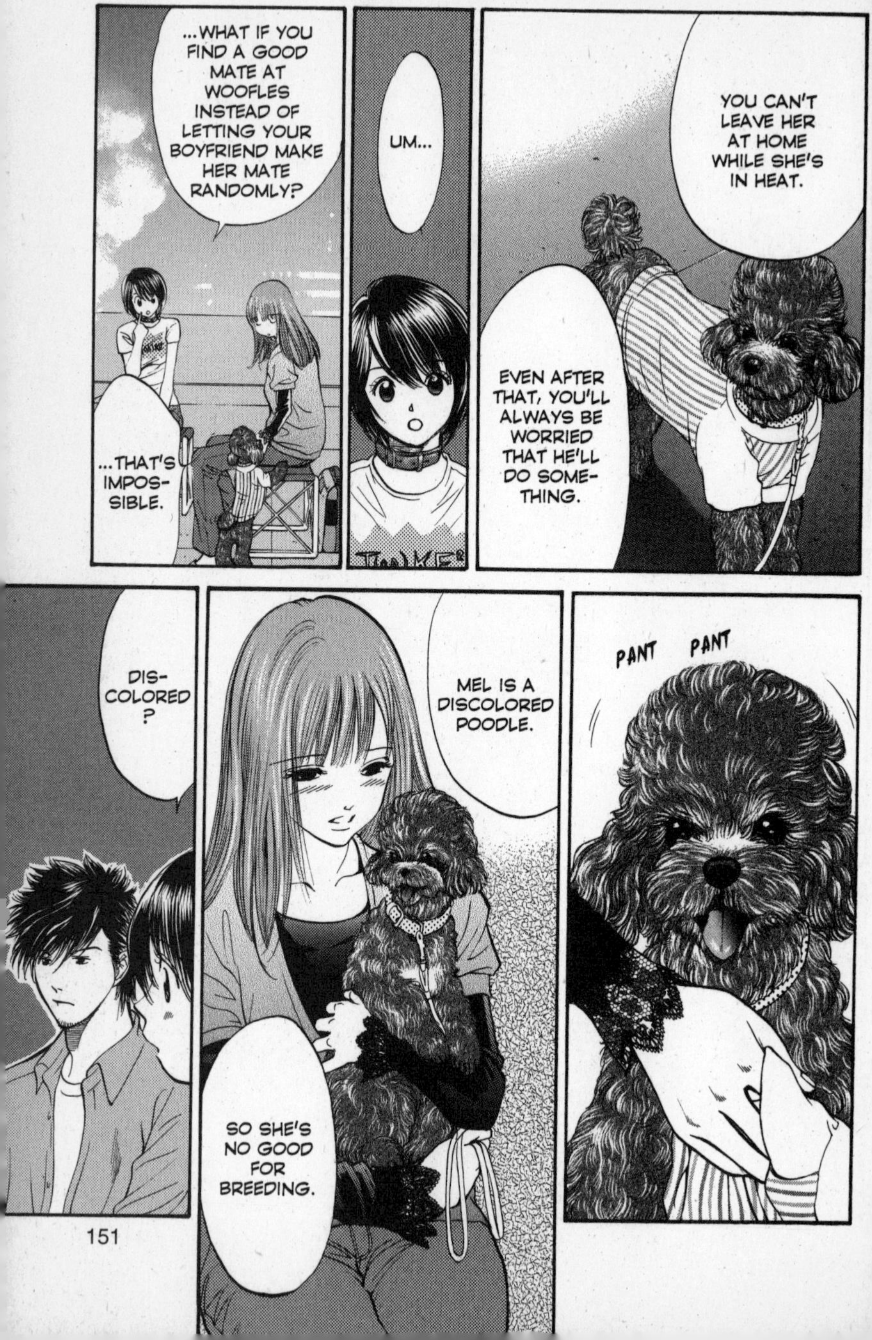
YOU CAN'T LEAVE HER AT HOME WHILE SHE'S IN HEAT.
EVEN AFTER THAT, YOU'LL ALWAYS BE WORRIED THAT HE'LL DO SOME-THING.
UM...
...WHAT IF YOU FIND A GOOD MATE AT WOOFLES INSTEAD OF LETTING YOUR BOYFRIEND MAKE HER MATE RANDOMLY?
...THAT'S IMPOS-SIBLE.
PANT PANT
MEL IS A DISCOLORED POODLE.
SO SHE'S NO GOOD FOR BREEDING.
DIS-COLORED?

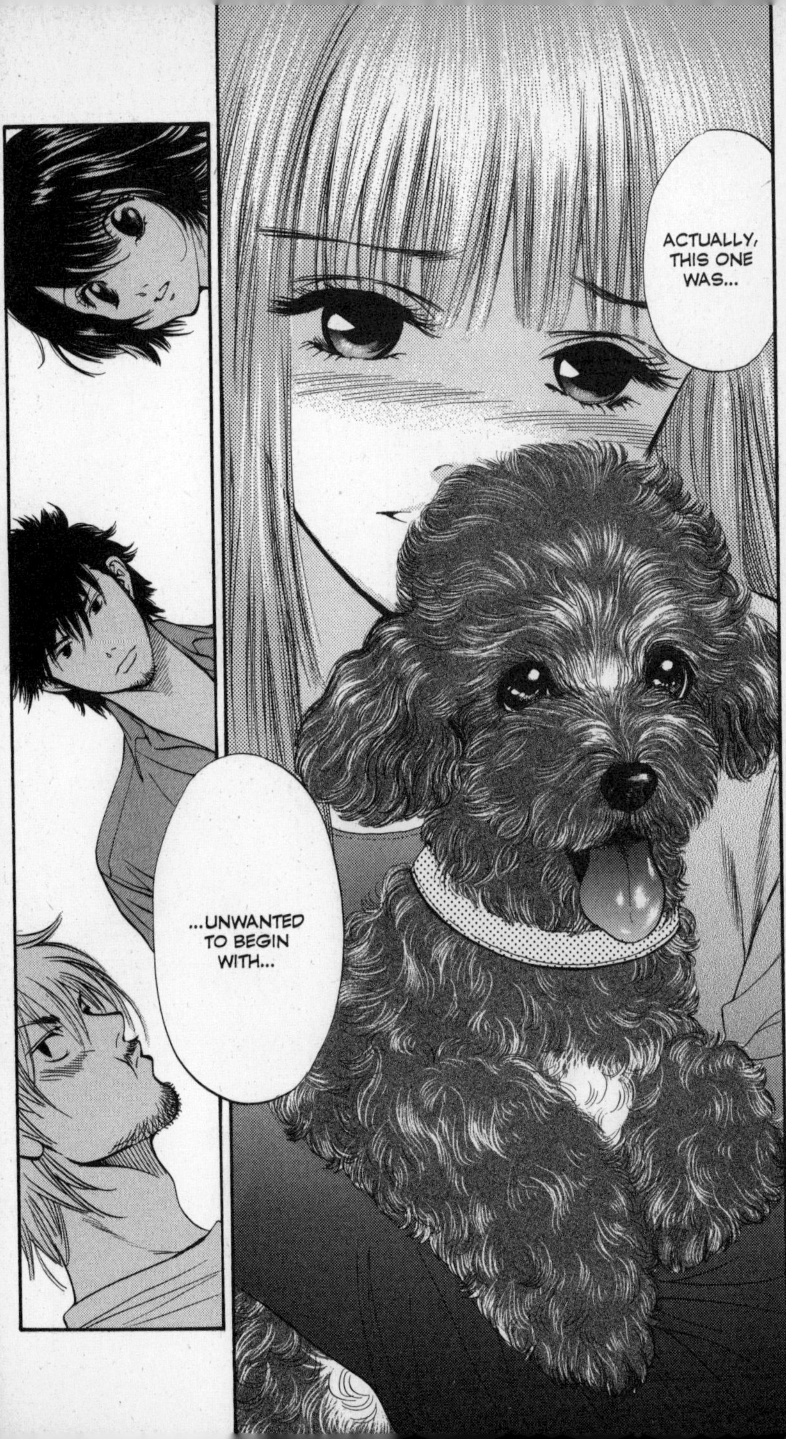
ACTUALLY, THIS ONE WAS...
...UNWANTED TO BEGIN WITH...

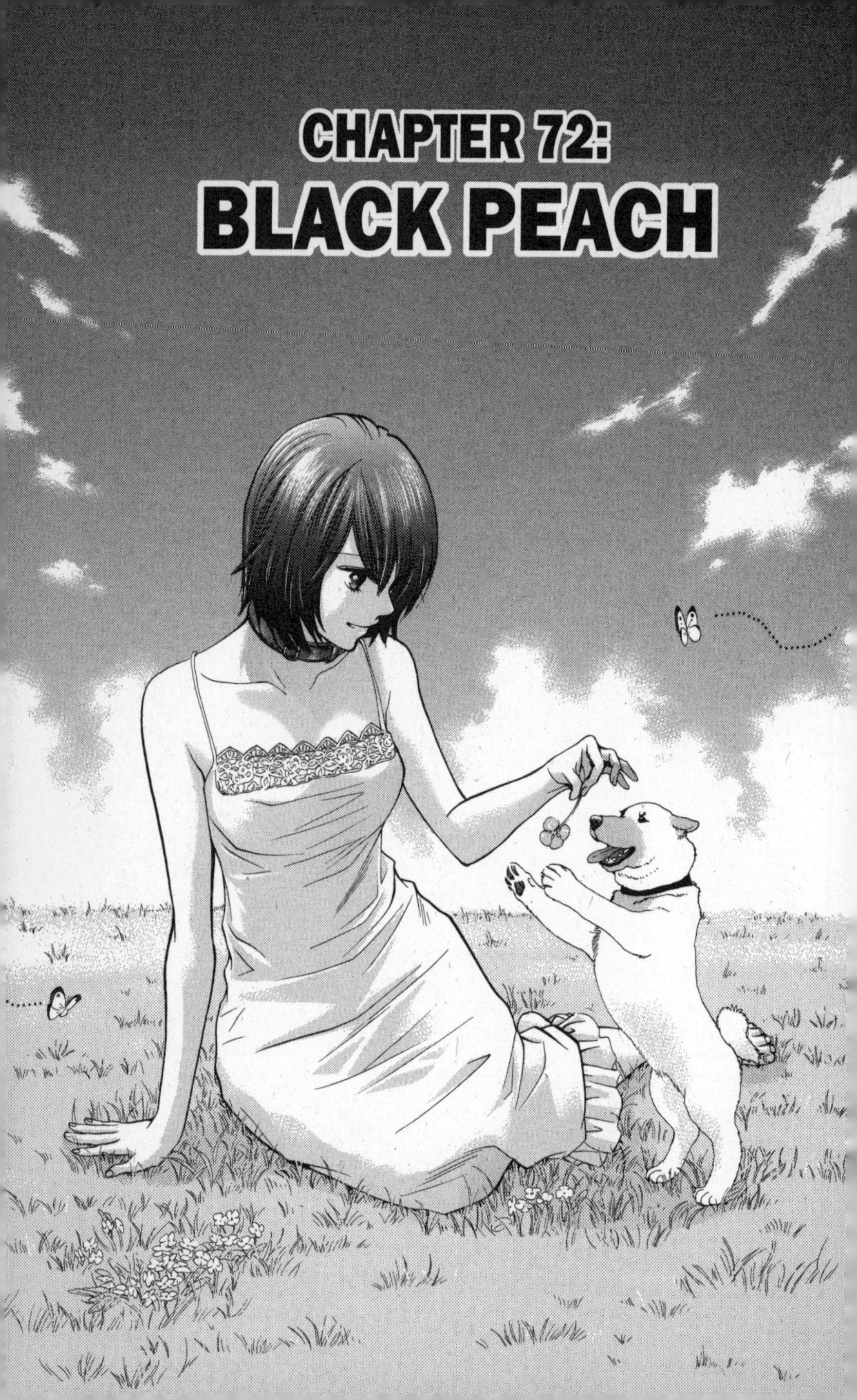
CHAPTER 72:
BLACK PEACH

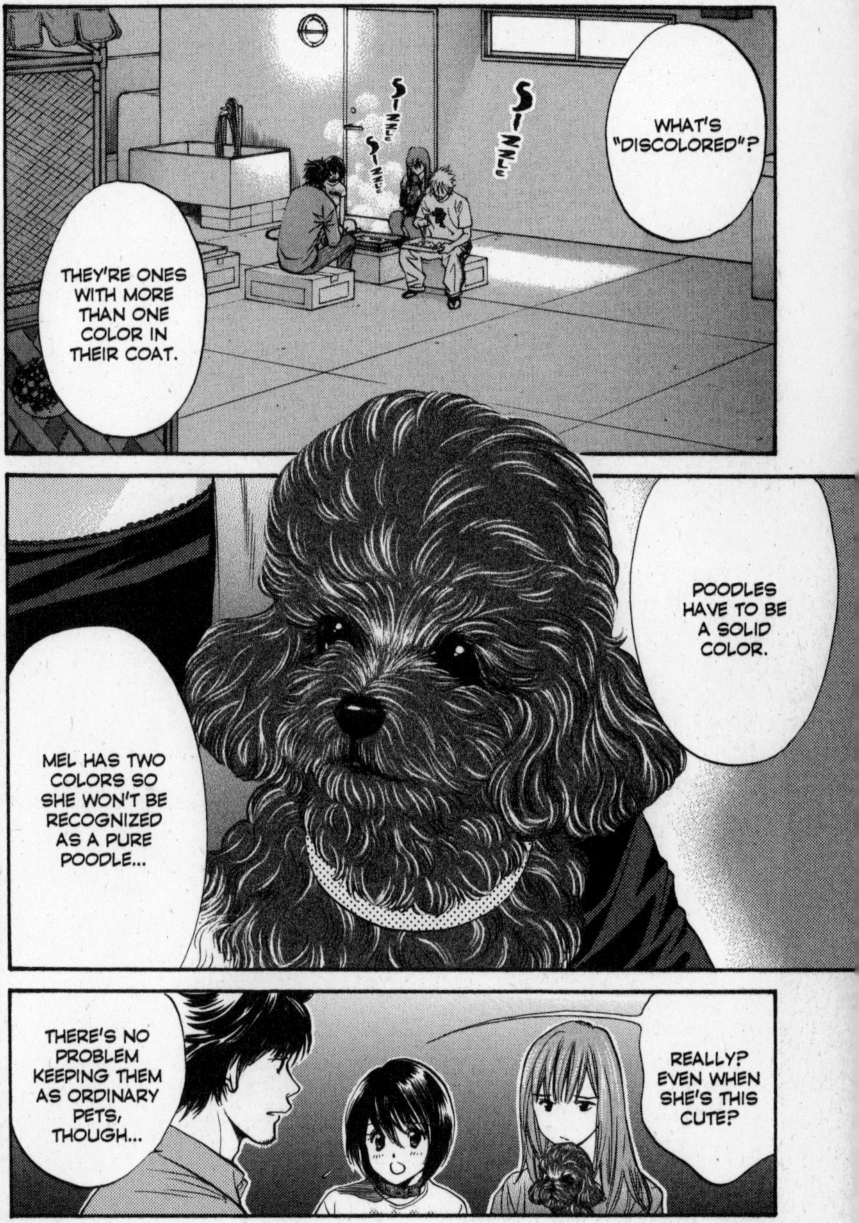
WHAT'S "DISCOLORED"?
SIZZLE
SIZZLE
SIZZLE
THEY'RE ONES WITH MORE THAN ONE COLOR IN THEIR COAT.
POODLES HAVE TO BE A SOLID COLOR.
MEL HAS TWO COLORS SO SHE WON'T BE RECOGNIZED AS A PURE POODLE...
REALLY? EVEN WHEN SHE'S THIS CUTE?
THERE'S NO PROBLEM KEEPING THEM AS ORDINARY PETS, THOUGH...

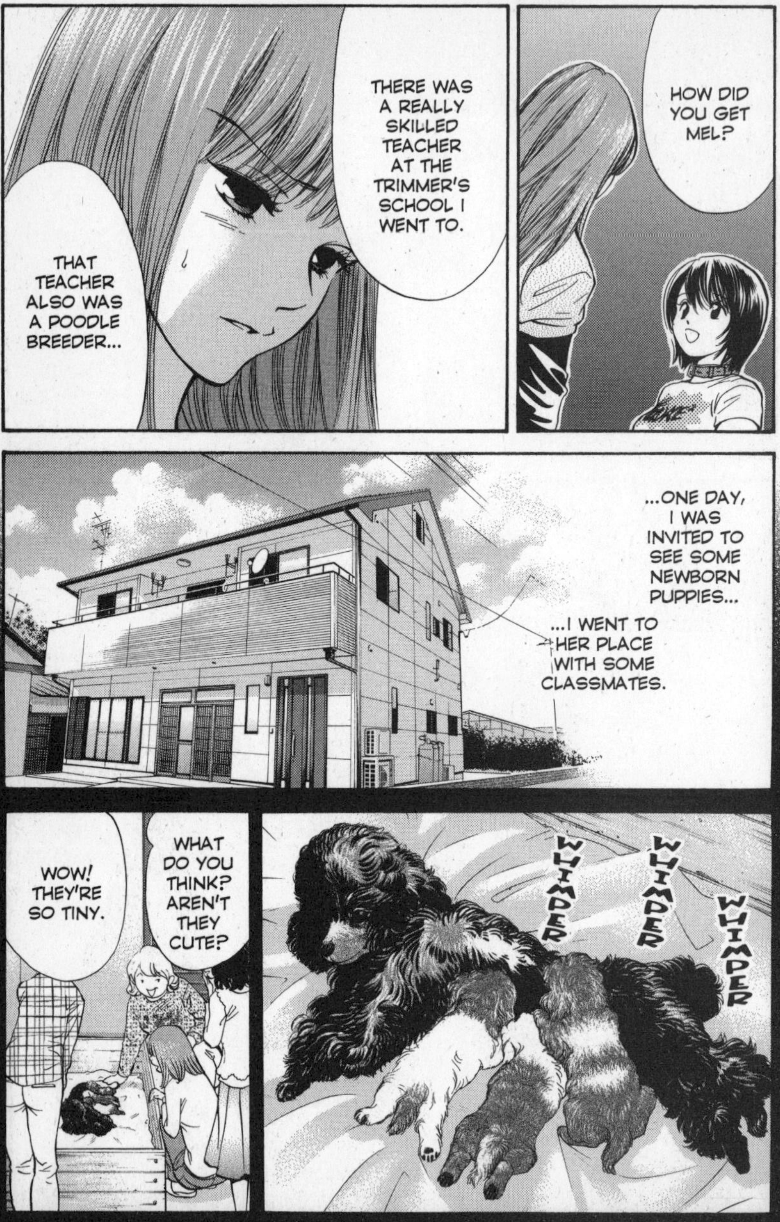
HOW DID YOU GET MEL?
THERE WAS A REALLY SKILLED TEACHER AT THE TRIMMER'S SCHOOL I WENT TO.
THAT TEACHER ALSO WAS A POODLE BREEDER...
...ONE DAY, I WAS INVITED TO SEE SOME NEWBORN PUPPIES...
...I WENT TO HER PLACE WITH SOME CLASSMATES.
WHIMPER
WHIMPER
WHIMPER
WHAT DO YOU THINK? AREN'T THEY CUTE?
WOW! THEY'RE SO TINY.

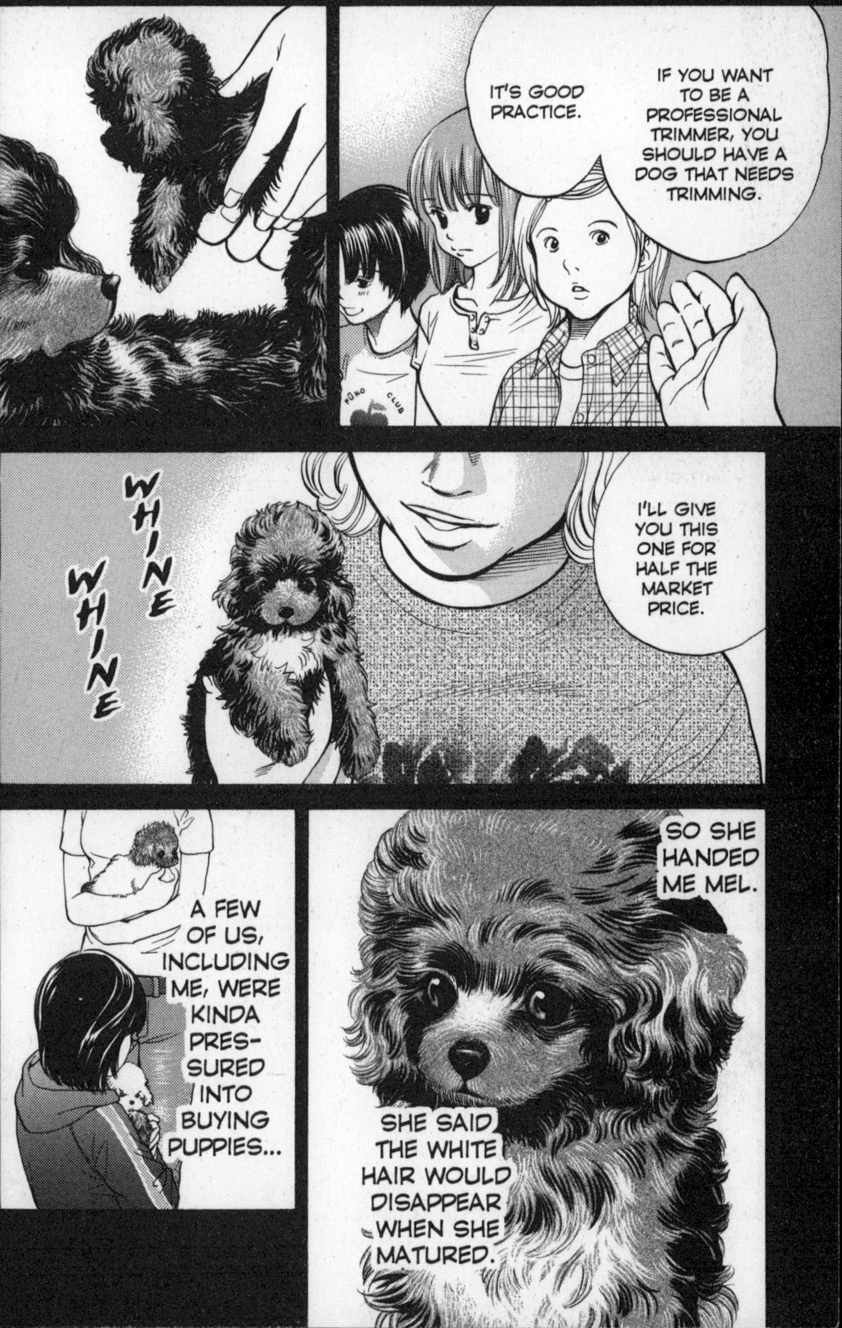
IF YOU WANT TO BE A PROFESSIONAL TRIMMER, YOU SHOULD HAVE A DOG THAT NEEDS TRIMMING.
IT'S GOOD PRACTICE.
I'LL GIVE YOU THIS ONE FOR HALF THE MARKET PRICE.
WHINE
WHINE
SO SHE HANDED ME MEL.
SHE SAID THE WHITE HAIR WOULD DISAPPEAR WHEN SHE MATURED.
A FEW OF US, INCLUDING ME, WERE KINDA PRES-SURED INTO BUYING PUPPIES...

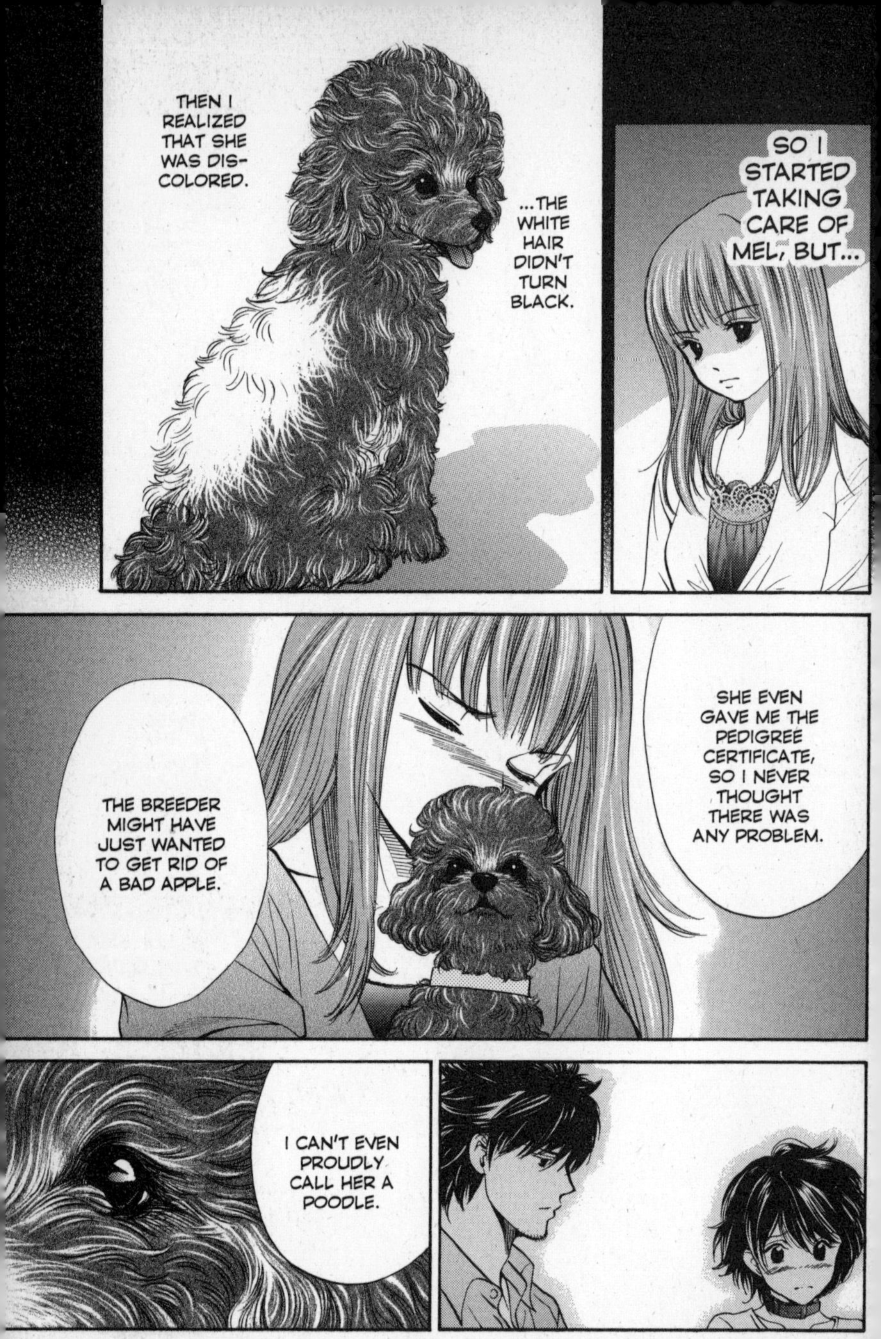
SO I STARTED TAKING CARE OF MEL, BUT...
THEN I REALIZED THAT SHE WAS DIS-COLORED.
...THE WHITE HAIR DIDN'T TURN BLACK.
SHE EVEN GAVE ME THE PEDIGREE CERTIFICATE, SO I NEVER THOUGHT THERE WAS ANY PROBLEM.
THE BREEDER MIGHT HAVE JUST WANTED TO GET RID OF A BAD APPLE.
I CAN'T EVEN PROUDLY CALL HER A POODLE.

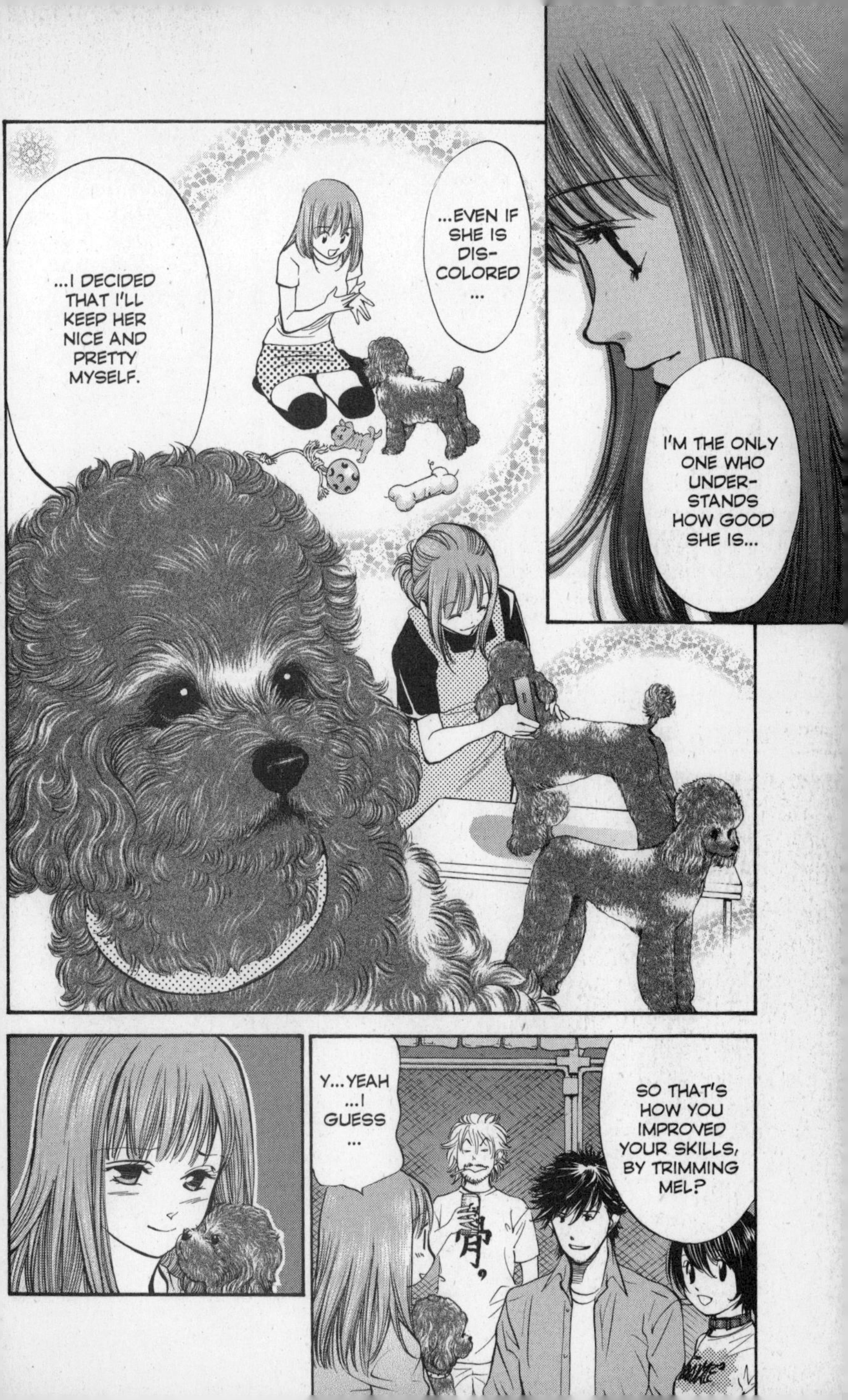
I'M THE ONLY ONE WHO UNDER-STANDS HOW GOOD SHE IS...
...EVEN IF SHE IS DIS-COLORED ...
...I DECIDED THAT I'LL KEEP HER NICE AND PRETTY MYSELF.
SO THAT'S HOW YOU IMPROVED YOUR SKILLS, BY TRIMMING MEL?
Y...YEAH ...I GUESS ...

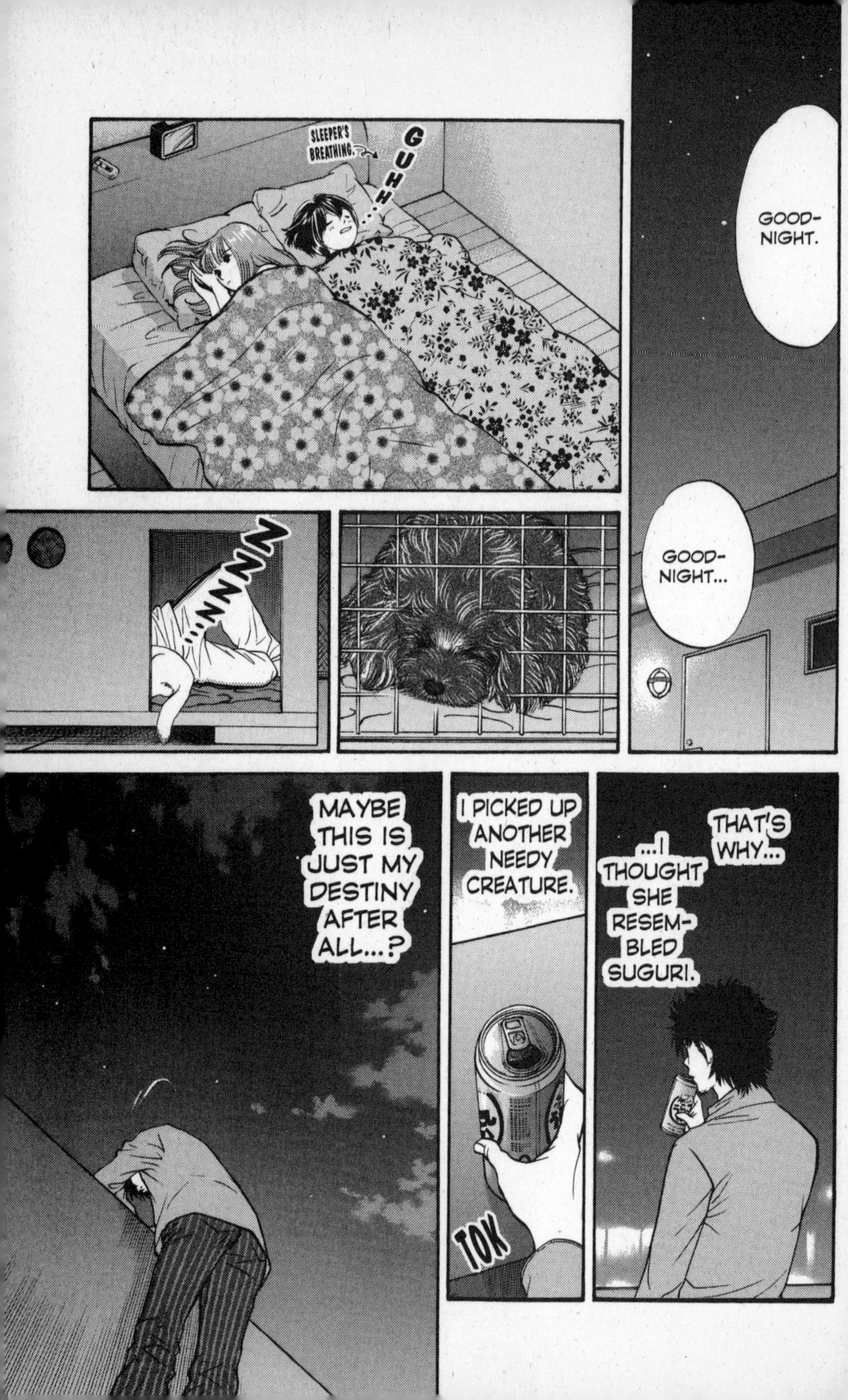
GOOD-NIGHT.
GOOD-NIGHT...
SLEEPER'S BREATHING.
GUHH...
ZNNNN...
THAT'S WHY...
...I THOUGHT SHE RESEMBLED SUGURI.
I PICKED UP ANOTHER NEEDY CREATURE.
TOK
MAYBE THIS IS JUST MY DESTINY AFTER ALL...?

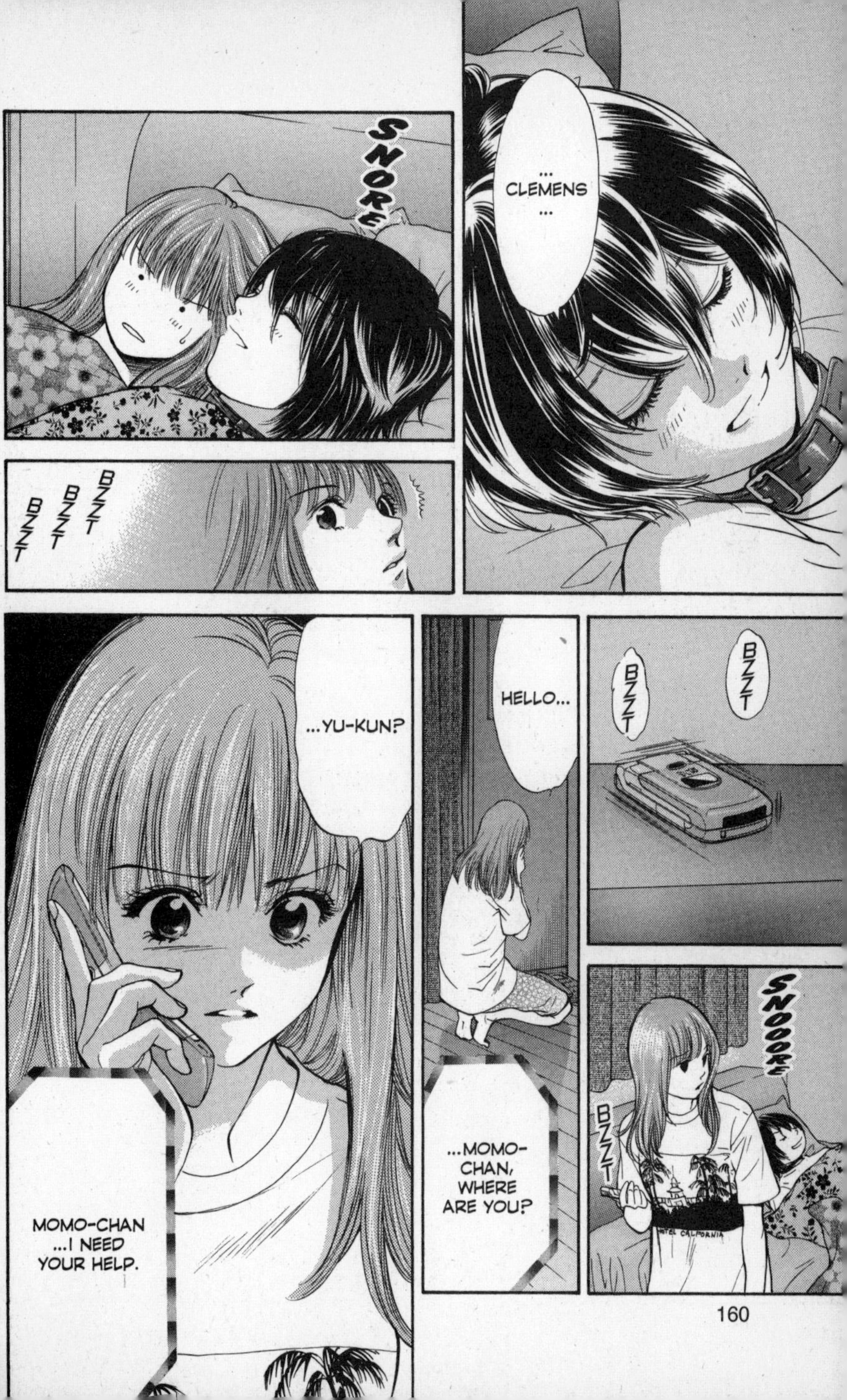

... CLEMENS ...
SNORE
BZZT BZZT BZZT
BZZT BZZT
SNOOORE
BZZT
HELLO...
...MOMO-CHAN, WHERE ARE YOU?
...YU-KUN?
MOMO-CHAN ...I NEED YOUR HELP.

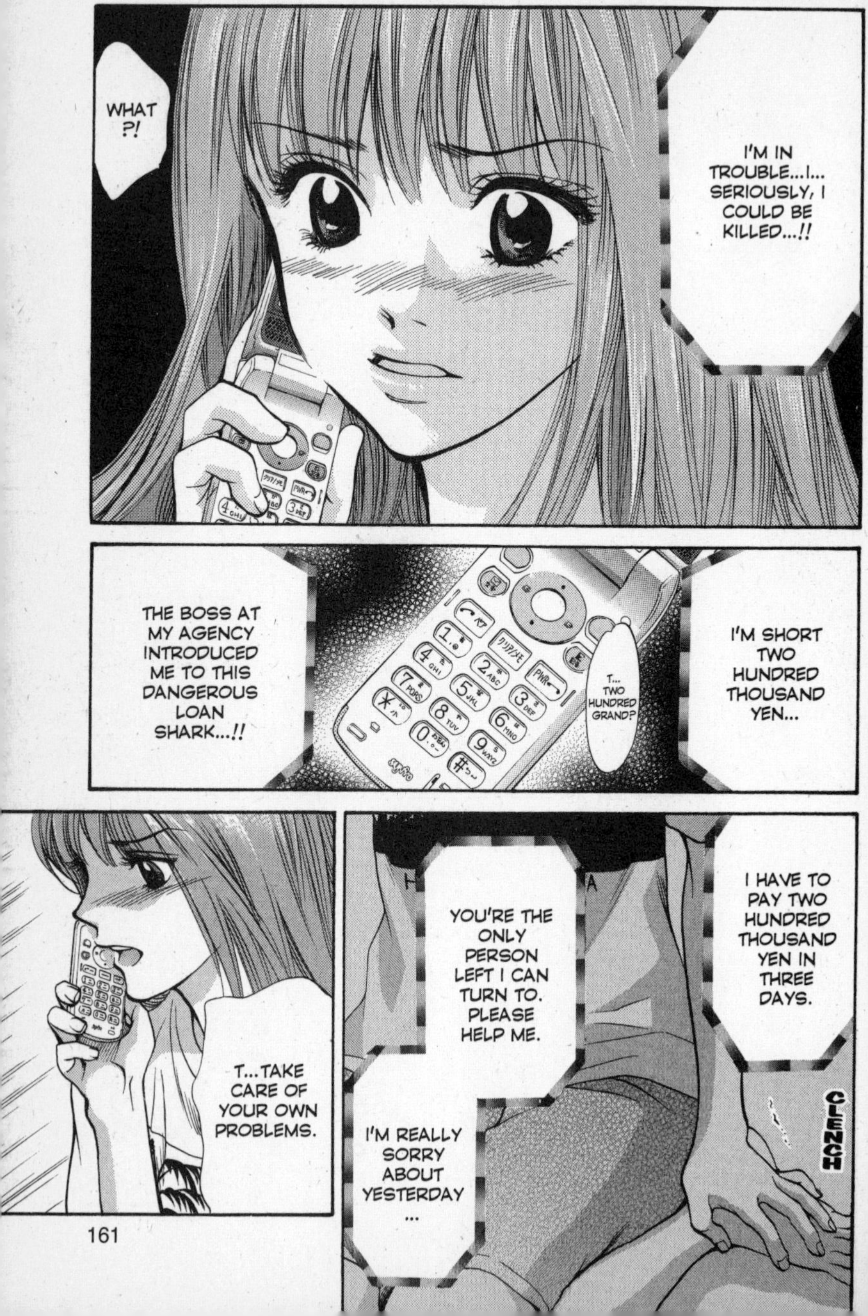
I'M IN TROUBLE...I... SERIOUSLY, I COULD BE KILLED...!!
WHAT?!
I'M SHORT TWO HUNDRED THOUSAND YEN...
T... TWO HUNDRED GRAND?
THE BOSS AT MY AGENCY INTRODUCED ME TO THIS DANGEROUS LOAN SHARK...!!
I HAVE TO PAY TWO HUNDRED THOUSAND YEN IN THREE DAYS.
YOU'RE THE ONLY PERSON LEFT I CAN TURN TO. PLEASE HELP ME.
CLENCH
I'M REALLY SORRY ABOUT YESTERDAY ...
T...TAKE CARE OF YOUR OWN PROBLEMS.

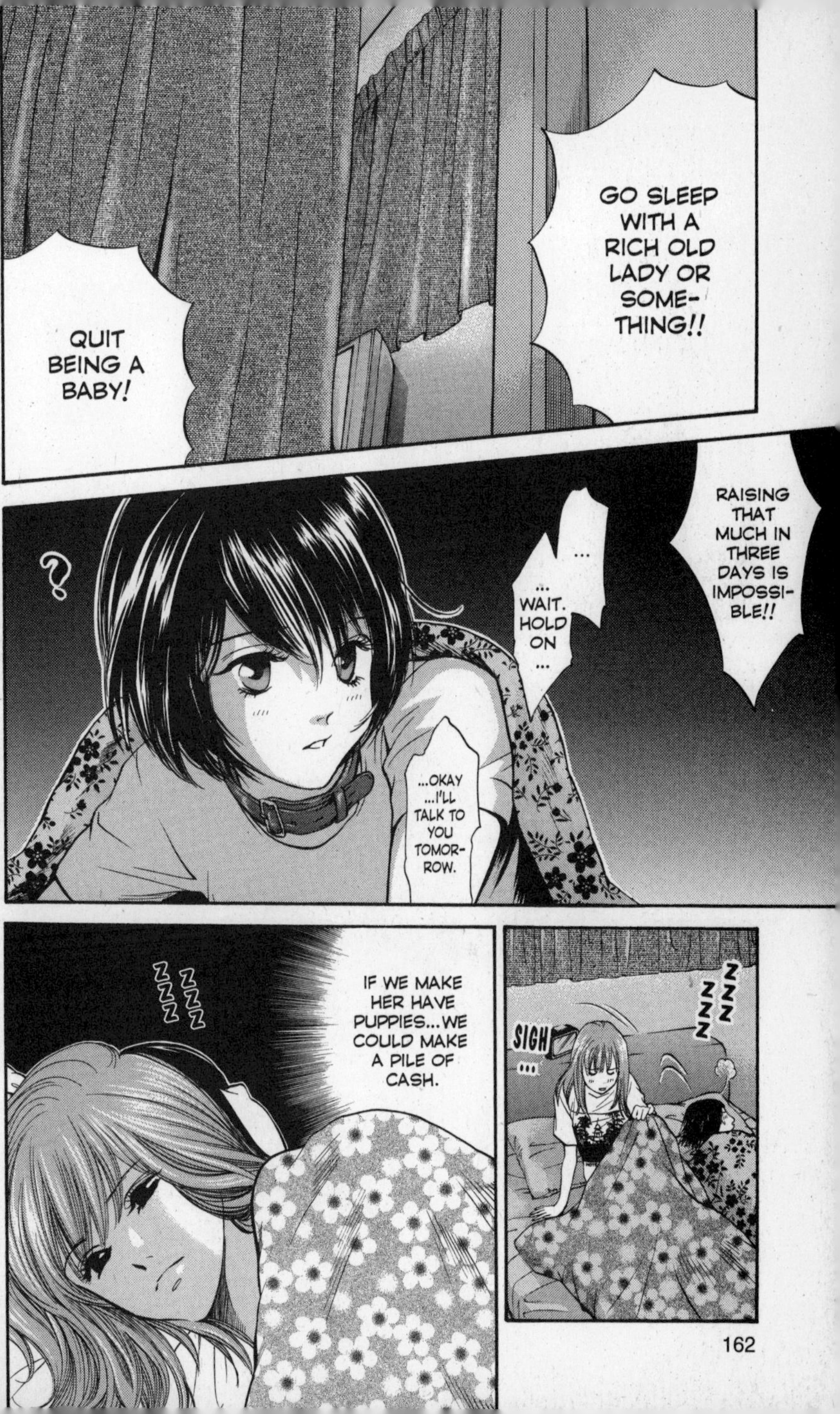
GO SLEEP WITH A RICH OLD LADY OR SOME-THING!!
QUIT BEING A BABY!
RAISING THAT MUCH IN THREE DAYS IS IMPOSSI-BLE!!
...
... WAIT. HOLD ON ...
...OKAY ...I'LL TALK TO YOU TOMOR-ROW.
?
Z Z Z Z
SIGH ...
IF WE MAKE HER HAVE PUPPIES...WE COULD MAKE A PILE OF CASH.
Z Z Z Z Z Z

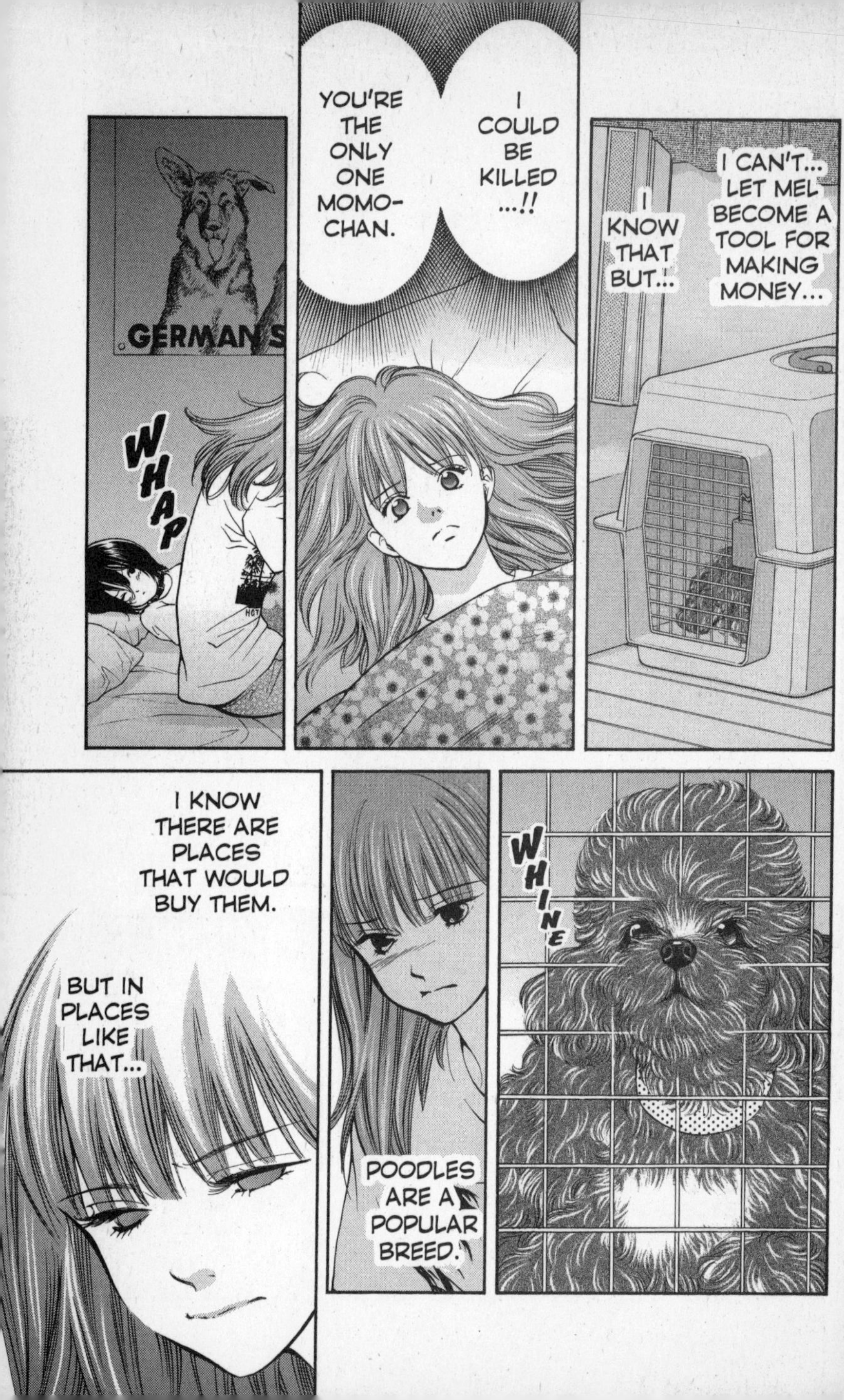
I CAN'T... LET MEL BECOME A TOOL FOR MAKING MONEY...
I KNOW THAT BUT...
I COULD BE KILLED ...!!
YOU'RE THE ONLY ONE MOMO-CHAN.
GERMAN S
WHAP
WHINE
POODLES ARE A POPULAR BREED.
I KNOW THERE ARE PLACES THAT WOULD BUY THEM.
BUT IN PLACES LIKE THAT...

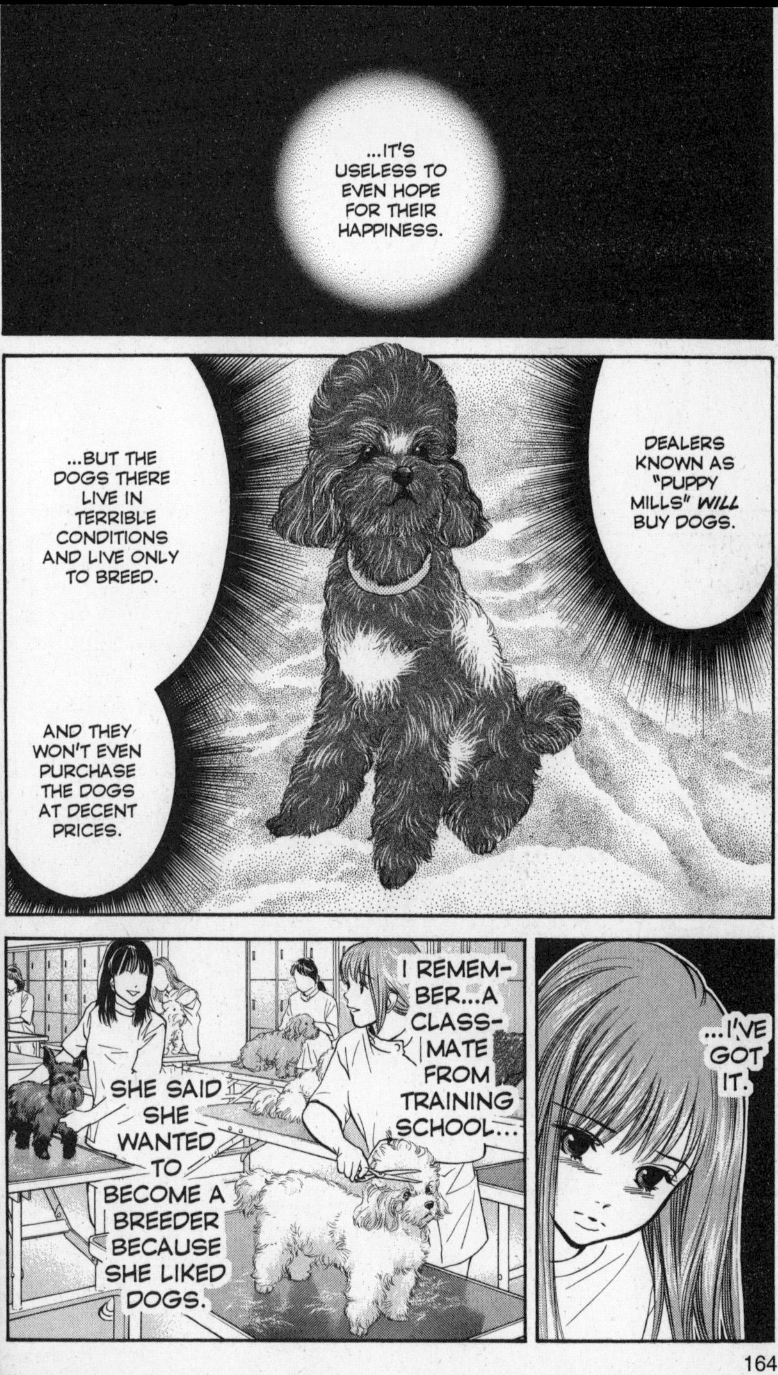
...IT'S USELESS TO EVEN HOPE FOR THEIR HAPPINESS.
DEALERS KNOWN AS "PUPPY MILLS" *WILL* BUY DOGS.
...BUT THE DOGS THERE LIVE IN TERRIBLE CONDITIONS AND LIVE ONLY TO BREED.
AND THEY WON'T EVEN PURCHASE THE DOGS AT DECENT PRICES.
...I'VE GOT IT.
I REMEMBER...A CLASSMATE FROM TRAINING SCHOOL...
SHE SAID SHE WANTED TO BECOME A BREEDER BECAUSE SHE LIKED DOGS.

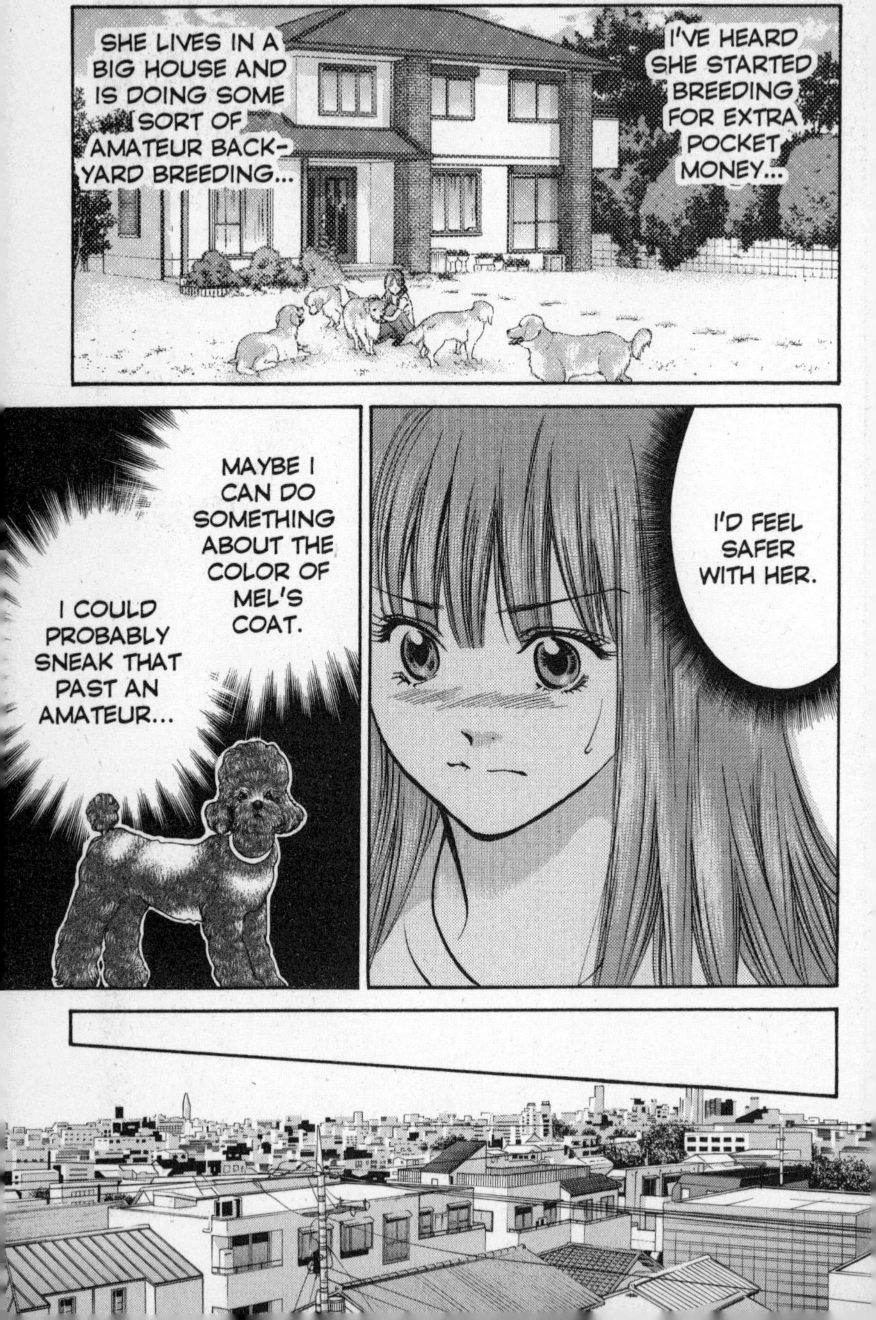
I'VE HEARD SHE STARTED BREEDING FOR EXTRA POCKET MONEY...
SHE LIVES IN A BIG HOUSE AND IS DOING SOME SORT OF AMATEUR BACK-YARD BREEDING...
I'D FEEL SAFER WITH HER.
MAYBE I CAN DO SOMETHING ABOUT THE COLOR OF MEL'S COAT.
I COULD PROBABLY SNEAK THAT PAST AN AMATEUR...

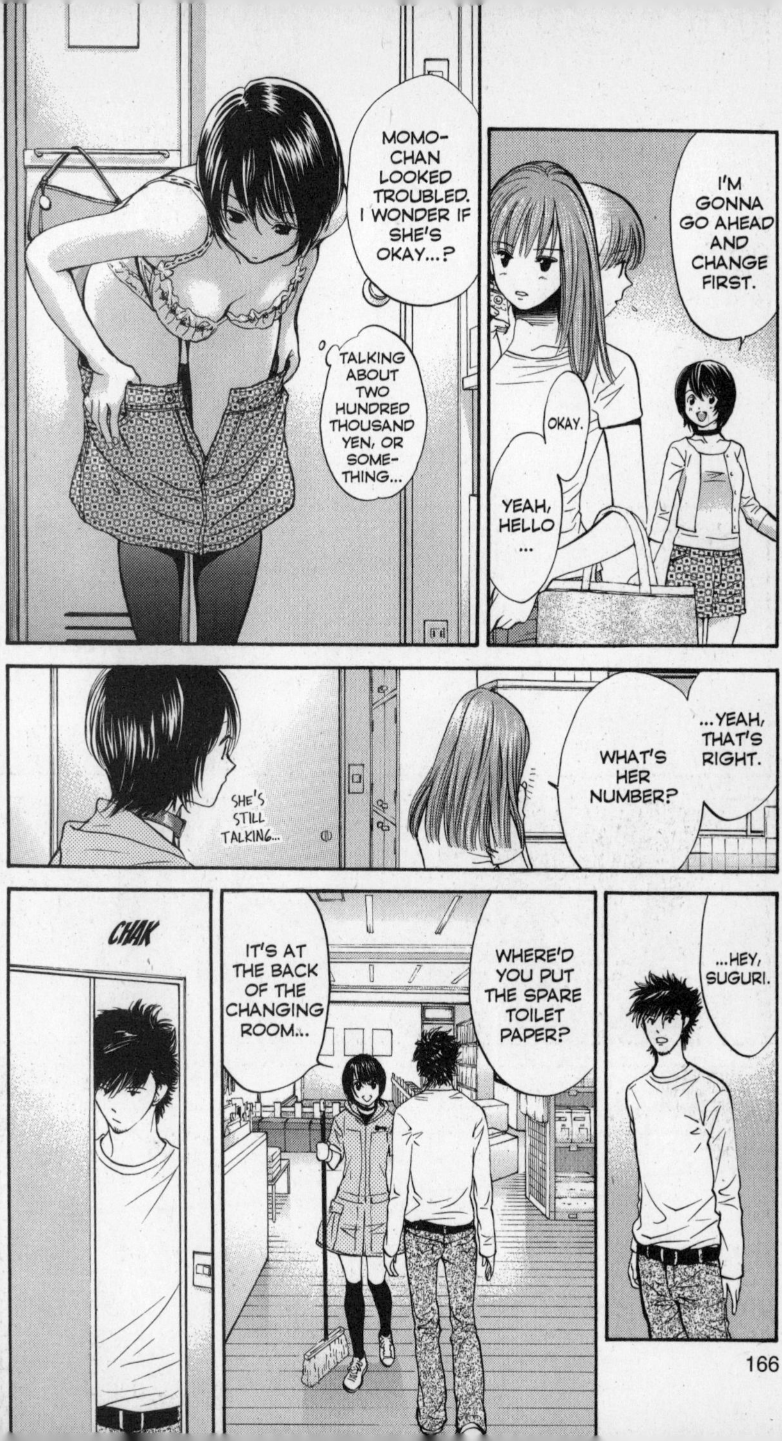
I'M GONNA GO AHEAD AND CHANGE FIRST.
OKAY.
YEAH, HELLO...
MOMO-CHAN LOOKED TROUBLED. I WONDER IF SHE'S OKAY...?
TALKING ABOUT TWO HUNDRED THOUSAND YEN, OR SOME-THING...
...YEAH, THAT'S RIGHT.
WHAT'S HER NUMBER?
SHE'S STILL TALKING...
...HEY, SUGURI.
WHERE'D YOU PUT THE SPARE TOILET PAPER?
IT'S AT THE BACK OF THE CHANGING ROOM...
CHAK

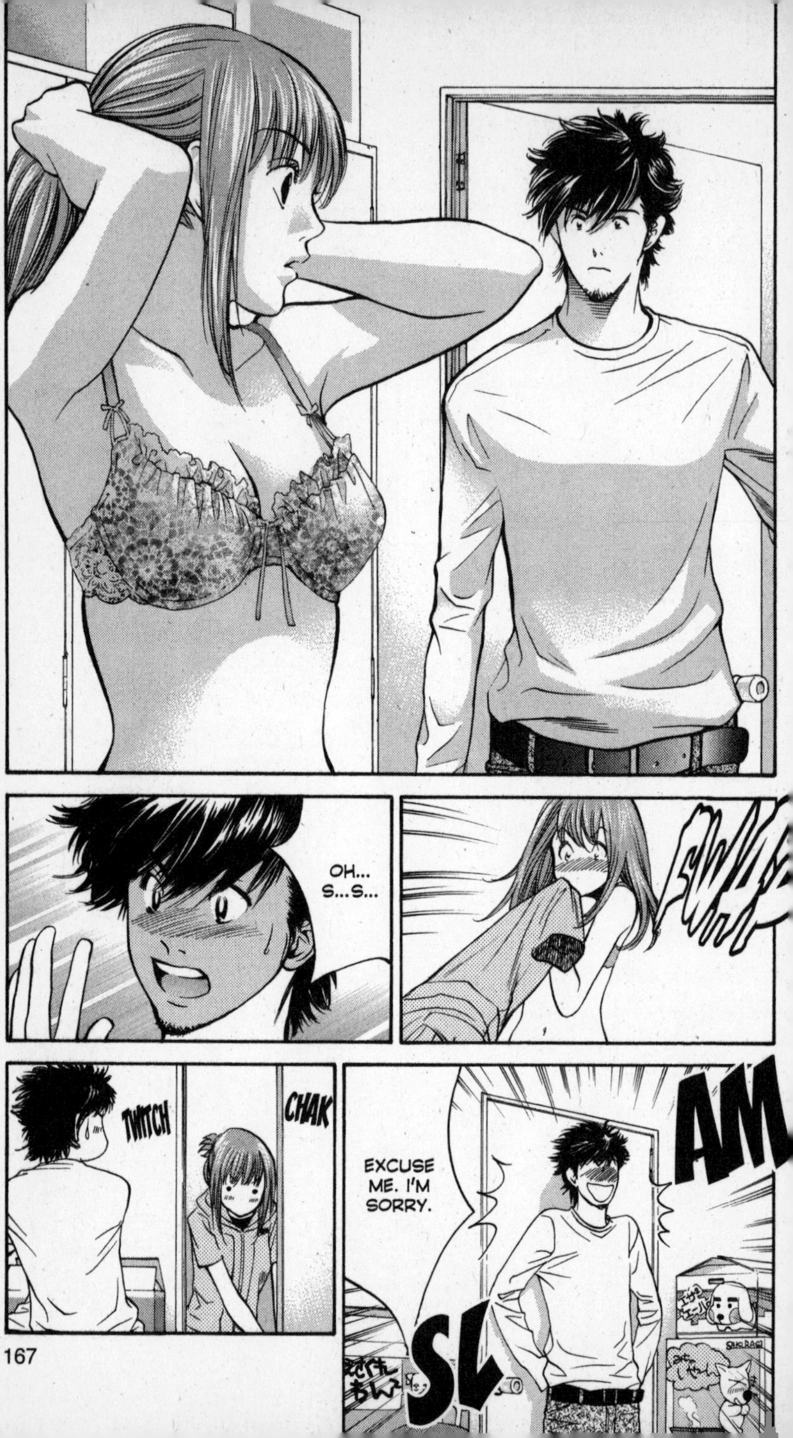
OH... S...S...
EXCUSE ME. I'M SORRY.
AM
SL
CHAK
TWITCH

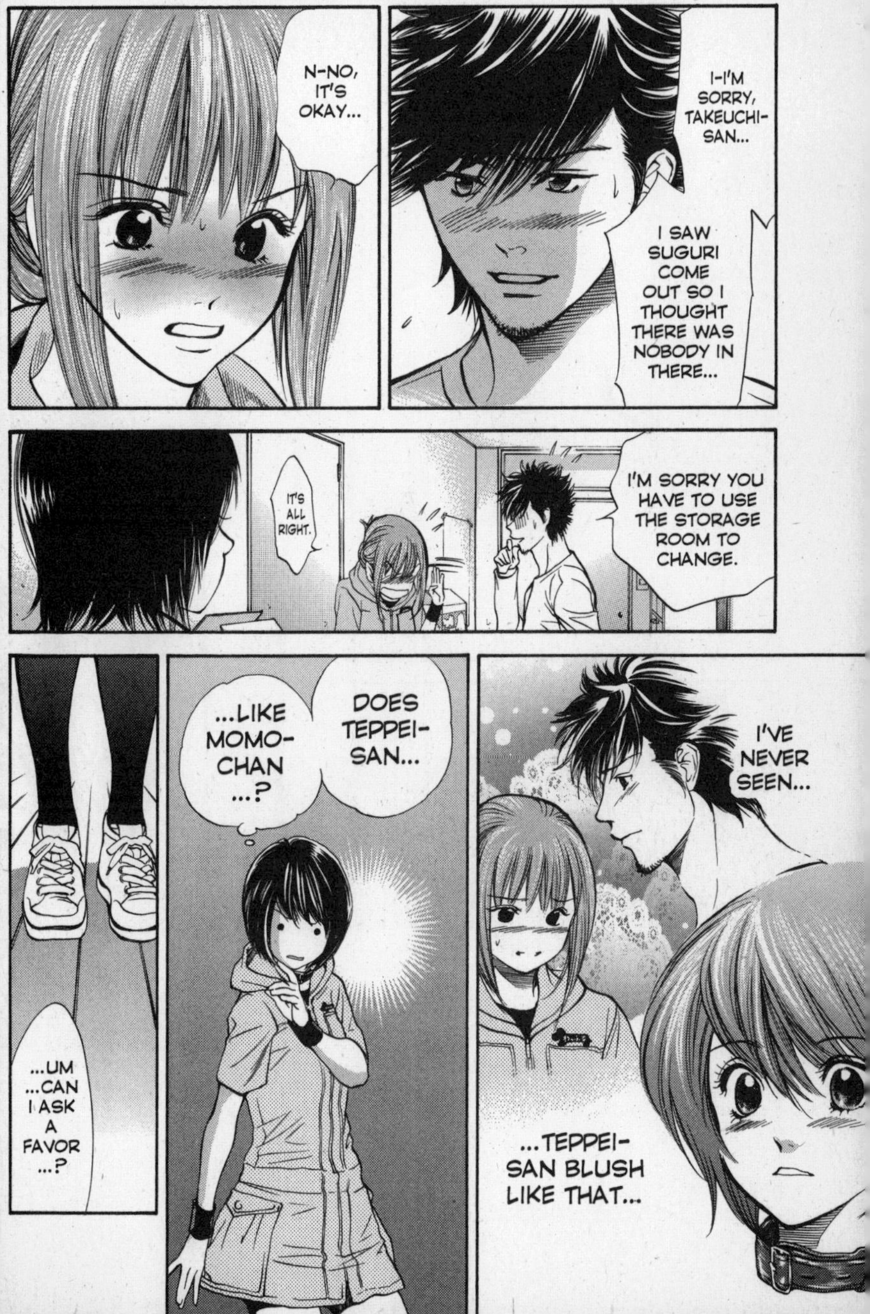
I-I'M SORRY, TAKEUCHI-SAN...
I SAW SUGURI COME OUT SO I THOUGHT THERE WAS NOBODY IN THERE...
N-NO, IT'S OKAY...
I'M SORRY YOU HAVE TO USE THE STORAGE ROOM TO CHANGE.
IT'S ALL RIGHT.
I'VE NEVER SEEN...
...TEPPEI-SAN BLUSH LIKE THAT...
DOES TEPPEI-SAN...
...LIKE MOMO-CHAN ...?
...UM ...CAN I ASK A FAVOR ...?

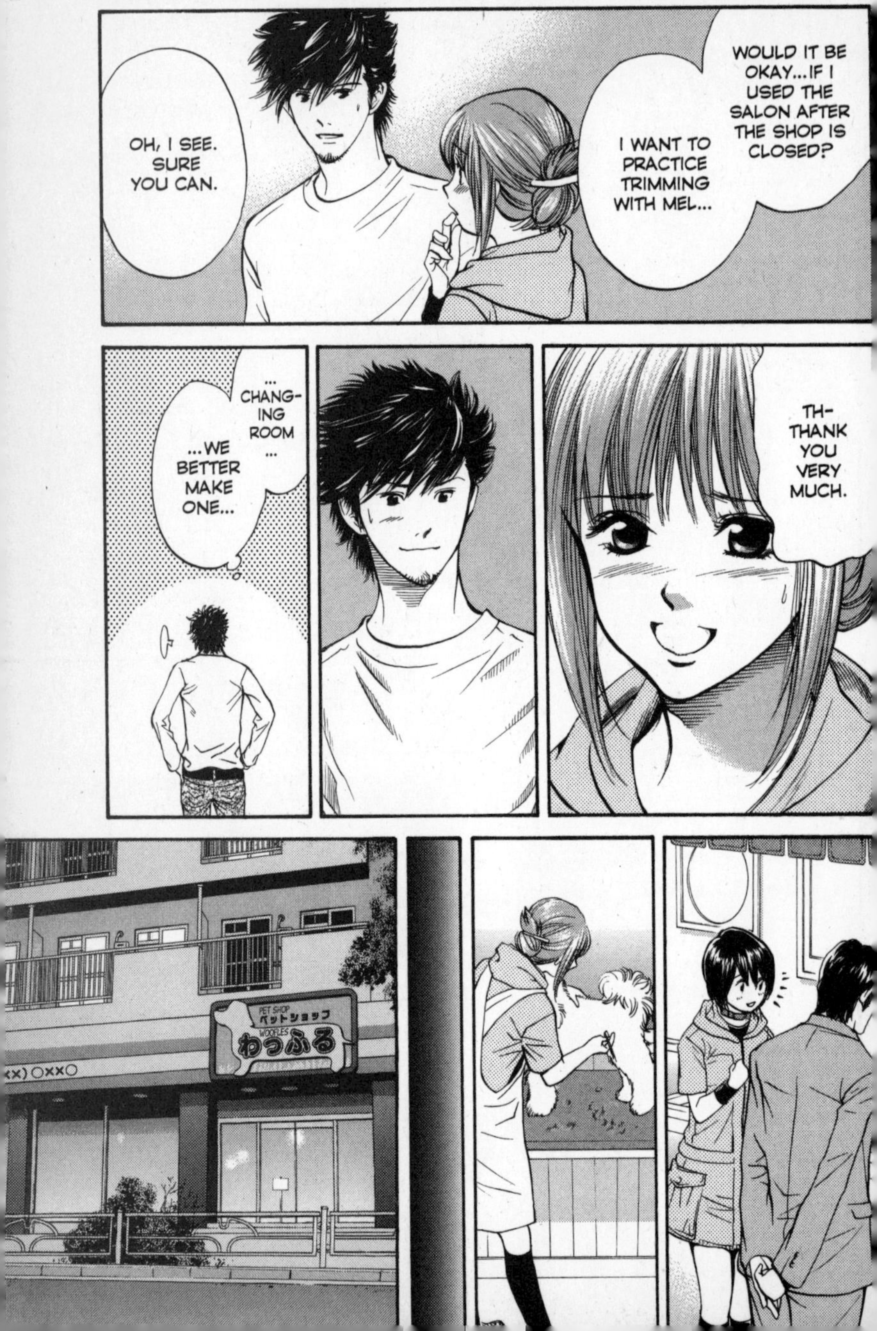
WOULD IT BE OKAY...IF I USED THE SALON AFTER THE SHOP IS CLOSED?
I WANT TO PRACTICE TRIMMING WITH MEL...
OH, I SEE. SURE YOU CAN.
TH-THANK YOU VERY MUCH.
... CHANGING ROOM ...
...WE BETTER MAKE ONE...
PET SHOP
ペットショップ
WOOFLES
わっふる

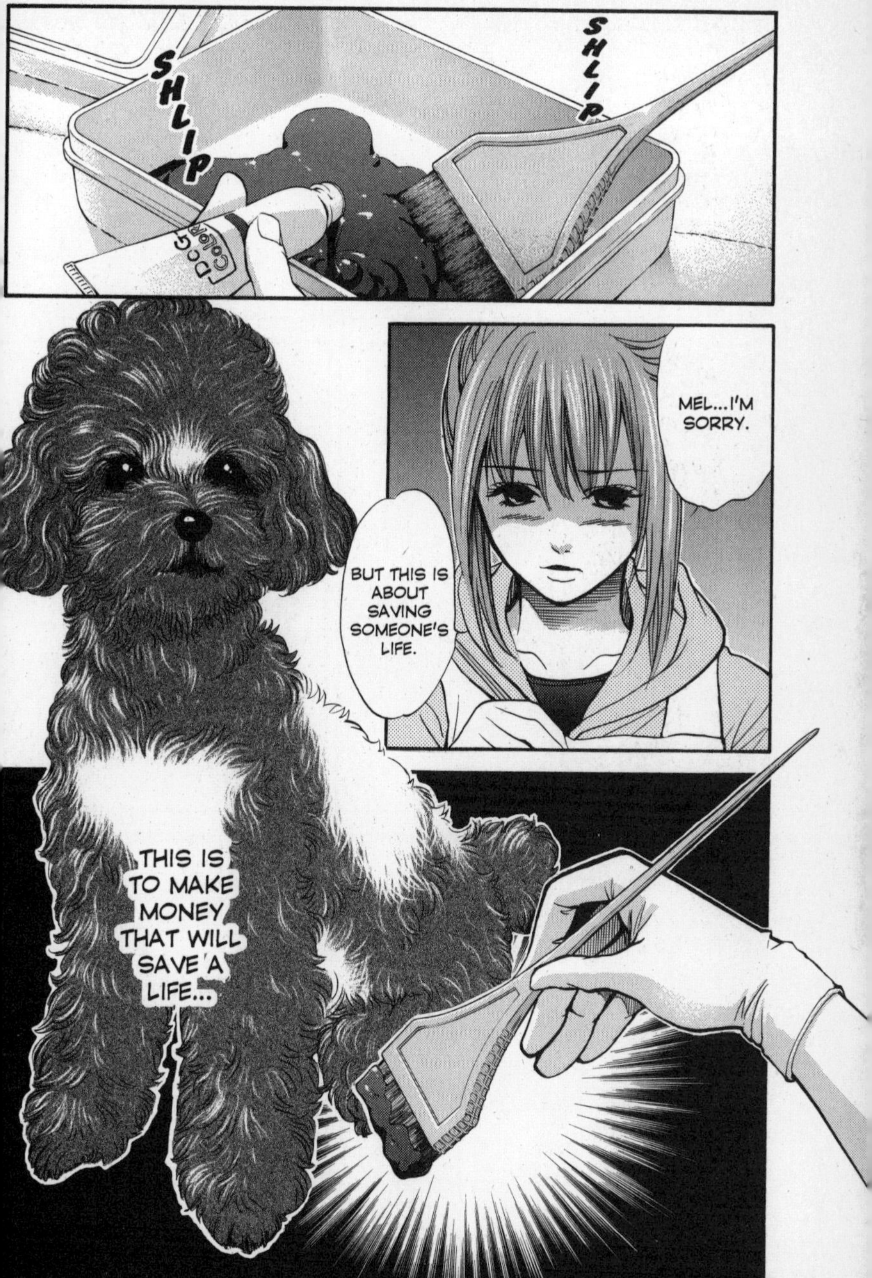
SHLIP
SHLIP
MEL...I'M SORRY.
BUT THIS IS ABOUT SAVING SOMEONE'S LIFE.
THIS IS TO MAKE MONEY THAT WILL SAVE A LIFE...

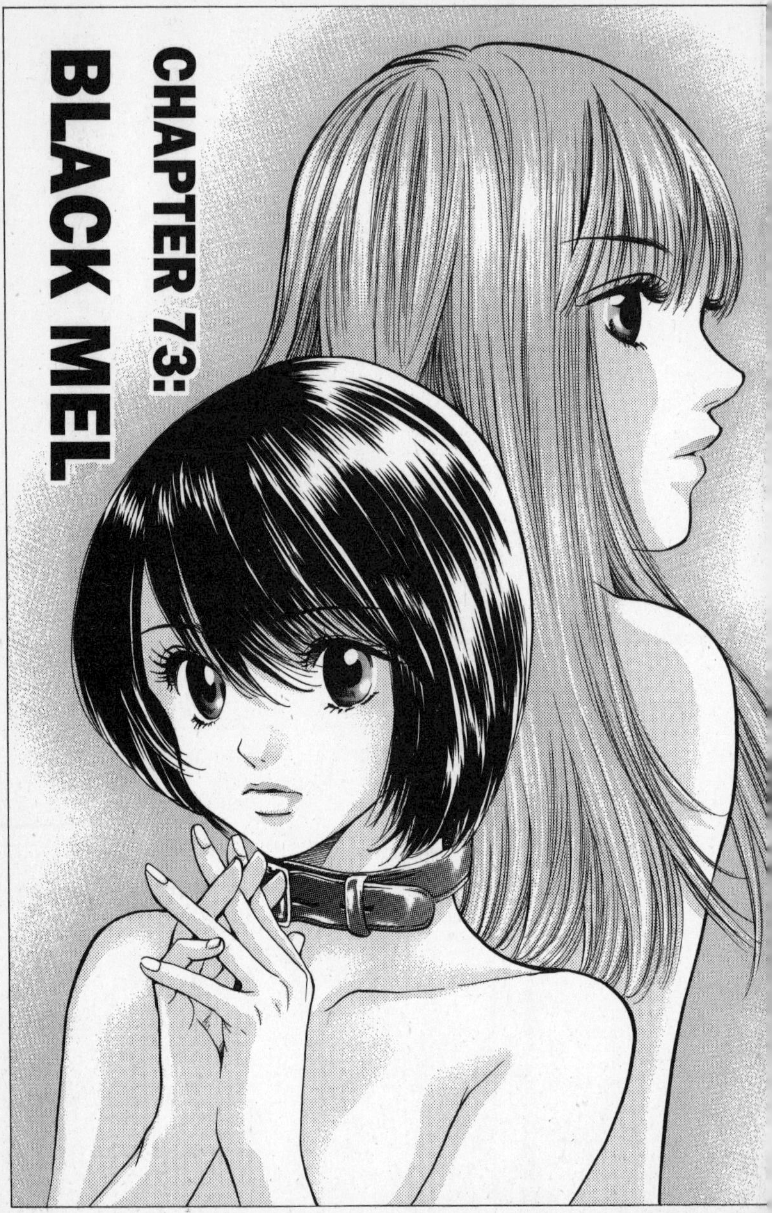
CHAPTER 73:
BLACK MEL

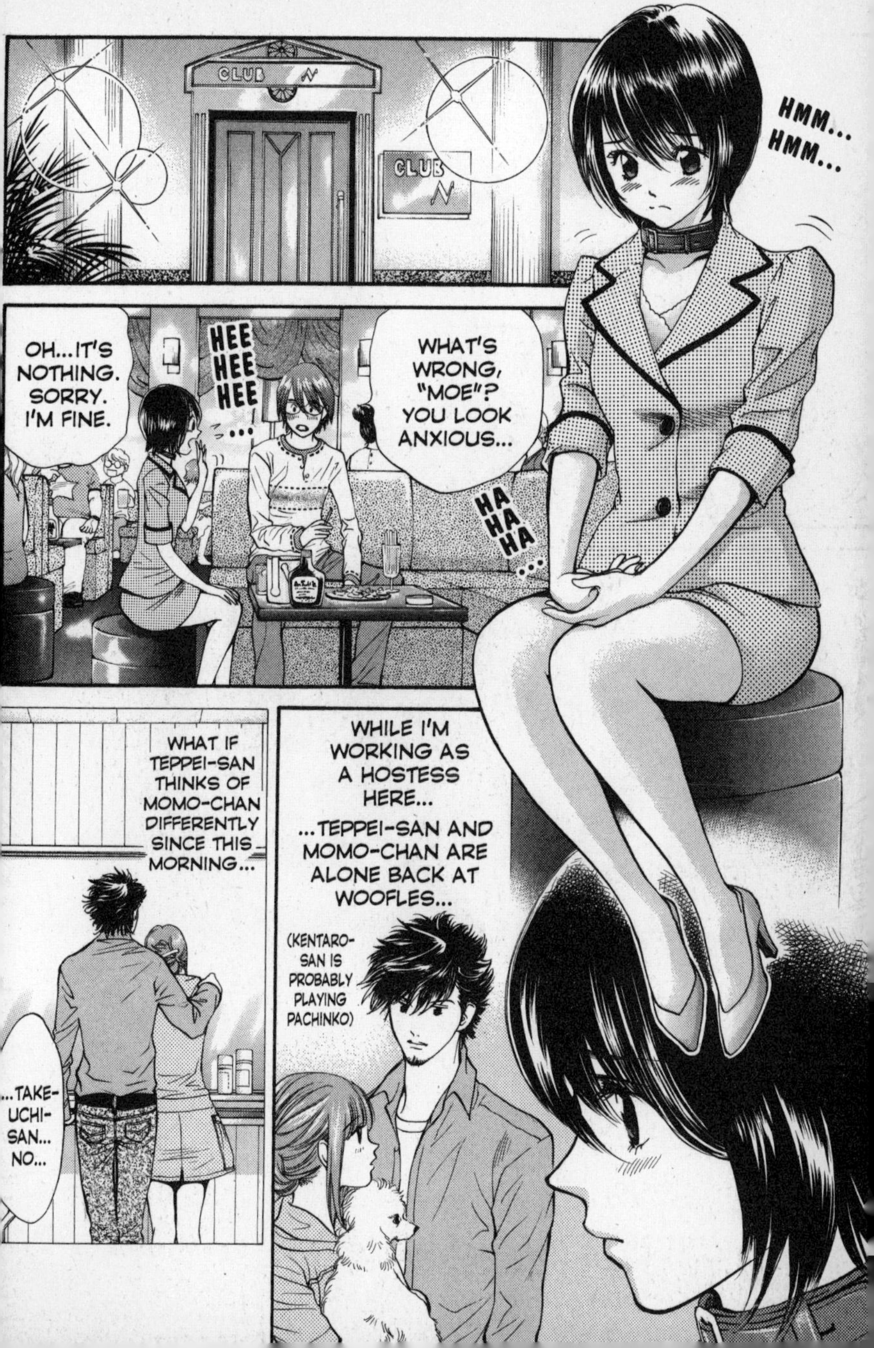
HMM... HMM...
CLUB
CLUB
WHAT'S WRONG, "MOE"? YOU LOOK ANXIOUS...
HA HA HA...
HEE HEE HEE...
OH...IT'S NOTHING. SORRY. I'M FINE.
WHILE I'M WORKING AS A HOSTESS HERE...
...TEPPEI-SAN AND MOMO-CHAN ARE ALONE BACK AT WOOFLES...
(KENTARO-SAN IS PROBABLY PLAYING PACHINKO)
WHAT IF TEPPEI-SAN THINKS OF MOMO-CHAN DIFFERENTLY SINCE THIS MORNING...
...TAKE-UCHI-SAN... NO...

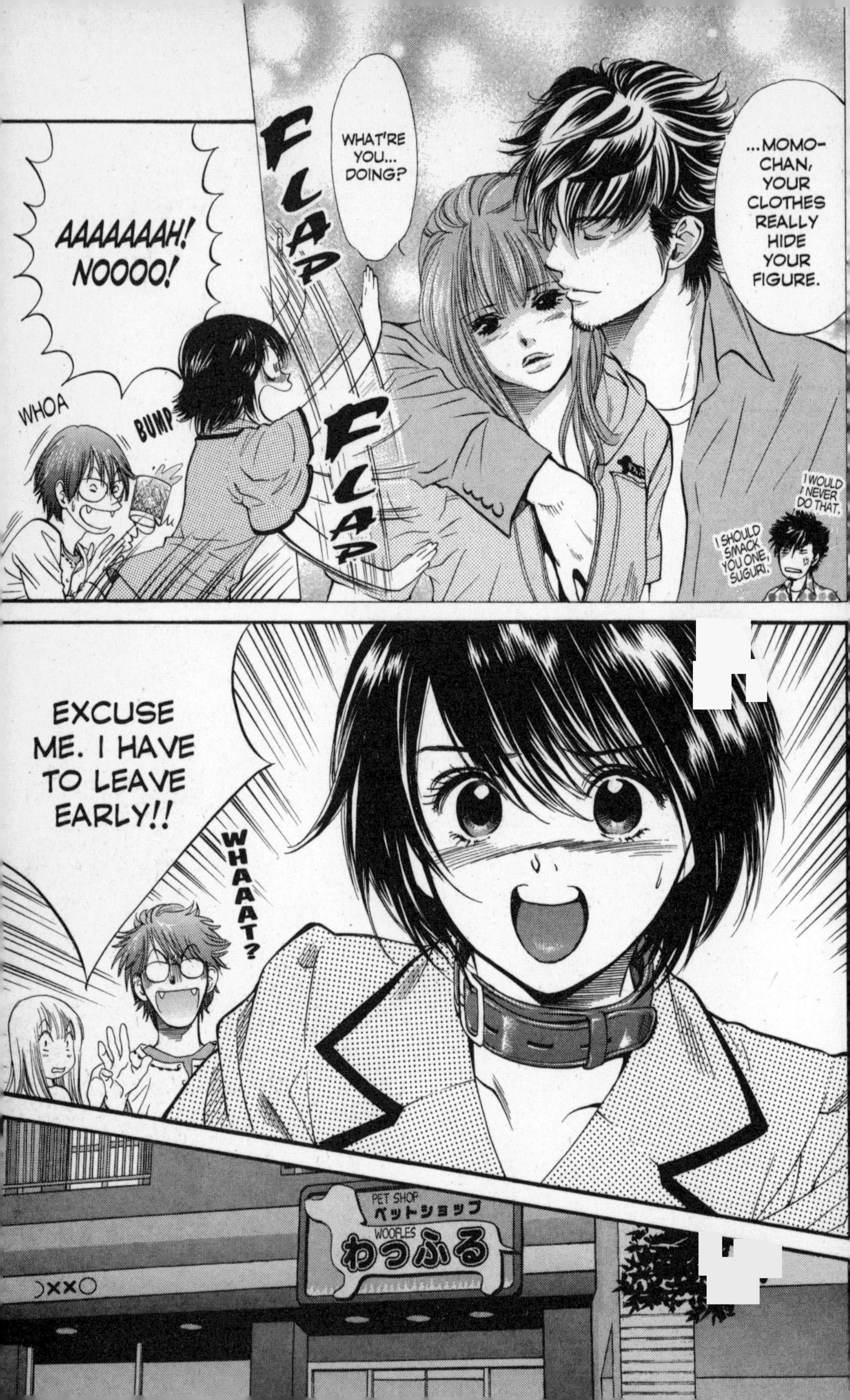
...MOMO-CHAN, YOUR CLOTHES REALLY HIDE YOUR FIGURE.
WHAT'RE YOU... DOING?
FLAP
FLAP
I WOULD NEVER DO THAT.
I SHOULD SMACK YOU ONE, SUGURI.
AAAAAAAH! NOOOO!
BUMP
WHOA
EXCUSE ME. I HAVE TO LEAVE EARLY!!
WHAAAT?
PET SHOP
ペットショップ
WOOFLES
わつふる

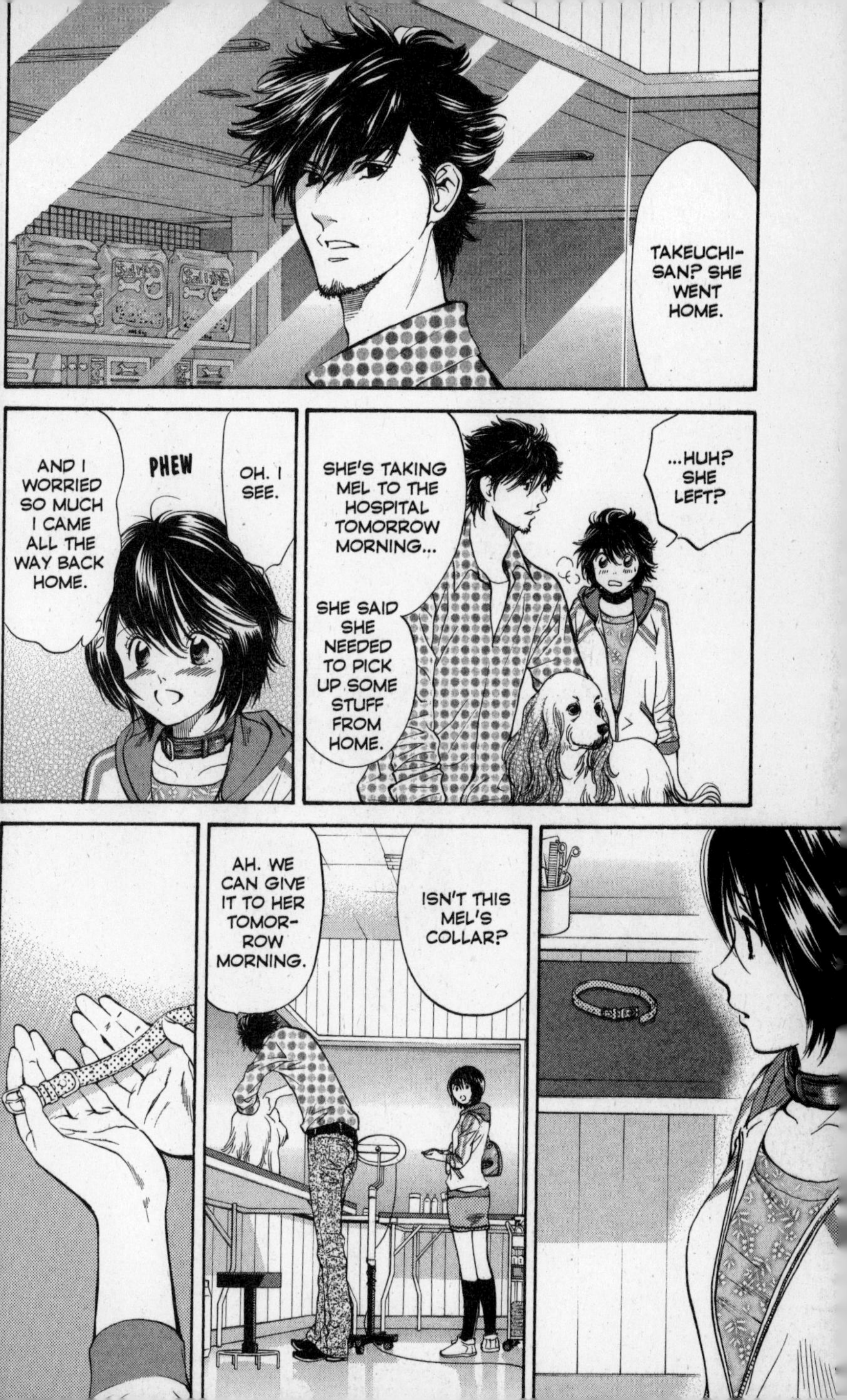
TAKEUCHI-SAN? SHE WENT HOME.
...HUH? SHE LEFT?
SHE'S TAKING MEL TO THE HOSPITAL TOMORROW MORNING...
SHE SAID SHE NEEDED TO PICK UP SOME STUFF FROM HOME.
OH. I SEE.
PHEW
AND I WORRIED SO MUCH I CAME ALL THE WAY BACK HOME.
ISN'T THIS MEL'S COLLAR?
AH. WE CAN GIVE IT TO HER TOMOR-ROW MORNING.

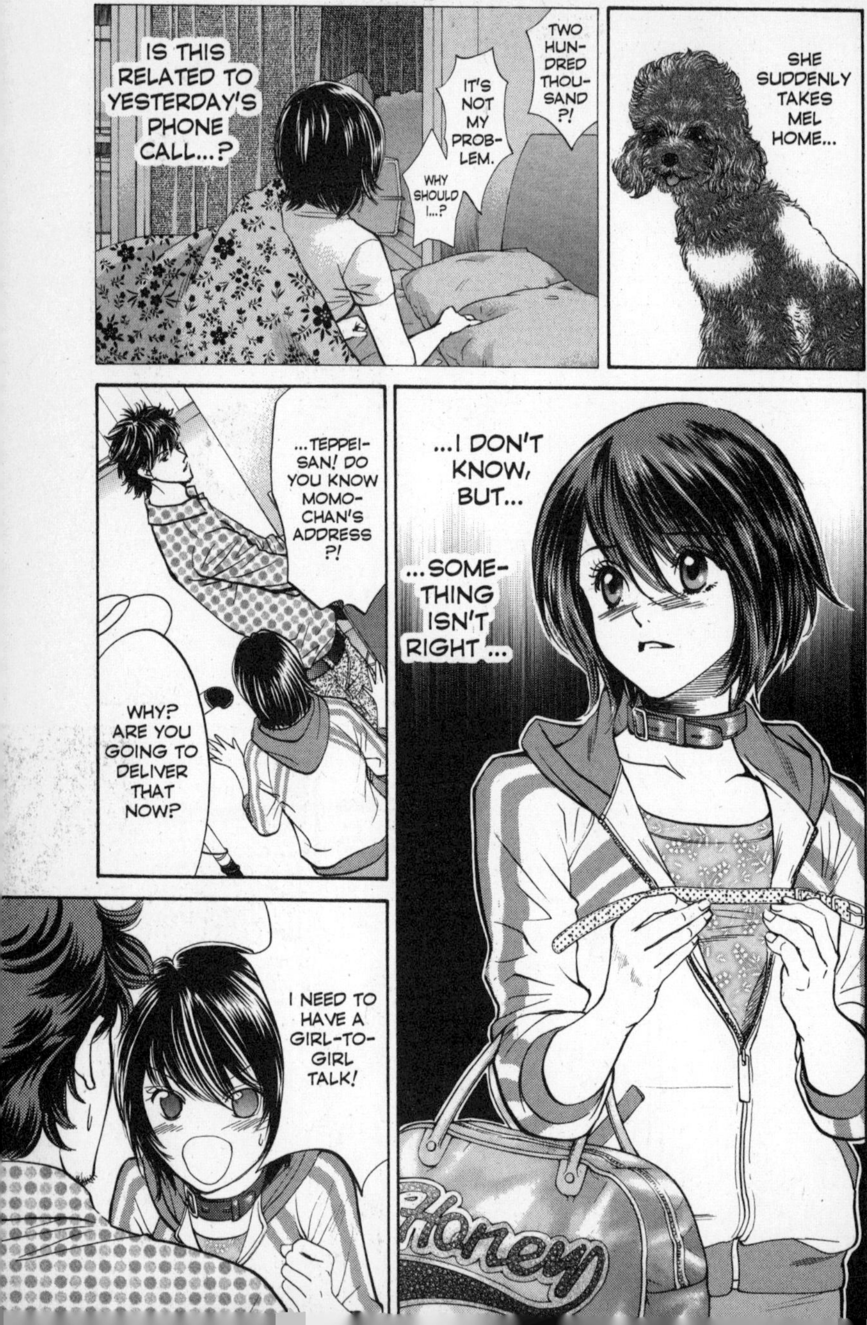
SHE SUDDENLY TAKES MEL HOME...
TWO HUNDRED THOUSAND ?!
IT'S NOT MY PROBLEM.
WHY SHOULD I...?
IS THIS RELATED TO YESTERDAY'S PHONE CALL...?
...I DON'T KNOW, BUT...
...SOMETHING ISN'T RIGHT...
Honey
...TEPPEI-SAN! DO YOU KNOW MOMO-CHAN'S ADDRESS ?!
WHY? ARE YOU GOING TO DELIVER THAT NOW?
I NEED TO HAVE A GIRL-TO-GIRL TALK!

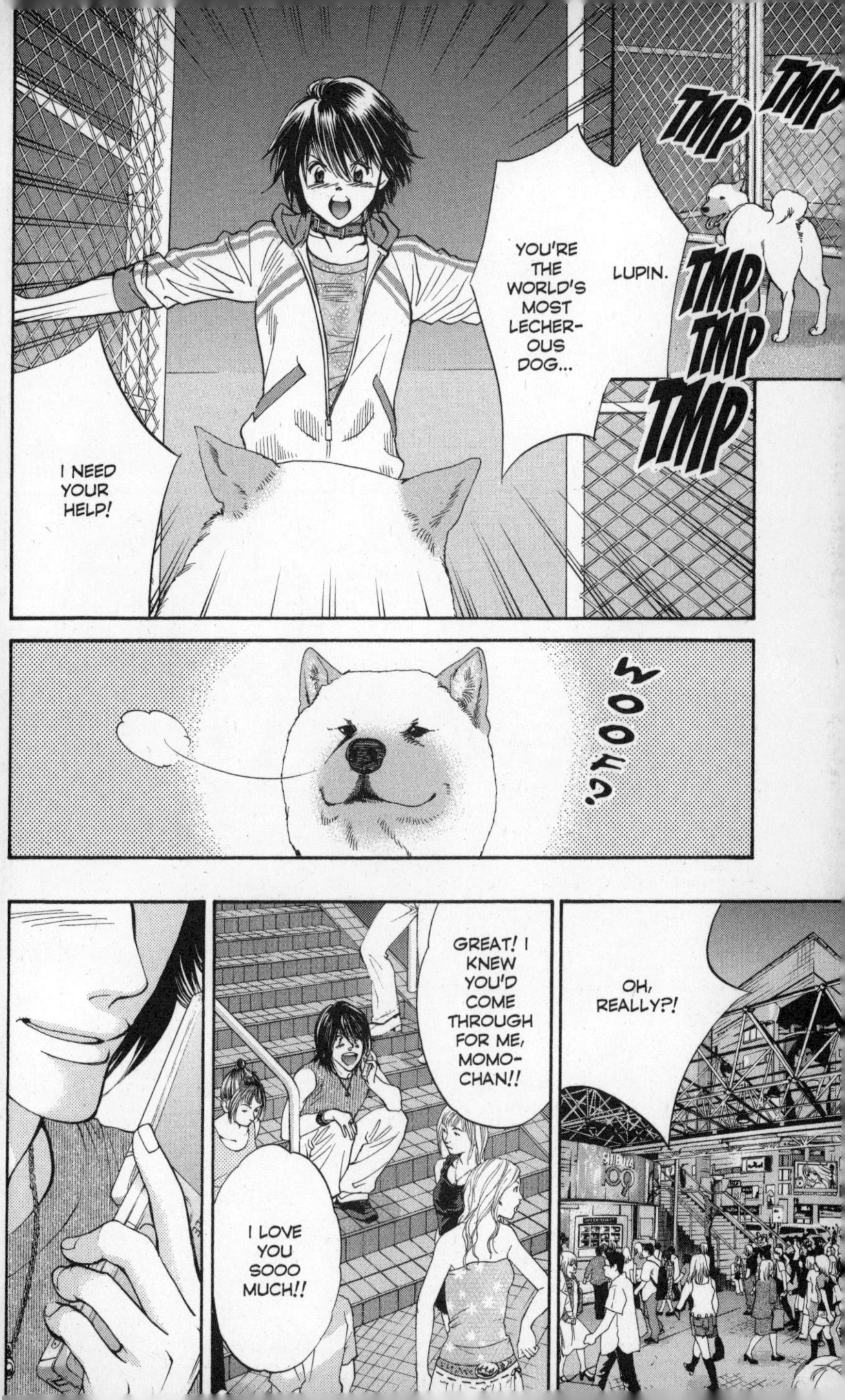
TMP TMP
TMP TMP TMP
LUPIN.
YOU'RE THE WORLD'S MOST LECHER-OUS DOG...
I NEED YOUR HELP!
WOOF?
OH, REALLY?!
GREAT! I KNEW YOU'D COME THROUGH FOR ME, MOMO-CHAN!!
I LOVE YOU SOOO MUCH!!

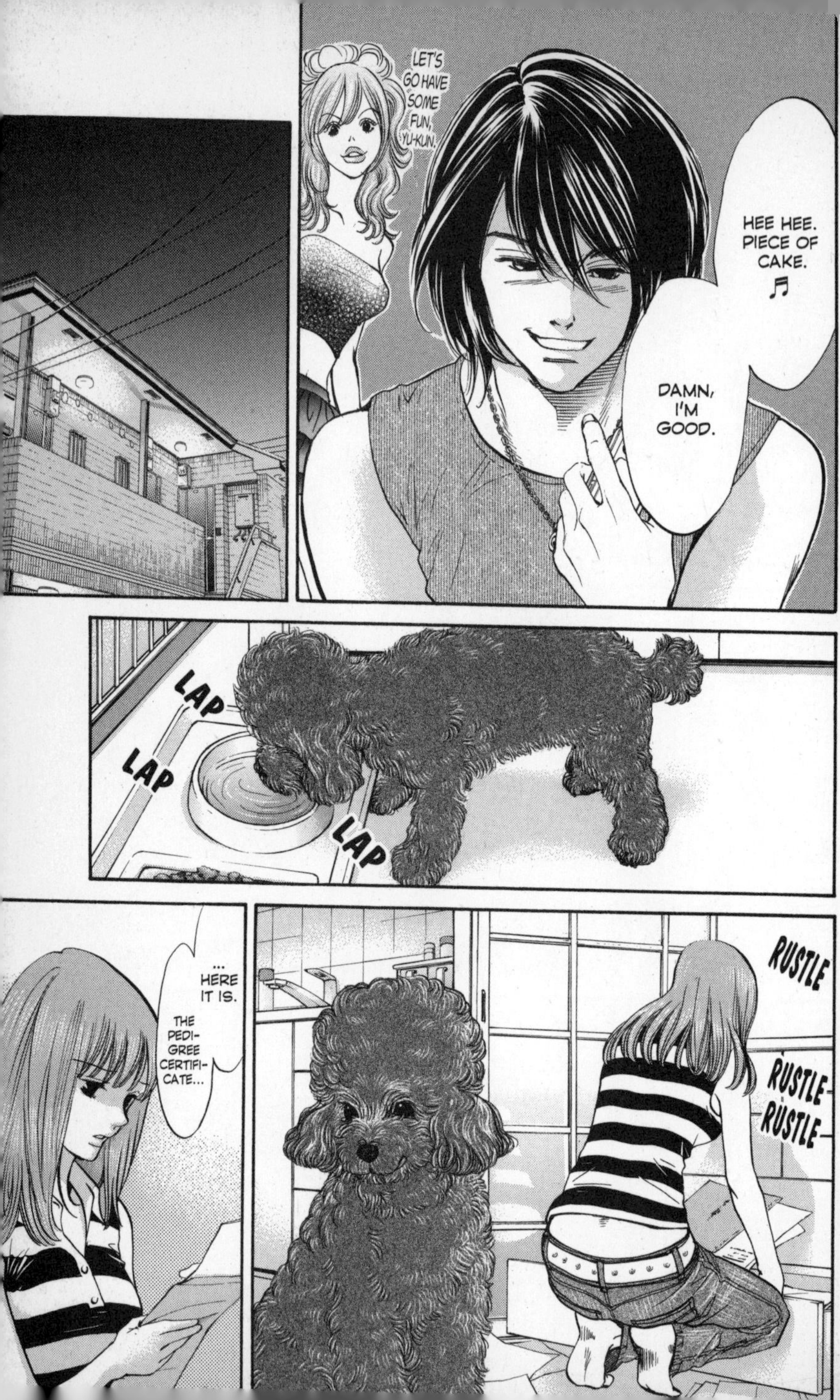
LET'S GO HAVE SOME FUN, YU-KUN.
HEE HEE. PIECE OF CAKE. ♬
DAMN, I'M GOOD.
LAP
LAP
LAP
RUSTLE
RUSTLE-RUSTLE-
... HERE IT IS.
THE PEDIGREE CERTIFICATE...

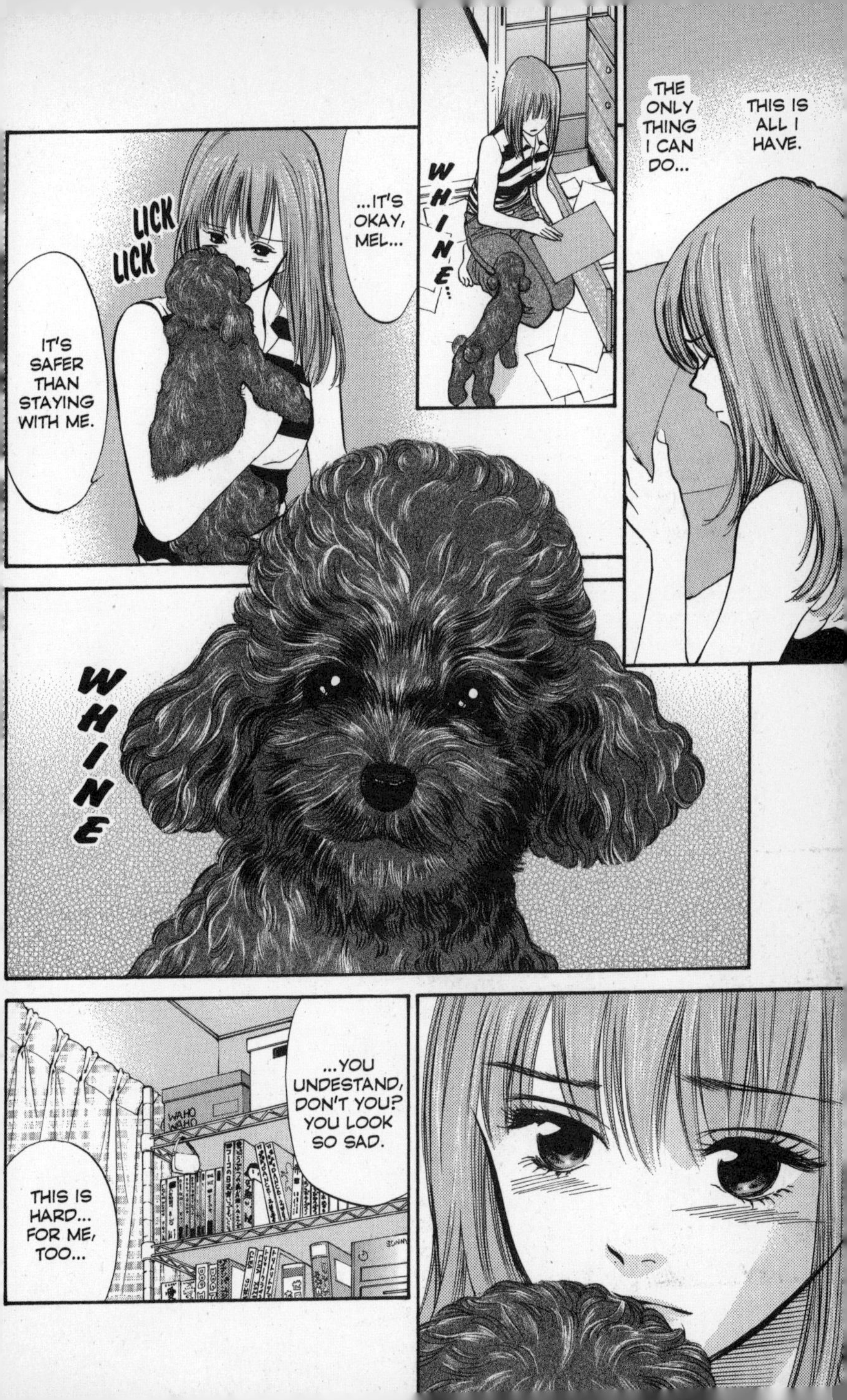
THIS IS ALL I HAVE.
THE ONLY THING I CAN DO...
WHINE...
...IT'S OKAY, MEL...
LICK LICK
IT'S SAFER THAN STAYING WITH ME.
WHINE
...YOU UNDESTAND, DON'T YOU? YOU LOOK SO SAD.
THIS IS HARD... FOR ME, TOO...

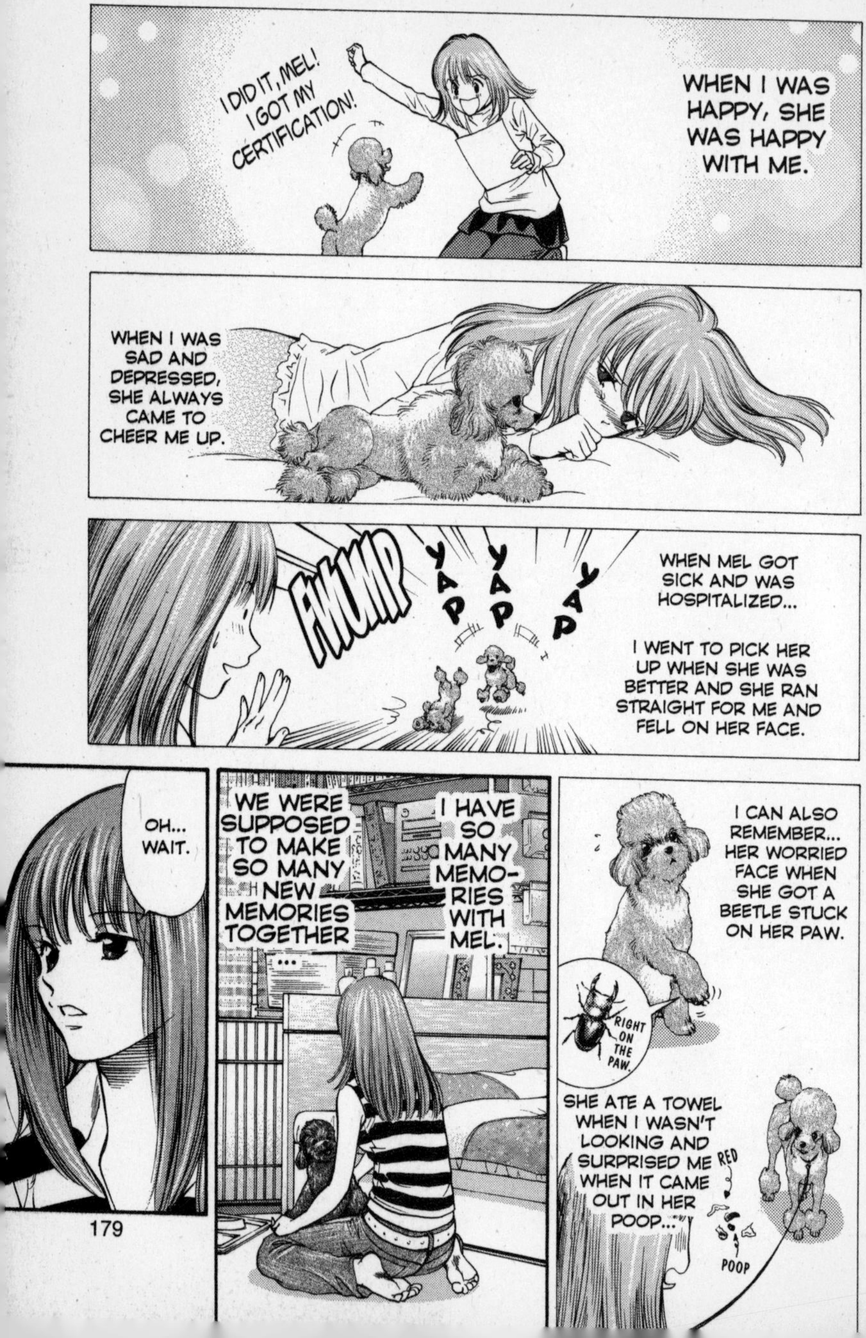
WHEN I WAS HAPPY, SHE WAS HAPPY WITH ME.
I DID IT, MEL! I GOT MY CERTIFICATION!
WHEN I WAS SAD AND DEPRESSED, SHE ALWAYS CAME TO CHEER ME UP.
WHEN MEL GOT SICK AND WAS HOSPITALIZED...
I WENT TO PICK HER UP WHEN SHE WAS BETTER AND SHE RAN STRAIGHT FOR ME AND FELL ON HER FACE.
YAP YAP YAP
FWUMP
I CAN ALSO REMEMBER... HER WORRIED FACE WHEN SHE GOT A BEETLE STUCK ON HER PAW.
RIGHT ON THE PAW.
SHE ATE A TOWEL WHEN I WASN'T LOOKING AND SURPRISED ME WHEN IT CAME OUT IN HER POOP...
RED
POOP
I HAVE SO MANY MEMORIES WITH MEL.
WE WERE SUPPOSED TO MAKE SO MANY NEW MEMORIES TOGETHER
...
OH... WAIT.

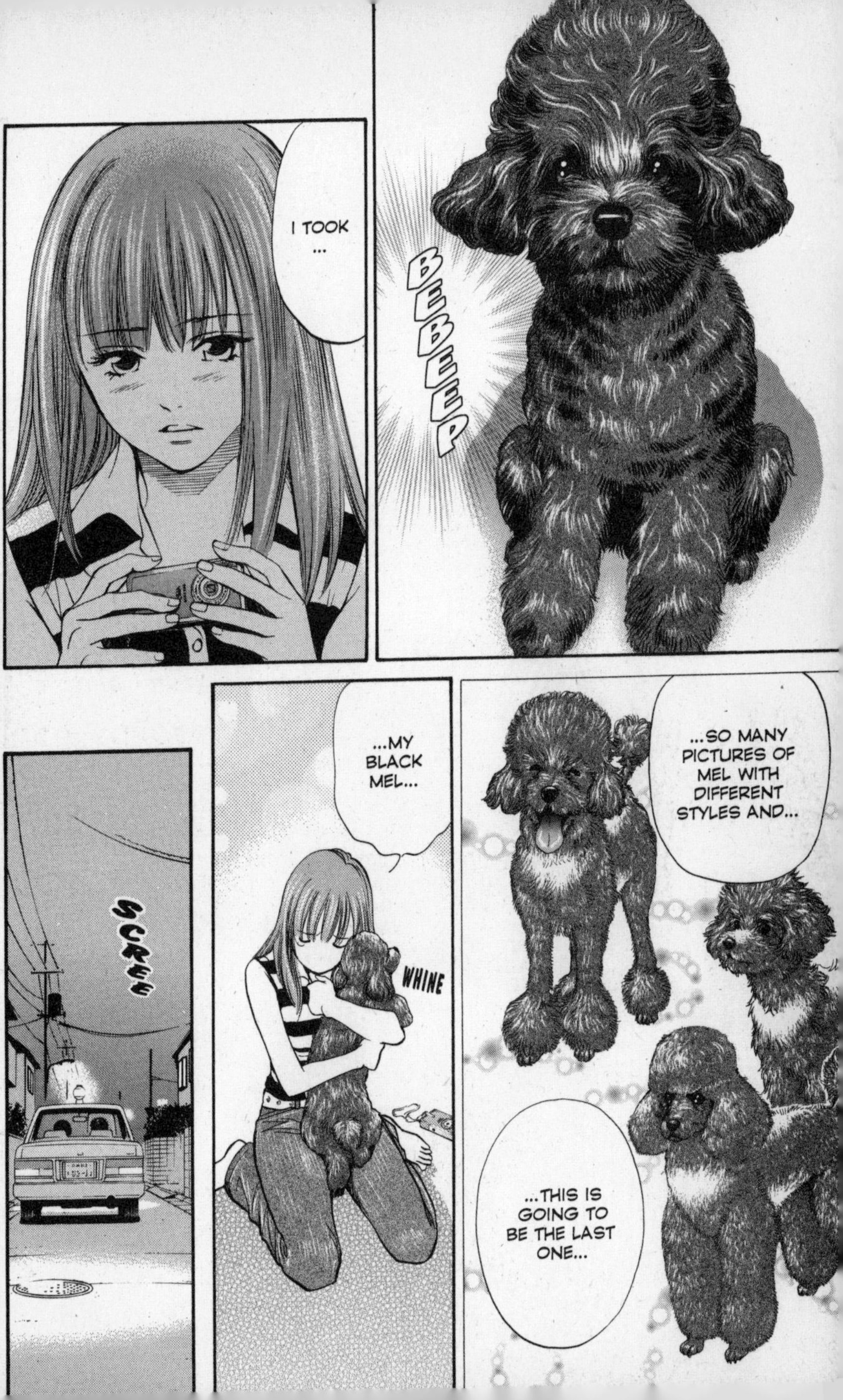
BEBEEP
I TOOK ...
...SO MANY PICTURES OF MEL WITH DIFFERENT STYLES AND...
...THIS IS GOING TO BE THE LAST ONE...
...MY BLACK MEL...
WHINE
SCREE

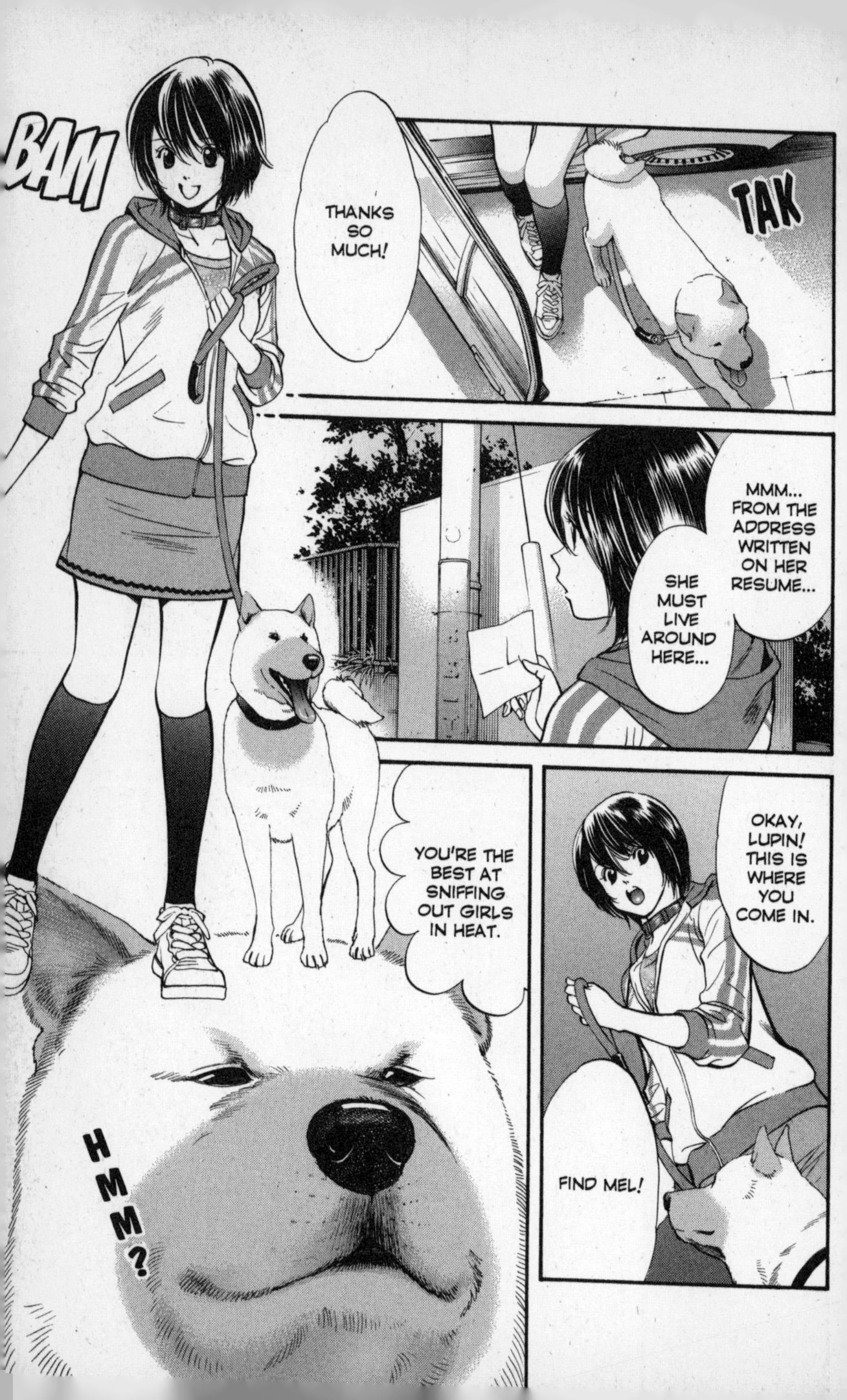
TAK
THANKS SO MUCH!
MMM... FROM THE ADDRESS WRITTEN ON HER RESUME...
SHE MUST LIVE AROUND HERE...
BAM
OKAY, LUPIN! THIS IS WHERE YOU COME IN.
FIND MEL!
YOU'RE THE BEST AT SNIFFING OUT GIRLS IN HEAT.
HMM?

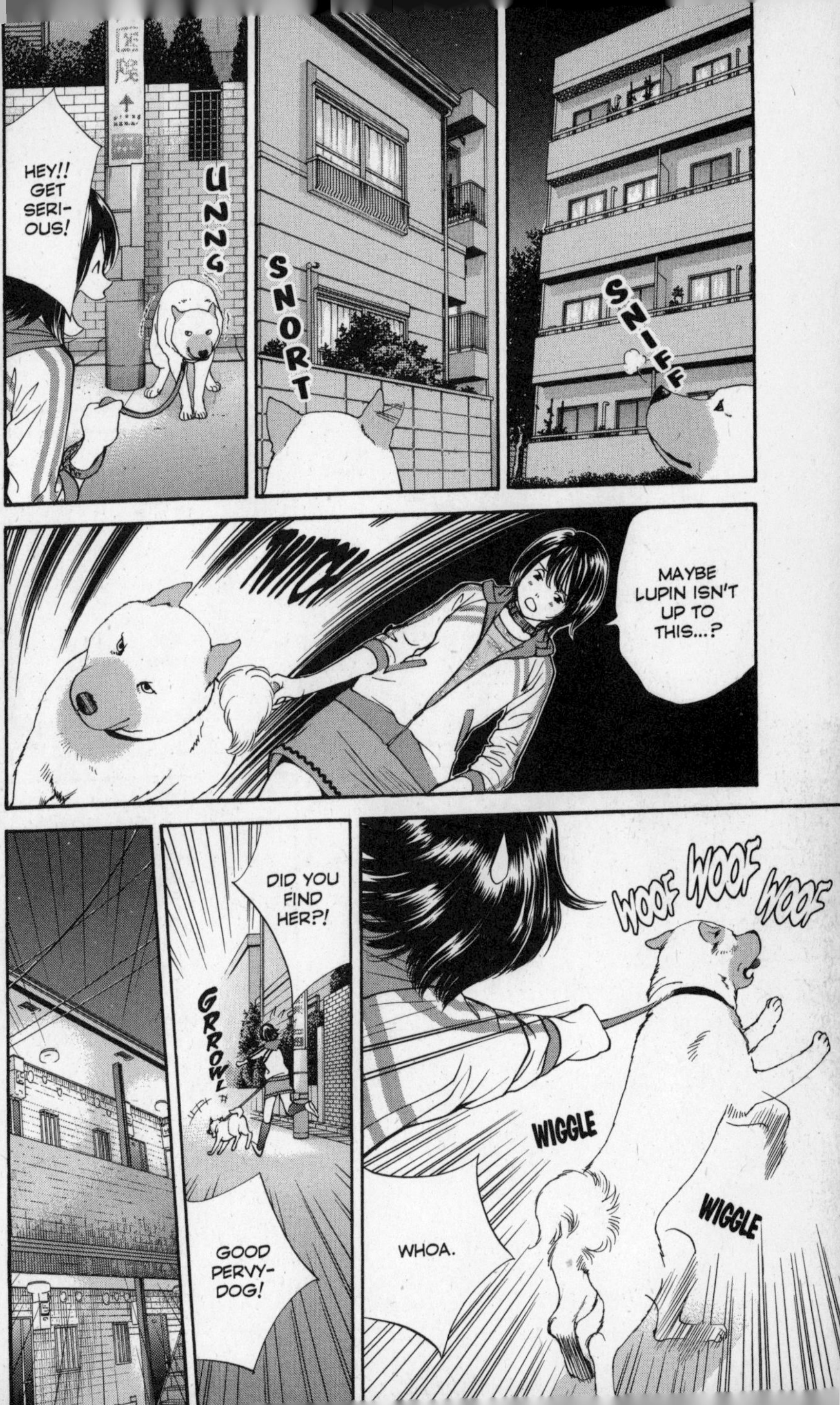
SNIFF
SNORT
HEY!! GET SERI-OUS!
UNNG
MAYBE LUPIN ISN'T UP TO THIS...?
TWITCH
WOOF WOOF WOOF
WIGGLE
WIGGLE
WHOA.
DID YOU FIND HER?!
GRROWL
GOOD PERVY-DOG!

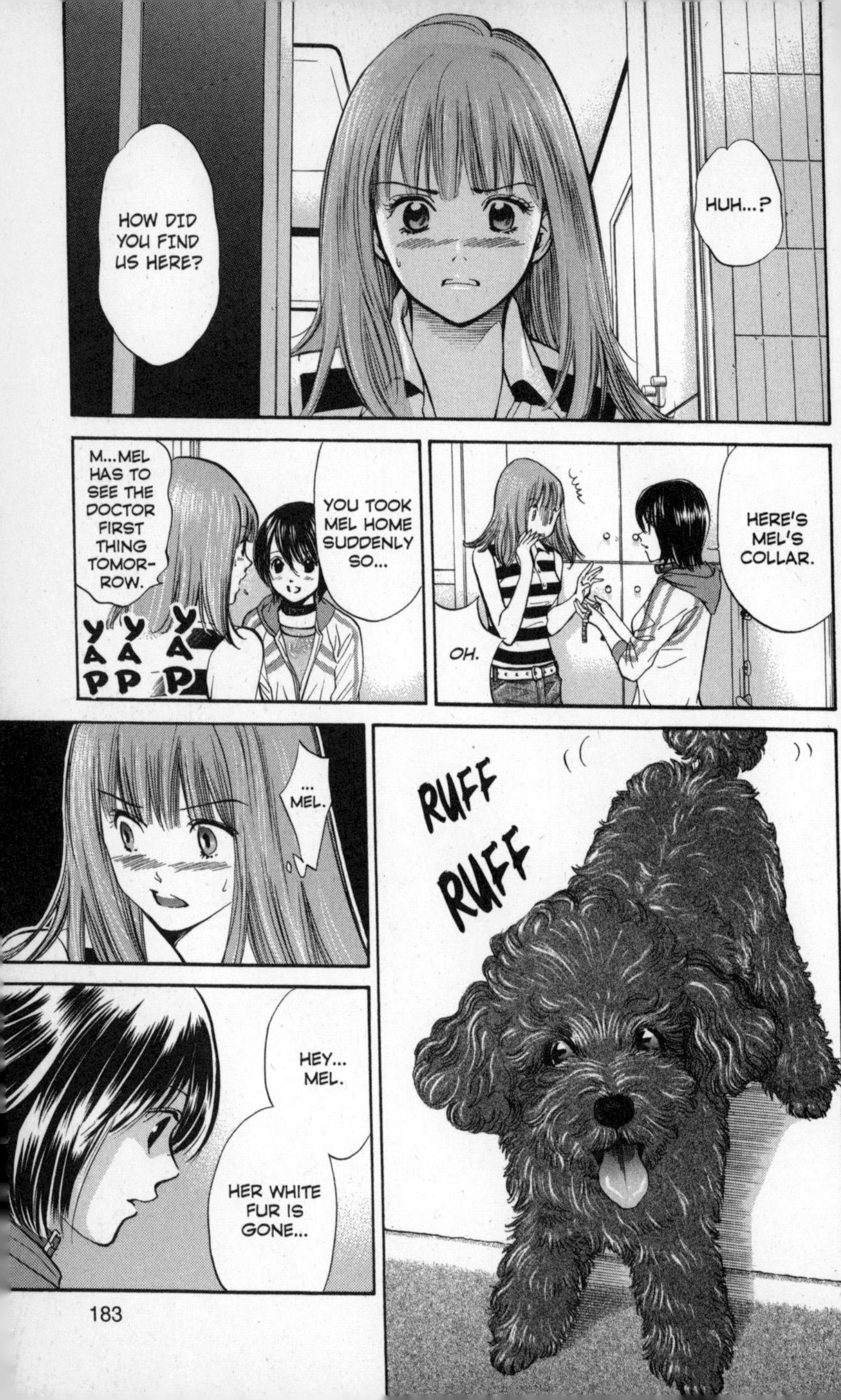
HUH...?
HOW DID YOU FIND US HERE?
HERE'S MEL'S COLLAR.
OH.
YOU TOOK MEL HOME SUDDENLY SO...
M...MEL HAS TO SEE THE DOCTOR FIRST THING TOMORROW.
YAP YAP YAP
RUFF RUFF
... MEL.
HEY... MEL.
HER WHITE FUR IS GONE...

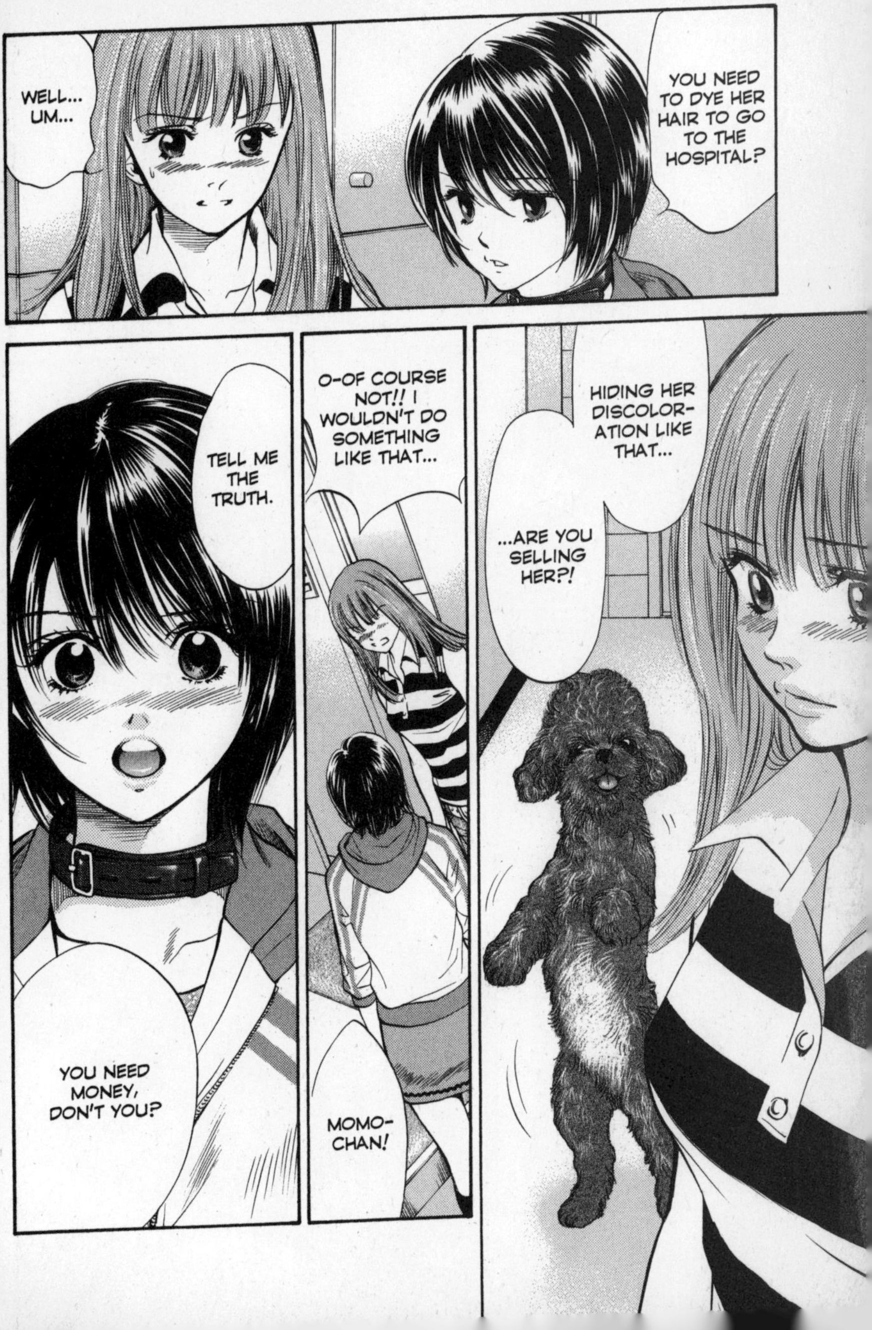
YOU NEED TO DYE HER HAIR TO GO TO THE HOSPITAL?
WELL... UM...
HIDING HER DISCOLOR-ATION LIKE THAT...
...ARE YOU SELLING HER?!
O-OF COURSE NOT!! I WOULDN'T DO SOMETHING LIKE THAT...
MOMO-CHAN!
TELL ME THE TRUTH.
YOU NEED MONEY, DON'T YOU?

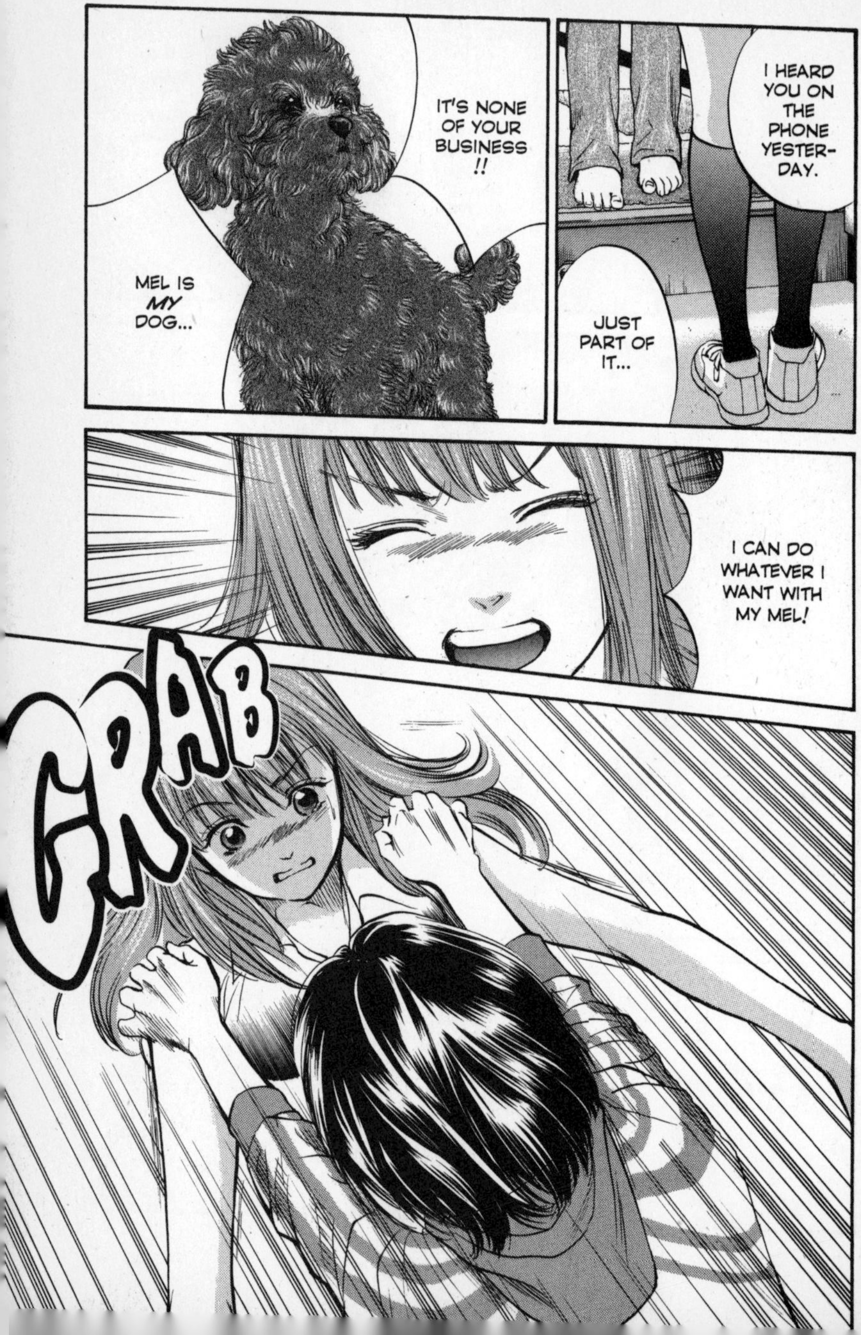
I HEARD YOU ON THE PHONE YESTERDAY.
JUST PART OF IT...
IT'S NONE OF YOUR BUSINESS!!
MEL IS *MY* DOG...
I CAN DO WHATEVER I WANT WITH MY MEL!
GRAB

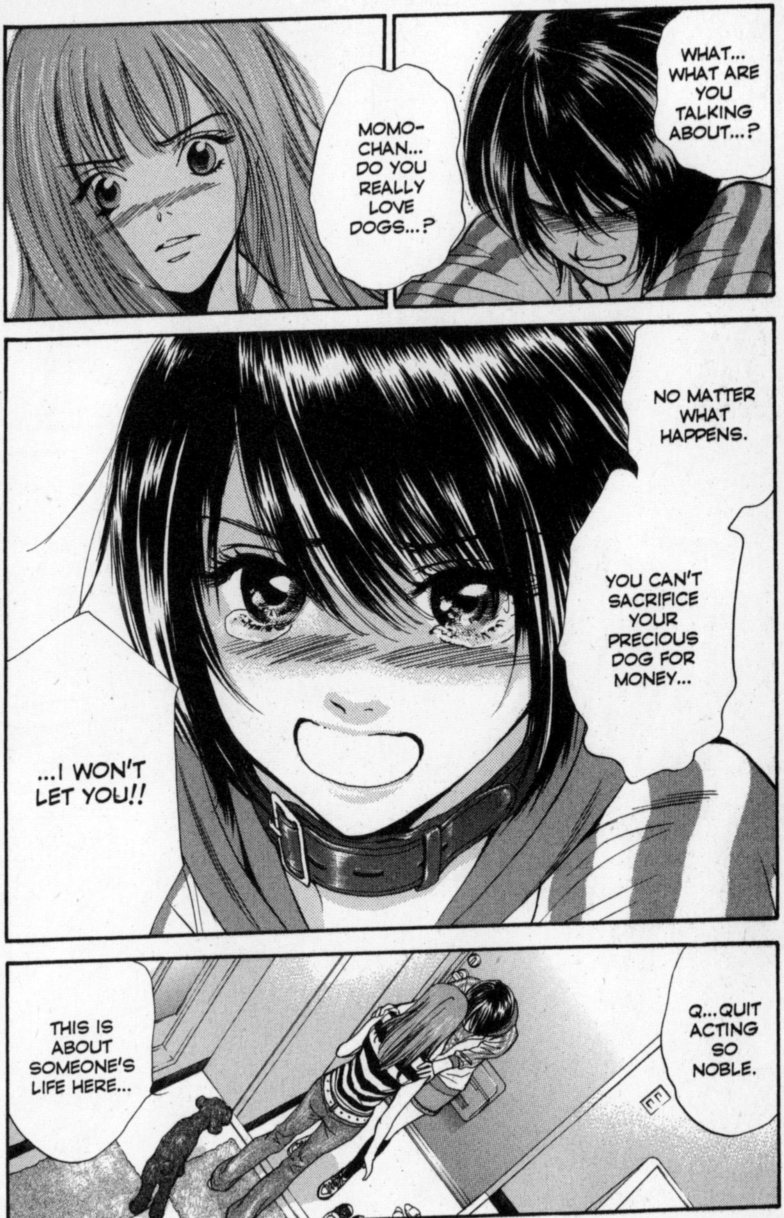
WHAT... WHAT ARE YOU TALKING ABOUT...?
MOMO-CHAN... DO YOU REALLY LOVE DOGS...?
NO MATTER WHAT HAPPENS.
YOU CAN'T SACRIFICE YOUR PRECIOUS DOG FOR MONEY...
...I WON'T LET YOU!!
Q...QUIT ACTING SO NOBLE.
THIS IS ABOUT SOMEONE'S LIFE HERE...

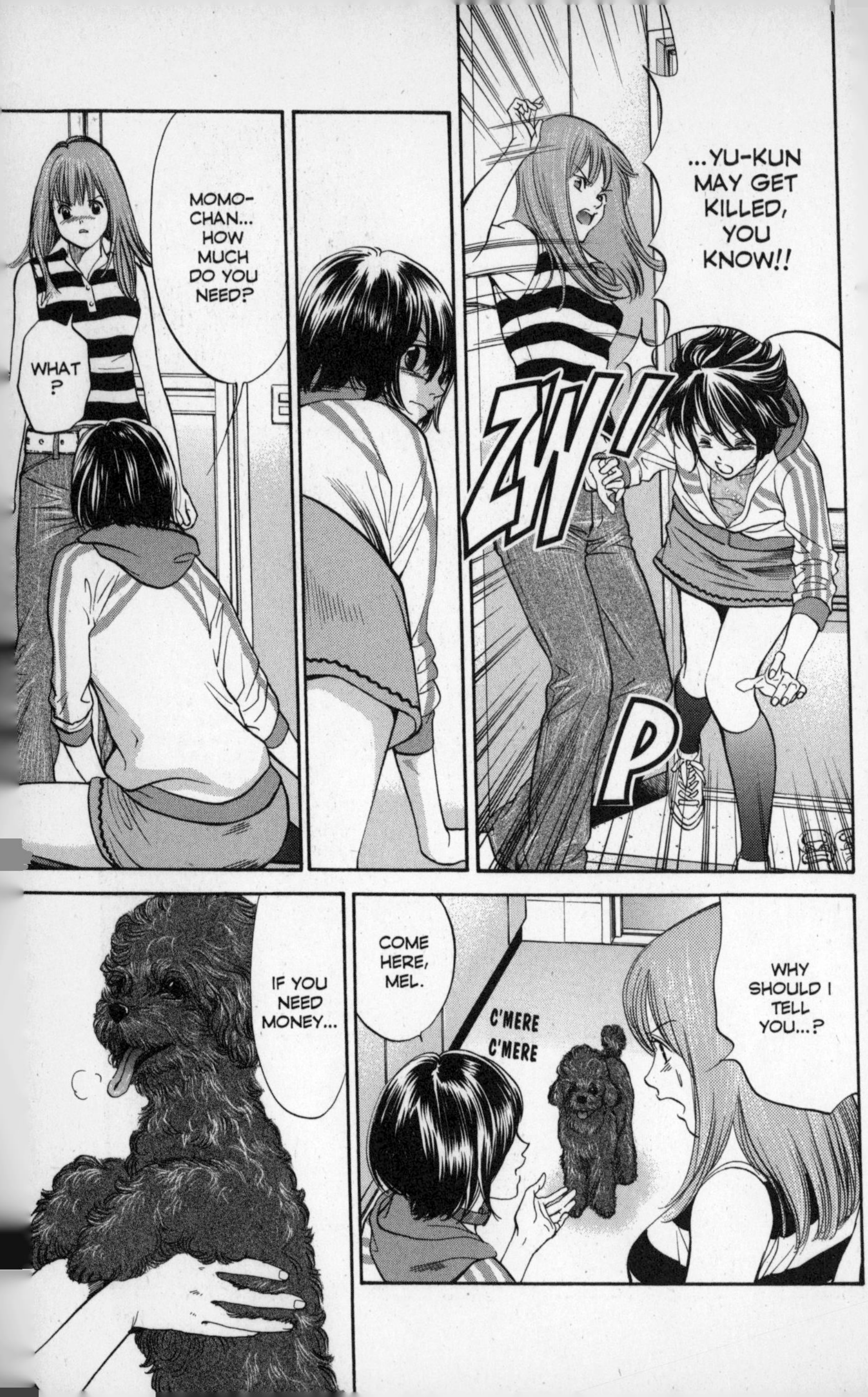
...YU-KUN MAY GET KILLED, YOU KNOW!!
ZW
!
P
MOMO-CHAN... HOW MUCH DO YOU NEED?
WHAT?
WHY SHOULD I TELL YOU...?
C'MERE C'MERE
COME HERE, MEL.
IF YOU NEED MONEY...

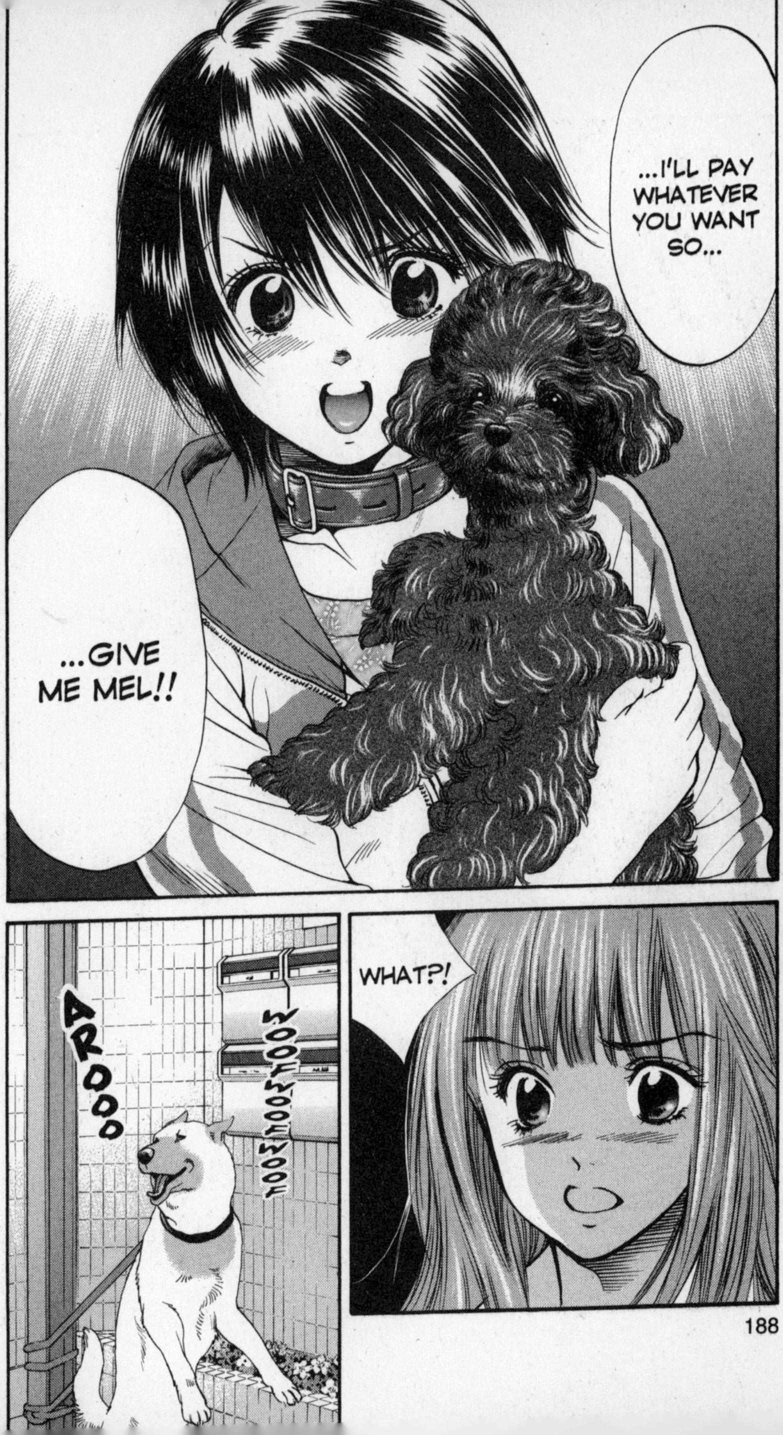
...I'LL PAY WHATEVER YOU WANT SO...
...GIVE ME MEL!!
WHAT?!
WOOFWOOFWOOF
AROOOO

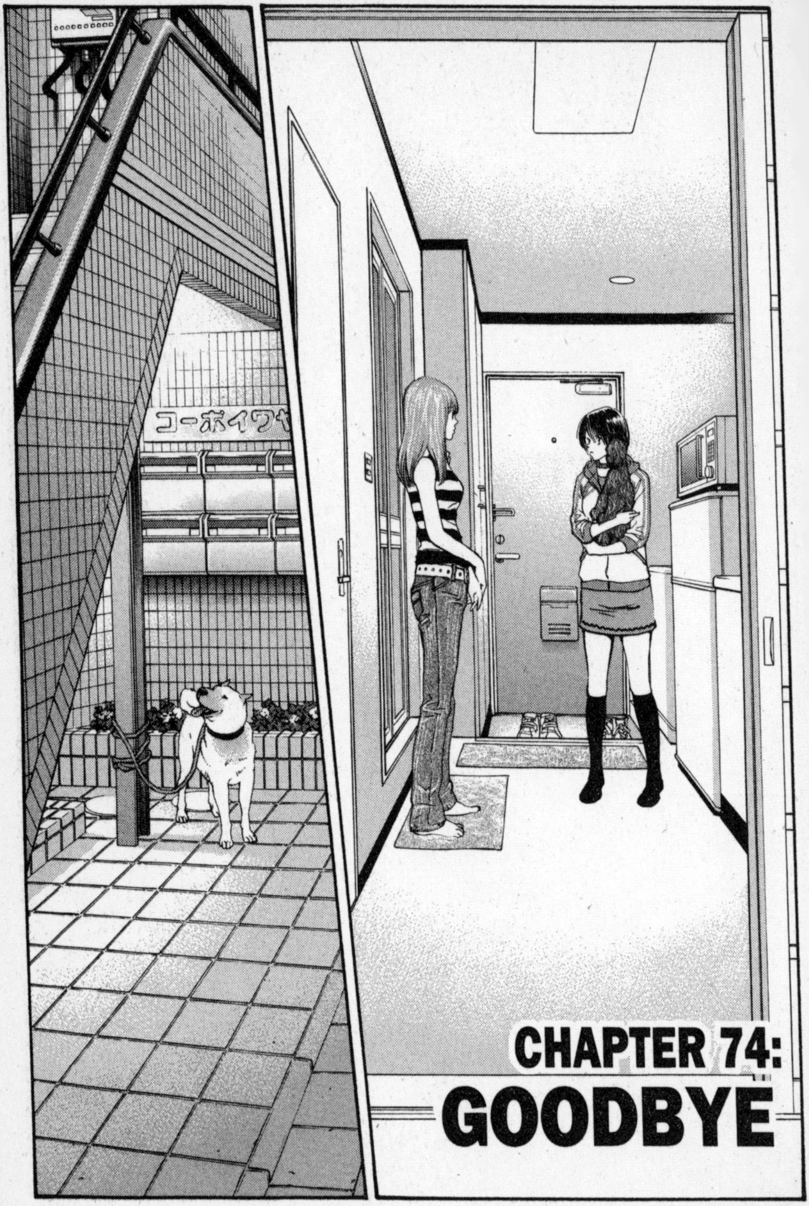
CHAPTER 74:
GOODBYE

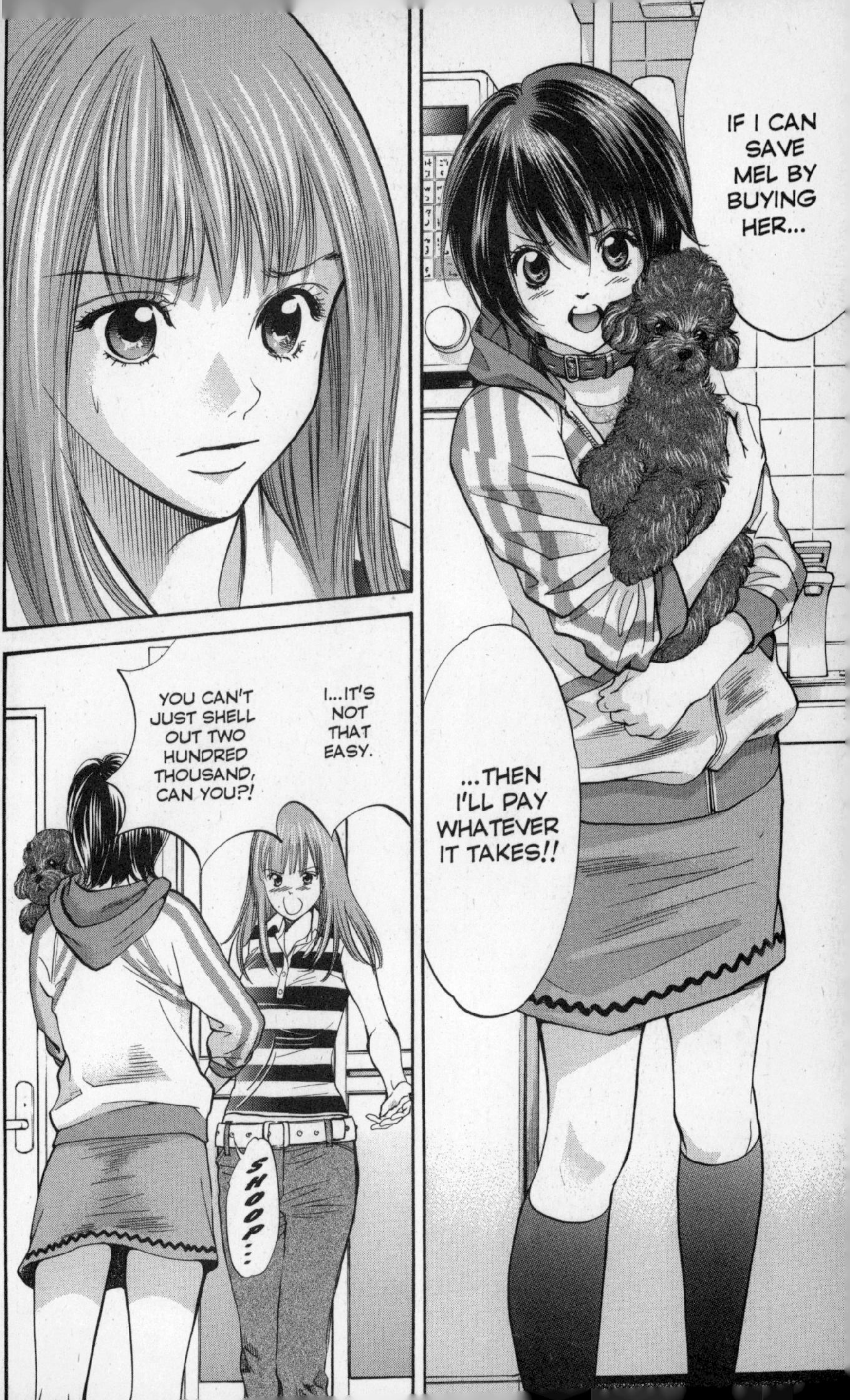
IF I CAN SAVE MEL BY BUYING HER...
...THEN I'LL PAY WHATEVER IT TAKES!!
I...IT'S NOT THAT EASY.
YOU CAN'T JUST SHELL OUT TWO HUNDRED THOUSAND, CAN YOU?!
SNOOP...

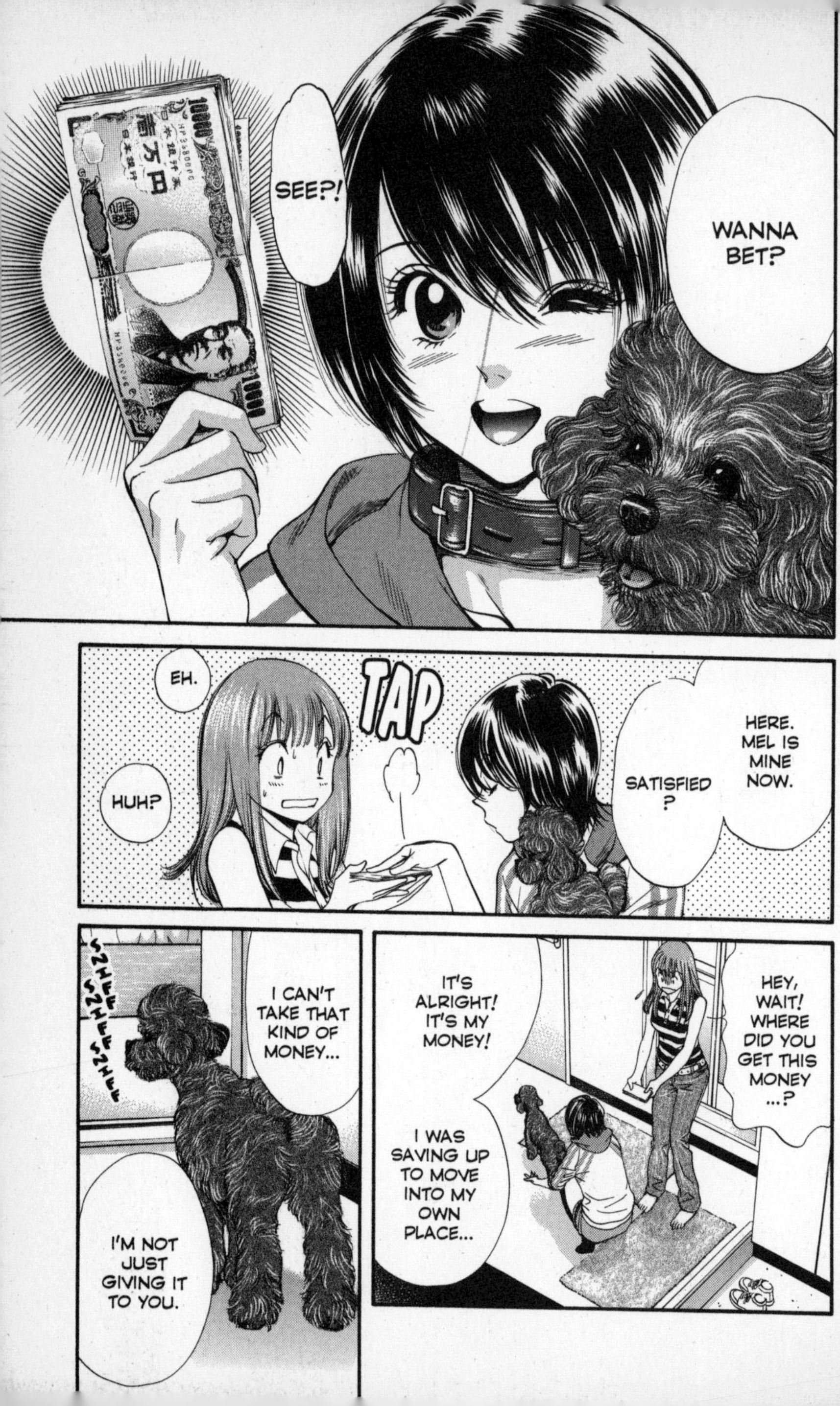
WANNA BET?
SEE?!
HERE. MEL IS MINE NOW.
SATISFIED?
TAP
EH.
HUH?
HEY, WAIT! WHERE DID YOU GET THIS MONEY ...?
IT'S ALRIGHT! IT'S MY MONEY!
I WAS SAVING UP TO MOVE INTO MY OWN PLACE...
I CAN'T TAKE THAT KIND OF MONEY...
SNIFF SNIFF SNIFF
I'M NOT JUST GIVING IT TO YOU.

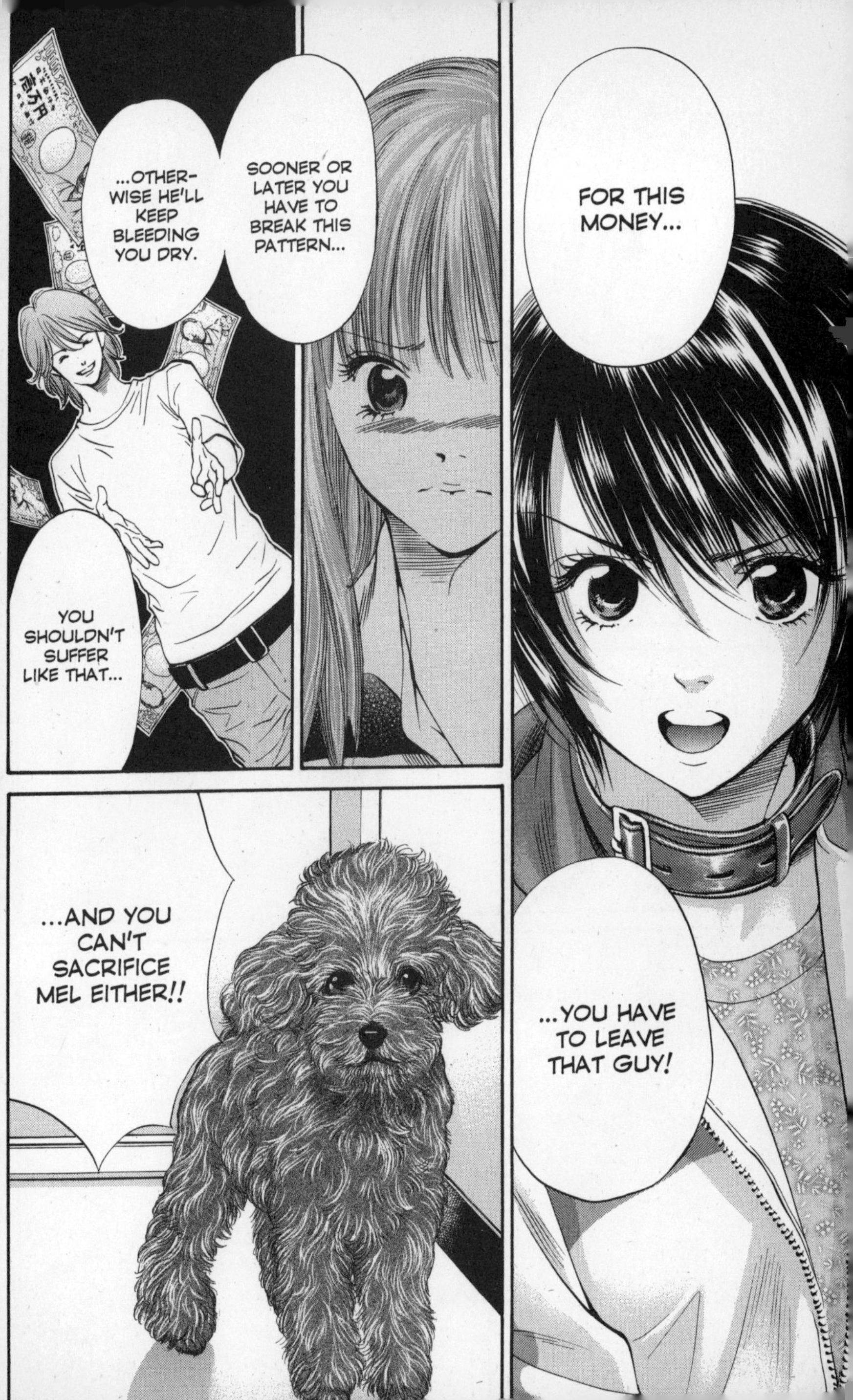
FOR THIS MONEY...
...YOU HAVE TO LEAVE THAT GUY!
SOONER OR LATER YOU HAVE TO BREAK THIS PATTERN...
...OTHER-WISE HE'LL KEEP BLEEDING YOU DRY.
YOU SHOULDN'T SUFFER LIKE THAT...
...AND YOU CAN'T SACRIFICE MEL EITHER!!

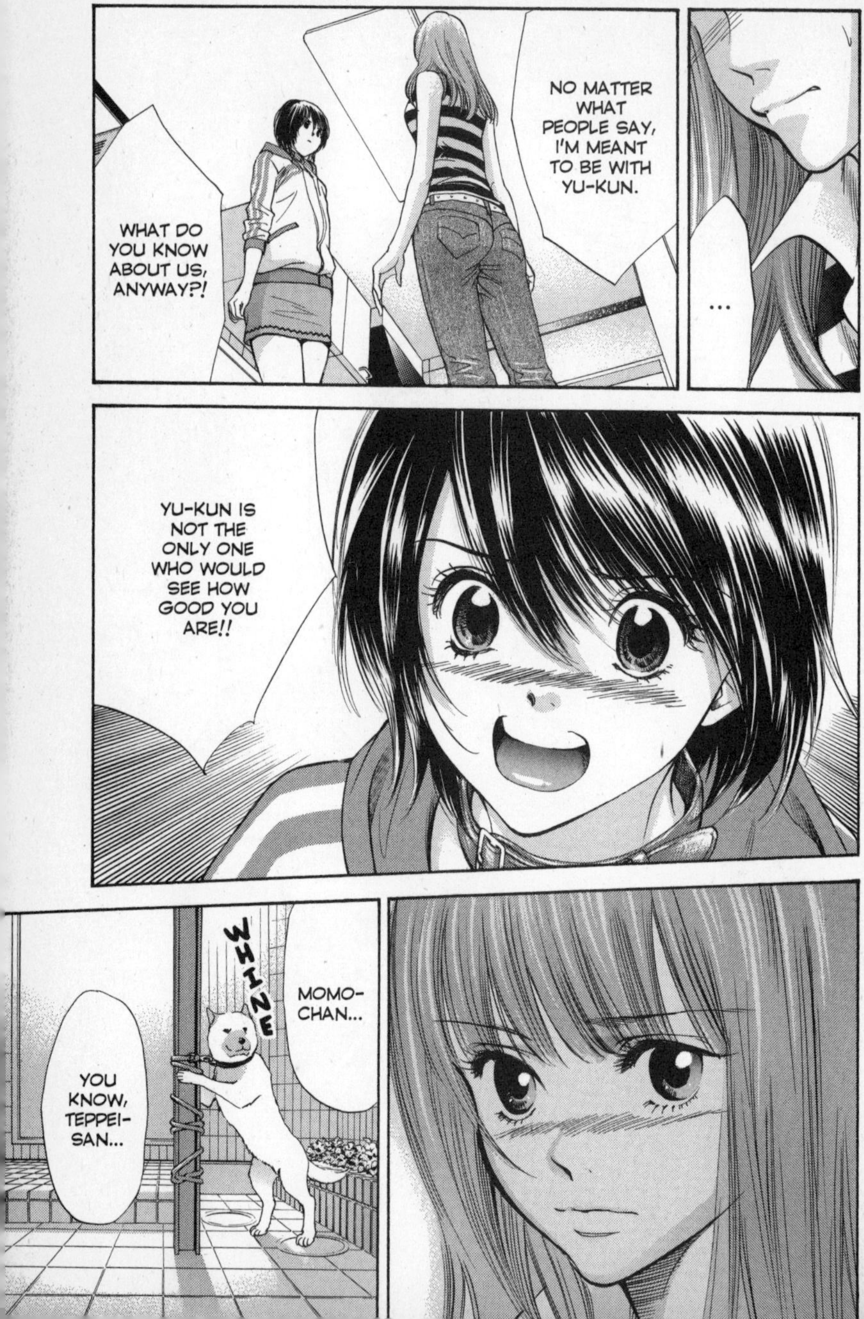
...
NO MATTER WHAT PEOPLE SAY, I'M MEANT TO BE WITH YU-KUN.
WHAT DO YOU KNOW ABOUT US, ANYWAY?!
YU-KUN IS NOT THE ONLY ONE WHO WOULD SEE HOW GOOD YOU ARE!!
MOMO-CHAN...
WHINE
YOU KNOW, TEPPEI-SAN...

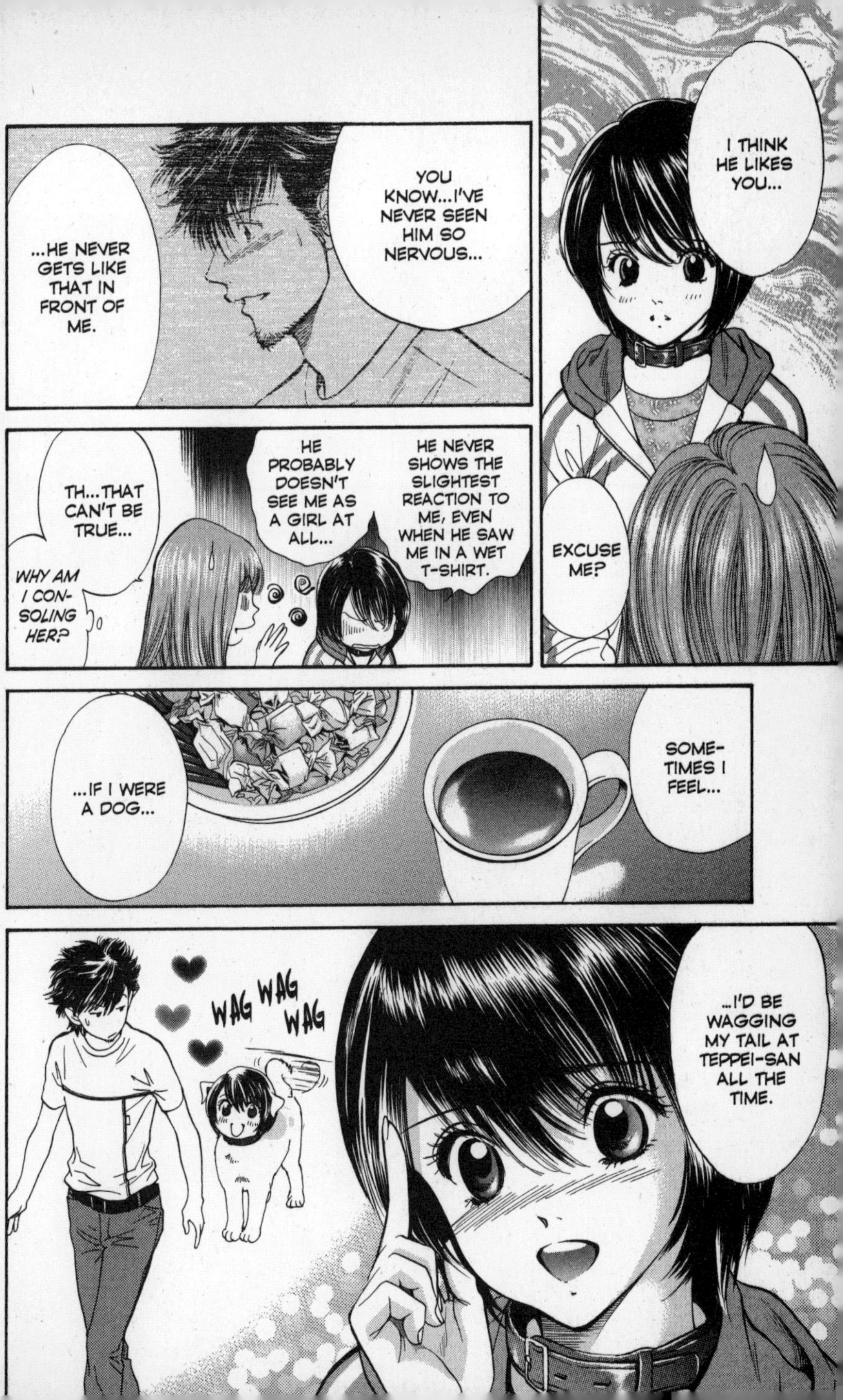
I THINK HE LIKES YOU...
EXCUSE ME?
YOU KNOW...I'VE NEVER SEEN HIM SO NERVOUS...
...HE NEVER GETS LIKE THAT IN FRONT OF ME.
HE NEVER SHOWS THE SLIGHTEST REACTION TO ME, EVEN WHEN HE SAW ME IN A WET T-SHIRT.
HE PROBABLY DOESN'T SEE ME AS A GIRL AT ALL...
TH...THAT CAN'T BE TRUE...
WHY AM I CON-SOLING HER?
SOME-TIMES I FEEL...
...IF I WERE A DOG...
...I'D BE WAGGING MY TAIL AT TEPPEI-SAN ALL THE TIME.
WAG WAG WAG

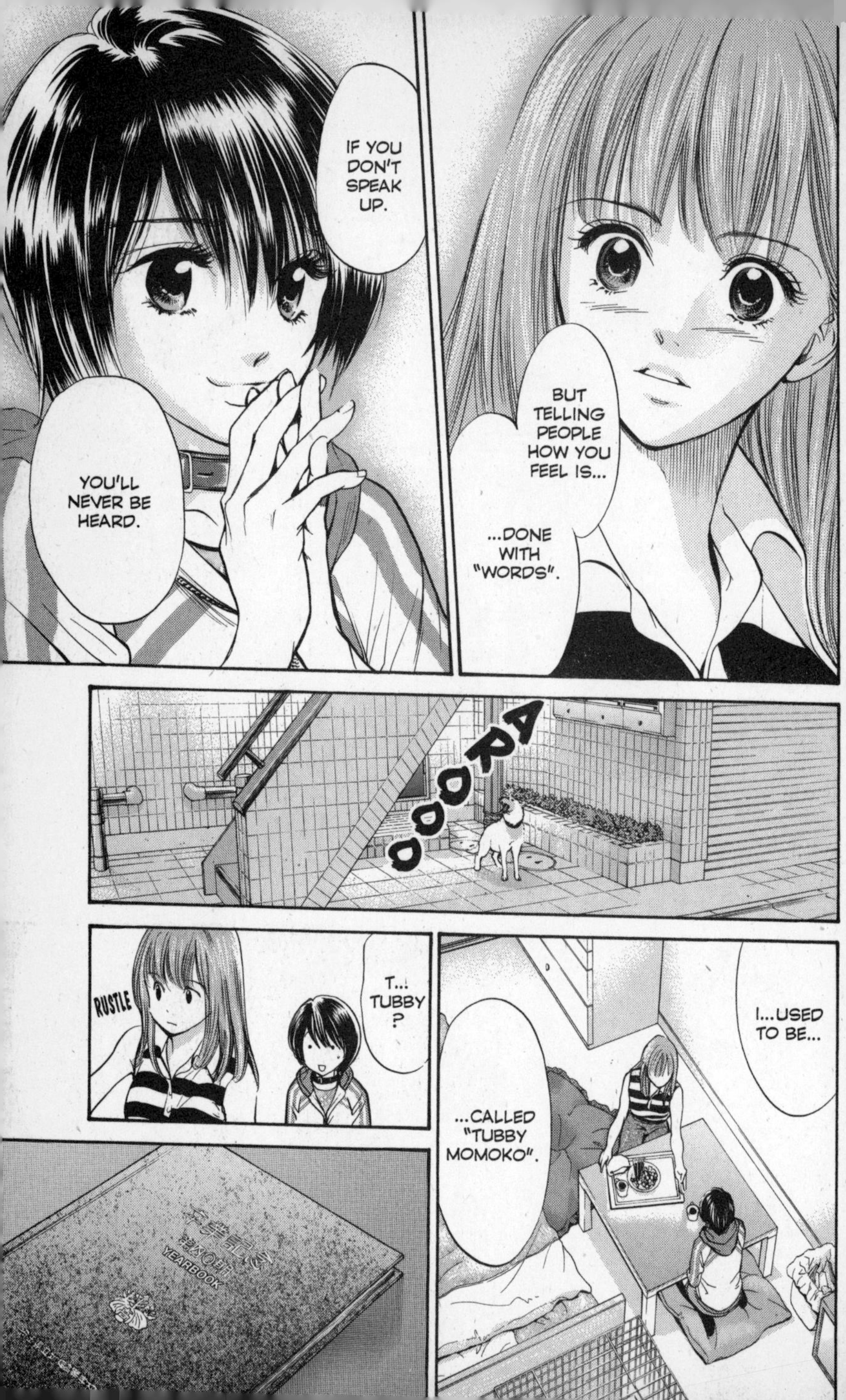
IF YOU DON'T SPEAK UP.
YOU'LL NEVER BE HEARD.
BUT TELLING PEOPLE HOW YOU FEEL IS...
...DONE WITH "WORDS".
DODORA
RUSTLE
T...! TUBBY?
YEARBOOK
I...USED TO BE...
...CALLED "TUBBY MOMOKO".

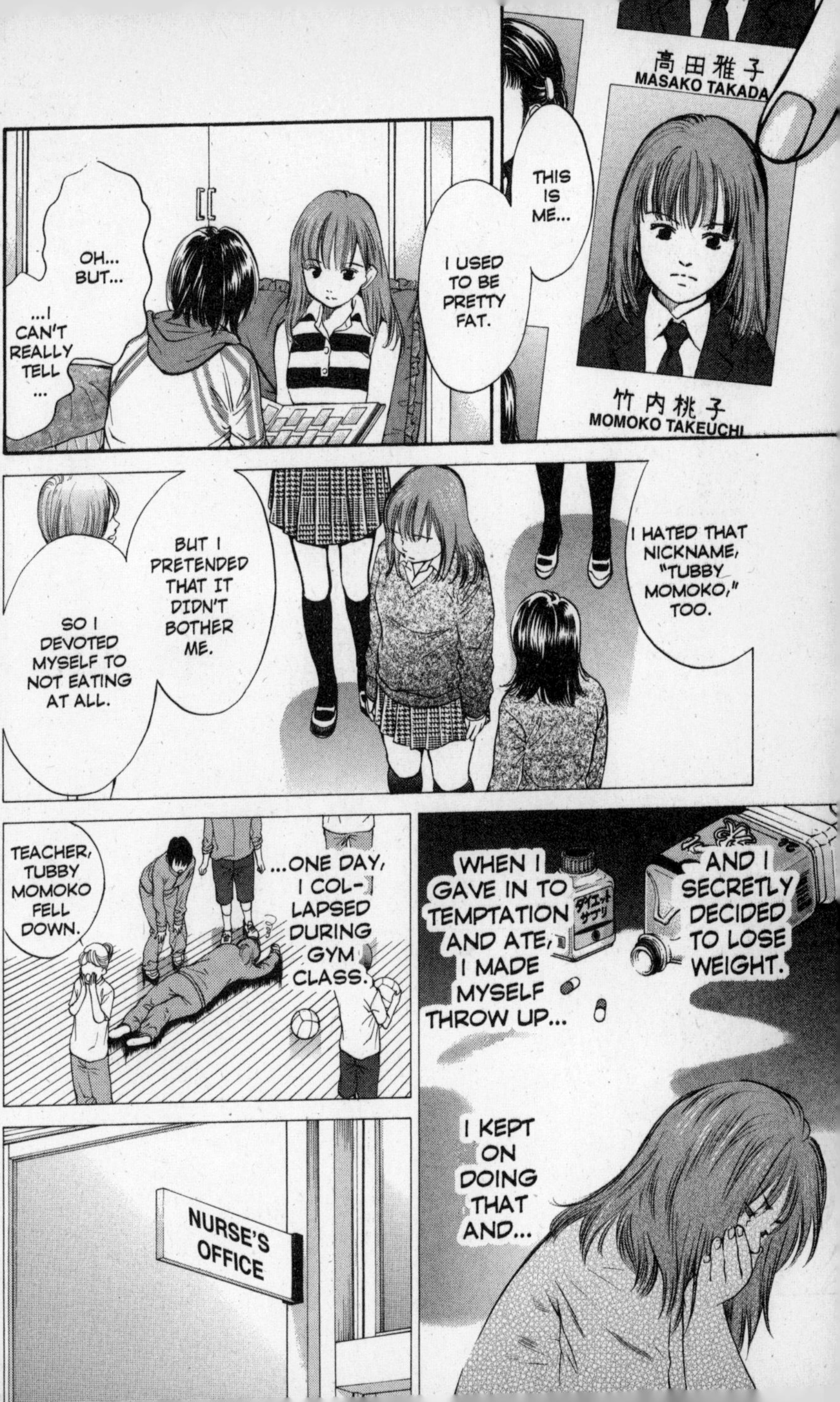
高田雅子
MASAKO TAKADA
THIS IS ME...
I USED TO BE PRETTY FAT.
竹内桃子
MOMOKO TAKEUCHI
OH... BUT...
...I CAN'T REALLY TELL ...
I HATED THAT NICKNAME, "TUBBY MOMOKO," TOO.
BUT I PRETENDED THAT IT DIDN'T BOTHER ME.
SO I DEVOTED MYSELF TO NOT EATING AT ALL.
AND I SECRETLY DECIDED TO LOSE WEIGHT.
WHEN I GAVE IN TO TEMPTATION AND ATE, I MADE MYSELF THROW UP...
I KEPT ON DOING THAT AND...
...ONE DAY, I COL-LAPSED DURING GYM CLASS.
TEACHER, TUBBY MOMOKO FELL DOWN.
NURSE'S OFFICE

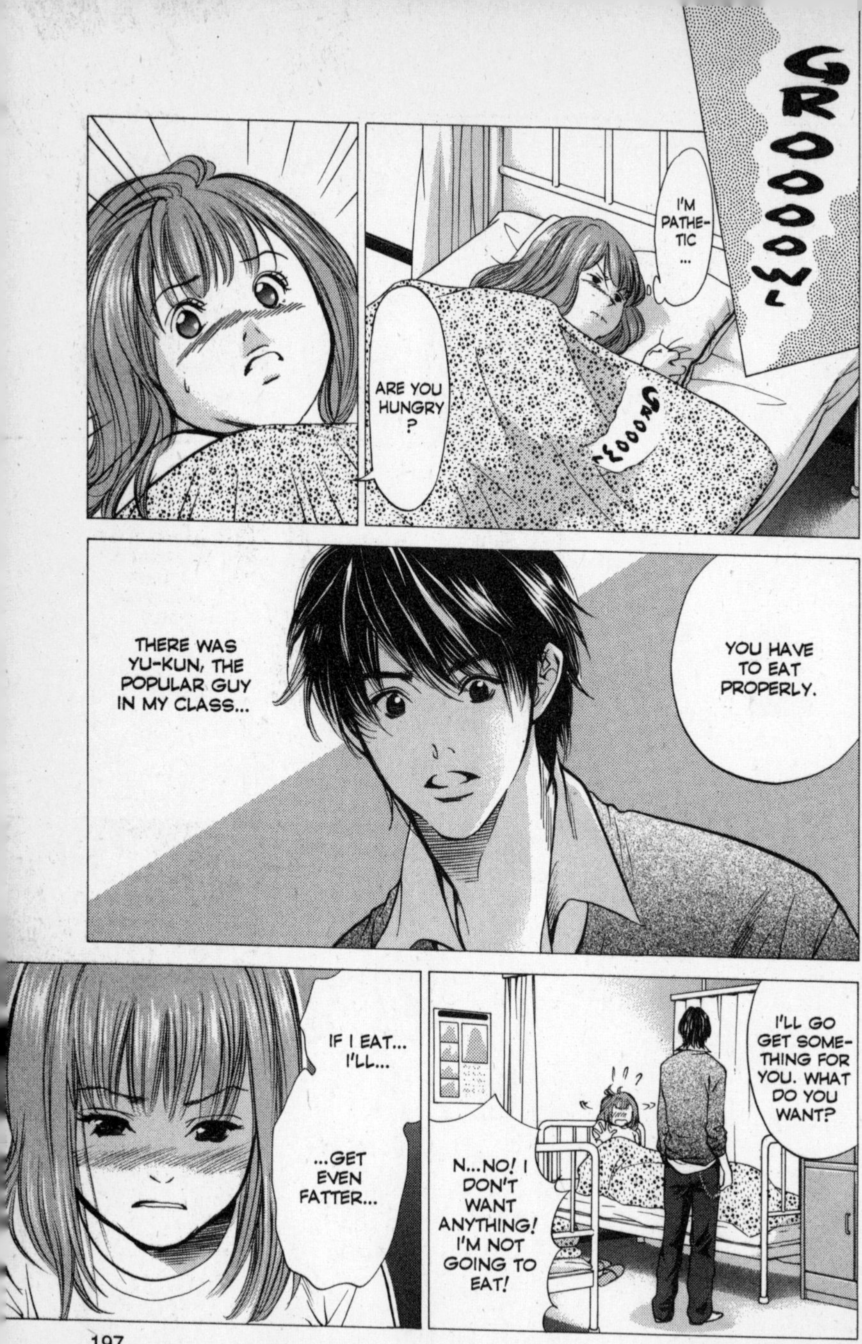
GROOOOOWL
I'M PATHETIC...
GROOOO
ARE YOU HUNGRY?
YOU HAVE TO EAT PROPERLY.
THERE WAS YU-KUN, THE POPULAR GUY IN MY CLASS...
I'LL GO GET SOMETHING FOR YOU. WHAT DO YOU WANT?
N...NO! I DON'T WANT ANYTHING! I'M NOT GOING TO EAT!
IF I EAT... I'LL...
...GET EVEN FATTER...

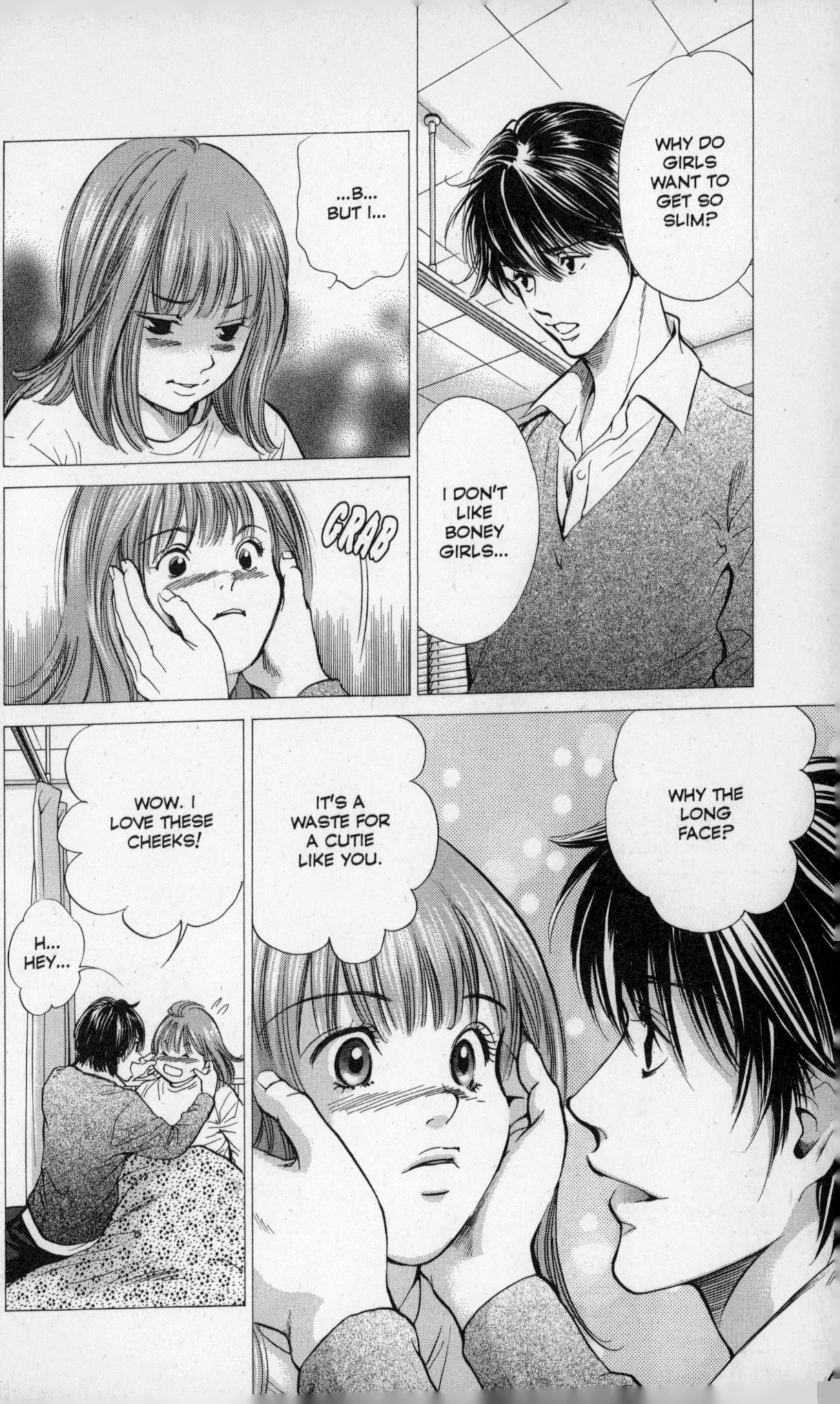
WHY DO GIRLS WANT TO GET SO SLIM?
I DON'T LIKE BONEY GIRLS...
...B... BUT I...
GRAB
WHY THE LONG FACE?
IT'S A WASTE FOR A CUTIE LIKE YOU.
WOW. I LOVE THESE CHEEKS!
H... HEY...

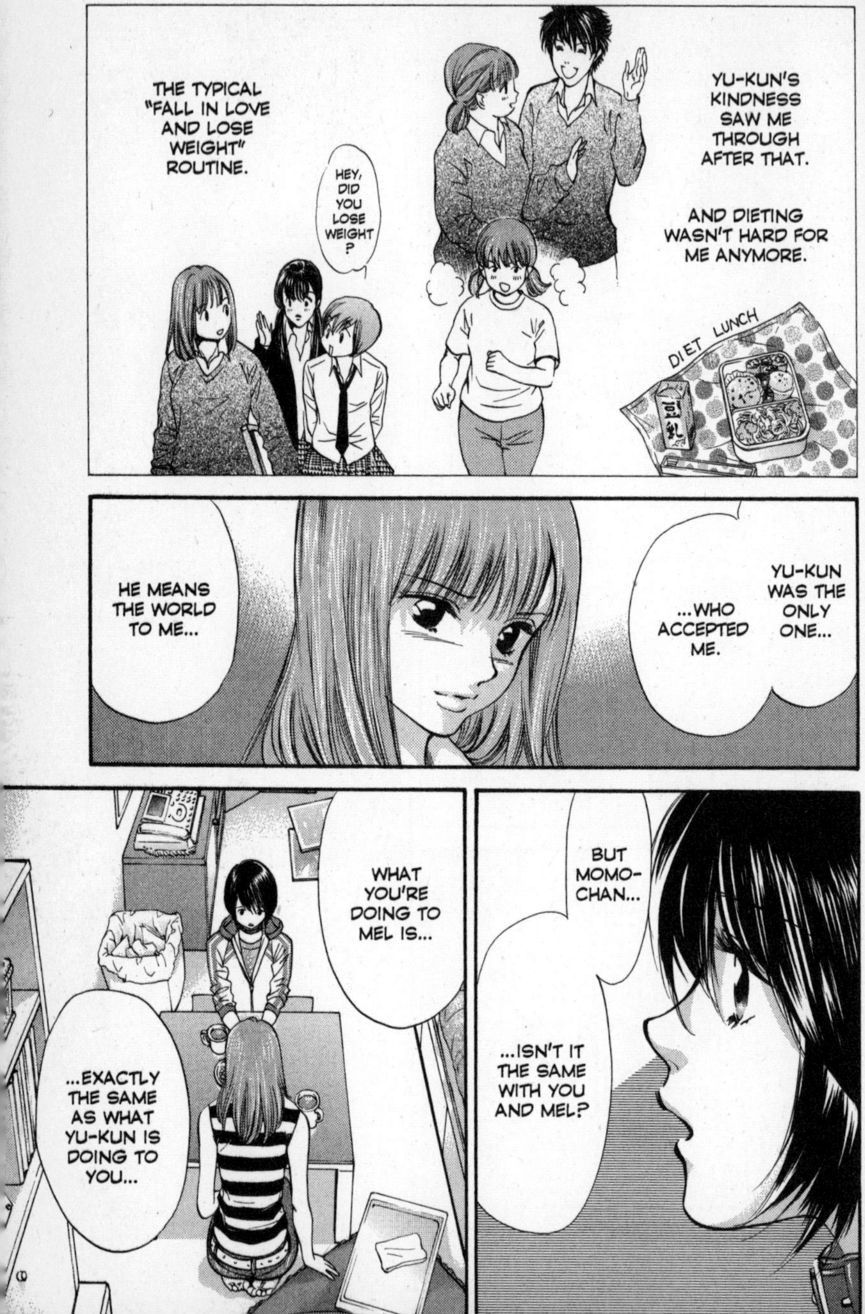
YU-KUN'S KINDNESS SAW ME THROUGH AFTER THAT.
AND DIETING WASN'T HARD FOR ME ANYMORE.
DIET LUNCH
HEY, DID YOU LOSE WEIGHT?
THE TYPICAL "FALL IN LOVE AND LOSE WEIGHT" ROUTINE.
YU-KUN WAS THE ONLY ONE...
...WHO ACCEPTED ME.
HE MEANS THE WORLD TO ME...
BUT MOMO-CHAN...
...ISN'T IT THE SAME WITH YOU AND MEL?
WHAT YOU'RE DOING TO MEL IS...
...EXACTLY THE SAME AS WHAT YU-KUN IS DOING TO YOU...

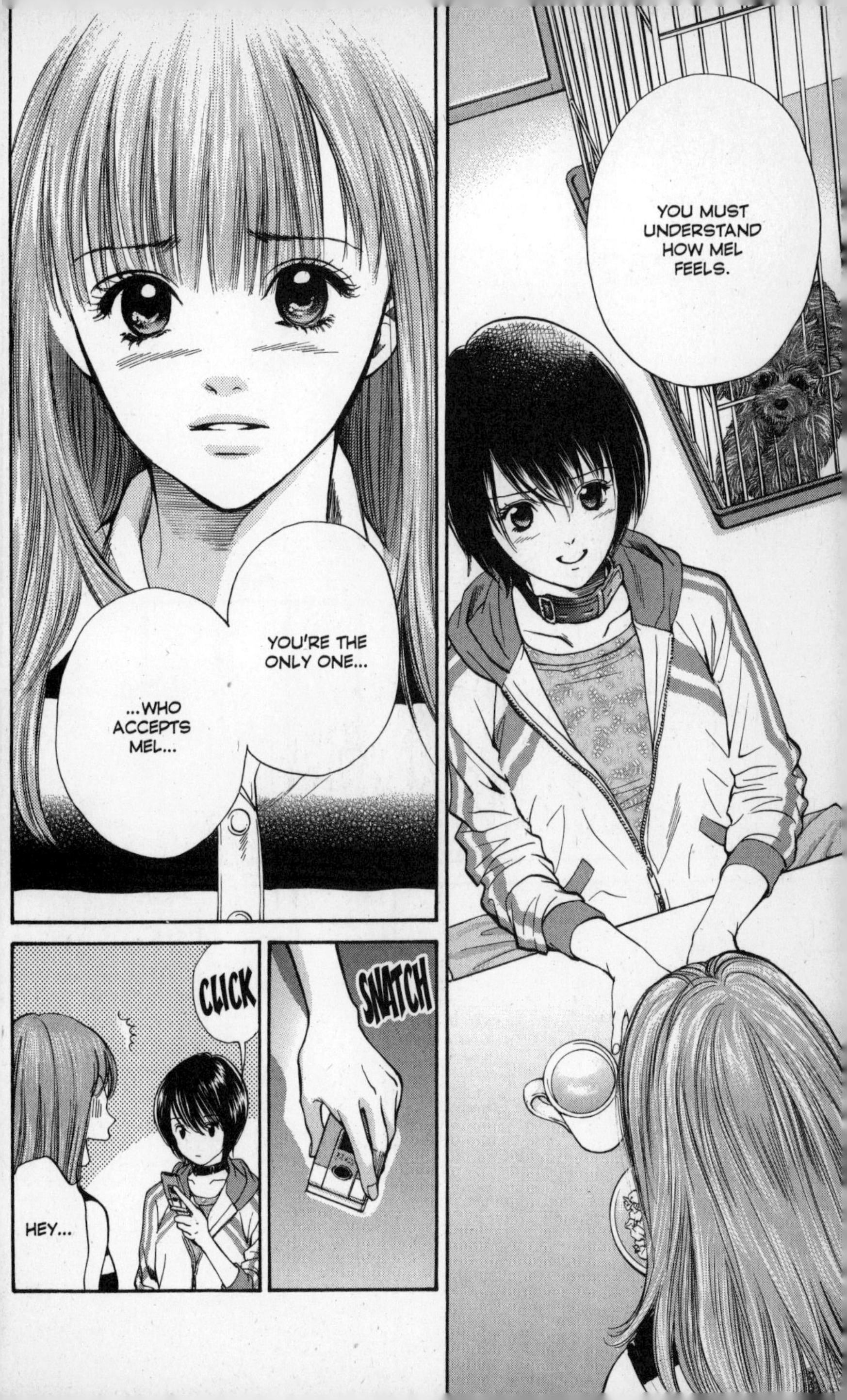
YOU MUST UNDERSTAND HOW MEL FEELS.
YOU'RE THE ONLY ONE...
...WHO ACCEPTS MEL...
SNATCH
CLICK
HEY...

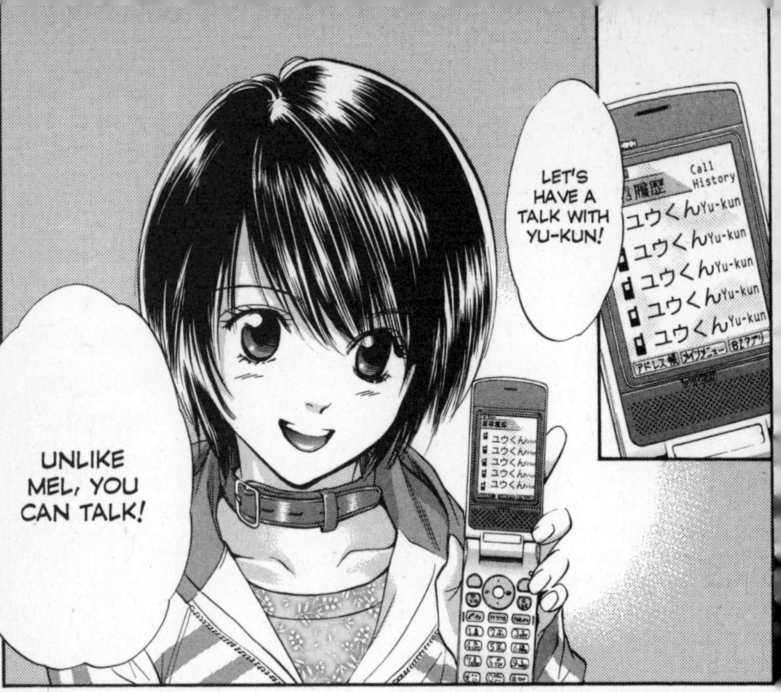
Call History
ユウくんYu-kun
ユウくんYu-kun
ユウくんYu-kun
ユウくんYu-kun
ユウくんYu-kun
LET'S HAVE A TALK WITH YU-KUN!
UNLIKE MEL, YOU CAN TALK!

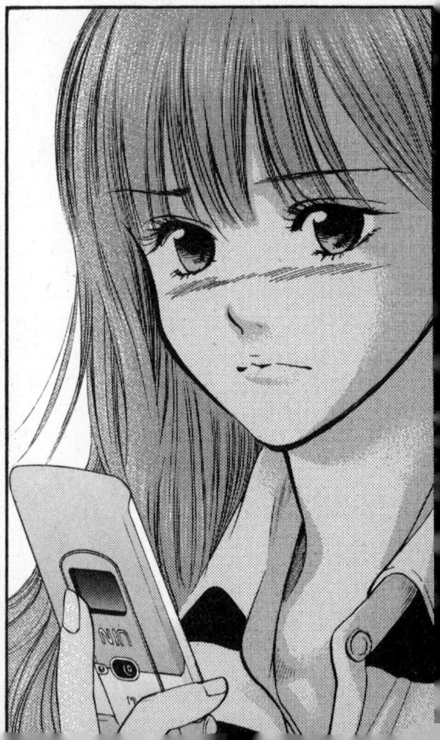

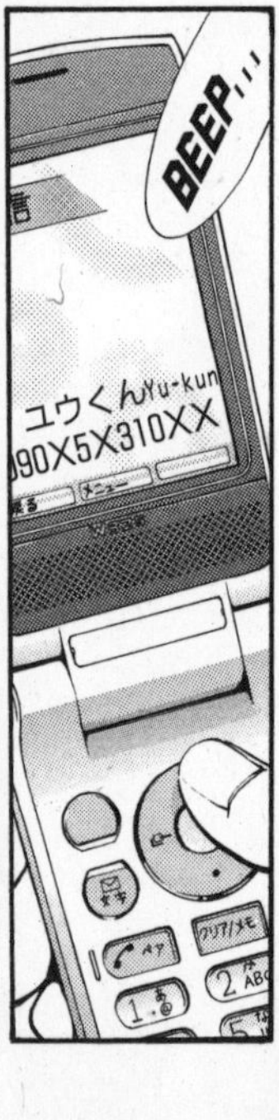
BEEP...
ユウくんYu-kun

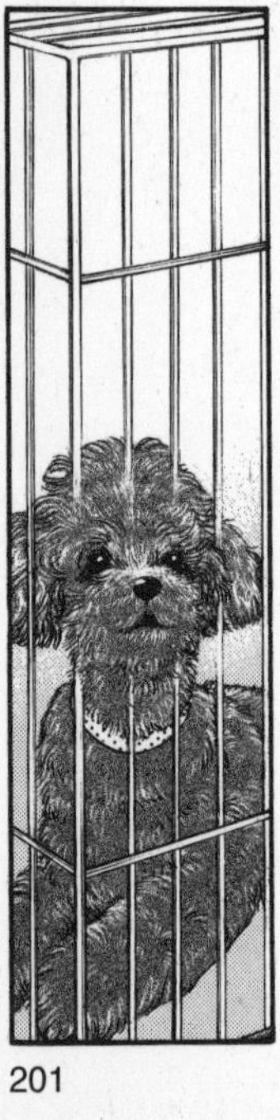

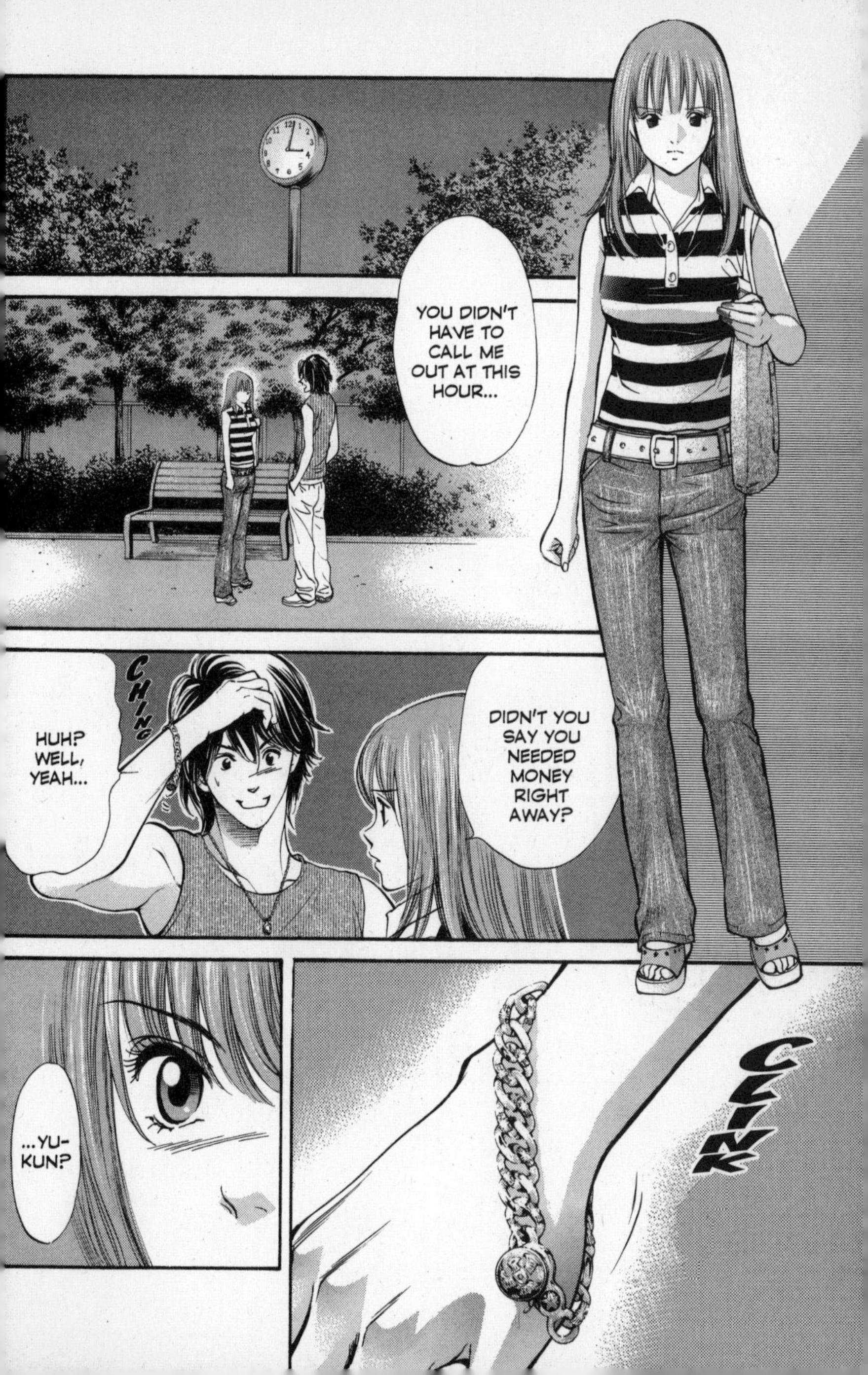
YOU DIDN'T HAVE TO CALL ME OUT AT THIS HOUR...
DIDN'T YOU SAY YOU NEEDED MONEY RIGHT AWAY?
CHING
HUH? WELL, YEAH...
CLINK
...YU-KUN?

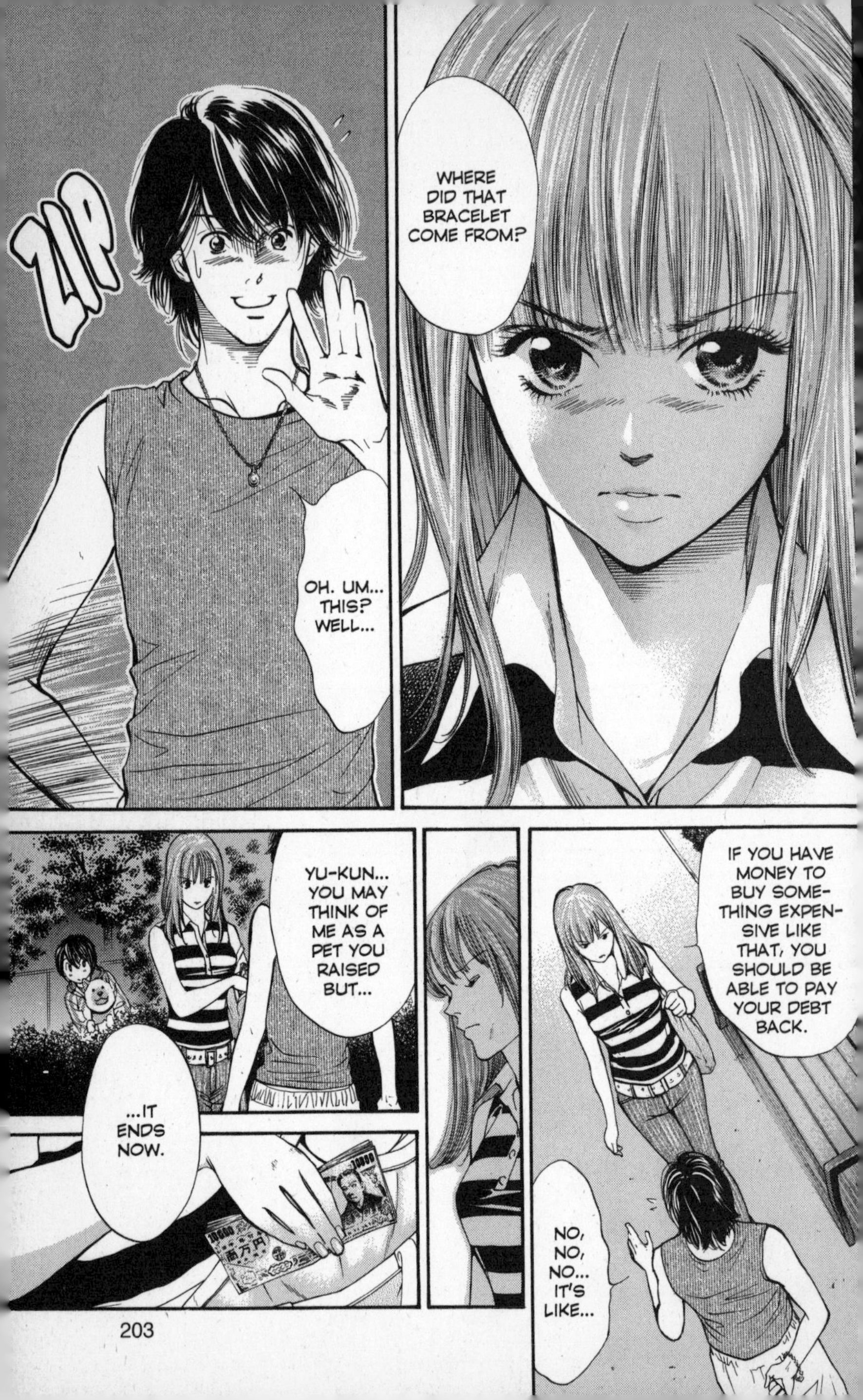
WHERE DID THAT BRACELET COME FROM?
ZIP
OH. UM... THIS? WELL...
IF YOU HAVE MONEY TO BUY SOME-THING EXPEN-SIVE LIKE THAT, YOU SHOULD BE ABLE TO PAY YOUR DEBT BACK.
NO, NO, NO... IT'S LIKE...
YU-KUN... YOU MAY THINK OF ME AS A PET YOU RAISED BUT...
...IT ENDS NOW.

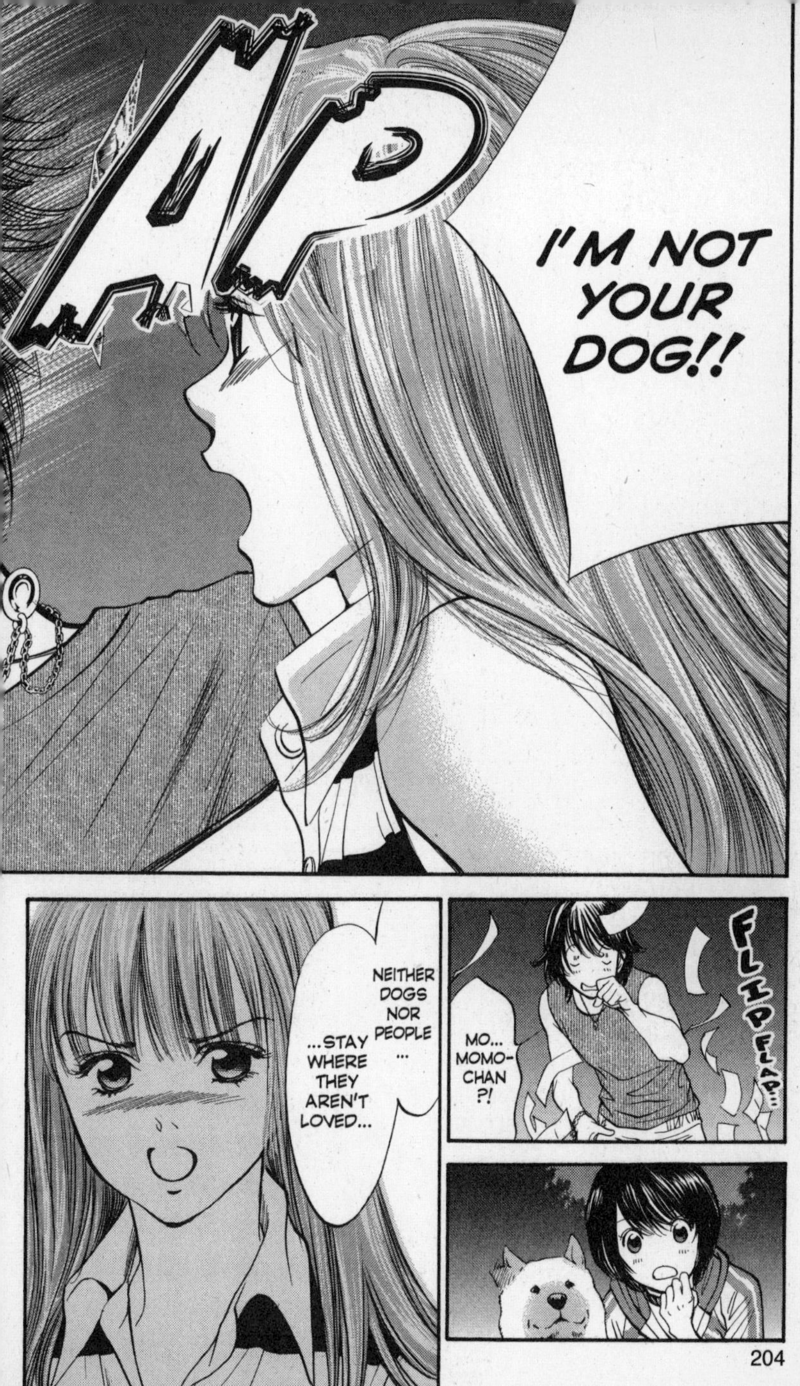
AP
I'M NOT YOUR DOG!!
FLIP FLAP...
MO... MOMO-CHAN ?!
NEITHER DOGS NOR PEOPLE ...
...STAY WHERE THEY AREN'T LOVED...

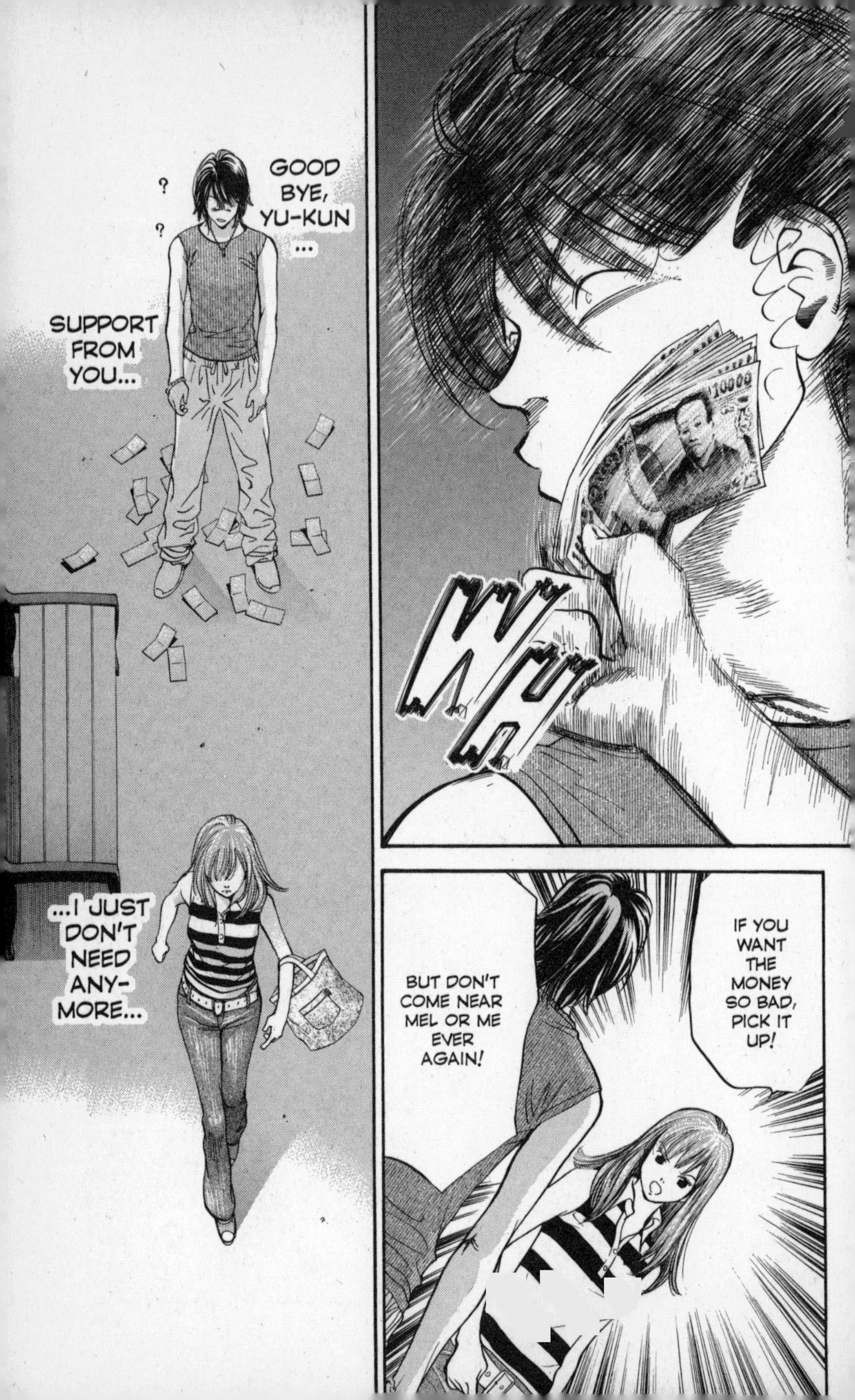
IF YOU WANT THE MONEY SO BAD, PICK IT UP!
BUT DON'T COME NEAR MEL OR ME EVER AGAIN!
GOOD BYE, YU-KUN ...
SUPPORT FROM YOU...
...I JUST DON'T NEED ANY-MORE...

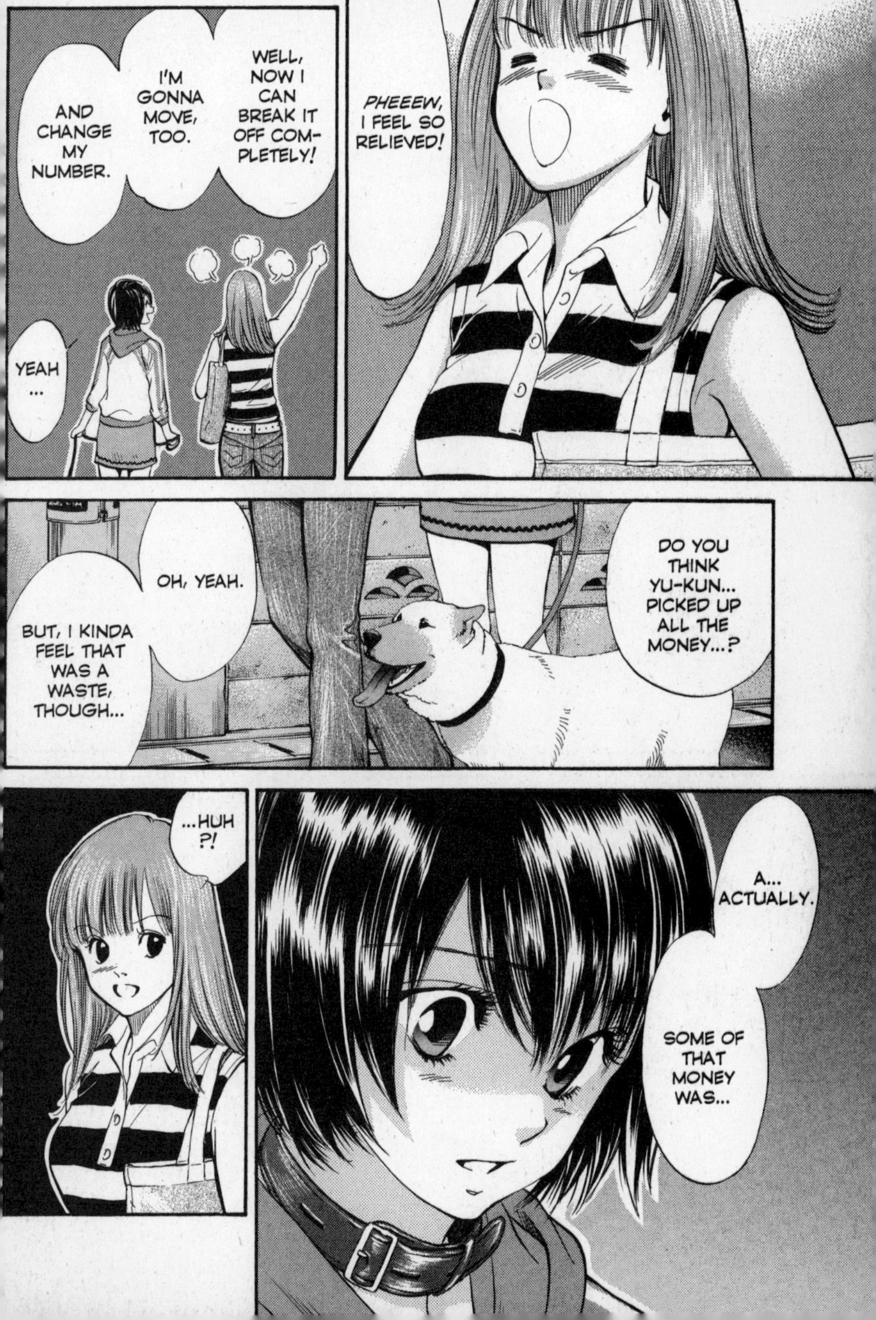
PHEEEW, I FEEL SO RELIEVED!
WELL, NOW I CAN BREAK IT OFF COM-PLETELY!
I'M GONNA MOVE, TOO.
AND CHANGE MY NUMBER.
YEAH ...
DO YOU THINK YU-KUN... PICKED UP ALL THE MONEY...?
OH, YEAH.
BUT, I KINDA FEEL THAT WAS A WASTE, THOUGH...
A... ACTUALLY.
SOME OF THAT MONEY WAS...
...HUH ?!

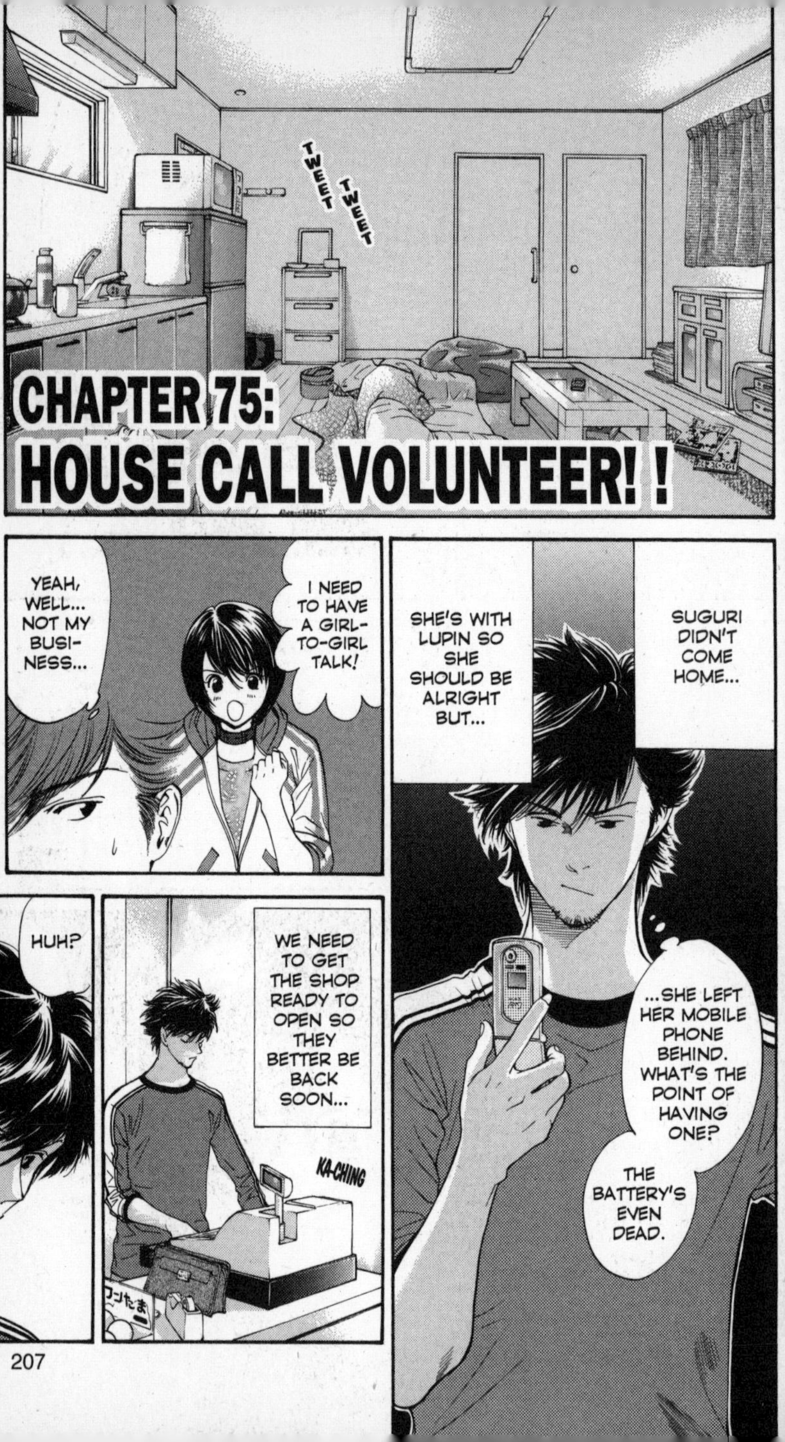
TWEET TWEET
CHAPTER 75:
HOUSE CALL VOLUNTEER! !
SUGURI DIDN'T COME HOME...
SHE'S WITH LUPIN SO SHE SHOULD BE ALRIGHT BUT...
...SHE LEFT HER MOBILE PHONE BEHIND. WHAT'S THE POINT OF HAVING ONE?
THE BATTERY'S EVEN DEAD.
I NEED TO HAVE A GIRL-TO-GIRL TALK!
YEAH, WELL... NOT MY BUSI-NESS...
WE NEED TO GET THE SHOP READY TO OPEN SO THEY BETTER BE BACK SOON...
KA-CHING
HUH?

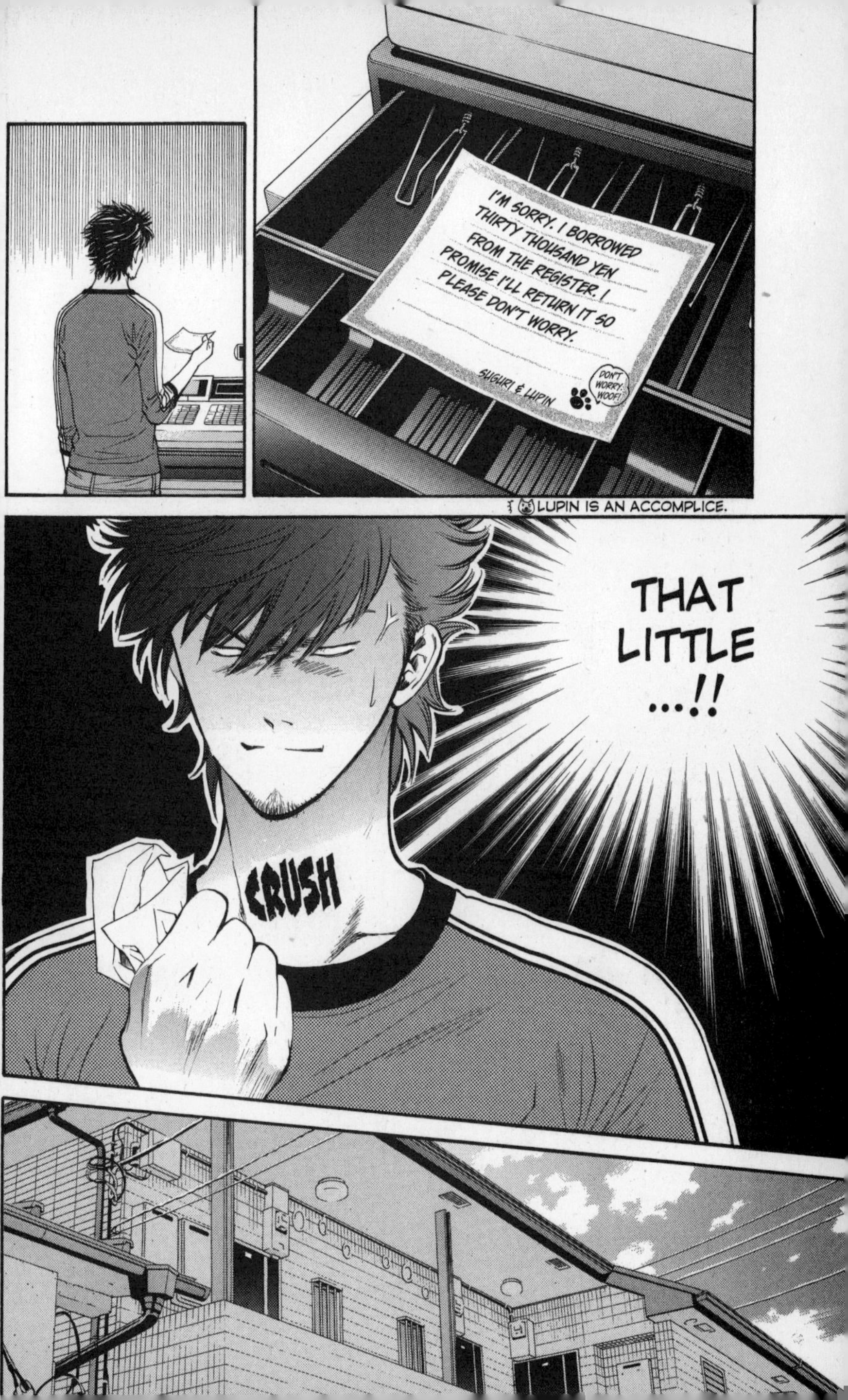
I'M SORRY. I BORROWED THIRTY THOUSAND YEN FROM THE REGISTER. I PROMISE I'LL RETURN IT SO PLEASE DON'T WORRY.
SUGURI & LUPIN
DON'T WORRY. WOOF!
LUPIN IS AN ACCOMPLICE.
THAT LITTLE ...!!
CRUSH

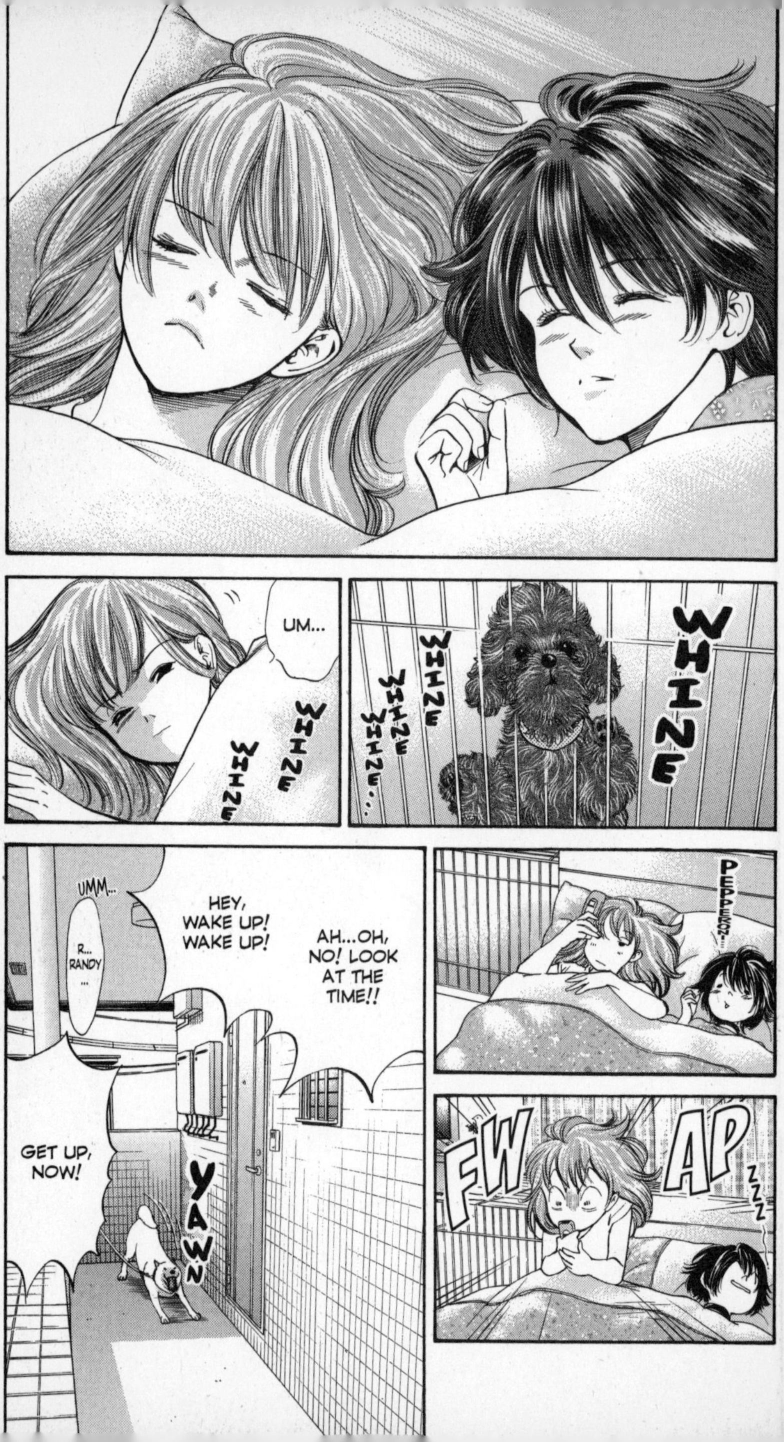
WHINE
WHINE
WHINE
WHINE...
UM...
WHINE
WHINE
PEPPERONI...
FWAP
ZZZ
AH...OH, NO! LOOK AT THE TIME!!
HEY, WAKE UP! WAKE UP!
UMM...
R... RANDY...
GET UP, NOW!
YAWN

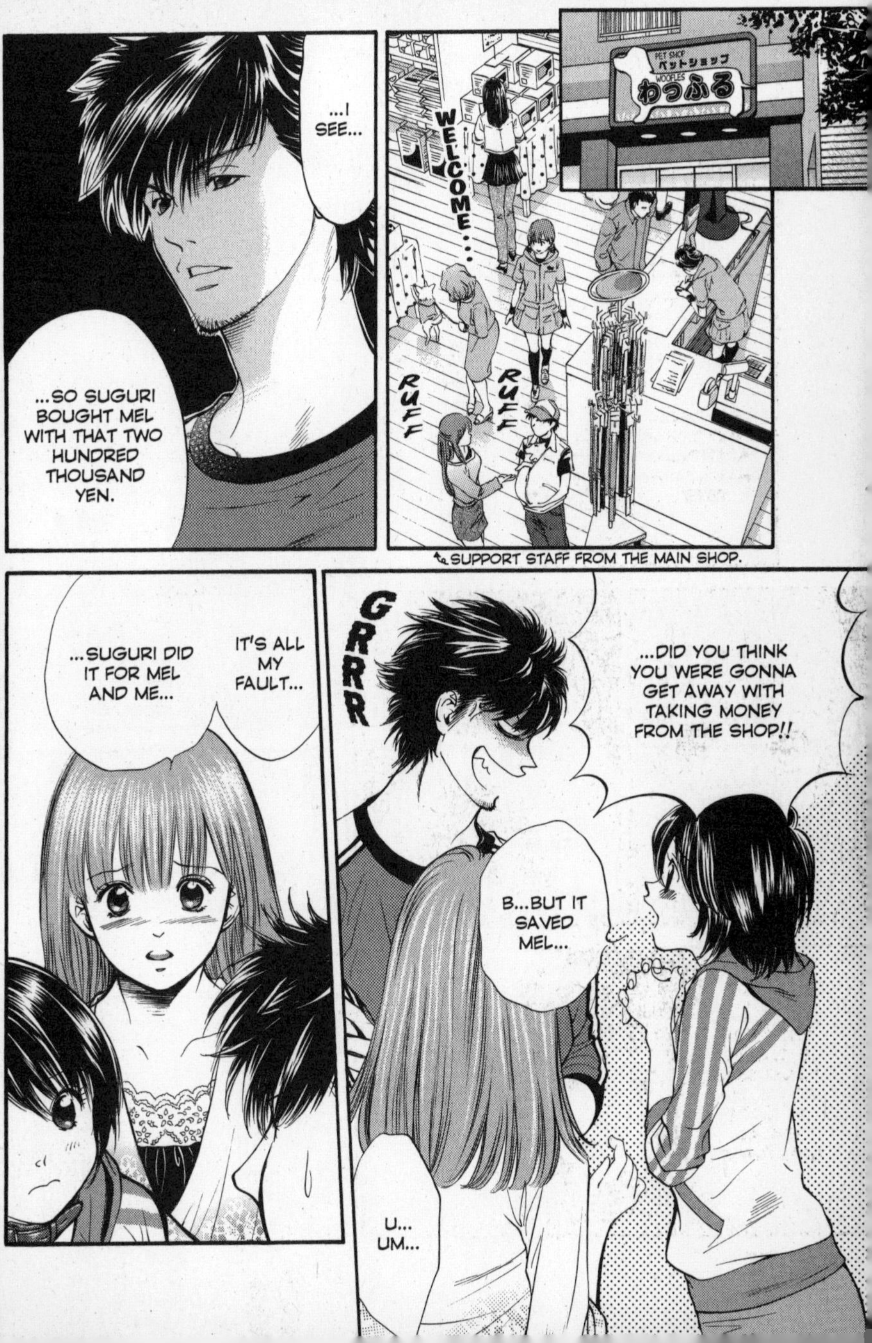
PET SHOP ペットショップ
WOOFLES わっふる
WELCOME...
RUFF
RUFF
SUPPORT STAFF FROM THE MAIN SHOP.
...I SEE...
...SO SUGURI BOUGHT MEL WITH THAT TWO HUNDRED THOUSAND YEN.
GRRR
...DID YOU THINK YOU WERE GONNA GET AWAY WITH TAKING MONEY FROM THE SHOP!!
B...BUT IT SAVED MEL...
U... UM...
IT'S ALL MY FAULT...
...SUGURI DID IT FOR MEL AND ME...

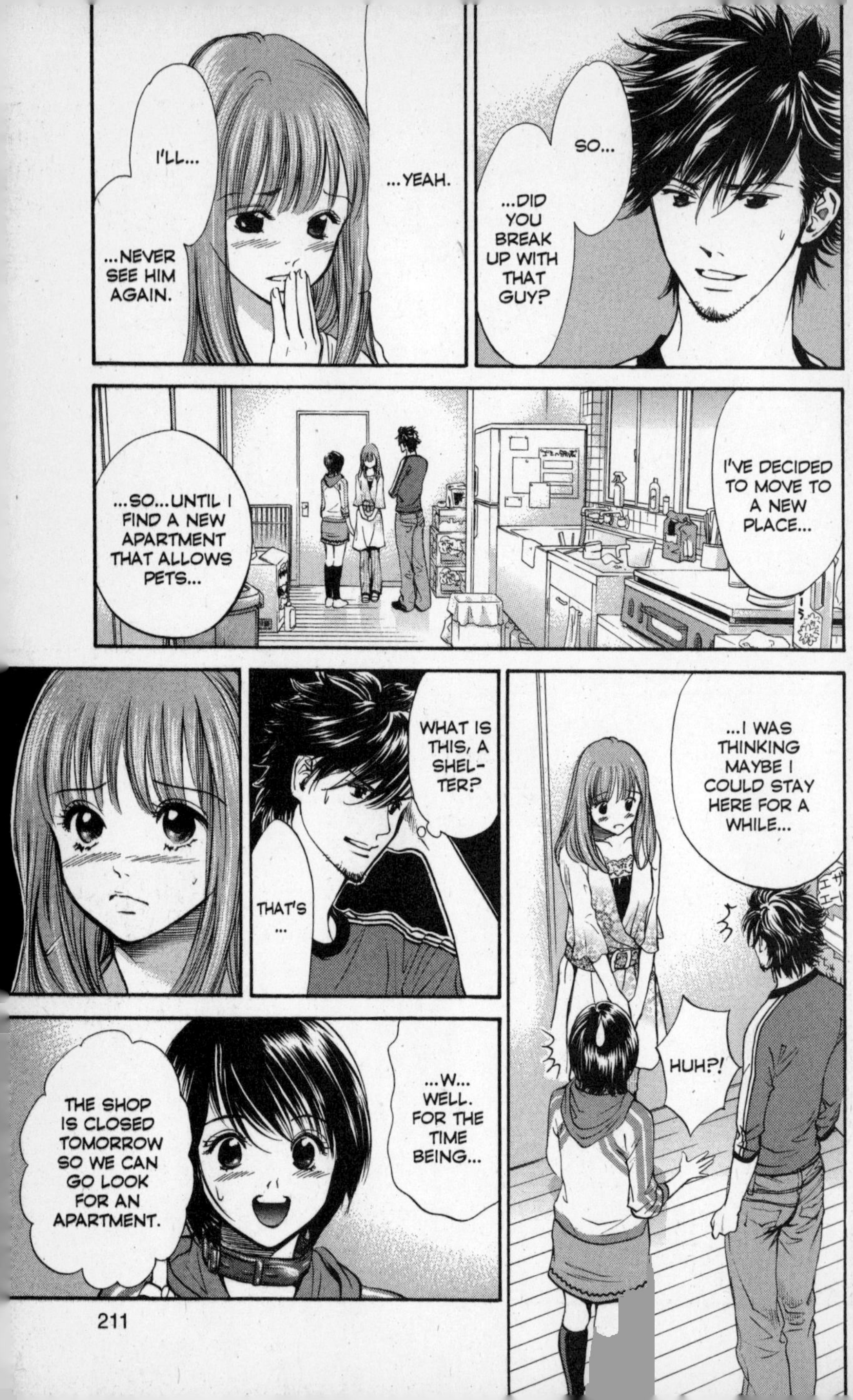
SO...
...DID YOU BREAK UP WITH THAT GUY?
...YEAH.
I'LL...
...NEVER SEE HIM AGAIN.
I'VE DECIDED TO MOVE TO A NEW PLACE...
...SO...UNTIL I FIND A NEW APARTMENT THAT ALLOWS PETS...
...I WAS THINKING MAYBE I COULD STAY HERE FOR A WHILE...
HUH?!
WHAT IS THIS, A SHELTER?
THAT'S...
...W... WELL. FOR THE TIME BEING...
THE SHOP IS CLOSED TOMORROW SO WE CAN GO LOOK FOR AN APARTMENT.

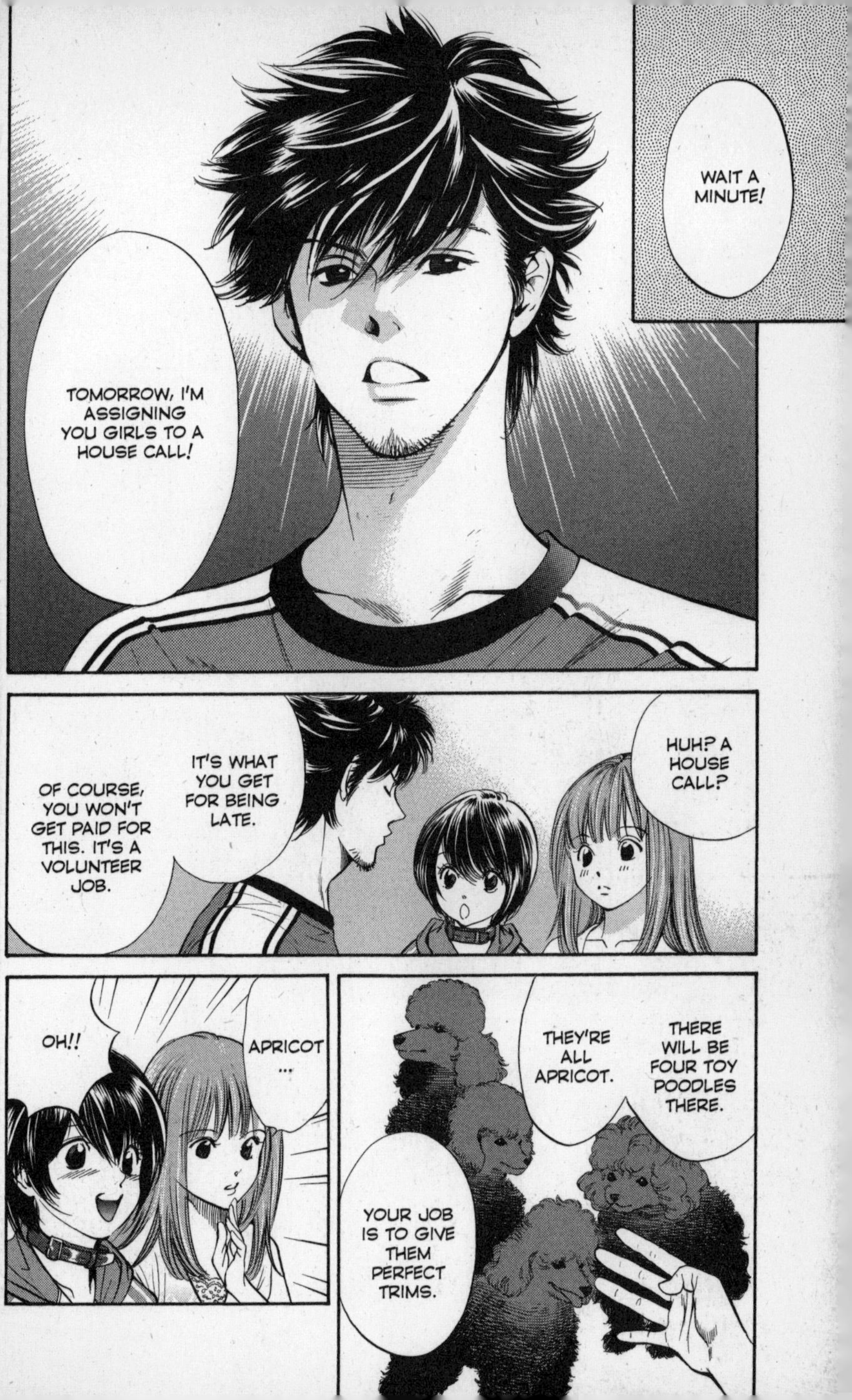
WAIT A MINUTE!
TOMORROW, I'M ASSIGNING YOU GIRLS TO A HOUSE CALL!
HUH? A HOUSE CALL?
IT'S WHAT YOU GET FOR BEING LATE.
OF COURSE, YOU WON'T GET PAID FOR THIS. IT'S A VOLUNTEER JOB.
THERE WILL BE FOUR TOY POODLES THERE.
THEY'RE ALL APRICOT.
YOUR JOB IS TO GIVE THEM PERFECT TRIMS.
APRICOT ...
OH!!

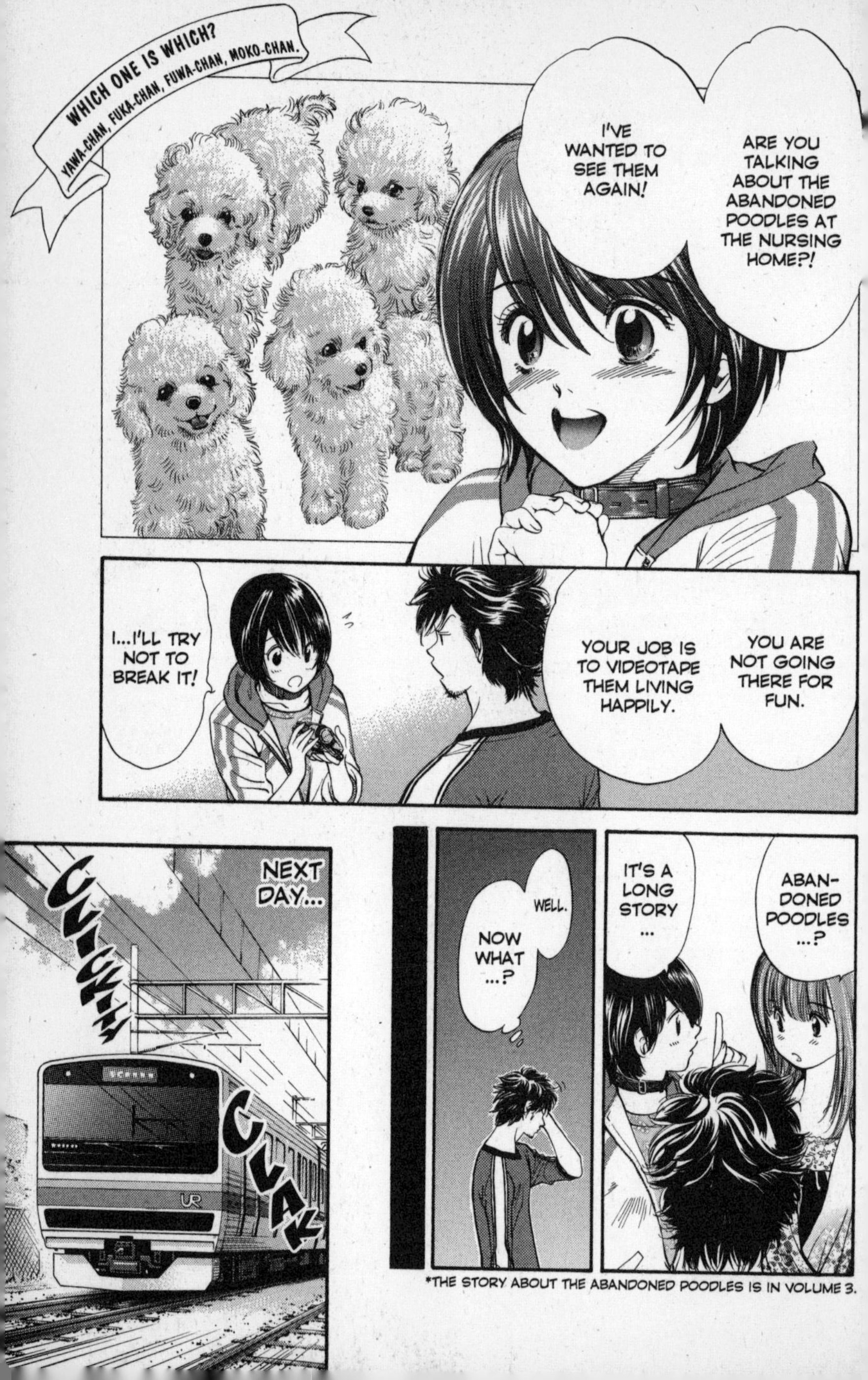
ARE YOU TALKING ABOUT THE ABANDONED POODLES AT THE NURSING HOME?!
I'VE WANTED TO SEE THEM AGAIN!
WHICH ONE IS WHICH?
YAWA-CHAN, FUKA-CHAN, FUWA-CHAN, MOKO-CHAN.
YOU ARE NOT GOING THERE FOR FUN.
YOUR JOB IS TO VIDEOTAPE THEM LIVING HAPPILY.
I...I'LL TRY NOT TO BREAK IT!
ABAN-DONED POODLES ...?
IT'S A LONG STORY ...
WELL.
NOW WHAT ...?
NEXT DAY...
CLICKITY
CLAK

*THE STORY ABOUT THE ABANDONED POODLES IS IN VOLUME 3.

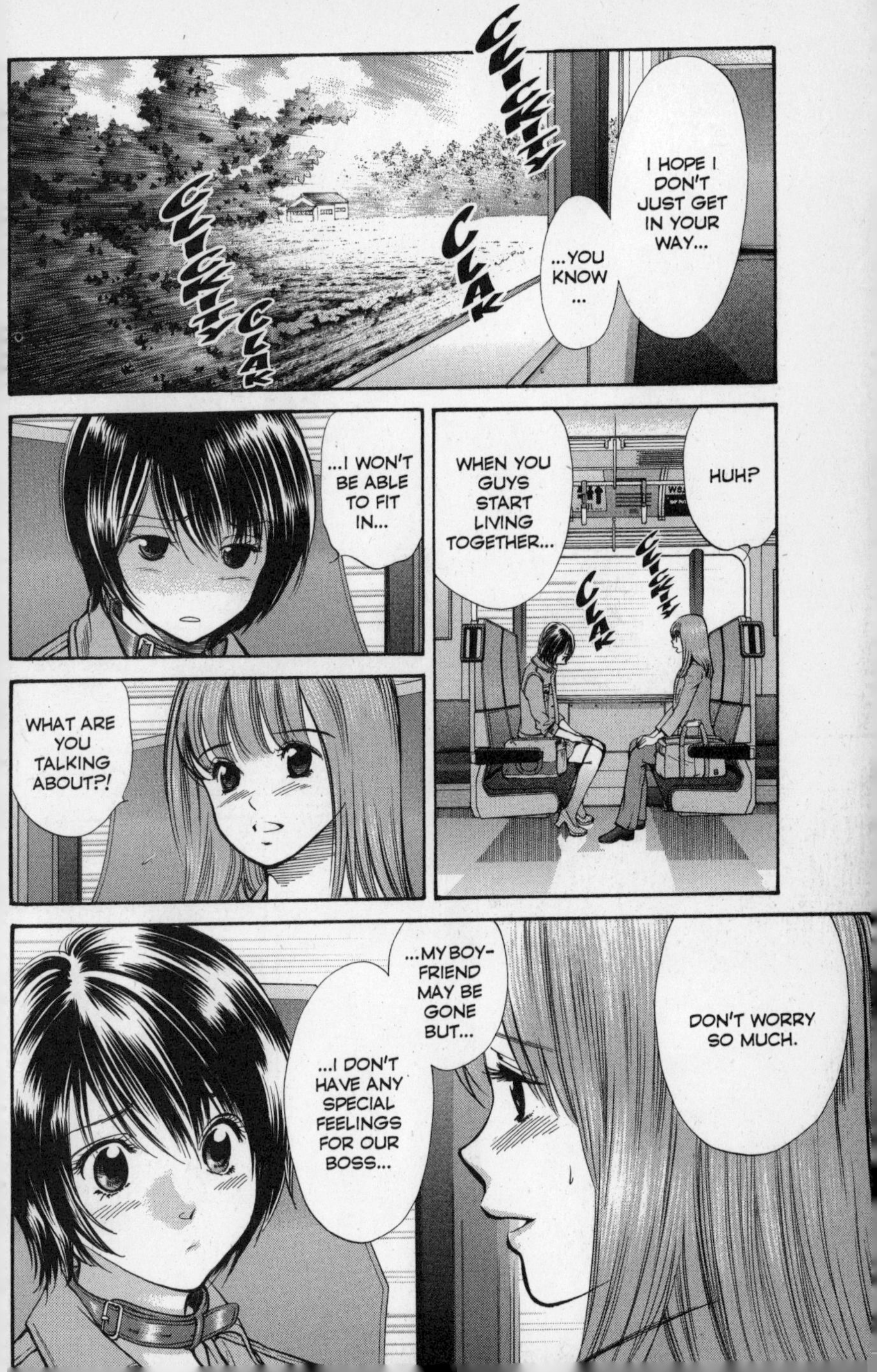
CLICKITY
I HOPE I DON'T JUST GET IN YOUR WAY...
...YOU KNOW...
CLAK
CLICKITY CLAK
HUH?
WHEN YOU GUYS START LIVING TOGETHER...
CLICKITY CLAK
...I WON'T BE ABLE TO FIT IN...
WHAT ARE YOU TALKING ABOUT?!
DON'T WORRY SO MUCH.
...MY BOY-FRIEND MAY BE GONE BUT...
...I DON'T HAVE ANY SPECIAL FEELINGS FOR OUR BOSS...

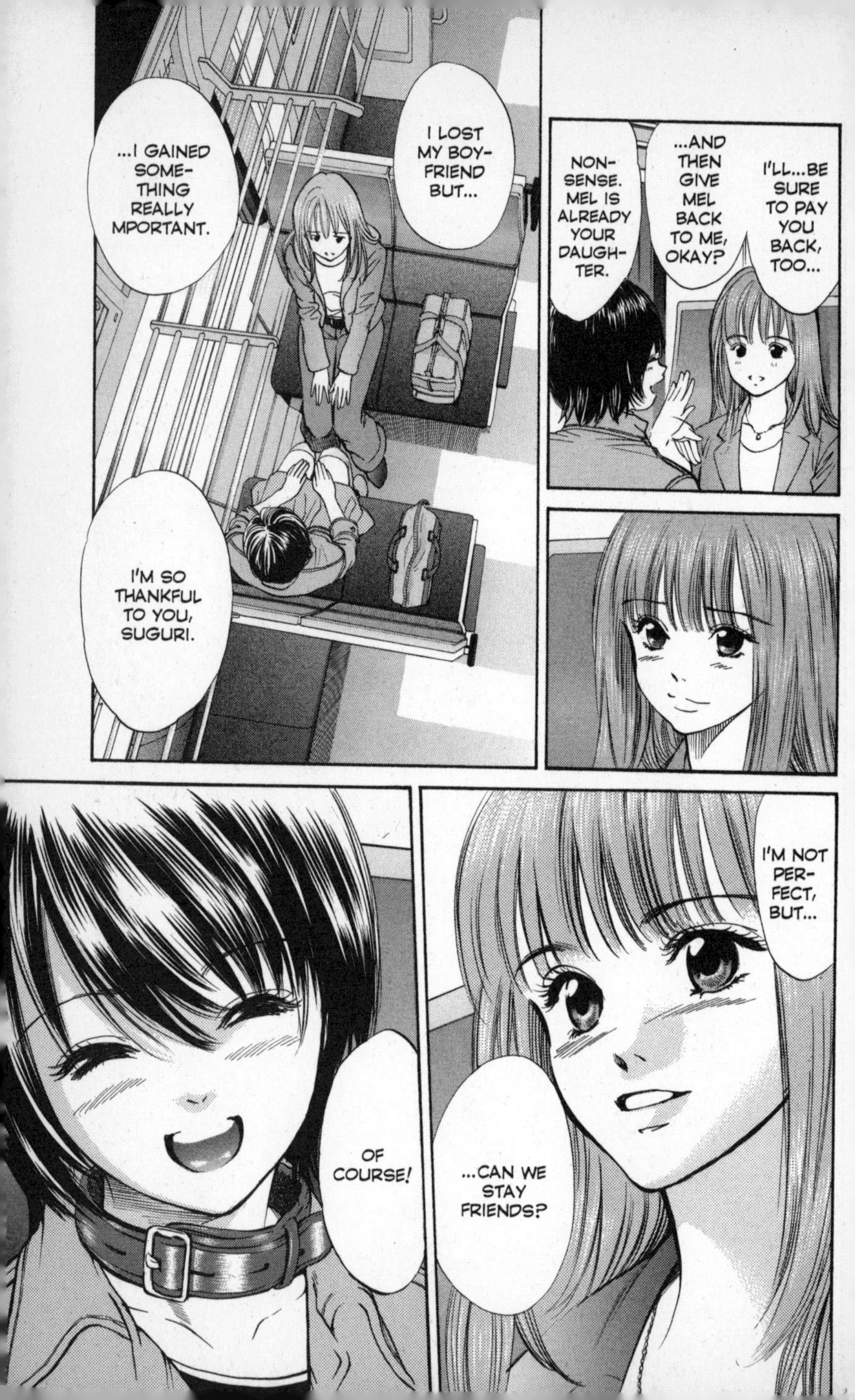
I'LL...BE SURE TO PAY YOU BACK, TOO...
...AND THEN GIVE MEL BACK TO ME, OKAY?
NON-SENSE. MEL IS ALREADY YOUR DAUGH-TER.
I LOST MY BOY-FRIEND BUT...
...I GAINED SOME-THING REALLY MPORTANT.
I'M SO THANKFUL TO YOU, SUGURI.
I'M NOT PER-FECT, BUT...
...CAN WE STAY FRIENDS?
OF COURSE!

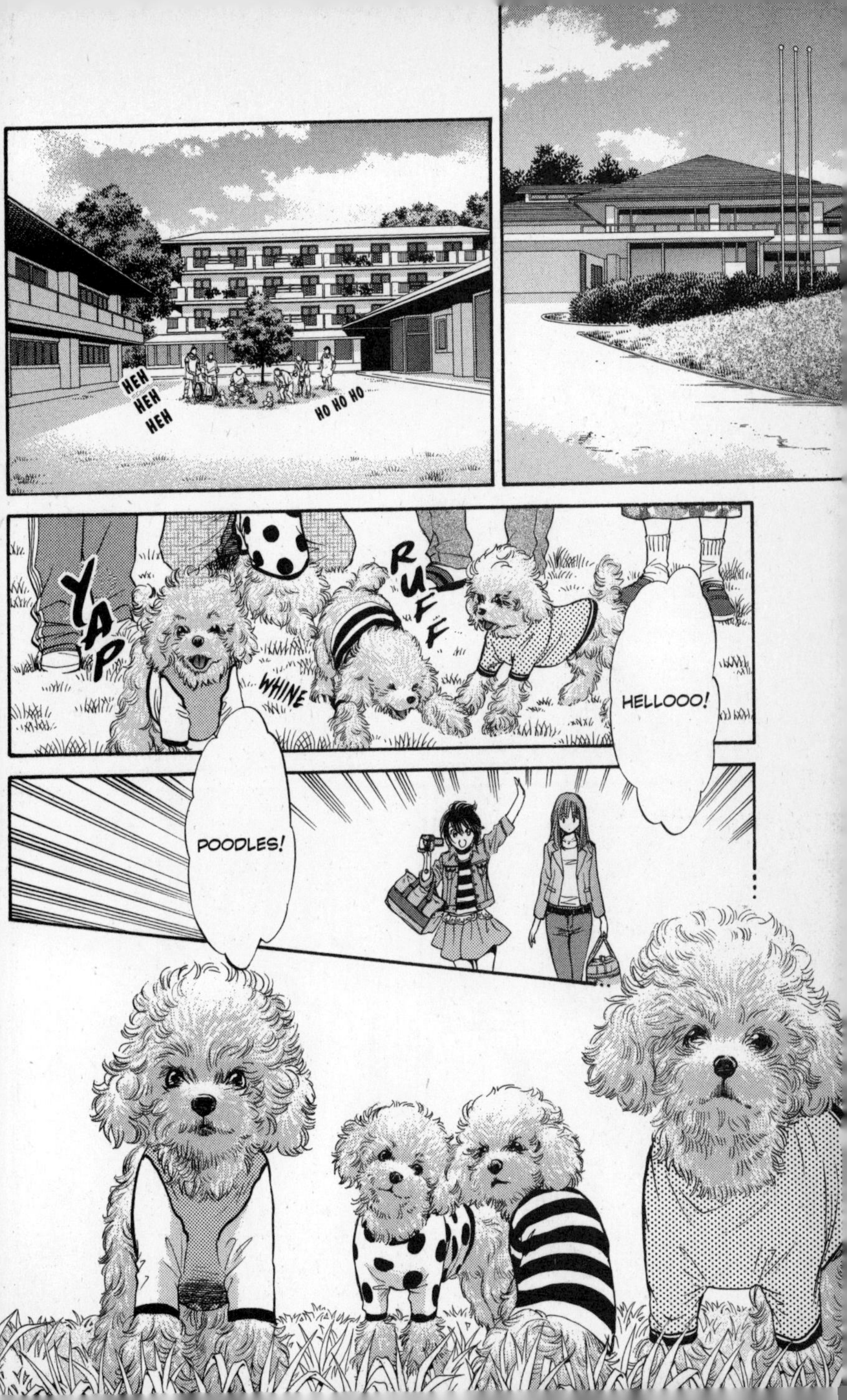
HO HO HO
HEH HEH HEH
RUFF RUFF
WHINE
YAP
HELLOOO!
POODLES!

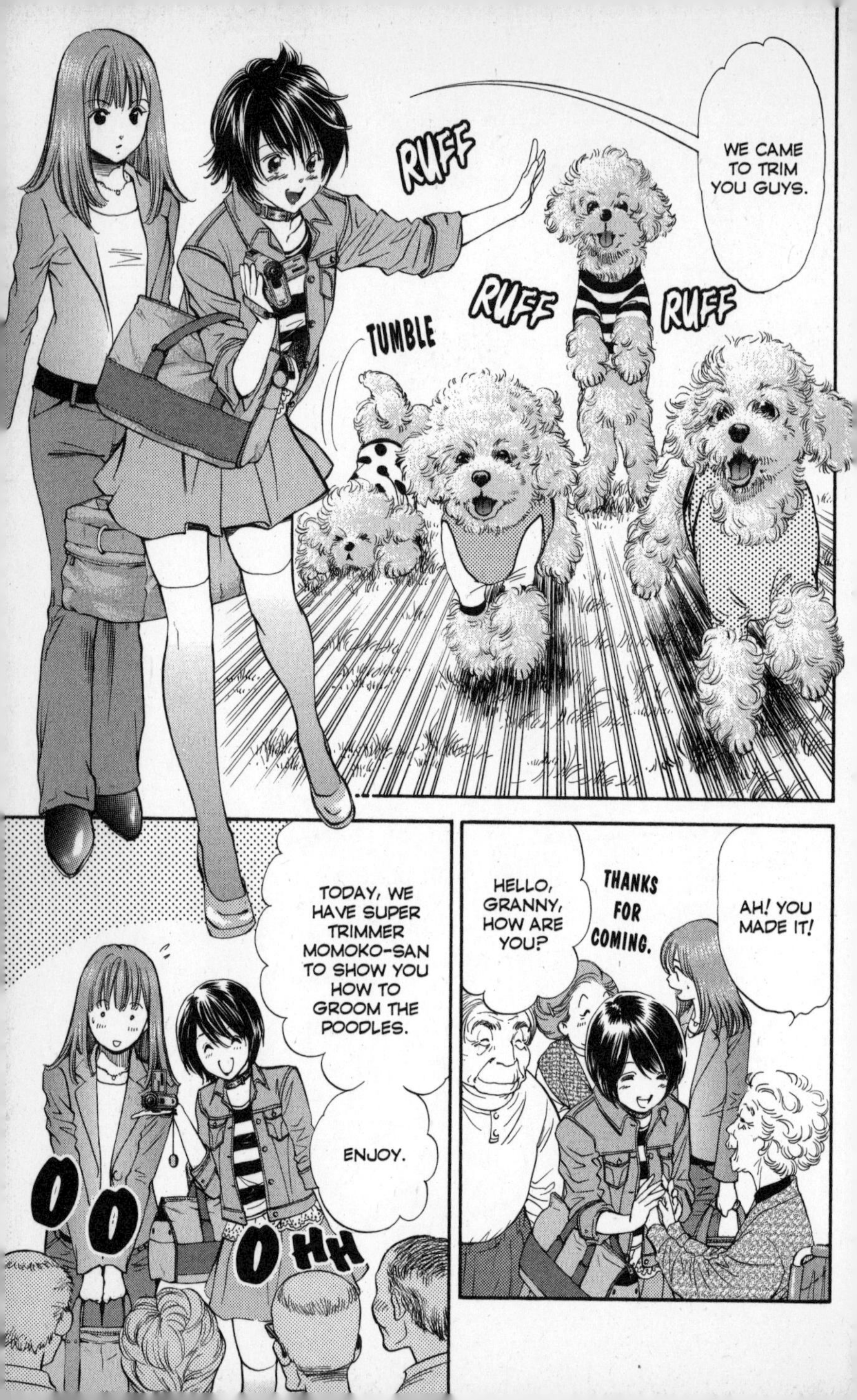
WE CAME TO TRIM YOU GUYS.
RUFF
RUFF
RUFF
TUMBLE
AH! YOU MADE IT!
THANKS FOR COMING.
HELLO, GRANNY, HOW ARE YOU?
TODAY, WE HAVE SUPER TRIMMER MOMOKO-SAN TO SHOW YOU HOW TO GROOM THE POODLES.
ENJOY.
OOOOHH

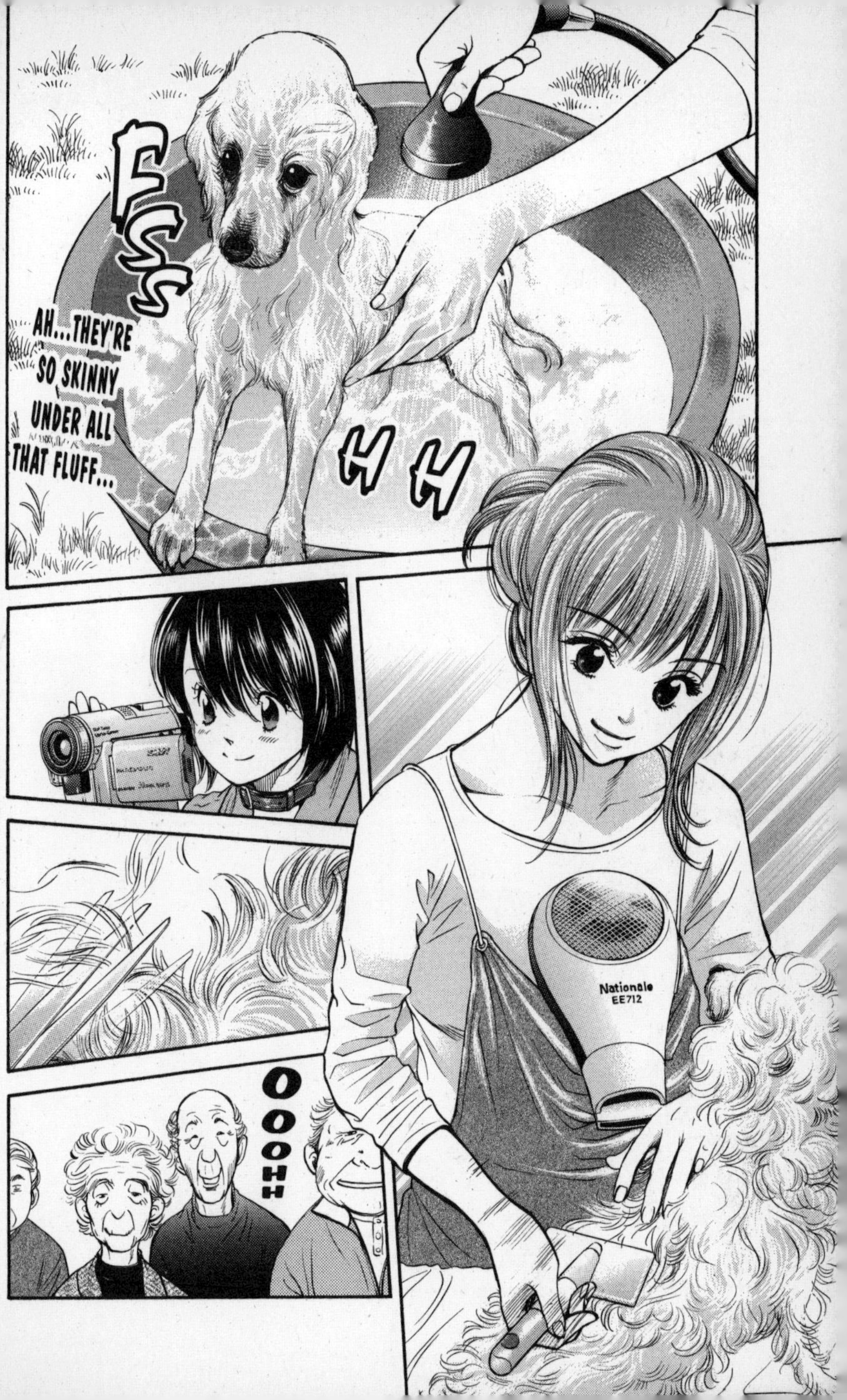
FSS
AH...THEY'RE SO SKINNY UNDER ALL THAT FLUFF...
HH
Nationale
EE712
OOOOHH

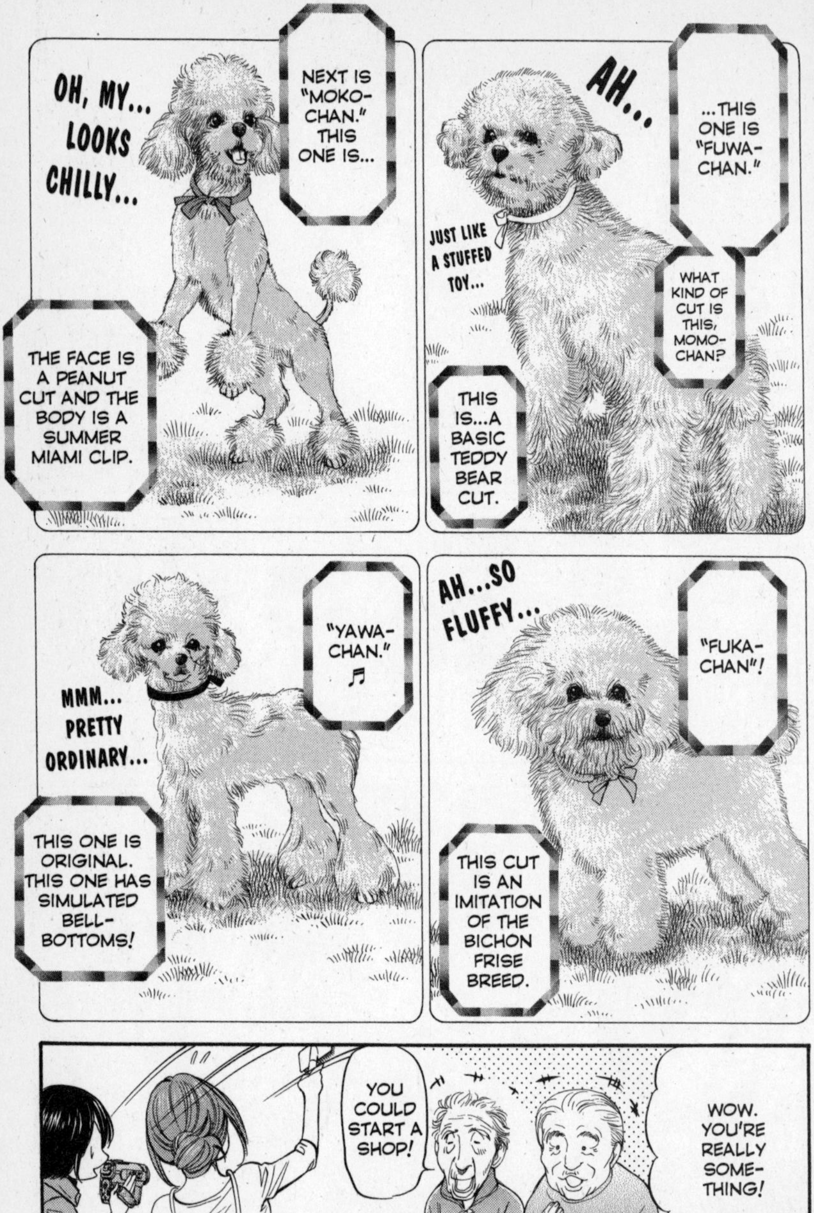
...THIS ONE IS "FUWA-CHAN."
AH...
WHAT KIND OF CUT IS THIS, MOMO-CHAN?
JUST LIKE A STUFFED TOY...
THIS IS...A BASIC TEDDY BEAR CUT.
NEXT IS "MOKO-CHAN." THIS ONE IS...
OH, MY... LOOKS CHILLY...
THE FACE IS A PEANUT CUT AND THE BODY IS A SUMMER MIAMI CLIP.
"FUKA-CHAN"!
AH...SO FLUFFY...
THIS CUT IS AN IMITATION OF THE BICHON FRISE BREED.
"YAWA-CHAN." ♬
MMM... PRETTY ORDINARY...
THIS ONE IS ORIGINAL. THIS ONE HAS SIMULATED BELL-BOTTOMS!
WOW. YOU'RE REALLY SOME-THING!
YOU COULD START A SHOP!

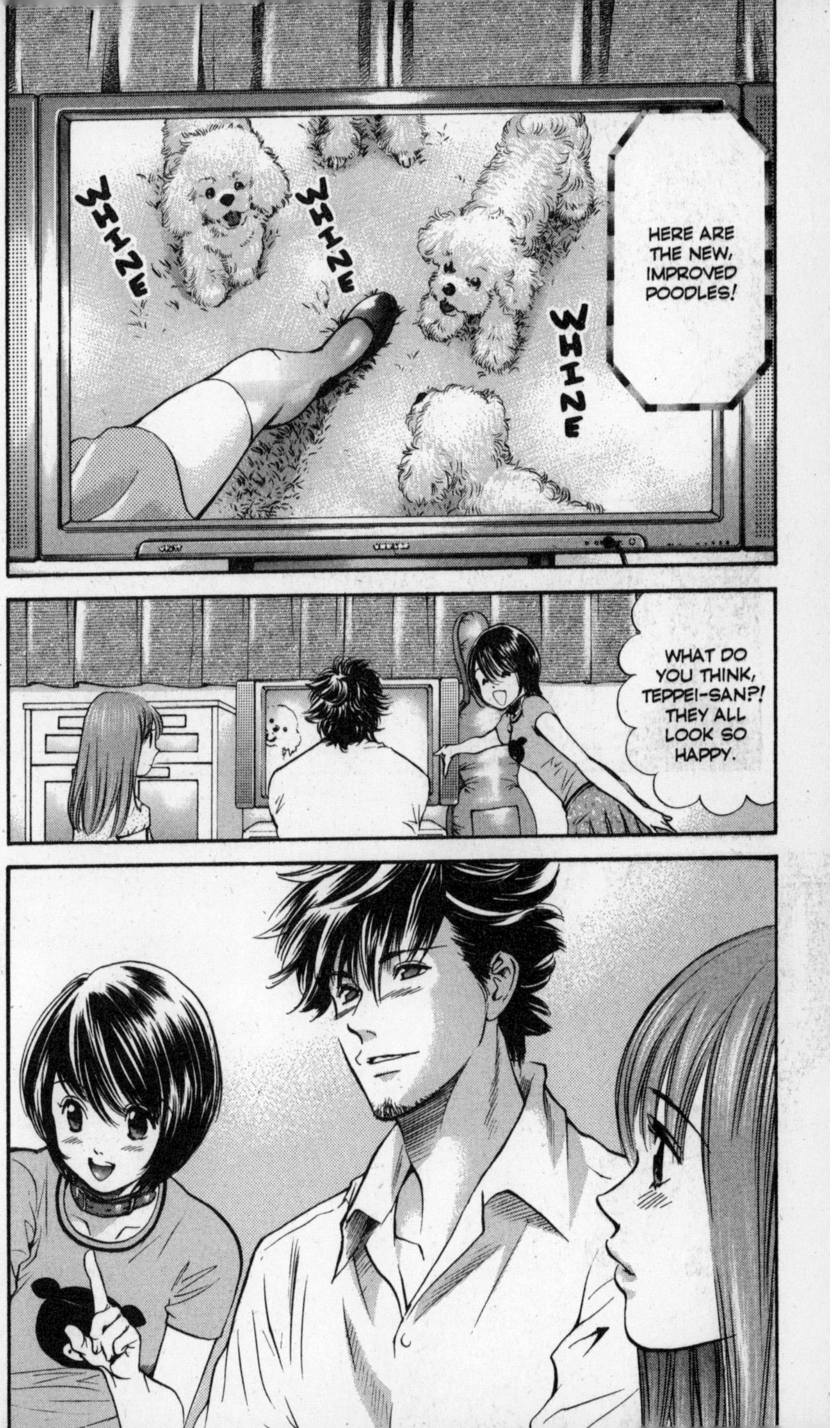
HERE ARE THE NEW, IMPROVED POODLES!
WHINE
WHINE
WHINE
WHAT DO YOU THINK, TEPPEI-SAN?! THEY ALL LOOK SO HAPPY.

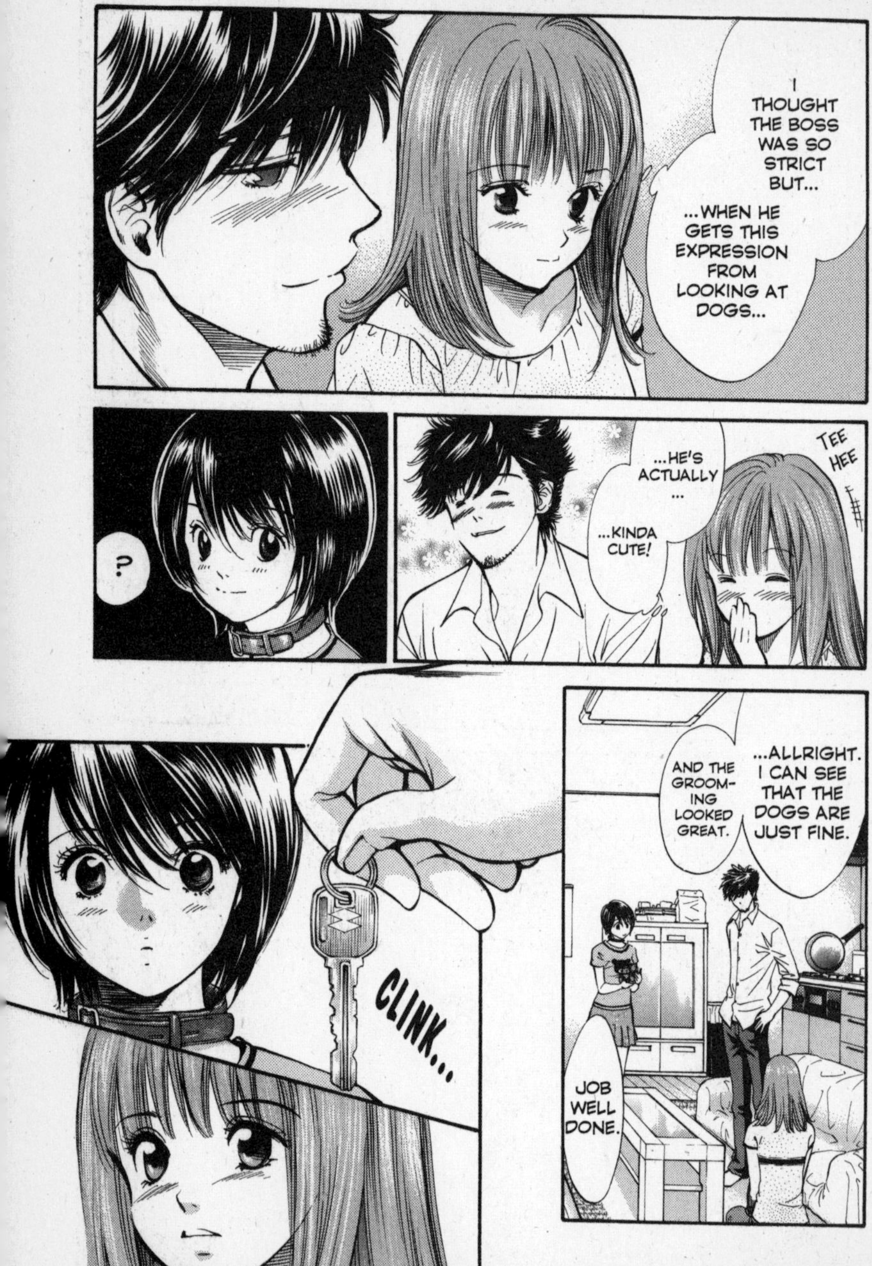

I THOUGHT THE BOSS WAS SO STRICT BUT...
...WHEN HE GETS THIS EXPRESSION FROM LOOKING AT DOGS...
TEE HEE
...HE'S ACTUALLY ...
...KINDA CUTE!
?
...ALLRIGHT. I CAN SEE THAT THE DOGS ARE JUST FINE.
AND THE GROOM-ING LOOKED GREAT.
JOB WELL DONE.
CLINK...

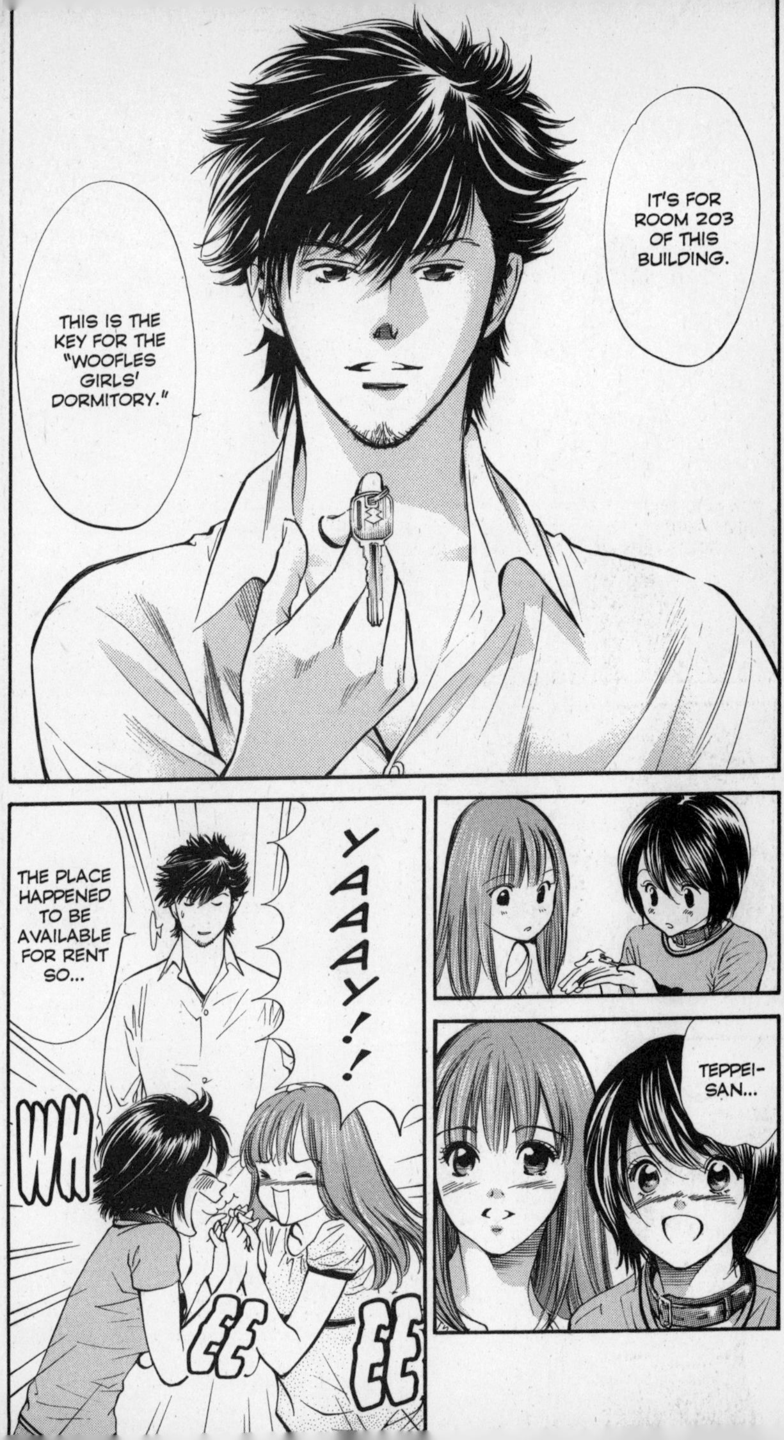

IT'S FOR ROOM 203 OF THIS BUILDING.
THIS IS THE KEY FOR THE "WOOFLES GIRLS' DORMITORY."
TEPPEI-SAN...
YAAAY!!
THE PLACE HAPPENED TO BE AVAILABLE FOR RENT SO...
WH
EE
EE

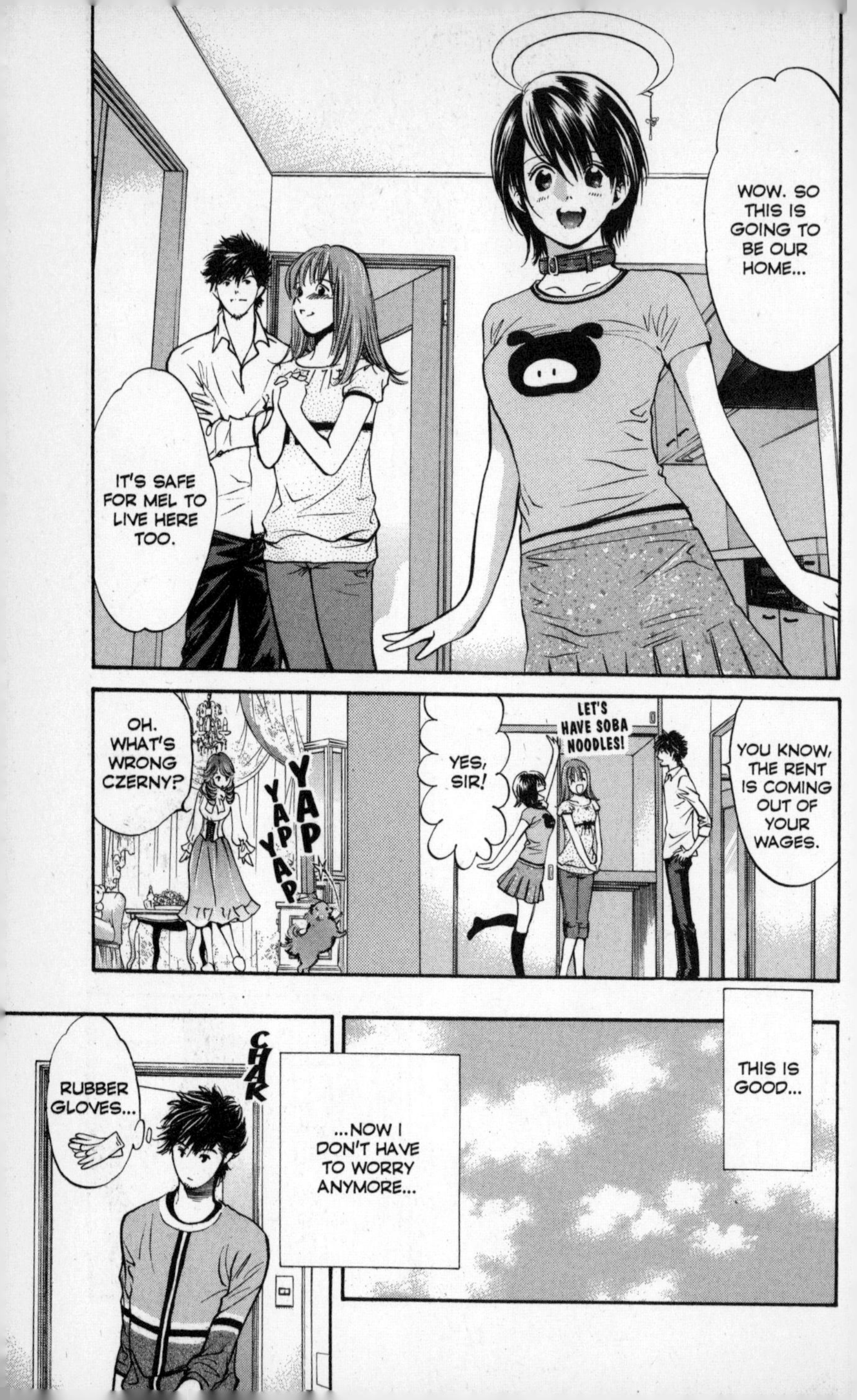
WOW. SO THIS IS GOING TO BE OUR HOME...
IT'S SAFE FOR MEL TO LIVE HERE TOO.
YOU KNOW, THE RENT IS COMING OUT OF YOUR WAGES.
LET'S HAVE SOBA NOODLES!
YES, SIR!
YAP YAP
YAP YAP
OH. WHAT'S WRONG CZERNY?
THIS IS GOOD...
...NOW I DON'T HAVE TO WORRY ANYMORE...
CHAK
RUBBER GLOVES...

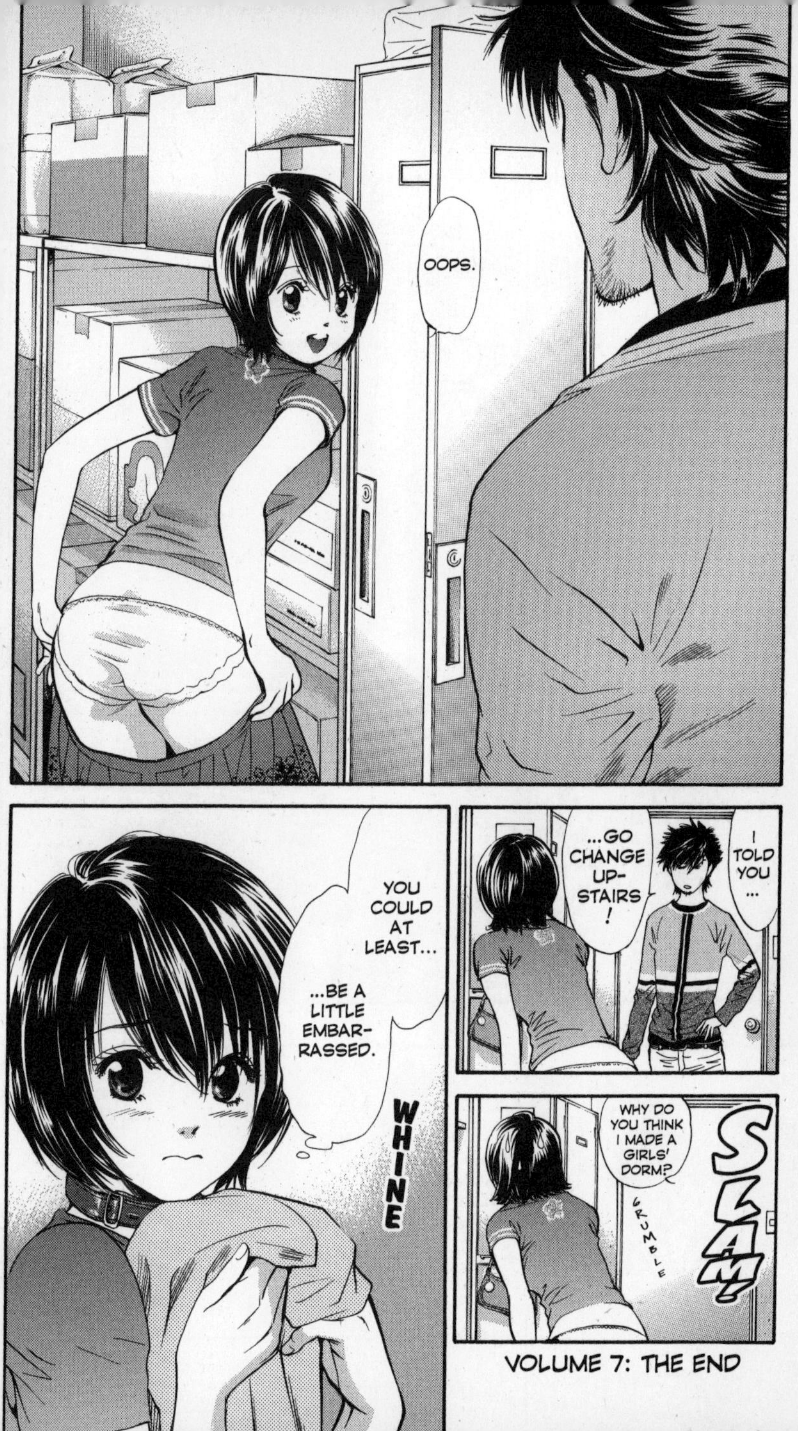
OOPS.
I TOLD YOU...
...GO CHANGE UPSTAIRS!
SLAM!
WHY DO YOU THINK I MADE A GIRLS' DORM?
GRUMBLE
YOU COULD AT LEAST...
...BE A LITTLE EMBARRASSED.
WHINE

VOLUME 7: THE END

INUBAKA

INUBAKA

Everybody's Crazy for Dogs!

From Kaho-san in Saitama prefecture

🐾 Gulliver-chan (Papillon)

This dog is crazy for the hair dryer! When the dog feels wet somewhere, it turns that area toward the hair drier. Here's another story about this willful dog— when someone wanted to buy it, it wouldn't come out of the cage and ended up unsold in the shop!

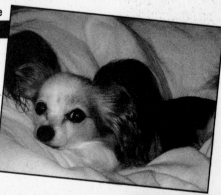

Yukiya Sakuragi

Amazing! There are so many dogs that really hate hair dryers. (My dog, too.) Longhaired doggies have to dry their hair thoroughly; otherwise it'll get tangled. Good doggy!

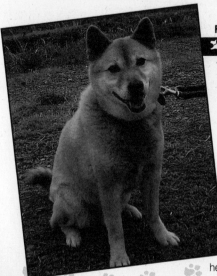

From Okumura-san in Aichi prefecture

🐾 Ryu-kun (mix)

People call Okumura-san crazy for dogs. Okumura's beloved Ryu-kun can bring the newspaper. "It may be just because I'm crazy for my dog, but doesn't it look like Lupin...?" comments Okumura-san.

Yukiya Sakuragi

Wow! The silhouette is just like Lupin's (lol). But it has an air of maturity that Lupin lacks. But they really do look alike... It's not shown here, but Okamura-san also has another very nice dog named Nero-chan (Newfoundland).

From Matsumoto-san in Shizuoka prefecture

🐕 Chiro-chan & Hana-chan
(Shiba & French Bulldog)

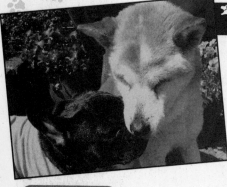

Shockingly, Chiro-chan, the Shiba, will turn 18 years old this July. Hana-chan (1 year old) came and kept giving Chiro-chan love bites, which weren't appreciated. But Chiro-chan eventually gave up and they became good friends.

Yukiya Sakuragi

Wow! Chiro-chan is long-lived!! Awesome! Possibly in competition with young Hana-chan? The picture of Hana-chan in the bath is just like a manga and made me laugh so hard.

From Ozaki-san in Aichi prefecture

🐕 Coron-chan (Kaninchen Dachshund)

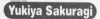

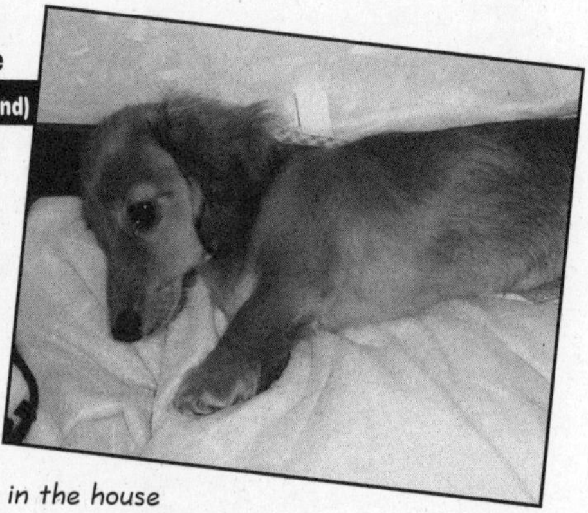

Coron-chan is a Kaninchen Dachshund, which is even smaller than a Miniature Dachshund. It just turned two months old but it's really clever and has already mastered "sit" and "come." Father first objected to keeping the dog in the house but now he is totally into it because it's so cute.

Yukiya Sakuragi

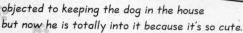

It's so tiny! It's amazing how cute it is even though it's no longer a puppy (lol). Plus, it's clever, too... But I think such goodness is owed to a good owner.

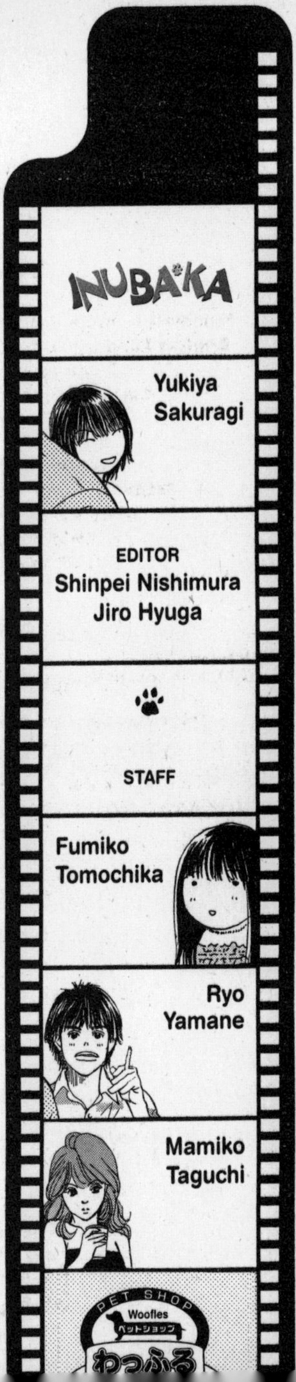
INUBAKA
Yukiya Sakuragi
EDITOR
Shinpei Nishimura
Jiro Hyuga
STAFF
Fumiko Tomochika
Ryo Yamane
Mamiko Taguchi
PET SHOP
Woofles
ペットショップ
わっふる
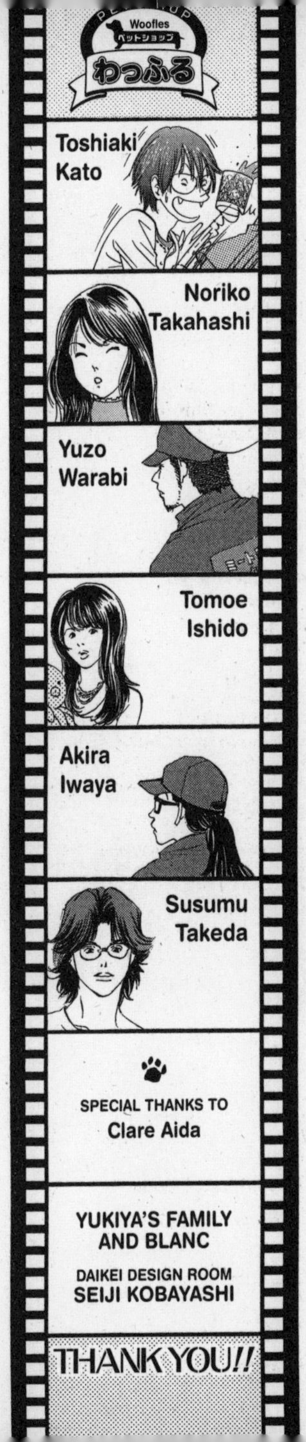
Woofles
ペットショップ
わっふる
Toshiaki Kato
Noriko Takahashi
Yuzo Warabi
Tomoe Ishido
Akira Iwaya
Susumu Takeda
SPECIAL THANKS TO
Clare Aida
YUKIYA'S FAMILY AND BLANC
DAIKEI DESIGN ROOM
SEIJI KOBAYASHI
THANK YOU!!

Inubaka
Crazy for Dogs
Vol. #7
VIZ Media Edition

Story and Art by
Yukiya Sakuragi

Translation/Hidemi Hachitori, HC Language Solutions, Inc.
English Adaptation/Ian Reid, HC Language Solutions, Inc.
Touch-up Art & Lettering/Kelle Han
Cover and Interior Design/Hidemi Sahara
Editor/Ian Robertson

Editor in Chief, Books/Alvin Lu
Editor in Chief, Magazines/Marc Weidenbaum
VP of Publishing Licensing/Rika Inouye
VP of Sales/Gonzalo Ferreyra
Sr. VP of Marketing/Liza Coppola
Publisher/Hyoe Narita

Printed in the U.S.A.

Published by VIZ Media, LLC
P.O. Box 77010
San Francisco, CA 94107

10 9 8 7 6 5 4 3 2 1
First printing, February 2008

www.viz.com
store.viz.com

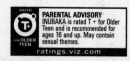

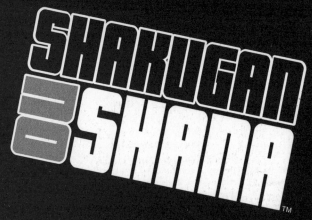
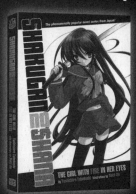
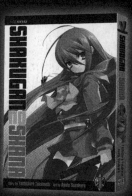

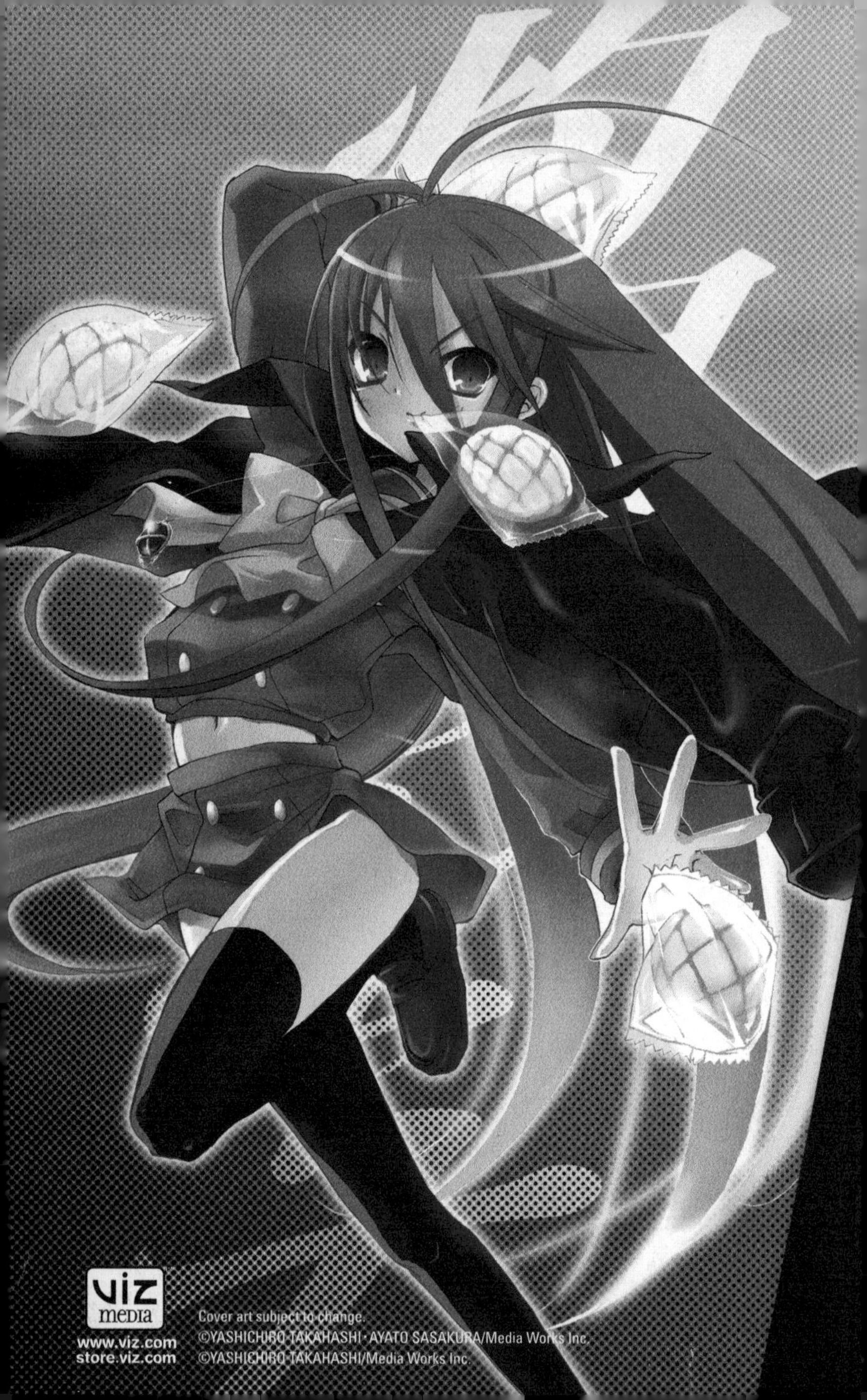

LOVE MA

LET US KNOW WHAT YOU THINK!

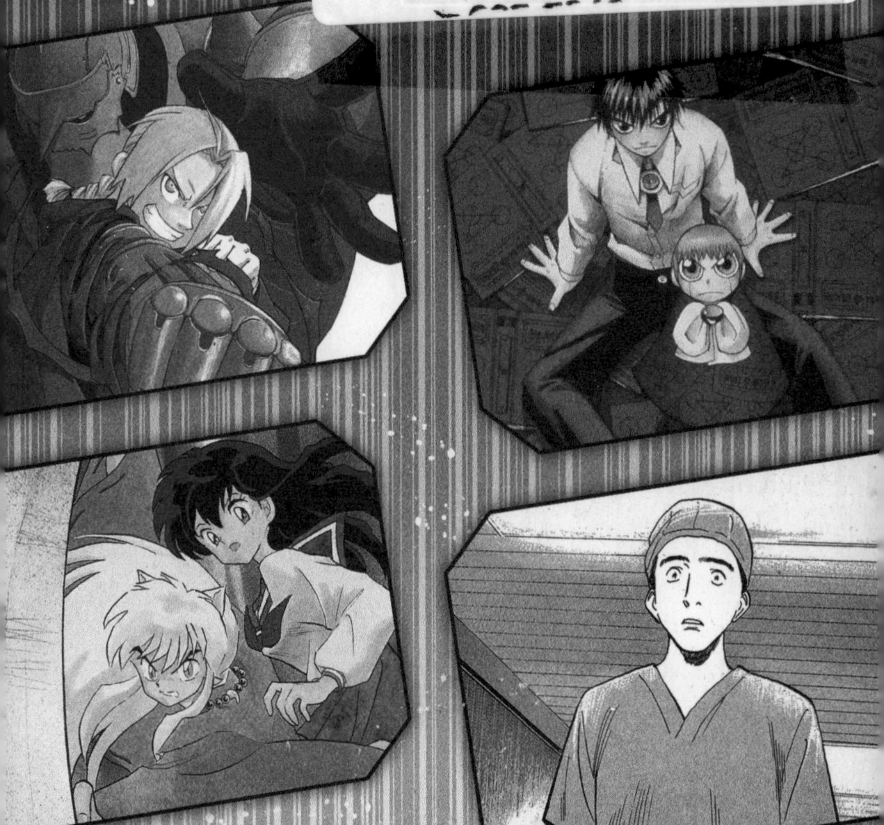

HELP US MAKE THE MANGA YOU LOVE BETTER!